SCOTTISH INDEPENDENCE

SCOTTISH INDEPENDENCE

A PRACTICAL GUIDE

Jo Eric Murkens with Peter Jones and Michael Keating

EDINBURGH UNIVERSITY PRESS

© The Constitution Unit, University College London, 2002

Edinburgh University Press Ltd
22 George Square, Edinburgh

Typeset in Goudy Old Style
by Hewer Text Ltd, Edinburgh, and
printed and bound in Great Britain by
MPG Books Ltd, Bodmin

A CIP record for this book is
available from the British Library

ISBN 0 7486 1699 3 (paperback)

The right of The Constitution Unit, University College London
to be identified as author of this work
has been asserted in accordance with
the Copyright, Designs and Patents Act 1988.

Contents

Part Four: The Realities and the Limits of Independence
Jo Eric Murkens (Chapter 14) and Michael Keating (Chapter 15)

Analytical Table of Contents

Part One: The Road to Independence
Jo Eric Murkens

Acknowledgements

This book is the result of a study undertaken by the Constitution Unit during 2000–1. A project on Scottish independence was first conceived by Robert Hazell back in 1998. David Sinclair did the early research, and obtained funding for the project from the Esmée Fairbairn Foundation in 1999. We are very grateful for their generous support, which was essential to the project. The book which has resulted is the product of an independent initiative by the Constitution Unit which has not been influenced by any government body or political party.

The work would not have been possible without help and support from a large number of individuals. The study relied in part on study visits to Scotland, Denmark, and Quebec, and benefited hugely from the interviews conducted in the course of the research. Acknowledging the assistance of everyone involved does not in any way imply their agreement with the overall content and conclusions. Any errors remain the authors' own.

I am extremely grateful for the generous help and continued involvement of Alan and Caroline Boyle, Eileen Denza, Tony Aust, Matthew Happold, Abby Innes, Brendan O'Leary, William Walker, Louis Forget, Beth Richardson, Emmanuel Kattan, Denis Turcotte, Johanne Poirier, Jeremy Jenkins, and Simon Partridge. I am indebted to Michael Keating who produced an inspirational conclusion at very short notice and thus added an extra dimension to the book.

Thanks are also due to Martin Reid, Bill Lawton, Amanda Sloat, Elizabeth Holt, Andrew Scott, Caitríona Carter, Robert Lane, Clive Archer, James Mitchell, Neil Walker, Iain MacWhirter, Kirsty Milne, George Kerevan, John Goodlad, David Spence, Frederik Harhoff, Vibeke Roosen, Per Lachman, Árni Olafsson, Jenny Hartley, Diane Stephenson, Paula Cohen, James Cant, Richard Hogben, David Nelson, Naseef Huda, John Bachtler, Tim Figures, Karen Henderson, Heather Grabbe, Keith Patchett, Shaun Bowler, Mads Qvortrup, Angus Robertson, Neil Mac-

Cormick, Ben Wallace, Andrew Rogerson, Natalie Lichtenstein, Gwynneth Williams, William Wallace, Romesh Vaitilingam, Quentin Thomas, and Gwynneth and Douglas Frame.

Particular thanks are owed to the interviewees in Canada: Mark Walters (and all attendants of his lunch-time discussion group), Daniel Turp, Robert Young, Warren J. Newman, Mary Dawson, Ghislain Otis, Leslie Seidle, Graham Flack, Andrew Bennett, Joël Lépine, Guy Lachapelle, Michel Venne, Yves-Marie Morissette, Jean François Gaudreault-Desbiens, Guy Laforest, Joseph Facal, Francine Barry, Michel Seymour, Serge Joyal, André Joli-Coeur, Jacques Frémont, Benoît Pelletier, Ronald L. Watts, Hudson Meadwell, Peter Leslie, Dan Soberman, as well as Fiona and Philip Mason, Joanne Bayly, Julian Feldman, and Daniel Sanger.

The Director of the Constitution Unit, Professor Robert Hazell, as well as my colleague Alan Trench read and commented on every piece of work in progress, and offered steady back up and encouragement. Roger Masterman deserves special credit for copy-editing every chapter of the book and for generally chipping in bits of information at the right moment. Other members of the Constitution Unit and the School of Public Policy at University College London offered support and help at various junctures. These included: Jeremy Croft, Meg Russell, Ben Seyd, Clare Delap, Mark Sandford, Scott Greer, Rebecca Blackwell, Gareth Lewes, as well as Allyson Pollock, Melanie Mason and James Lancaster. David Sinclair's excellent earlier research, as well as his briefing 'Issues Around Scottish Independence' (The Constitution Unit, September 1999), were invaluable and made possible the speedy completion of this project. His briefing has largely been incorporated into this work.

A seminar on Chapters 1–3 was held at Edinburgh University which was attended by David Nelson, Alex Wright, Eberhardt Bort, Simon Wakefield, Gordon Mulholland, Craig Milroy, Alasdair Allan, Robert Seaton, Stephen Tierney, Elizabeth Watson, Barry Winetrobe, Eileen Denza, Magnus Linklater, William Walker, Peter Jones and Robert Hazell. The Constitution Unit and Peter Jones would like to thank the attendants for their critical comments and useful suggestions.

Finally, thanks are due to my other colleagues, acquaintances, friends, and family. I would like to single out Arthur Schafer, Jennifer August, Romie Singh and Hans Murkens for their stimulus and subtle support.

Peter Jones has asked us to acknowledge the invaluable contributions and assistance which he has received from many sources. In particular, he would like to single out Matty Schreck for his help with sources on Czechoslovakia, and Robert Gill for his many hours of work on financial data and unearthing of material on Quebec. Thanks for advice and help are also due to Gavin McCrone, Jeremy Peat, Hervey Gibson, James Mitchell, Donald MacRae, Neil Hood, John McLaren, Andrew Wilson, David Bell, Dan Mulhall, Conor O'Riordan, Denis Turcotte, William Lawton, Alice Brown and Iain McNicoll. Thanks also go to staff at the National Statistics Office, the economics and statistics division of the Scottish Executive, the economics department of the Royal Bank of Scotland, and to Wood Mackenzie. An especial note of thanks is insufficient recognition of the toleration of Rhona, Peter's wife, for the many nights he spent hunched over a keyboard.

Jo Eric Murkens
The Constitution Unit
London
March 2002

Notes on the Authors

Jo Eric Murkens worked as a Research Assistant at the Constitution Unit from September 2000 to August 2001. As the lead researcher on the Scottish Independence project he published a briefing on 'Scotland's Pace in Europe' in February 2000 and contributed the Europe section to the Unit's quarterly monitoring reports. Born in Bristol to a German father and an Anglo-Indian mother, Jo holds dual (British and German) citizenship. He went to school in Hanover and Cologne, but returned to Britain for higher education. Jo read English and European Law at Queen Mary and Westfield College, London, and the University of Copenhagen. He is currently a researcher at the European University Institute, Florence.

jo.murkens@iue.it

Peter Jones has been the Scotland and North of England correspondent of *The Economist* since 1995. Prior to that, he was the Scottish Political Editor of *The Scotsman* for eight years. Other publications include (with Christopher Harvie) *The Road to Home Rule*, a popular history of the Scottish home rule movement, published in 2000 by Edinburgh University Press, and several articles on Scottish politics in *Scottish Affairs*, a quarterly journal. He is an honours graduate in geography of St Andrews University. Peter lives in Edinburgh and is married to Rhona Brankin, the Labour Member of the Scottish Parliament for Midlothian since 1999. The views expressed in this and all other publications are his, and his alone.

Pjones@ednet.co.uk

Michael Keating graduated from the University of Oxford and gained his PhD at Glasgow College (now Glasgow Caledonian University) in 1975. He is Professor of Regional Studies at the European University Institute,

Florence, and Professor of Scottish Politics at the University of Aberdeen. He previously taught at the universities of Strathclyde and Western Ontario and has held visiting posts in the United States, France, Spain and Norway. He has published widely in the field of regionalism, nationalism, Scottish politics, and urban politics and policy, and his most recent book is *Plurinational Democracy: Stateless Nations in a Post-Sovereignty Era* (Oxford University Press, 2001).

'A functioning democracy requires a continuous process of discussion . . . No one has a monopoly on truth, and our system is predicated on the faith that in the marketplace of ideas, the best solutions to public problems will rise to the top. Inevitably, there will be dissenting voices. A democratic system of government is committed to considering those dissenting voices, and seeking to acknowledge and address those voices in the laws by which all in the community must live.'

The Supreme Court of Canada,
Reference re Secession of Quebec
[1998] 2 S.C.R. 217, paragraph 68.

'It should be borne in mind that there is nothing more difficult to arrange, more doubtful of success, and more dangerous to carry through than initiating changes in a state's constitution. The innovator makes enemies of all those who prospered under the old order, and only lukewarm support is forthcoming from those who would prosper under the new. Their support is lukewarm partly from fear of their adversaries, who have the existing laws on their side, and partly because men are generally incredulous, never really trusting new things unless they have tested them by experience. In consequence, whenever those who oppose the changes can do so, they attack vigorously, and the defence made by others is only lukewarm. So both the innovator and his friends are endangered together.'

Niccolo Machiavelli, *The Prince*, Chapter VI

'Politics is perhaps the only profession for which no preparation is thought necessary.'

Robert Louis Stevenson (1850–1894),
'Yoshida-Torajiro,'
Familiar Studies of Men and Books, 1882.

Introduction

The political landscape in Scotland has changed. Even though the Scottish National Party (SNP) did slightly worse than expected in the May 1999 elections, and lost one seat at Westminster in the June 2001 general election, the possibility remains that one day Scotland may seek independence from the rest of the United Kingdom (UK). The SNP will continue to argue the case for independence and the chances are that it may form an administration in Edinburgh sometime in the next ten years. SNP leader John Swinney targets 2007 (the three-hundredth anniversary year of the Treaty of Union) as a possible year for independence.[1] Most opposition parties take their turn in government; and in devolved and federal systems abroad – such as Catalonia or Quebec – nationalist parties frequently govern at the sub–national level.

The Parti Québécois (PQ) became the Government of Quebec for the first time in 1976 and has served terms in power since then. But after 25 years as a major political force in Quebec the PQ has still not achieved its goal of sovereignty. In comparison, the SNP had very little political leverage until 1997 – when devolution was put on the legislative agenda by the new Labour government. The 1999 Scottish parliament elections established the SNP as a serious political player. Whilst it still has no experience of holding power in office it now has power within arms' reach. This is not to suggest that a referendum on independence or that independence itself is imminent; but every time the SNP does well in the polls, or uses its voice effectively in the new Scottish Parliament, the question will re-surface. And if the SNP win an election in Scotland independence will move sharply onto the political agenda.

But what exactly does 'independence' mean? The SNP has not defined its meaning with complete clarity. SNP leader John Swinney wants Scotland to be 'a normal independent country'.[2] But what is the substance of independence? We do not hesitate to recognise the work the SNP, and others, have done in this area. An interesting but now dated collection of essays on *Independence and Devolution: the Legal Implications for Scotland* was edited by John Grant and published in 1976 by W. Green & Son. More recent publications in this area are:

- a chapter by Robert Lane called ' "Scotland in Europe": An Independent Scotland in the European Community' (Lane 1991);
- a paper by the Scottish Centre for Economic and Social Research in 1996 called *Scotland's Government – the transition to Independence* (Scottish Centre for Economic and Social Research 1996);
- a journal article by Matthew Happold called 'Independence: In or Out of Europe?' (Happold 2000); and
- a journal article by Neil MacCormick in 2000 entitled 'Is There A Constitutional Path to Scottish Independence?' (MacCormick 2000).

But many questions remain to be answered. What are the key functions of a state? What difference would independence make? How much greater would Scotland's autonomy be? William Wallace, Professor in International Relations at the London School of Economics, sums up the core functions of the state as the following:

> The preservation of internal order, the maintenance of national boundaries and the defence of national territory against foreign attack; the provision of 'legitimate' government, through an established and well-ordered state apparatus, equipped with the symbols and institutions needed to 'represent' the nation and to give its citizens a sense of participation in the national community; the provision of services, and of welfare, to reinforce this sense of national community; and the promotion of national prosperity – which in the Keynesian era became the pursuit of balanced and sustained economic growth (Wallace 1997: 33).

The question then becomes how much autonomy states have in the modern globalised and interdependent economy. The idea of the nation-state in Western Europe as the locus of social and political identity was central to the French revolution, and developed in the nineteenth century. The second half of the twentieth century has (arguably) witnessed the gradual demise of the state, instigated and assisted by the European Community (MacCormick 1999: 125).

Does the SNP want to create an independent Scotland based on a nineteenth century model of the nation-state? Does it want to establish its own network of embassies, its own foreign policy, its own armed forces, and its own currency? Or is it more of a European federalist party? There are conflicting tendencies within the SNP. Some would like an independent Scotland to be a completely different country – even outside the European Union. Others do not want it to change much at all and would like to keep pensions, the National Health Service, and the Queen. At the very least, an independent Scotland would distinguish itself from its current form in three ways:

1. The Scottish state would have exclusive or overriding legislative and judicial power, that is the power to make the laws for and interpret the laws of the land.
2. The Scottish state would have exclusive power over levying taxes and public spending.
3. The Scottish state could enter into, renegotiate, and revoke international treaties.

The problem is that in an increasingly inter-dependent world the idea of national sovereignty has been diminished. Even a much larger player like the United Kingdom cannot, for example, unilaterally negotiate an external trade agreement with a third country that bypasses the European Union. An independent Scotland would be even more constrained by the economic realities. Scotland would not obtain exclusive control of its fisheries industry or farming policy if it achieved sovereign statehood within the European Union. Building on more than 30 years of European integration, the Maastricht Treaty (1992) reinforced and recognised the gradual erosion of all traditional core functions of the West European states. No longer would Member States have sole control over national territory and borders, police, citizenship and immigration, currency, taxation, financial transfers, management of the economy, promotion of industry, representation and accountability, foreign policy and defence. Wallace notes that only welfare remained in the domain of the nation state, although arguably the Social Chapter impinged on that (Wallace 1997: 35).

And how would Scotland achieve independence? Can it be attained by constitutional evolution rather than revolution? The presumption of the modern state is one of indivisibility, and countries do not generally provide for their own demise. Indeed, between 1920 and 1989 there was only one significant case of secession (that of East Pakistan, now Bangladesh, in 1971). But after the fall of the Iron Curtain in 1989 there have been, as Professor Allen Buchanan of the University of Arizona points out, 'at least a dozen secessionist attempts and more than twenty-five new states have been formed out of fragments of old ones' (Buchanan 1998: 14).

The purpose of this book is not to offer an opinion on the imminence of secession or a grant of independence for Scotland. Rather, it assumes that such an event might come about and then proceeds to examine what would be entailed by such an event. Many of these questions are frequently raised in British political debate, especially at election times. A high degree of uncertainty surrounds all predictions as to the future consequences – political, economic, and social. Would Scotland inherit membership of the European Union? How much of the national debt would be assigned to Scotland upon independence? Would the Scottish economy prosper like that of the Celtic tiger across the Irish sea? Would Scots still be free to live and work in England, and *vice versa*? These and many other questions will be addressed in this book. It is not a comprehensive account but we believe that it is more detailed than any other guide produced so far.

This work has striven to be strictly neutral on the desirability of independence. It is not a party political document. It should not be read as an endorsement either for or against Scottish independence. It is a technical and we hope expert contribution to the independence debate, but one that will undoubtedly need to be developed and refined should independence one day become a realistic prospect. Our approach is deliberately logical and sequential. We are setting out how Scottish independence could be attained within the UK's constitutional framework and under the rule of law. For the sake of analysis, we have to assume that all players would abide by the rules of the game. That is not to say that the whole process would not be intensely political and would likely be much messier than the logical path we have mapped out here.

The book has four parts. Part One is about the road leading up to independence and has a sharp domestic focus. The central feature of the first three chapters is 'referendums'. Chapter 1 introduces some preliminary but important issues to do with referendums in the Scottish context. Chapter 2 is about the *macro* use of referendums in the UK (for example, the doctrine of parliamentary sovereignty and the role of the Electoral Commission) whereas Chapter 3 examines the *micro* issues (for example, thresholds and the wording of the question). Chapter 4 highlights the main points that would need to be negotiated before Scotland could become an independent state.

The second part of the book is about the road leading from independence and has a sharp international focus. Chapter 5 asks what effect Scottish independence would have on the United Kingdom. Chapter 6 addresses at some length the question whether Scotland would inherit membership of the European Union. Chapter 7 considers two case studies which have had an impact on the European Communities, and Chapter 8 analyses the scenario whereby Scotland would formally have to accede to the EU. Chapter 9 is about the rules of state succession to international treaties as well as international organisations.

The final two parts take a different perspective. Part Three, by Peter Jones, examines the economics of independence using the available evidence about Scotland and the lessons to be learned from Canada and Czechoslovakia. Chapter 10 looks at where, economically, an independent Scotland would be starting from. Chapter 11 considers how the assets and liabilities of the UK could be divided and Chapter 11 debates how much economic uncertainty might be caused by the process of moving to independence. Chapter 12 sets out the institutions that would be needed by Scotland to manage its economic independence and considers how much economic freedom Scotland would have.

Part Four moves beyond the process of independence. Chapter 14 examines post-independence relations between Scotland and the remainder of the United Kingdom, with citizenship as its focal point. Chapter 15, contributed by Michael Keating, examines the present condition of Scottish nationalism and sets it in the context of a changing international political environment.

Finally, terminology should be clarified. This book argues that if Scotland became independent, the rump (or remainder) of the United Kingdom (rUK) would step into the footsteps of the current United Kingdom. In other words, rUK would be the continuing State of the United Kingdom. This acronym may be unsightly and even annoying. But it serves its purpose and, for better or worse, is used throughout.

– Notes –

1. *The Scotsman*, 25 September 2000, p. 6.
2. Scottish Parliament Official Report, Session 1, 21 June 2001, Col. 1768.

Part One: The Road to Independence

Jo Eric Murkens

CHAPTER I

Preliminary Issues

– INTRODUCTION –

Scottish independence is the *raison d'être* of the SNP. But even though independence is envisaged as the ultimate goal, the SNP says very little about how it can be achieved and how it will get past the sovereign guardian of the United Kingdom constitution, the Westminster Parliament. It is especially not clear how independence will affect the United Kingdom as a whole. Even though the withdrawal of Scotland from the United Kingdom is sometimes understood as a case of 'secession', that is probably not what Scottish nationalists have in mind. One definition of secession is 'the creation of a State by the use or threat of force and without the consent of the former sovereign' (Crawford 1979: 247). Secession is thus not the same as a 'grant of independence', by which a particular territory and people are granted independence through legislative or other means by the parent state. Secession is a unilateral process. The grant of independence is a bilateral and consensual process (Crawford 1998: 86) that is consistent with most people's understanding of how independence for Scotland should be achieved. James Crawford, who is Professor of International Law at the University of Cambridge, makes a further distinction 'between immediately effective grants of independence, and gradual erosion or accretion of power in a local unit, such that the latter eventually is classified as a separate State' (Crawford 1979: 215). In short, independence could either be attained in one fell swoop, or gradually and over time as a process of further devolution.

The chapters of Part One will examine the constitutional path by which Scotland would attain independence in greater detail. The main focus will be on the use of independence referendums and the negotiations for independence. But there are three preliminary questions to be asked before the conduct of referendums can be considered:

- does Scotland have a right in law to be independent?
- does the Scottish Parliament have the power to hold a referendum on independence?
- under what circumstances will a referendum be politically persuasive? What constitutes a mandate for independence?

– Does Scotland have a right in law to be independent? –

The right to self-determination is commonly understood to mean that a group or people have a right in law to secede from their parent state, that is the state to which they are affiliated.[1] But, outside the colonial context, public international law does not recognise such a right. On the contrary, one of the objectives of international law is to maintain the territorial integrity of states, which implies that governments of a state must be allowed to resist the secession of a part of its territory using lawful means (Crawford 1998: 87). Article 1(1) of the International Covenant on Civil and Political Rights (ICCPR) and of the International Covenant on Economic, Social and Cultural Rights (ICESCR), adopted by the General Assembly in 1966, provides that:

> All peoples have the right to self-determination. By virtue of that right they freely determine their political status and freely pursue their economic, social and cultural development.

A significant number of states, however, insisted that this provision did not amount to a right to secede.[2] Here, there is an obvious inconsistency between, on the one hand, allowing a people to freely determine its political status but, on the other, preventing them from establishing an independent state. As Quane notes, 'the reference to "political status" is broad enough to encompass the right to independence or any other international status' (Quane 1998: 560). The reach of Article 1 was therefore limited by the categories of people to which it applies, namely peoples organised as states and colonial peoples, thus rendering the *legal* right to secession in the Covenants 'largely irrelevant' (Ibid. at 562).

Articles 1 and 55 of the UN Charter refer to the principle of self-determination as a basis for the development of friendly relations among nations. For many states, including the UK, the principle has 'very strong moral force, but it was too complex to be translated into legal terms'.[3] Arguably the UK has gone beyond what is strictly necessary by repeatedly asserting, 'its support in the United Nations for the right of self-determination, and the exercise of that right within the United Kingdom itself[4].

Undoubtedly the UK would have refrained from such a broad endorsement of self-determination knowing that so doing would give licence to the Scots, for example, to break away and become independent.

If there is no right to secede under international law, does such a right exist in the constitutional law of the United Kingdom? The United Kingdom's constitutional laws neither permit nor preclude Scottish independence. Article 1 of the Acts of Union 1706–7 purports to create a Union lasting in perpetuity, and some interpret certain provisions of the Acts as laying down 'fundamental law' which cannot be altered (see Smith 1957; Mitchell 1968). The constitutional principle of parliamentary sovereignty, however, states that a subsequent parliament can undo the decision of a previous parliament. In fact, the Act of Union itself has been frequently amended by Parliament (for a discussion of the alterability of the Acts of Union see Munro 1994). The United Kingdom of Great Britain and Northern Ireland is the result of the union of Great Britain (England, Wales and Scotland) with Ireland following the 1801 Act of Union. It is not the product of the previous Acts of Union which produced Great Britain. So does the 1707 legislation amount to a 'Constitution'? Elizabeth Wicks, of the University of Birmingham, concludes that:

> To regard the Union legislation as a constitution but to permit it to be breached if there is popular consent for the breach is a serious error, which if correct would not only undermine the significance of the Union legislation, but also the significance of constitutions generally (Wicks 2001: 125).

The Acts of Union are, therefore, better thought of as 'constituent documents' which give effect to the UK constitution. The Union manifests itself in the existence of a joint Parliament, but also in the protection of Scotland's own laws and institutions for the judiciary, the church, education and local government, which recognises Scotland's distinctiveness within the United Kingdom.

The constitutional position in the United Kingdom must be contrasted with Canada where the Supreme Court dealt at great length with the question whether, under the Constitution of Canada, the right to secession could be effected unilaterally by Quebec – the implications of their opinion are discussed in the next section. In the United Kingdom, the absence of a written constitution and the fact that the right to self-determination is not mentioned in the European Convention on Human Rights and so is not caught by the Human Rights Act 1998 means that there is no *locus* in which a right to secede might be found.

Having established that there is no legal right to secession in either international or constitutional law, the next step is to consider the existence of a political or moral right of the Scottish people to choose independence. The United Kingdom has, like Canada, not shied away from discussing the possible parting of Scotland on a political level. The *Claim of Right for Scotland*, adopted at the inaugural meeting of the Scottish Constitutional Convention asserts 'the sovereign right of the Scottish people to determine the form of Government best suited to their needs' (Scottish Constitutional Convention 1995: 10). This is something that even opponents of Scottish devolution or independence have accepted. Former Prime Minister Margaret Thatcher wrote in her memoirs that:

> As a nation, they have an undoubted right to national self–determination; thus far they have exercised that right by joining and remaining in the Union. Should they determine on independence no English party or politician would stand in their way, however much we might regret their departure (Thatcher 1993: 624).

Similarly, Thatcher's successor John Major said that independence would be an 'unimaginable disaster' but that it could nonetheless happen. In an interview with the Glasgow *Herald* he said:

> The future of Scotland is your decision. If, after all the arguments that have been carefully weighed, the people of Scotland want to break the bonds that bind us then it can be done. No nation can be held within a Union against its will.[5]

There would appear to be support across any political divide for the proposition that Scottish independence should not, for example, be subject to an English veto. The implication is that, if Scotland opted for independence in a democratic manner, then Westminster would co-operate in letting Scotland leave the Union. The Labour Party is a Unionist party that introduced devolution but continues to oppose separatism. Prior to the 1997 May election, Labour's leader Tony Blair said:

> We support devolution; we oppose separation. The enemy of the Union is no change, not devolution. To insist that the only choice open to Scotland is separation or the status quo is to defy wit, instinct and history. Of course we can celebrate and recognise the differences in our nations within the UK, because the unity of the UK should be based not on conformity, but on diversity.[6]

In government, the view has become clouded by the fact that the Scotland Act 1998 does not include a ceiling. The implications of this have been expounded most succinctly by the former Secretary of State for Wales, Ron Davies, who argued that devolution is a 'process' rather than a settled 'event' (Davies 1999), and by Tam Dalyell MP, who believes that devolution is 'a motorway without exit to an independent state'.[7]

Within national law the principle of self-determination has long been accepted in relation to Northern Ireland, and is now firmly enshrined in Section 1 of the Northern Ireland Act 1998.[8] As a matter of equality it would be difficult to deny that right to Scotland. However, on closer inspection, the self-determination offered by the UK Government to the people of Northern Ireland is not for full independence, but the right to rejoin the Republic of Ireland. As Hazell and O'Leary note, 'it is a more limited right of reunification, not a right of unconstrained self-determination' (Hazell and O'Leary 1998: 23). Such a legal right plainly does not exist in the context of Scotland. When the Referendums (Scotland and Wales) Bill was published, the Secretary of State for Scotland, the late Donald Dewar, said that:

> the only way in which we could move to independence would be if people voted for independence. That is clearly their right and I would not wish to deny them that right (*The Herald* 16 May 1997, p. 1).

Of interest in all the above citations is the general confusion of terms. It has already been shown that while Scotland may enjoy a 'right' to self-determination that does not mean that the Scots have a 'right' to secede and become independent. According to the opinion of the International Commission of Jurists in 1920 on the Åland Islands[9], self-determination was a political principle that could not justify the breaking-up of functioning States. On the contrary, it was only during periods of unstable or uncertain State sovereignty that self-determination should be invoked to re-establish the political normality of statehood.[10] But can self-determination really only be expressed 'in the normal functioning of existing participating processes' (Koskenniemi 1994: 246)? After the Åland Islands opinion, jurists limited the secessionist potential of the right to self-determination to the context of decolonisation. However, Martti Koskenniemi, Counsellor (Legal Affairs) for the Ministry of Foreign Affairs of Finland, noted that self-determination was increasingly being interpreted along more generous lines because:

> the conception of 'abnormality' has been widened to include not only situations in which there has been a revolutionary international transformation such as took place in 1914–1919 or again in 1989 but also situations

where the internal constitution of 'clearly established States' has been found completely unacceptable (Koskenniemi 1994: 247).

Additionally, the anti-statist character of self-determination has been reinforced by the legal requirement that, even if the national entity does not have a right to secede, the parent State must protect its identity and its members' ability to 'enjoy their own culture, to profess and practice their own religion, or to use their own language'.[11] Self-determination, in other words, both supports and challenges statehood. The general consensus as regards the application of self-determination in the UK is that such a right would be a political as opposed to a legal right.[12] There is no right in law to secede from the United Kingdom, although there is a political understanding that such an entitlement exists as regards Scotland.[13]

– Does Quebec have a right to secede unilaterally from Canada? –

Canada is a close parallel as it shows how a country that has been shaped by the common law has dealt with the prospect of secession by one of its constituent parts, namely Quebec. Because Quebec provides many close points of comparison it is given extended treatment in this book and in this opening chapter. The rise of Quebec nationalism since the 'quiet revolution' in the 1960s, and of the separatist Parti Québécois (PQ) which came to power under René Lévesque in 1976, has led to two sovereignty referendums in Quebec. The referendum of 20 May 1980 was called by the PQ Government for a mandate to negotiate 'sovereignty-association' with Canada, the results of which would then have been put to the electorate for approval in a second referendum. The proposal was rejected by 59.6 per cent to 40.4 per cent, and the Liberals returned to provincial power in 1985. After the failure of the Meech Lake talks in 1990 and the Charlottetown Accord of 1992, where Quebec sought recognition as a 'distinct society', the provincial separatist party PQ and the newly-formed federal separatist party Bloc Québécois (BQ) experienced a surge in support. The PQ won the provincial elections in 1994 and pledged to hold another referendum.

On 30 October 1995, Canada came within an ace of losing Quebec after a province-wide sovereignty referendum. Unlike the 1980 referendum, which had received a substantial federalist majority, the federalists clinched the 1995 referendum only by the narrowest of margins (50.58 per cent to 49.42 per cent).[14] After years of dismissing a separatist referendum victory as unlikely and not wanting to have an open debate about the merits of the PQ's sovereigntist[15] claims, Canada's federal Government was woken up by the result. It subsequently resorted to attack as the best form of defence and came up with two complementary plans to take the wind out of the separatists' sails. Plan A was developed as the 'soft' option by which Quebec's cultural and legal differences were recognised and expressly embraced by the federation. Plan B in contrast was more proactive, not to say aggressive, and the Government decided that it would:

- consistently reject sovereigntist claims;
- emphasise the prospect of long and protracted negotiations (were Quebec to vote 'Yes' next time);
- question the legitimacy of a referendum that was restricted to the voters of Quebec but had constitutional implications for Canada as a whole;
- bring to the people's attention the consequences of territorial division, namely that if Canada is divisible, so is Quebec.[16]

It was under Plan B that the federal Government referred the question of the legality of Quebec's secession to the Supreme Court of Canada. Justice Minister Alan Rock emphasised that the federal Government was not implying that Quebec could never become sovereign:

> The leading political figures of all our provinces and the Canadian public have long agreed that the country cannot be held together against the will of Quebecers. This government agrees with that . . .[17]

What the Canadian Government did advocate was that sovereignty be obtained within the constitutional framework and under the rule of law. With this in mind the federal Government sought advice from the Supreme Court which released its opinion almost two years later in August 1998. The principal implications of the *Reference re Secession of Quebec*[18] lie in Canadian constitutional law and in public international law. But since the judgement of the Supreme Court is based upon certain legal and constitutional principles on which the entire judgement rests, the implications of their reasoning may be wider felt. There are striking similarities between Quebec and Scotland. As Mark D. Walters, Professor of Constitutional Law at Queen's University in Canada, notes, 'efforts by Canadian and British judges to identify constitutional rules and principles of a common law nature are analogous, even though one system has a written constitution and the other does not' (Walters 1999: 383). This chapter draws extensively on the main features of the *Quebec Secession Reference* case, because it is relatively little known in Scotland.

As in Scotland, the legal issues relating to independence, sovereignty and secession have tended to be ignored. Quebec sovereigntists as well as Scottish nationalists prefer to argue that independence from the federation/union is entirely a matter of politics to be decided by the people of the part wanting to secede. However, by asking the Supreme Court of Canada to rule on the legality of Quebec's secession the federal Government stressed the primacy of law over politics as regards the democratic governance within Canada and its constitutional integrity (see Howse and Malkin 1997). The federal Government sought clarification on three questions:

1. Under the Constitution of Canada, can the National Assembly, legislature or government of Quebec effect the secession of Quebec from Canada unilaterally?
2. Does international law give Quebec the right to effect secession from Canada unilaterally? In this regard, is there a right to self-determination under international law that would give Quebec the right to secession?
3. In the event of a conflict between domestic and international law on the right of Quebec to effect secession from Canada unilaterally, which would take precedence in Canada?

The Court gave substantive answers to the first two questions, finding unanimously that there was no basis, either under Canadian or under international law, on which to rest a legal right of Quebec to secede from Canada. On the third point, it did not see any potential conflict between constitutional and international law. The Court could have given a very short opinion in answer to the questions put before it, concentrating purely on matters of law. It went on, however, to discuss matters that are related to the above questions which enabled the Court to give a more comprehensive and rounded, yet also a more political, opinion.

The Court addressed the historical context of Canada's Constitution[19] before examining:

> four foundational constitutional principles that are most germane for resolution of this reference: federalism, democracy, constitutionalism and the rule of law, and respect for minority rights. These defining principles function in symbiosis. No single principle can be defined in isolation from the others, nor does any one principle trump or exclude the operation of any other.[20]

The Court contended that in a federal system 'no one majority is more or less "legitimate" than the others as an expression of democratic opinion'.[21] It would, therefore, be 'a grave mistake to equate legitimacy with the "sovereign will" or majority rule alone, to the exclusion of other constitutional values'.[22] Since the Constitution Act 1982 allows each participant in the federation to initiate constitutional change:

> the existence of this right imposes a corresponding duty on the participants in Confederation to engage in constitutional discussions in order to acknowledge and address democratic expressions of a desire for change in other provinces. This duty is inherent in the democratic principle which is a fundamental predicate of our system of governance.[23]

But the Court gave short shrift to the argument that a majority vote in a province-wide referendum could legitimately by-pass the Constitution. This is an important point. The will of the majority does not automatically trump the will of the minority. Referendums in Quebec (and so far in Scotland) are instruments of consultation not policy making. But they are also an expression of the popular voice. Since popular sovereignty underlies the legitimacy of the constitutional settlement, does it follow that the same popular sovereignty could lead to secession by majority vote alone?

The Court unequivocally rejects such a conclusion. Majoritarianism is only 'superficially persuasive'. The Court's substantive answer is worth citing in full:

> Constitutional government is necessarily predicated on the idea that the political representatives of the people of a province have the capacity and the power to commit the province to be bound into the future by the constitutional rules being adopted. These rules are 'binding' not in the sense of frustrating the will of a majority of a province, but as defining the majority which must be consulted in order to alter the fundamental balances of political power (including the spheres of autonomy guaranteed by the principle of federalism), individual rights, and minority rights in our society. Of course, those constitutional rules are themselves amenable to amendment, but only through a process of negotiation which ensures that there is an opportunity for the constitutionally defined rights of all the parties to be respected and reconciled.[24]

In other words, democracy (or majoritarianism) is not an overriding value but has to be reconciled with constitutionalism and the protection of minority rights. For these reasons an 'enhanced majority' is required to achieve constitutional change – although the Court does not spell out what that means in practice.[25]

Having established the pertinent principles, the Court analyses their operation with respect to secession which it defines as:

the effort of a group or section of a state to withdraw itself from the political and constitutional authority of that state, with a view to achieving statehood for a new territorial unit on the international plane.[26]

The Court concedes that 'the Constitution is silent as to the ability of a province to secede from Confederation' and that it 'neither expressly authorizes nor prohibits secession'. That said, 'an act of secession would purport to alter the governance of Canadian territory' and consequently secession would 'require an amendment to the Constitution, which perforce requires negotiation.'[27] As a result, secession could be achieved by 'the power of the people of Canada acting through their various governments duly elected and recognized under the Constitution'.[28] The Court here is at pains to uphold the integrity of the Canadian federation without appearing to be undemocratic. Thus unilateral secession which is:

1. Premised solely on a positive result in a referendum, however clear; and
2. Without prior negotiations with both the other provinces and the federal Government

would be unconstitutional. The referendum result would, however, carry 'considerable weight' and it would 'confer legitimacy on the efforts of the government of Quebec to initiate the Constitution's amendment process in order to secede by constitutional means'.[29] The Court insists that the result has to be 'clear', which it defines as 'free of ambiguity both in terms of the question asked and in terms of the support it achieves'.[30] The Court later abbreviates the formulation to 'a clear majority . . . on a clear question',[31] and holds that this standard would be subject to 'political evaluation' rather than judicial consideration.[32] Crucially, it does not specify an actual percentage or threshold. A 'qualitative evaluation',[33] rather than a numerical specification, is called for. This would take account of extraneous factors, such as how the referendum campaign was conducted and whether voting procedures were adhered to.

– Significance of the Supreme Court's judgement –

The judgement of the Supreme Court cuts to the core of the relationship between law and politics (see Toope: 1999). The Court was all too aware that simply declaring that Quebec could not unilaterally effect secession by no means pre-empted a unilateral declaration of independence. In a judgement that pleased and upset both federalists and sovereigntists in equal measure, the Court found that whilst secession was clearly unconstitutional, the unequivocal rejection of the federation would, however, give rise to 'a reciprocal obligation on all parties . . . to negotiate constitutional changes to respond to that desire'.[34]

The federalism principle and the democratic principle (which gives the referendum its weight) go hand in hand, and it is this combination that gives rise to the legal duty to negotiate and to amend the constitution. The four key principles of the unwritten Canadian constitution (federalism, democracy, the rule of law and minority rights) are structured non-hierarchically and would at all times have to be adhered to in negotiations. Walters sums up the situation as follows:

> Quebec could not rely upon democracy to insist upon a legal entitlement to secede; its legal right would extend only to bona fide negotiations [paragraphs 87–93]. Conversely, other parties could not rely upon federalism, the rule of law or minority rights to refuse to negotiate secession: as long as Quebec itself 'respects the rights of others' they would be under a legal duty to negotiate with Quebec [paragraph 92] (Walters 1999: 378–9).

Thus, the Court here transforms the PQ Government's long-held view that Canada would be under a moral or political duty to negotiate independence with Quebec after a sovereigntist referendum victory into a legal obligation. In so doing, the Supreme Court's judgement went beyond what was strictly necessary to rule on the legality of a prospective unilateral declaration of independence. It chose to rule as well under what circumstances Quebec might lawfully secede from Canada, and made pronouncements on the legal framework for secession. To Walters the Court's response amounts to 'judicial activism aimed ultimately at reconciling . . . "legality" with (democratic) "legitimacy"' (Walters 1999: 375).

Finally, it should be noted that the Canadian Government's decision to refer the question of secession to its Supreme Court was an act of political strength. Wheeling in the strong arm of the law at this stage not only helped to defuse the political debate but it also had the same effect as the habitual and familiar reassertion of domestic 'law and order' policies which successive Anglo-American governments have relied on. By invoking the traditional culture of deference, whereby the people are expected to obey the law uncritically, the implication is that secession would be a (quasi-) revolutionary act, and hence illegal, which only people who disregard the law could possibly support.

– Could Scotland declare independence unilaterally? –

In striking contrast to Quebec, which has consistently fought for recognition as a 'nation' or as a 'distinct society', the Scots are unquestionably recognised as one of four nations within the United Kingdom. The drive for Scottish independence is largely rooted in the belief that nationhood and statehood are twins who should no longer be kept apart. Scottish civic identity has not only continued to exist within the United Kingdom but, as Professor Neil MacCormick of the University of Edinburgh notes, has also become more localised so that Scots now recognise highland and lowland, Gaelic and Scots, country and town, East and West, North and South (MacCormick 1999: 60). The clarity of Scotland as a territorial and political unit and the national identity of the Scottish people mean that no one can seriously dispute that Scotland possesses all the necessary ingredients for statehood.

However, it is also clear that statehood could not be achieved unilaterally by the devolved Scottish parliament. Without having secured agreement from the United Kingdom the purported Act by the Scottish Parliament declaring the country's independence would be *ultra vires* and void. A unilateral declaration of independence (UDI), although the conventional way to initiate secession, is not a constitutional option for Scotland as it is a 'hostile' declaration of independence. The most obvious recent UDI was by Southern Rhodesia on 11 November 1965. After this declaration of political dissent by the white government, the United Kingdom immediately imposed economic sanctions, and the UN later imposed a total embargo on trade with the country. Rhodesia declared itself a republic in 1970 but was not recognised by the United Kingdom or by any other State. In other words, the consequences of a UDI are worlds apart from the smooth transition to independence that mainstream Scottish nationalists have in mind.

– Lessons from Quebec –

The situation in Quebec is also instructive for Scotland. Quebec provides the only instance of a secession referendum in a modern liberal democracy.[35] The Parti Québécois (PQ) may even be prepared to attain sovereignty by issuing a UDI – if all else fails. In the second and most recent Quebec referendum on sovereignty in 1995, draft legislation was in place to negotiate a new economic and political partnership with Canada. Agreement was to be reached within one year. In the event that agreement was not reached or Canada refused to negotiate, the PQ proposed that the Quebec National Assembly would unilaterally declare Quebec to be a 'sovereign country' and request international State recognition.[36] Of interest is that, unlike the SNP, the PQ was not just talking of leaving the federation but had draft legislation as well as a strategy in place. That was more than enough to send resounding shockwaves to the federal

Government, which responded by referring the question of the legality of a UDI to the Supreme Court of Canada and by passing the Clarity Act, details of which are discussed in Chapter 3.

In terms of strategy there is now a stark choice for the Quebec government between attaining sovereignty constitutionally (that is by amending the Canadian constitution) or unconstitutionally by issuing a UDI. The Clarity Act is framework legislation enacted by Parliament in Ottawa that sets out a process for secession of any Canadian province. It lays down the conditions that must be met before the federal government will negotiate secession. In so doing it contradicts fundamental beliefs of the PQ Government in Quebec, for instance about the feasibility of a UDI or the requisite size of a majority in a sovereignty referendum.

Although the federal Government insists that it would not hold Quebec in Canada against its will, it is nevertheless clear that the strategies of the two sides pull in opposite directions. And even within the PQ there are different views on how sovereignty should be attained. Whilst sovereignty through constitutional amendment is the preferred route, others argue that Canada would never let Quebec go on PQ terms and fear that Quebec's fate would be forged by Canada's dominance in the negotiation process. A UDI is *prima facie* a clearer statement of Quebec's desire to be a sovereign State but this ignores the fact that Quebec's fate would still be forged by extraneous forces, namely the international community which does not take kindly to UDI's except in extreme circumstances which do not apply to Quebec. The Supreme Court of Canada identified three circumstances where public international law recognises the possibility of unilateral secession under the right of self-determination:

1. Where 'a people' is governed as part of a colonial empire;
2. Where 'a people' is subject to alien subjugation, domination or exploitation;
3. And possibly where 'a people' is denied any meaningful exercise of its right to self-determination within the state of which it forms part.

This is a very liberal interpretation of the right to self-determination. Mary Dawson, who is the Associate Deputy Minister in the Department of Justice of the Government of Canada and was the lead legal advisor to the Government of Canada in relation to the *Quebec Secession Reference* case, surmises that 'there is little doubt that the opinion will be cited with interest by international observers focussing on the development of this area of the law' (Dawson 1999: 33).

– Relevance for Scotland –

A UDI is, as the Quebec case shows, not an option for the Scots either. The Scottish Parliament would have to secure consent from the United Kingdom first, otherwise the purported Act by the Scottish Parliament declaring the country's independence would be *ultra vires* and void. To become independent by a constitutional route would require the United Kingdom's equivalent to a 'constitutional amendment', that is an Act of Parliament either stating that Scotland shall henceforth be a sovereign State and/or stating that all legislation stemming from Westminster shall henceforth not apply to Scotland. All UK governments have been unequivocal in upholding the Union. But both Conservative and Labour Prime Ministers have accepted publicly that Scotland could not be kept in the Union against its will. The United Kingdom's stance on Scottish independence derives from three premisses:

- Scotland is a territorially distinct nation;
- the people of Scotland have a right to national self-determination;
- to exercise that right, the people of Scotland must express their desire for independence democratically.

In other words, if the Scots decided to withdraw their support for the Union, then Scotland could leave the Union it once chose to join. This concession by the United Kingdom is a politically generous one and not one required by either constitutional or international law. If the above position is accepted, namely that Scotland is entitled to withdraw from the United Kingdom if it so desires, then only two practical questions remain:

- does the Scottish Parliament have the power to hold a referendum on independence?
- what constitutes a mandate for independence?

Does the Scottish Parliament have the power to hold a referendum on independence?

– Political issues –

Under the Scotland Act 1998, the UK Parliament remains sovereign and retains control over such matters as foreign affairs, defence, national security, the UK's fiscal and monetary policy, and social security policy and administration.[37] However, the Scottish Parliament can debate any matter and could use this ability to put a particular issue on the political agenda in Westminster.

As a matter of law, a referendum on the Union is outside its powers. Sections 28 and 29 of the Scotland Act 1998 and Schedules 4 and 5 impose explicit restrictions and reservations on the Scottish Parliament's general legislative jurisdiction. In particular, it is not within the competencies of the Scottish Parliament to amend the Scotland Act (section 29(2) and Schedule 4, Part I, paragraph 4(1)), or to enact legislation on reserved matters (section 29(2)(b)). Such reserved matters include 'the Union of the Kingdoms of Scotland and England' and the UK Parliament (Schedule 5, Part I, paragraph 1(b) and (c)), international relations (Schedule 5, Part I, paragraph 7(1)), and nationality (Schedule 5, Part II, section B6).

A referendum on Scotland's future within the Union lies outside the powers of the Scottish Parliament if used as a means to change the constitutional set-up, but does it lie outside as a mechanism of consultation? Secretary of State for Scotland, Donald Dewar, clearly thought it did, although he was not oblivious to the political weight of a successful referendum on independence:

> A referendum that purported to pave the way for something that was *ultra vires* is itself *ultra vires* . . . But . . . the sovereignty of the people, which is often prayed in aid, is still there in the sense that, if they vote for a point of view, for change, and mean that they want that change by their vote, any elected politician in this country must very carefully take that into account.[38]

Dewar rejects an 'indirect' referendum on independence. A Trojan-horse style question, one that is formally within the ambit of the Scotland Act but whose objective is outside the Act, is rejected. But interestingly Dewar does accept that the people could 'vote for a point of view, for change'. The question is whether that 'vote for change' should be confined to general and Holyrood elections or whether a referendum might not also be used as a vehicle for change.

The general consensus amongst commentators regarding the delineation of powers is as follows: whilst the Scottish Parliament may not make laws that challenge the integrity of the United Kingdom, it can nonetheless debate matters such as Scottish independence and even authorise a referendum to gauge public opinion. As Professor Neil MacCormick says:

> The Scottish Executive has unlimited powers to negotiate with the Westminster government about any issues which could be the subject of discussion between them, therefore it could seek an advisory referendum (MacCormick 2000: 726).

Colin Munro, Professor of Constitutional Law at the University of Edinburgh, appears to confirm this. In an article in *The Scotsman* he was quoted as saying:

> You have to make the distinction between the reserved powers and what parliament can debate and discuss. There is nothing to stop the parliament arranging to hold a referendum, because that would not involve a change in the law. The actual separation of Scotland from the rest of the UK would be a Westminster decision, but Labour have already said that they would regard a majority vote in favour of the SNP as a vote for independence (*The Scotsman*, 11 March 1998).

Mark D. Walters, Professor of Law at Queen's University in Canada, writes that:

> a consultative referendum – even on secession – would not conflict with the policy of the [Scotland] Act so long as its purpose is to assist the Scottish Parliament in determining the democratic will of the electorate (Walters 1999: 387).

To draw things together, the Scottish Parliament has the power to debate any issue it likes and consult widely, regardless of whether the subject matter actually falls within its remit. There is nothing to stop it debating the Act of Settlement, nuclear proliferation or other matter not within its legislative powers. As a matter of politics, Parliament is there to express the views of the people.

– Legal issues –

But holding a referendum on independence is, of course, different from debating it. Referendums cost money: in Scotland the cost would be approximately £5 million. The Scottish Executive has no more rights than the British Government to spend money on holding a referendum without first obtaining legislative authority. The procedure would be that the Scottish Executive would need to introduce a Bill in the Scottish Parliament to hold a referendum. But this Bill would be subject to scrutiny and possible challenge under the Scotland Act by:

1. The member of the Executive who is in charge of the Bill (Section 31(1));
2. The Presiding Officer (Section 31(2));
3. The Advocate General, the Lord Advocate or the Attorney General (Section 33(1)) who can refer the question whether the Bill is within the

powers of the Scottish Parliament to the Judicial Committee of the Privy Council;

4. The Secretary of State (Section 35) who can intervene where she reasonably believes that the Bill would (a) be incompatible with any international obligations, or the interests of defence or national security, or which (b) refers to a reserved matter. This amounts to a political veto whereby the Secretary of State 'may make an order prohibiting the Presiding Officer from submitting the Bill for Royal Assent'.

Third parties, such as ordinary citizens or political parties opposed to independence cannot challenge a Bill introduced by the Executive: this early right of challenge is limited to the officers listed above. But they could seek a declaration that the Act of the Scottish Parliament is invalid (see below), or seek an interdict[39] to prevent the holding of the referendum. The other public official who might be called on to intervene is the Auditor General for Scotland. The validity of the legislation will be determined by reference to the 'purpose' of the Referendum Bill (Section 29(3) of the 1998 Act). If the outcome of the proposed referendum means independence then it will be classified as a reserved matter and therefore *ultra vires*. However, where the referendum is purely advisory in nature and does not pre-determine the effect of the outcome of the referendum, then the Bill has a chance of survival. Its purpose is determined by the wording of the referendum question.

The legislative competence of the Scottish Parliament can also be questioned in relation to an Act – as opposed to a Bill. Section 29(1) of the Scotland Act states that '[a]n Act of the Scottish Parliament is not law so far as any provision of the Act is outside the legislative competence of the Parliament.' It must be for the courts to decide whether or not the contested provision was within or outside legislative competence. The Scotland Act itself does not determine all the possible parties who could raise issues of competence. Chris Himsworth and Colin Munro, both from the University of Edinburgh, state that:

[i]t may be that the proceedings will be raised by the UK Government to challenge the validity of an Act of the Parliament – producing a case between the Government and a devolved institution. Equally, however, it might be a citizen or group of citizens who wish to make the challenge – usually producing, therefore, a case between individuals and a devolved institution. In either of these circumstances the most likely but not inevitable form of proceedings would be judicial review in the Court of Session (Himsworth and Munro 1999: 194).

Depending on the wording of the referendum (considered at pp. 62–8 below) the Scottish Parliament could probably arrange for the referendum to be held. The result, however, would not be legally binding on Westminster. The Select Committee on Scottish Affairs considered the question of power in its examination of the Scotland Act. Their report states that:

> greater power can only be granted to Scotland by the UK Parliament and here there is potential for conflict. To take the extreme example, constitutional matters are reserved but it is hard to see how the Scottish Parliament could be prevented from holding a referendum on independence should it be determined to do so. If the Scottish people expressed a desire for independence the stage would be set for a direct clash between what is the English doctrine of sovereignty and the Scottish doctrine of the sovereignty of the people.[40]

The Committee believes that, both in political and in practical terms, it would be difficult to prevent a referendum on independence.

To conclude this section, the strength of the direct and democratic expression of the people's will is not derived from the constitutional position but from political legitimacy. Reform does not always conform to the rule of law and formal legitimacy. It is true that the powers of the Scottish parliament are limited and do not extend to creating the platform for constitutional change in the United Kingdom. And it is also true that the nascent Scottish doctrine of sovereignty (of the people) will, once wakeful, clash with the formal United Kingdom doctrine of sovereignty (of Parliament). But all that is anticipated and is part and parcel of constitutional development and reform. The danger with over-emphasising formalism and legalism is a Catch 22 situation whereby the UK Government publicly recognises Scotland's entitlement to independence and to hold a referendum but does not in practice provide the constitutional mechanism to give effect to those rights, rendering them futile.

The last preliminary question to be considered is under what conditions a referendum would be called.

– What constitutes a mandate for independence? –

If one accepts the above two propositions, namely that Scotland could break away from the United Kingdom and that the Scottish Parliament has powers vested in it that might initiate that process, the next question is what would trigger the process. Since the SNP is the biggest party by far advocating independence, with a real chance of one day becoming the largest party in the Scottish Parliament, its strategy is obviously of key importance.

There are essentially two kinds of mandate: from a vote in elections (either to the UK or Scottish Parliament), and from a vote in a referendum. A referendum can either be held before negotiations for independence begin (to initiate those negotiations) or after they have been concluded (to accept or reject their outcome). It would of course be possible to hold referendums at both points. Since it first came to provincial power in Quebec in 1976 the PQ has not argued that winning a majority of seats in the Quebec Parliament constitutes a mandate to commence negotiations. It is committed to seeking a mandate in a subsequent referendum. In contrast, the SNP's *Policy intentions for the 1999 Elections* implied that had it received a majority in the Scottish Parliament elections it would have taken that 'as a mandate for Independence negotiations . . . At the conclusion of negotiations the proposed settlement would be put to the Scottish people in a referendum for their approval.'[41]

There are advantages to both approaches. A single–issue referendum to initiate the independence process provides a greater degree of clarity regarding voters' views on the principle of independence than victory or defeat in a multi-issue election ever could. However, a referendum on the principle of independence would be incomplete without knowing some of the terms. As the Scottish Centre for Economic and Social Research (SCESR) noted in its 1996 report, 'independence in this context is not an abstract concept, but must be framed as a concrete proposal for a duly constituted State with a clearly stated constitution standing in a defined relationship to its neighbours and enjoying a definite position in relation to international and transnational organisations.' The report argued that a referendum would ideally be held once negotiations are complete on a 'precise proposal for a duly constituted independent Scotland' (SCESR 1996: paragraph 14). One option would be for Scottish ministers to indicate broadly what terms they are hoping to negotiate with the UK. There are people who might support independence on some terms but not on others and they should be presented with a specific proposal on which to cast judgement. This would be politically astute because it would strengthen the subsequent negotiations.

It will be argued here that referendums relating to Scottish independence need to take place both before and after the envisaged negotiations. The first one will trigger the negotiations and the second will seek approval of the result of the negotiations. The details are considered more fully below. Who negotiates for each side, the contents of the negotiations, and how long the negotiations should be allowed to take are discussed in Chapter 4.

– The SNP's strategy –

The SNP's traditional stance was that independence would be the result of a process in three stages:

1. They would need to win either a majority of Scotland's seats at Westminster or a majority in the new Scottish Parliament;
2. The terms of independence would then be negotiated;
3. The question of independence would be put to the test in a referendum.

In a document setting out policy intentions for the 1999 elections to the Scottish Parliament the SNP stated that, were it to win with:

> a majority of the seats (65 or more) . . . then we will take that as a mandate for Independence negotiations. We will start those negotiations as soon as practicable after the May election. At the conclusion of negotiations the proposed settlement would be put to the Scottish people in a referendum for their approval.[42]

The belief was that negotiations would be triggered by the SNP winning a majority of seats in Scotland and that a referendum was needed (if not for legal then for political reasons) only to complete the transition to full independence. This strategy can be summed up as:

Option 1: Majority – Negotiations – Referendum
However, in 1999 the SNP also had a contingency plan in the event that it failed to gain a majority but formed the Executive (either as a minority Executive or as senior partner in a coalition). In that case the plan was to 'hold an independence referendum within the first term. If the Scottish people so choose we would then go into negotiations which would lead to Independence'.[43] The then SNP leader Alex Salmond also expressed his desire to hold a referendum, albeit in vague terms:

> No party this century has won a majority of both seats and votes in Scotland but obviously that would be our aim and objective. If we do win an overall majority with 50 per cent, then of course we would ask Westminster to negotiate but the decision would still come back to the people in a referendum. If we are in an administration then we'll hold a referendum and again it would be within the context of the four-year term of the Scottish Parliament (*The Scotsman*, 7 April 1999).

The SNP recently retracted from its hard-line stance that independence could be achieved solely by voting for the SNP. The SNP National Council agreed on 25 March 2000 to modify the three-stage process and instead map out its independence vision, put it before the people in a referendum and, only if the outcome was favourable, proceed to negotiate the terms of independence with the UK government. The Council asserted that:

> Scotland is in the process of becoming an independent country, that our goal of national independence can be reached within a defined timescale and that this will be achieved when the people of Scotland vote for independence in a referendum (SNP 2000).

This is a step away from the traditional position that a majority vote for the SNP is synonymous with independence. It has caused some controversy amongst fundamentalist supporters and members. It thus no longer appears to be the case that holding a majority of Scottish seats in Westminster would constitute a mandate for independence but that only a positive referendum result will constitute such a mandate.[44] The shift in strategy has a number of diverse reasons. The main one is a rethink following the creation of the Scottish Parliament. Scottish Parliamentary elections are now the main focus for determining Scotland's future, and not the general elections at Westminster.

The SNP faces systemic difficulties in both the Westminster and the Scottish Parliament. They relate in the main to the electoral system under which members are elected. At Westminster, there are now 72 Scottish seats[45] to be fought for of which the SNP won five in the June 2001 elections. In the unlikely event that the SNP won a majority of Scottish seats it would, it claims, have a mandate to enter into negotiations on independence. However, this is only an option at each UK general election. Moreover, the Westminster first past the post system makes it exceedingly difficult for the SNP to win a majority of seats in Scotland.

Post-devolution, the Scottish Parliament has become the more important *locus* for Scottish politics. It reflects the prime expression of the voice of the Scottish electorate. The SNP is also more likely to do better there than in a Westminster election.[46] The SNP are currently the second biggest political party in the Scottish Parliament with 35 of the 129 seats, pipped by Labour with 55 seats. The SNP forms the main opposition to the Labour–Liberal Democrat coalition at Holyrood. The system of proportional representation (PR) has benefited the SNP in opposition but would make it harder for the SNP on its own to form a government with a working majority. PR makes overall majorities less likely.

In short, political reality motivated the SNP to change tack in March 2000. Previously under Option 1, the election victory itself would have led on to specific negotiations on independence, the outcome of which would then have been submitted for approval in a national referendum. The new strategy, whereby the election victory leads on to a referendum on the specific question of independence which then leads on to negotiations could be summed up as:

Option 2: Majority – Referendum – Negotiations

Option 2 is analogous to the procedure followed by the UK Government in setting up the Scottish Parliament and Welsh Assembly. The Labour Government, having achieved a majority in the 1997 general election, published White Papers proposing in some detail a plan for the devolved legislatures. Having obtained approval of these plans by referendums, the Government then legislated for their implementation.

The question then becomes under what conditions the UK Government would accept the legitimacy and political force of a Scots desire to be independent. Is it the political majority as defined in an election that compels the UK Government to engage in specific negotiations (Option 1)? Or is it the 'double whammy' of the political majority in the elections as well as in the referendum that so compels the UK Government (Option 2)?

Were the SNP to follow Option 1 and take a majority in elections as a mandate, it would assume that all those who voted for the SNP also voted for independence. This would imply that the SNP is a single-issue party (which it denies) with whom no other big party will want to form a coalition. Two other (minor) parties favour Scottish independence, the Scottish Green Party and the Scottish Socialist Party. A majority for the SNP, either alone or in coalition, could be interpreted as adequate support for negotiations to begin with the UK Government: but the SNP would enter the negotiations in a weak position, because of uncertainty about the nature of its mandate. The SNP would do well to ponder the example of the Blair government, which greatly strengthened its mandate in 1997 to introduce the devolution legislation, and swept away any possible Conservative challenge in Parliament, by holding pre-legislative referendums in Scotland and Wales. Similarly any SNP government should consider strengthening its hand in advance of negotiations by confirming that independence is the 'settled will' of the Scottish people. For these reasons, a referendum before negotiations is needed.

It is too soon to anticipate the conduct of the SNP. Only the discarded Option 1 had any time to mature and so it is necessary to set out all available routes by which the SNP might enter into negotiations. Option 2 creates opportunities for the SNP. The Scottish Green Party and the Scottish Socialists both support independence, and both parties may be wooed to enter a coalition in the event that the SNP is the largest single party in the Scottish Parliament but fails to gain an overall majority of seats. In short, Option 2 constitutes a double-barrelled political force, with a political majority expressing itself in both election and referendum, and is marked by flexibility in terms of forming the Executive.

– Analysis –

There are political advantages and disadvantages to both Options 1 and 2. We suggest that for the independence process to proceed in an orderly and fair manner both options need to be combined: a referendum is required before and after the negotiations. The choice is not between Option 1 and Option 2 because both referendums would ask different questions. One has to distinguish clearly between the first referendum on the principle, giving authority to enter into negotiations, and the second referendum, on the details of the constitutional settlement which has been negotiated. Whereas Referendum 1 does not require a detailed document, Referendum 2 does. The Scottish people need a detailed prospectus setting out the terms of independence which have been negotiated with the UK Government, and ideally a draft constitution too. The prospectus will have to be drafted at the conclusion of the negotiations and before Scottish consent to independence is finally sought. It is the prospectus and draft constitution that makes up the specific proposition to be put to the electorate in a second referendum. The document would take the form of a White Paper. There is no 'ceiling' as to what might be included in the draft constitution but in order to be recognisable as such it should as a 'floor' 'declare Scotland's independent status, provide for establishing a Parliament of Scotland, define the institutions and procedures for the government of Scotland, and determine the fundamental rights of citizens of an independent Scotland' (SCESR 1996: paragraph 15). The suggested final process would then be:

Option 3: Majority – Referendum 1 – Negotiations – Referendum 2
This process indicates the different nature of the referendums. Whereas the focus in political literature tends to be on the first referendum as being the all-important hurdle to pass, it is in fact the second referendum which carries decisive weight. A positive result in Referendum 1 would be no more, and no less, than a politically compelling expression of support from the Scots for their Executive to enter into negotiations with the UK Government. Nothing would have been set in stone at this stage. It would be perfectly possible for voters in the first referendum to vote 'Yes' on

wanting negotiations leading to a new constitutional settlement to begin, but then to reject the terms of independence in Referendum 2 if they are deemed too harsh or too ineffective. Negotiations would either cease or continue, and a new referendum could be called at a later date.

Scottish Ministers would obviously try to avoid falling at the second hurdle. The dangers of a 'neverendum' are all too real and no one in Scotland would benefit from letting the matter go on for years. As Peter Jones shows in Chapter 12, prolonged uncertainty would be damaging to business confidence, inward investment and the Scottish economy. To guard against the risk of the second referendum backfiring, an SNP government could decide that the Scottish Parliament should be the arbiter of the terms of independence. Inviting the parliament to approve the terms that had been negotiated would be less cumbersome and less time consuming than holding a second referendum; but it would not necessarily be decisive. As is mentioned below, the close vote in the Dáil in 1921 on the Treaty did not resolve the matter, and Ireland slid into civil war. The only certain way to ascertain the views of the Scottish people about the acceptability of the terms which have been negotiated is to hold a second referendum. As an alternative proposal, there could be room for the Scottish Parliament to step in and endorse the terms of independence as negotiated by the Scottish and the UK sides. This would be much less cumbersome than holding a second referendum. However, it would only be a constitutional possibility if Westminster accepts to be bound by the endorsement of the Scottish Parliament. Since that is unlikely, would the holding of a second referendum not be the better bet?

This conclusion is strengthened if one takes into account the wider political context. There are now two electoral cycles which punctuate Scottish politics, with UK general elections currently falling in the mid-term of a Scottish parliament. What if a general election fell due, or was called, during or at the end of the independence negotiations which had followed the first referendum? This could be presented by the UK government as a second poll on the independence issue. The UK government could destabilise the negotiations or seek to undermine the result by calling a snap election and making the terms of Scottish independence a central issue. The only effective way to counter argument about whether the Scots wanted independence on the terms which had been negotiated would be for the Scottish Executive to hold their own poll, by having a second referendum.

Moreover, three UK precedents for major constitutional change point clearly towards the need for two referendums:

1. Irish independence. The political mandate for independence arrived in the 1918 general election when Sinn Fein won 73 of the Irish seats at Westminster, the Unionists won 26, and a devolutionist Home Rule Party took 6. The terms of Irish independence were agreed between the UK government and Irish Free State representatives in the 1921 Treaty. These terms were accepted by a bare majority of the Irish cabinet (4:3) and, after a fortnight's debate, by 64 votes to 57 in the Dáil. The anti-Treaty faction under De Valera did not accept the result, and civil war followed. It is not being suggested here that there might be civil war in Scotland; merely that a vote in the Scottish Parliament might not settle the issue of whether the terms of independence are acceptable to the Scottish people. The only certain way to ascertain the views of the Scottish people would be to hold a referendum. The point is only being made that there are many definitions of independence, and a referendum is the most painless way of finding out which is acceptable.

2. UK accession to the EEC. Terms of accession were negotiated by the 1970–4 Conservative government and were ratified by Parliament. The UK entered the EEC on 1 January 1973. But political debate about the acceptability of these terms continued. Eventually, the 1974–9 Labour government renegotiated the terms of accession and received ratification of them in a referendum in 1975. That referendum put an end to the debate about the terms of UK EEC membership and an end to the debate about the principle of UK EEC membership.

3. Scottish and Welsh devolution. It might be argued that in proposing Option 2, the SNP are merely following the precedent set by the UK Government in its devolution process. But there is a major difference between that and independence. Devolution was a process entirely within the control of one government. It was able to set out the terms of devolution and implement them. Achieving independence, however, requires negotiations between two governments. A Scottish government might set out what it intended to achieve and win approval for it in principle in the first referendum. But what it actually achieved might be so radically different from the original intention as to bear little resemblance to it. The eventual terms of the Irish Treaty were so unpalatable that the Irish delegation was deadlocked, and signed only with the greatest reluctance in the face of a surprise ultimatum from Lloyd George. In these circumstances, and to end political argument (which might be de-stabilising to the new Scottish state), a second referendum to ratify the negotiation outcome is the wisest course.

Option 3 also has a Canadian precedent. The referendum in Quebec of 20 May 1980 was called by the PQ Government for a mandate to negotiate 'sovereignty-association' with Canada. Had the PQ won that referendum and had subsequently negotiated with Canada, the results of those negotiations would have been put to the electorate for approval in a second referendum.

The only instance where it would be unnecessary to hold a second referendum would be where the Scots came out of the negotiations with everything they wanted, in other words, where the terms of independence matched the Scottish Executive's initial demands. Such an outcome is highly unlikely: just how unlikely is illustrated if one looks at the list of issues that will rank near the top:

1. No share of the national debt;
2. Expulsion of nuclear bases;
3. EU membership;
4. Rights to oil revenues;
5. Continued protection by UK defence force.

From current policy statements these are likely to be among the SNP's principal demands. They would need to have been endorsed, at least by implication, in the initial referendum (but in Chapter 3 we suggest a referendum question in much more general terms). Only if the five tests were met is it arguable that there would be no need to go back to the Scottish people to seek assent to the terms.

– Different approaches to each referendum –

As in the 1975 referendum on membership of the European Economic Community and in the 1997 devolution referendums, the enabling provisions would be set out in a free standing Bill solely concerned with holding the referendum.[47] There are two questions that govern each referendum:

- what is the referendum for?
- who is ordering it?

Legislative provision for the referendums would be made in the following two ways. The first case deals with a pre-legislative referendum. An Act of the Scottish Parliament will be needed as paving legislation before the first referendum can be held.

The second referendum could take the form of either a pre- or a post-legislative referendum. The referendum could be on a specific proposition (a

White Paper), which would be turned into an Act upon a positive vote. This was the strategy in the 1997 devolution referendums. Alternatively, Westminster could pass a Scotland (Independence) Act but make its implementation dependent on the public's approval. This was the strategy in the 1979 devolution referendums which resulted in the rejection of Parliament's legislation in the Scotland Act and Wales Act 1978, which were subsequently repealed.

Weighing up the 1979 and 1997 experiences it is suggested for the second referendum that Westminster should use a pre-legislative referendum to endorse the result of the negotiations, and put a prospectus and a draft constitutional document before the Scottish electorate. As in the 1970s, it would be a serious waste of parliamentary time to pass a difficult and controversial bill, only to see all efforts rejected in a referendum. A prospectus in the form of a detailed White Paper would give voters all the information they would need to make an informed choice.

The details about the conduct of the referendum will need to be decided by the Scottish Executive and Scottish Parliament for the first referendum, and the UK Government and Westminster for the second referendum (but in consultation with the Scottish Executive). Past practice has been to leave details, such as the timing of the referendum and adaptation of electoral machinery, to secondary legislation. The question of timing – which is of strategic relevance – is discussed in the next section.

– Timing –

Both referendums could be held within the life of a four-year Parliament. The timing of the first referendum is tied to the outcome of an election. The timing of the second referendum would be tied to the less predictable outcome of independence negotiations. The SNP manifesto for the 1999 elections of Scotland's Parliament was silent on the issue of timing other than saying that it would 'hold a referendum within the first four year term of the Parliament' (SNP 1999: 10).

The first referendum could be called within the first year of a new parliament. The time lapse between the general election in May 1997 and the Scottish referendum in September was 19 weeks. Within this period the Referendum (Scotland and Wales) Bill was passed, the practicalities for voting were sorted out, a White Paper on the Government's proposal was published, the referendum campaigns were launched, and finally the referendum held. A similarly tight schedule might not be possible or desirable if Scotland is preparing for independence, but the first referendum should be held early on in the four-year term of a new Scottish Parliament to allow plenty of time for negotiations.

– UK reaction –

A danger in the event of Scottish independence is not just the possibility of long and protracted negotiations, but also that negotiations never properly get off the ground. What if the UK Government drags its feet? The Prime Minister could claim not to have a mandate to negotiate secession with the Scottish Executive. There would be little, if any, international pressure on the UK Government to heed the referendum result. Firstly, it is a purely internal affair; secondly, no state has either a direct or indirect interest in the weakening of the United Kingdom; and thirdly, a number of states would be deeply concerned by the precedent that Scottish independence would set.

And yet would the UK Government be well advised to ignore a majority in a referendum? The turnout in the 1995 sovereignty referendum in Quebec was an astounding 93.52 per cent, and a properly organised referendum on Scottish independence might motivate similarly large numbers of voters. If a convincing majority voted for independence then a UK strategy not to negotiate could easily backfire. It would reinforce a perception in Scotland that their demands and wishes are not taken seriously and would be easy political capital for the SNP. What is more, it would fundamentally compromise the legitimacy of the UK Government and the UK state as one based on democracy and the consent of the people.

– Lessons from Quebec –

Once more, the thinking on these matters is more advanced in Canada. The Supreme Court of Canada made some observations about the mechanics of negotiating in the *Quebec Secession Reference* case. It found that:

> the clear repudiation by the people of Quebec of the existing constitutional order would confer legitimacy on demands for secession, and place an obligation on the other provinces and the federal government to acknowledge and respect that expression of democratic will by entering into negotiations and conducting them in accordance with the [four] underlying constitutional principles . . .[48]

In other words, the conduct of the negotiating sides would be governed by the same constitutional principles that gave rise to the duty to negotiate in the first place, namely federalism, democracy, constitutionalism and the rule of law, and respect for minority rights. Relying on those principles the Court rejects two absolutist propositions. Firstly, the notion that there would be a legal obligation on Canada or on the other provinces to accede to Quebec's secession, 'subject only to negotiation of the logistical details',[49] is rejected. Quebec does not enjoy a right of self-determination (as recognised by public international law within the colonial context) which would permit the imposition of the terms of secession on the other parties. Moreover, on its own, a majority in favour of secession would not be enough to act as justification. As the Court consistently emphasises:

> The democracy principle . . . cannot be invoked to trump the principles of federalism and the rule of law, the rights of individuals and minorities, or the operation of democracy in the other provinces or in Canada as a whole.[50]

In short, to argue that secession is 'an absolute legal entitlement'[51] is to 'undermine the obligation to negotiate and render it hollow'.[52]

Secondly, the opposite argument is also rejected, that a clear majority in an independence referendum would impose no obligations on Canada, or that Canada could 'remain indifferent' to a clear sovereigntist mandate in a referendum. In the Court's words, 'this would amount to the assertion that other constitutionally recognized principles necessarily trump the clearly expressed democratic will of the people of Quebec'.[53] The rights of the other provinces and Canada cannot thwart Quebec's pursuit of secession, provided it is supported by a clear majority on a clear question, and provided that Quebec respects the rights of others. This raises the importance of negotiations:

> Negotiations would be necessary to address the interests of the federal government, of Quebec and the other provinces, and other participants, as well as the rights of all Canadians both within and outside Quebec.[54]

The interests of both Quebec and Canada, as well as Scotland and the United Kingdom, would be furthered by both sides engaging in negotiations and trying to resolve all the issues.

Relevance for Scotland:
the UK Government cannot 'remain indifferent'

The repudiation of absolutist positions is essential. Of course the UK Government would not be duty-bound to negotiate Scottish independence. Taken on its own, the referendum result would not suffice to upset the constitution and break up the Union. Moreover, Scotland does not have a legal right to secession and the United Kingdom does not have a correlative duty to let them go. On the other hand, unless support for independence is unconvincing, it will not be right or responsible for the UK

Government to 'remain indifferent', to use the words of the Supreme Court. Even though the constitutional premise in Canada is different, the clearly expressed democratic will of the people of Scotland would carry similar political weight. The desire to maintain 'constitutionalism and the rule of law' is as great in the United Kingdom as it is in Canada, and this would respect the democracy principle that the Scots rely on.

We assume that the UK Government would negotiate in good faith. This, however, would not necessarily be the case and the UK would naturally do all it could to win the second referendum. But here the importance of the first referendum should be noted. The Scots would have, after all, spoken. If the referendum has been properly supervised, the UK Government would be ill-advised to snub it. The UK Government will not give the Scots an easy ride in negotiations, but there is a difference between being a tough negotiator and being an unprincipled negotiator. There is in the UK a respect for the rule of law, and it should be assumed that agreements would generally be honoured.[55] Lessons here clearly have to be learned from the dissolution of Czechoslovakia in which early agreements were later broken by the stronger side (see Chapter 4). Neither side can afford intransigence or indifference. To borrow again from the Supreme Court, negotiations would be necessary to address the interests of the UK Government, of Scotland and the other constituent parts of the United Kingdom, as well as the rights of all citizens of the United Kingdom both within and outside the UK.

The Supreme Court recognises that the outcome of the negotiations cannot be predicted and that a stalemate is a real possibility. A wide range of issues would be on the agenda immediately after a positive independence referendum result. Canada and Quebec are linked by history and, naturally, 'a high level of integration in economic, political and social institutions across Canada'.[56] The key issues to be negotiated are identified by the Court as national economy, national debt and boundary issues. The boundary issue is particular to Canada due to the presence of linguistic and cultural minorities, including aboriginal peoples. It has to be on the agenda because, according to the Court, 'nobody seriously suggests that our national existence, seamless in so many aspects, could be effortlessly separated along what are now the provincial boundaries of Quebec'.[57] It is not discussed in any greater detail here, because there is no equivalent problem over boundaries in Scotland – save maybe for the maritime boundary which is discussed in Chapter 4.

The difficulty of negotiating and the absence of an absolute legal entitlement to secession means that one cannot assume that 'an agreement reconciling all relevant rights and obligations would actually be reached'.[58]

A stalemate would still be possible if Quebec/Scotland entered into negotiations to achieve sovereignty/independence whilst Canada/UK still hoped to prevent it. The Supreme Court declined to speculate what would transpire in such a case.[59] The Court merely said that the negotiation process would require:

> the reconciliation of various rights and obligations by the representatives of two legitimate majorities, namely, the clear majority of the population of Quebec, and the clear majority of Canada as a whole, whatever that may be.[60]

One of these 'legitimate majorities' would ultimately have to give way to the other. Some form of political compromise would achieve this. The Court speaks of 'reconciliation' but gives no suggestion as to how the two diametrically opposed political stances might be harmonised.[61] This challenge is as relevant for Canada as it is for the United Kingdom.

– CONCLUSION –

- Outside the colonial context the principle in international law of self-determination does not legitimise unilateral declarations of independence by territories within a state. Even so, the Scots have a widely acknowledged entitlement to leave the United Kingdom and become an independent state if they so desire.
- The Scottish Parliament may arrange to hold a consultative referendum provided it does not challenge the state of the Union. The referendum itself could not lead to or justify (unilateral) secession. The actual separation of Scotland from the rest of the UK would be a Westminster decision.
- Independence will come about in various stages. The most likely sequence is:

1. SNP win sufficient seats to form a government in Scotland;
2. SNP government introduces bill for advisory referendum in the Scottish Parliament;
3. Advisory referendum held to determine the will of the Scottish people;
4. If the result is positive for the SNP and accepted by the UK Government, the negotiation process can begin;
5. The outcome of the negotiations is embodied in a prospectus and draft constitutional document;
6. Westminster legislates for the holding of a second referendum;

7. The prospectus and draft constitutional document is put before the electorate in the second referendum. The result in this referendum would, in practice, be binding;

8. The Westminster Parliament would then pass the necessary legislation to give effect to Scottish independence.

– NOTES –

1. The principal instruments that recognise the right are the Charter of the United Nations (1945) Articles 1 and 55; The UN International Covenant on Civil and Political Rights (1976) Article 1; The UN International Covenant on Economic, Social and Cultural Rights (1976) Article 1; The UN Declaration on Principles of International Law Concerning Friendly Relations and Co-operation Among States in Accordance with the Charter of the United Nations (1970); The Vienna Declaration and Programme of Action (adopted by the UN World Conference on Human Rights in 1993); The UN Declaration on the Occasion of the Fiftieth Anniversary of the United Nations (1995); The Final Act of the Conference on Security and Co-operation in Europe (Helsinki Final Act) (1975).

2. Saudi Arabia, Belgium, Greece, the Soviet Union, India, Chile, France, Afghanistan, Ecuador, Venezuela, Yugoslavia, Syria and New Zealand noted that the draft article, 'was not concerned with . . . the right of secession' (Bossuyt 1987: 27).

3. See statements by France, New Zealand, Australia, Turkey, Czechoslovakia, United Kingdom, Syria, Saudi Arabia, Norway (Bossuyt 1987: 23).

4. In compliance with Article 40 of the ICCPR and Article 16 of the ICESCR the UK submits periodic reports on its performance under the Covenants. See 'Consideration of Reports submitted by States Parties under Article 40 of the Covenant: International Covenant on Civil and Political Rights: Addendum: The United Kingdom of Great Britain and Northern Ireland', UN Doc. CCPR/C/UK/99/5; Article 1.

5. 3 March 1992, p. 6.

6. House of Commons Hansard, 20 February 1997, Col. 1072.

7. House of Commons Hansard, 4 March 1998, Col. 1081.

8. Section 1 provides: '(1) It is hereby declared that Northern Ireland in its entirety remains part of the United Kingdom and shall not cease to be so without the consent of the majority of the people of Northern Ireland voting in a poll . . . (2) But if the wish expressed by a majority in such a poll is that Northern Ireland should cease to be part of the United Kingdom and form part of a united Ireland, the Secretary of State shall lay before Parliament such proposals to give effect to that wish as may be agreed between her Majesty's Government and the Government of Ireland.'

9. The Åland Islands are an autonomous and Swedish-speaking province of Finland. They are situated in the eastern part of the Baltic Sea between Sweden and Finland and consist of more than 6,000 islands. After the collapse of the Russian Empire, the League of Nations in 1921 conferred sovereignty over the Åland Islands to Finland. The subsequent Autonomy Act between Sweden and Finland granted autonomy, demilitarisation and neutralisation to the Islands.

10. *Rapport de la Commission Internationale de juristes chargée par le Conseil de la Société des Nations de donner un avis consultatif sur certains aspects juridiques de la question des îles d'Aland, in La question des Îles d'Aland. Documents diplomatiques publiés par le Ministère des Affaires Étrangères* (1920: 68–70).

11. International Covenant on Civil and Political Rights, Article 27.

12. For more discussion on the evolution and legal applicability of the right to self-

determination see Koskenniemi 1994; Moore 1998; Quane 1998; Sullivan 2000; Crawford 2001. For a possibly contrasting view see McCorquodale (1995: 287): 'the United Kingdom now accepts that self-determination is a right, not merely a principle with strong moral force, which places legal obligations on the United Kingdom'. Under what circumstance the UK might feel constrained to negotiate Scottish independence is discussed further below in this chapter.

13. As an afterthought one might address the following question: the United Kingdom is a union of four nations and it has accepted that the principle of self-determination applies within its territory. But is the UK made up of only England, Scotland, Wales and Northern Ireland? This is certainly legally true and based on the constitution and legislation of the UK. Macartney's view, however, is more expansive. He sets out 'the following nationalities [in the British Isles] in order of size: England; Scotland; Ireland; Wales; Jersey; Guernsey; Man; Alderney; and Sark. Two problem areas are left out of [this] scheme – the six counties of NE Ireland which form part of the UK, and the ancient Celtic territory of Cornwall. It will be further noted that the Northern and Western Isles are here subsumed in the Scottish nation, albeit as a very distinctive part of the Scottish realm' (Macartney 1984: 11).

14. *Rapport des resultats officiels du scrutin: référendum du 30 octobre 1995* (Quebec: Directeur Général des élections du Québec, November, 1995).

15. 'Sovereigntist' is the term used in Canada.

16. The Government of Quebec rejects the possibility that certain geographical areas within Quebec (such as the vast north, which is the native habitat of the Cree Indians and Inuit people, or areas of Anglo-predominance) could choose to remain in Canada whilst Quebec becomes independent. Federal government polls, however, suggest that the majority of Quebecois believe that aboriginal communities in northern Quebec should be given the option of keeping their territory in Canada if Quebec secedes.

17. Statement to the House of Commons on 26 September 1996; see Rock, 'Does the Law Permit Quebec's Unilateral Secession?' *Globe and Mail*, 27 September 1996.

18. The opinion is reported as *Reference re Secession of Quebec*, [1998] 2 S.C.R. 217; (1998) 161 D.L.R. (4th) 385 [henceforth the *Quebec Secession Reference* case].

19. Ibid. Paragraphs 33–48.

20. Ibid. Paragraph 49.

21. Ibid. Paragraph 66.

22. Ibid. Paragraph 67.

23. Ibid. Paragraph 69.

24. Ibid. Paragraph 76.

25. Ibid. Paragraph 77.

26. Ibid. Paragraph 83.

27. Ibid. Paragraph 84.

28. Ibid. Paragraph 85.

29. Ibid. Paragraph 87.

30. Ibid.

31. Ibid. Paragraph 93.

32. Ibid. Paragraph 100.

33. Ibid. Paragraph 87.

34. Ibid. Paragraph 88.

35. There are other possible cases in Europe, such as in the Basque country (but see 'Spain vows to block Basque referendum', *The Guardian*, 31 July 2001), and on the Faeroe Islands (but see 'Danes quash Faeroes break-away bid', from the newsroom of the BBC *World Service website* http://news.bbc.co.uk/hi/english/world/europe/news-id_681000/681601.stm [visited 6 August 2001]

36. *An Act Representing the Sovereignty of Quebec*, Quebec National Assembly, 1st sess., 35th leg (draft bill issued on 6 December 1994 but not enacted); *An Act Respecting the Future of*

Canada, Quebec National Assembly, 1st sess., 35th leg Bill 1 (introduced in the provincial legislature on 7 September 1995 but not enacted).

37. The reserved matters are listed in Schedule 5 of the Scotland Act.
38. House of Commons Hansard, 12 May 1998, Col. 256.
39. 'Interdict' is the term used in Scotland for 'injunction'.
40. *The Operation of Multi-Layer Democracy*, Scottish Affairs Committee Second Report of Session 1997–1998, HC 460–I, 2 December 1998, paragraph 27.
41. Scottish National Party, *Towards the Scottish Parliament. Enterprise, Compassion and Democracy – Policy Intentions for the 1999 Elections* (Edinburgh, SNP, 1999), at 20. The SNP's *Manifesto for the Scottish Parliament 1999 Elections* was less clear on this issue simply pledging that 'an SNP administration will hold a referendum on independence within the first four years of the Parliament'.
42. *Towards the Scottish Parliament: Enterprise, Compassion, Democracy* (September 1998), at 20.
43. Ibid.
44. This approach is in line with European Community practice which demanded of the successor States to Yugoslavia that they seek popular approval in a referendum before they could be expected to be recognised as States.
45. The number of Scottish seats at Westminster will be reduced to about 60 at the next parliamentary boundary review: Scotland Act 1998, section 86 and Schedule 1.
46. The boost offered by devolution to the nationalist parties was predicted by Mitchell J. and Seyd B. (1999).
47. An alternative way would be to enact general legislation designed to provide permanent legislative provision for the holding of referendums – a generic Referendum Act – but there are no current proposals for this in Edinburgh or Westminster.
48. *Quebec Secession Reference*, paragraph 88.
49. Ibid. Paragraph 90.
50. Ibid. Paragraph 91.
51. Ibid.
52. Ibid.
53. Ibid. Paragraph 92.
54. Ibid.
55. During the talks between the UK and Spain over the future of Gibraltar, expected at the time of writing to lead to an agreement on joint sovereignty, Foreign Secretary Jack Straw said that the government would not renege on its pledge to put any agreement to a referendum in Gibraltar: see 'People of Gibraltar "will remain British"', *Financial Times*, 5 February 2002.
56. *Quebec Secession Reference*, paragraph 96.
57. Ibid.
58. Ibid. Paragraph 97.
59. Ibid.
60. Ibid. Paragraph 93.
61. The Court here appreciates its role as a judicial body and states that it 'has no supervisory role over the political aspects of constitutional negotiations' (paragraph 101). Its role is confined to establishing the framework in which secession can be dealt with. It does not see itself as responsible for stipulating the political outcome.

CHAPTER 2

The Process and Referendums[1]

It was argued in the previous chapter that two referendums, one before and one after the negotiations, would be needed to bring about independence. This chapter will consider the use of referendums in general as well as the conduct of the two independence referendums in particular. It will examine the recent emergence of referendums in UK politics and their compatibility with the doctrine of parliamentary sovereignty. Referendums are controversial but often effective devices in politics. It will be argued that so long as they are approved by Parliament there are no principled objections to their use.

– INTRODUCTION –

The referendum now stands high on the political agenda. It has been the vehicle for securing constitutional change in Northern Ireland, Scotland, Wales and London. This is a striking transformation. As recently as 30 years ago referendums were commonly said to be unconstitutional. The people, it was held, have no direct part to play in the legislative process. Since then there have been eight referendums in the UK. The argument that they have no place in the UK's constitutional set-up is hard to sustain. Yet their use remains controversial. The UK constitution is 'unwritten', with the doctrine of parliamentary sovereignty at its heart. Referendums will therefore continue to have an uncertain place within this system of government.

Referendums have so far only been used on issues of major constitutional importance. In 1975 a referendum was held regarding the United Kingdom's continued membership of the European Communities based on the Treaty of Accession 1972 and the Wilson Government's 'renegotiation' of those terms. Two further referendums were held in 1979 regarding the creation of assemblies in Scotland and Wales. The proposition in Scotland was for a devolved assembly whose powers were defined in the Scotland Act 1978. The referendum was unsuccessful in that, although the 'Yes' vote attracted 51.6 per cent, it was made up of less than a third of the electorate which was not enough to satisfy the threshold requirement in the Act of 40 per cent of those eligible to vote.

The referendums on the new Scottish Parliament and the Welsh Assembly in September 1997, the referendum on the Greater London Authority on 7 May 1998, and the concurrent referendums on 22 May 1998 in Northern Ireland and the Republic of Ireland are milestones in British constitutional history. When the Scots were given a second chance to vote for or against devolution, the proposition in place was the White Paper on *Scotland's Parliament*. Almost three in four of those who voted (74.3 per cent) came out in favour of a Scottish parliament, whilst 63.5 per cent wanted it to have tax-varying powers.

Outstanding issues on which referendums may be held include a possible change to the electoral system, adoption of the euro currency, regional government in England, and finally, Scottish independence. Almost all political parties support referendums on one or more of these issues. What seems certain is that the electorate today faces the prospect of further referendums to come.

Popular support for referendums is high. The 1995 MORI/Joseph Rowntree Reform Trust survey reported 77 per cent of respondents in favour of the use of referendums on certain issues.[2] Yet referendums are not embraced without due consideration in Scotland. The reason for this is the 1979 referendum and the inclusion of the 40 per cent hurdle by George Cunningham, a Labour backbencher, which was rightly regarded as a wrecking amendment. Referendums are therefore regarded with suspicion, especially if Westminster is involved.

Three points should, however, be noted. First, there is a broader tradition of holding referendums in Scotland. Other than the 1979 and 1997 referendums there have also been private initiatives. In 1994 Strathclyde Region authorised a referendum on the semi-privatisation of the local water utility. The Government's proposal was voted down by over 90 per cent. More controversially in 2000, Brian Souter, who is Chairman of Stagecoach, funded the 'Keep the Clause' campaign against the repeal of Section 28 of the Local Government Act 1988 (c. 9). Arguably, the use of referendums in Scotland reflects a greater sense of popular sovereignty, as opposed to parliamentary sovereignty, which can be traced back to the Declaration of Arbroath of 1320 (see MacCormick 1999: 55). Second, the first (and psychologically most important) referendum would be held not by Westminster but by Holyrood, leaving the Scottish Parliament a fair amount of freedom to consult its people. And finally, it is in fact SNP policy to hold a referendum on independence.

– PARLIAMENTARY SOVEREIGNTY –

Referendums in the UK also need to be considered in the context of the doctrine of parliamentary sovereignty. Before 1975 it was widely held that a referendum would be inconsistent with the sovereignty of Parliament because Parliament could not delegate its decisions to another body. That view appears to have lost validity. If Parliament has sovereign power it must have the power to call a referendum. The referendums so far held in the UK have been advisory, with Parliament formally retaining its right to reject the verdict. In practice, however, it has been accepted that Parliament could not ignore a decisive expression of popular opinion.

The use of referendums is likely to remain controversial. It has been argued that referendums divide parties and produce inconsistent government and that, by handing over decision-making to the electorate they detract from MPs' general role. It can be claimed that this not only undermines parliamentary sovereignty but also reduces the capacity of the electorate to hold the government to account. On the other hand, a referendum can, theoretically, provide a limited means of entrenchment not otherwise provided for in the UK's constitutional arrangements. Constitutional change in the form of Scottish independence calls for a referendum like few other matters do.

Any such entrenchment provided through a referendum is a political, rather than a legal, safeguard. In theory Parliament could ignore precedent or pass legislation reversing any formal requirement to hold a referendum. The political difficulties of doing so may mean that the referendum can help guard against hasty or unwanted change. A referendum cannot, however, settle issues once and for all. At best it can provide a considered measure of the electorate's view at the time it is held. It can give a decision an immediate legitimacy, but it cannot settle any matter permanently as the 1975 referendum on Europe and the 1979 referendums on devolution have shown.

– NOT A POLITICAL PANACEA –

Concern about referendums has perhaps been greater in the UK than in other democracies. Yet even the most institutionally conservative politicians look favourably on the device when they calculate that it may further their policies.

International experience offers examples of the different ways in which referendums can be conducted and some lessons to be learnt. However, the diversity of practice confirms that there is no single 'right' way to initiate and conduct a referendum. The use of referendums is shaped by the constitutional framework within which they are held, and by the specific political context in which they are called.

Referendums are not a political panacea. Some powerful arguments can be deployed against them. For example, political expediency rather than democratic principle has been an important factor in past UK referendums. Unless rules or conventions for the use of referendums are developed, it is likely to remain so. There are also no guarantees that the SNP, if it is able to hold a referendum, will get the result it wants, or that the UK Parliament will accept legislation that gives effect to the outcomes of referendums. Results may, in part, reflect the current popular standing of the Scottish Executive, not the considered view of the voters on the referendum issues. Referendums may also oversimplify issues. They require a 'Yes' or a 'No' answer and thus cannot reflect shades of opinion. The choice and precise wording of the question are crucial and their outcome may be affected by an unequal provision of information and resources. Referendums have also in the past been criticised because of their use by some authoritarian regimes to confer legitimacy on their policies.

Some of these difficulties can be minimised by the way in which questions are formulated, by adequate provision for the dissemination of information, and by the application of effective guidelines for their efficient and fair conduct. Referendums should, nevertheless, be recognised as blunt, but often effective instruments, with which to seek a resolution to complex political issues.

– THE FRAMEWORK –

The Political Parties, Elections and Referendums Act 2000 (c. 41; henceforth the 2000 Act) and the Representation of the People Acts govern the way in which elections are run in the UK and, through the provision of a consistent framework, ensure that they are fair. Referendums raise a number of different issues. For example, a key element in the fair conduct of referendums is to ensure that the way they are run is independent of party political interest. The Government of the day may take ad hoc measures to that end. The 2000 Act aims to ensure that the rules governing the conduct of all referendums should, as far as possible, be consistent and widely understood, and produce efficiency and fairness.

Whereas past UK referendums have been organised and administered by

UK Government departments, this will not be the case in the future. The introduction and application of governing rules will not be the direct responsibility of the UK Government. Their development and implementation now belongs to the new Electoral Commission, which is an independent body established under the 2000 Act.

– THE ELECTORAL COMMISSION –

The functions of the Electoral Commission include overseeing the conduct of referendums authorised by Westminster in all parts of the United Kingdom including Scotland (Section 101(6)). In particular, it will regulate donations to political parties and establish national expenditure limits. In order to ensure that referendum results are accepted they should be conducted efficiently and ensure the fair representation of competing views.

There has for long been a strong case for giving responsibility for the conduct for referendums to an independent body like the new Electoral Commission. Public confidence in the neutrality of the conduct of a referendum is essential if the result is to be accepted as legitimate, particularly where the Government is pledged to support a specific outcome. The functions of the Electoral Commission are set out in the 2000 Act:

- advising on the wording of the question;
- allocating funding to campaign groups;
- monitoring balanced access to the broadcast media;
- supervising the organisation for each polling station;
- counting the votes and declaring the result.

It is important to note, however, that the Electoral Commission would probably not have a role in supervising referendums held by the Scottish Parliament. The 2000 Act is not explicit on this point, although section 6(3) does provide that:

> The Commission shall not . . . carry out any review (or make any report) under this section with respect to any of the following matters, namely . . . the conduct of referendums held in pursuance of any provision made by or under an Act of the Scottish Parliament . . .

So whilst the Scottish Parliament could hold a referendum on independence, the conduct of the referendum would be outside the powers of the Commission.

– LEGISLATION –

All referendums need parliamentary approval. Since devolution the source of the enabling legislation is no longer pre–determined. Westminster now faces competition from Holyrood although Westminster retains sole jurisdiction over reserved matters. Legislation is required to enable the UK Government or the Scottish Executive to spend money and exercise powers not otherwise provided for. Election machinery must be adapted and the cost of organising the ballot and any grants to campaigning groups must be voted for by the relevant Parliament. In the past, Westminster legislation for holding referendums has:

- defined persons eligible to vote;
- specified the wording of the question;
- provided for returning officers;
- provided for the appointment of an Electoral Officer with responsibility for counting the votes and announcing the result (this function now falls to the Electoral Commission);
- specified grants to be made towards the cost of campaigning – where grants were made (this function now falls to the Electoral Commission);
- provided powers to adapt existing electoral machinery as necessary (this function now falls to the Electoral Commission);
- excluded legal challenges to the result certified by the Chief Counting Officer;
- provided machinery for the determination of the date of the referendum.

It was argued in Chapter 1 that Scottish independence could only be brought about after positive results in two referendums. Each referendum would be different in nature and would originate from two different sources. Whereas the first referendum could be initiated and authorised by the Scottish Parliament (and would not involve the Electoral Commission), the second referendum on the terms of independence would have to be authorised by the Westminster Parliament (and would involve the Electoral Commission). Although Scottish independence could happen after a simultaneous legal process in both parliaments that reverses – as far as possible – the effects of the 1707 Act of Union, it would be the Westminster Act which is legally decisive. As the Union legislation is expressly reserved under the Scotland Act this is not an issue in English or Scottish law.

Authority for this assertion is rooted in precedence as well as in constitutional theory. Historically, the UK's constitution has been very resilient to change. The grant of independence to former colonies but also to component parts of the United Kingdom was done with relative ease. Having merged with the United Kingdom of Great Britain in 1801 to become the United Kingdom of Great Britain and Ireland[3], the constituent assembly (Dáil Éireann) articulated a constitution for the Irish Free State in 1921.[4] When the constitution was adopted by the Westminster Parliament in 1922,[5] the Irish Free State was granted the status of a self-governing body within the British Empire[6] and the UK became the United Kingdom of Great Britain and Northern Ireland.

As a matter of legal theory, the so-called rule of recognition is very much in dispute in this case. What created the Irish Free State? Was it Dáil Éireann's constitution of 1921 (the Republican view), or was it the Westminster Act of 1922 (the British view)? MacCormick too notes that even though two Acts of Union were needed to create the United Kingdom of 1707, it is the English enabling legislation that is always referred to as the Act of Union. He likens England to a majority shareholder whose (legislative) acts are decisive. As far as English common law is concerned, it is the Act of Union passed by the Parliament of England that is legally relevant (MacCormick 2000: 727–8). This view is supported by classic Diceyan legal thought, whereby the acquired status and legitimacy of the United Kingdom stems from English law and practice, whereas the Irish Free State derived its standing from the Westminster parliament. All things considered, an Act of the Westminster Parliament would be required to bring about Scottish independence.

– NOTES –

1. The following two chapters borrow in parts from The Constitution Unit, UCL, *Report of the Commission on the Conduct of Referendums* (1996). On the use of the term 'referendums' the then editor of the Oxford English Dictionary wrote: 'Usage varies, even in high places, and both *referendums* and *referenda* are found in print. My own view is that *referendums* is logically preferable as a plural form meaning ballots on one issue (as a Latin gerund, *referendum* has no plural). The Latin plural gerundive *referenda*, meaning "things to be referred", necessarily connotes a plurality of issues . . . By preferring *Referendums* as your title you have the angels of Rome and of the O.E.D on your side' (in Butler and Ranney 1978: 4, n. 2).
2. The Joseph Rowntree Reform Trust/MORI, *State of the Nations survey*, 1995. Subsequent *State of the Nations* surveys were made in collaboration with ICM but have not included a question on referendums.
3. Act for the Union of Great Britain and Ireland 1800 c. 67 (GB); Act for the Union of Great Britain and Ireland 1800 c. 38 (Ireland).
4. Constitution of the Irish Free State (Saorstát Éireann) Act 1922 (No. 1 of 1922).
5. Irish Free State (Constitution) Act 1922 (Sess 2) c. 1.
6. Ireland shed its dominion status completely with the passing of the Ireland Act 1949.

CHAPTER 3

The Practice of Referendums

— THE ELECTORATE —

The questions considered in this chapter are (a) where should the independence referendum be held and (b) who should be entitled to vote. Should it be held throughout the UK or in Scotland only? And should the electorate be those entitled to vote in general elections, or limited to those entitled to vote in local elections?

— UK-WIDE OR REGIONAL —

The first issue is whether to hold a UK-wide referendum, or to limit the ballot to Scotland. The UK has held only one national referendum – the 1975 referendum on remaining in the Common Market. In Denmark nationwide votes were held on the status of a part of the country (cession of the Virgin Islands, 1916), although the 1982 referendum on Greenland remaining a part of the European Communities was held only in Greenland. France (Algeria, 1961; New Caledonia, 1988) offers more examples of nationwide referendums.

Yet, there are a far greater number of instances where voting has been restricted to the areas where change is contemplated, as in Quebec, 1980 and 1995; Gibraltar 1967; Algeria, 1962. Once sub-national referendums in the United States and Switzerland are put to one side, the majority of sub-national referendums have been on issues relating to different degrees of self-determination. The most recent Northern Ireland, Scottish and Welsh devolution referendums were held only in those parts of the UK that were directly concerned, although some Members of Parliament argued that the referendums should have been UK-wide since they affected the 'constitution' of the UK as a whole. Tom Nairn, however, gives short shrift to their objections:

The same objections were made on behalf of Russia during the break-up of the USSR, and they were equally futile. In practice a 'say' for the commanding majority would amount to their right to forbid the change of status altogether – which they would almost certainly do (Nairn 2000: 312, n. 8).

Figure 3.1. Referendums on the constitutional status of a region or dependent territory.

Year	Country	Region/ Territory	Issue	Vote in Region only	'Yes' Vote %	Turnout %
1933	Australia	Western Australia	Secede from Australian Constitutional Convention	Yes	66.2	92
1967		New England, New South Wales	Proposed new state area	Yes	45.8	92.5
1984		Cocos Islands	Integrate with mainland	Yes	88.5	n/a
1980	Canada	Quebec	Independence	Yes	40.4	84.1
1982		Northwest Territory	Divide Territory	Yes	55.9	n/a
1995		Quebec	Independence	Yes	49.4	93.5
1916	Denmark	Virgin Islands	Cession from Denmark	No	64.2	38.0
1920		Schleswig	Incorporation	No	96.9	50.1
1979		Greenland	Approve home rule	Yes	73.1	63.2
1961	France	Algeria	Self determination	No	75.3	76.5
1987		New Caledonia	Remain part of France	Yes	94.6	N/a
1988		New Caledonia	New Caledonia deal	No	80.0	37.0
1979	Spain	Basque Region	Increased autonomy	Yes	94.7	58.9
1979		Catalonia	Increased autonomy	Yes	88.1	59.7
1980		Andalusia	Increased autonomy	Yes	93.3	60.4
1980		Galicia	Increased autonomy	Yes	77.3	26.2
1967	UK	Gibraltar	Keep link with UK	Yes	99.6	95.8
1973		Northern Ireland	Stay in UK	Yes	98.9	58.7
1979		Scotland	Approve devolution	Yes	51.6	63.6
1979		Wales	Approve devolution	Yes	20.9	58.8
1997		Scotland	Scottish Parliament	Yes	74.3	60.4
1997		Wales	Welsh Assembly	Yes	50.3	50.1
1998		London	Elected Mayor/ Authority	Yes	72.0	34.0
1998		Northern Ireland	Support for Belfast Agreement	Yes	71.1	80.1

Source: David Butler and Austin Ranney (eds), *Referendums Around the World*, 1994; Michael Gallagher and Pier Vincenzo Uleri, *The Referendum Experience in Europe*, 1996.

The UK precedents established in the 1970s and the 1990s, international practice and, last but not least, the principle of fairness indicate that an independence referendum should be held in Scotland only.

– THE ELECTORAL REGISTER –

A related question is whether Scots residing elsewhere in the UK/EU should be allowed to vote on an issue affecting the future of Scotland. In 1999, there were over two million British citizens who had lived abroad for less than twenty years, but only 13,700 of these had chosen to appear on the electoral register for that year.[1]

The electorate will either be defined as those in the region eligible to vote in general elections or in local elections. The relevant electorate for referendums has generally been the one entitled to vote in general elections – UK citizens, other Commonwealth citizens, citizens of the Irish Republic and overseas electors – with the addition of members of the House of Lords (who are entitled to vote in local elections). This means that a Scot living in France while on the electoral register in Scotland would be able to vote on independence, while a Scot living and registered in a London constituency would not. Indeed, anyone registered to vote in a Scottish constituency as an overseas voter, be they Scottish, Welsh, Northern Irish or English (but not an EU citizen), would be eligible to vote in a referendum held only in Scotland.

The notable exception is the Referendums (Scotland and Wales) Act 1997.[2] By virtue of Section 1(3) the referendum franchise was granted to those entitled to vote in local government elections in Scotland. The Government of the day refused to extend the franchise to the entire UK electorate, those born in Scotland or with a parent or grandparent born in Scotland, and those who had lived in Scotland at any given time over the last 20 years. In other words, any British or EU national resident in Scotland could have exercised her vote but any Scottish person not living in Scotland could not have.[3]

Importantly, in local and regional referendums voting rights can be extended to EU nationals resident for longer than one year. This is current practice in local and European elections (but not general elections). The usual postal and proxy facilities should be available. Provision should also be made for the late inclusion of eligible electors on the electoral register.

Both independence referendums in Scotland should use the same electorate as local elections. This was practised in 1997, and it also gives greater voice to those resident in Scotland (including EU nationals). That still leaves some space for a compromise solution whereby people born in

Scotland but resident abroad could register to vote. Given the significance of the independence referendums in Scotland the electoral register should be inclusive rather than exclusive.

– THRESHOLDS –

There are various ways and means by which central governments can try to protect themselves from uncomfortable results in referendums. One way is by 'shifting the goalposts', for example by demanding a higher majority than 50 per cent plus 1. Whether to demand a supermajority, and how to justify its imposition, is explored in this section.

The general rule in the UK, with just one exception, is that referendums are decided by simple plurality, with no threshold. Simple pluralities (that is majorities of those voting) were required province-wide in the 1973 Northern Ireland referendum and UK–wide in the 1975 European referendum. The 40 per cent threshold which applied in the Scottish and Welsh referendums in 1979 was inserted against the wishes of the government by a backbench amendment. It added an extra hurdle by requiring a substantial turnout.

The next referendums that were held followed in relatively quick succession after the Labour Party was elected in May 1997. The results are set out in Figure 3.2.

In none of these referendums were thresholds in place. As a result a Greater London Authority was created even though only 24.5 per cent of the electorate actually voted for it. The application of a threshold in future referendums is likely to be one of the most difficult issues to resolve. There are three main options:

- a simple majority of one;
- a proportion of those voting;
- a proportion of those entitled to vote.

A simple majority of those who cast their votes carries a natural authority. But it may be desirable to achieve a substantial majority of a specific size, that is a threshold stipulated by either the Scottish Parliament (in the first referendum) or Westminster (in the second referendum), to provide a measure of effective entrenchment of the decision. The case for thresholds advanced in those countries where they are used to approve constitutional amendments, and the question for the United Kingdom would be whether referendums on constitutional questions should be decided by supermajorities. There are two cogent arguments to be made. First, the people need to be protected from politicians trying to change the rules of the political game. Second, changing the constitution is a fundamental decision. It should not be affected by political changes but only by the settled will of the people. In other words, thresholds provide a safeguard against changing the basic laws of the State too easily.

Figure 3.2. UK Referendum results 1997–8.

Scotland referendum, 11 September 1997

Q1) Should there be a Scottish parliament?
Agree	1,775,045	(74.3%)
Disagree	614,400	(25.7%)

Q2) Should the parliament have tax varying powers?
Agree	1,512,889	(63.5%)
Disagree	870,263	(36.5%)

Turnout 60.4%

Referendum in Wales, 18 September 1997

Q1) I agree that there should be a Welsh Assembly.
    559,419   (50.3%)

Q2) I do not agree that there should be a Welsh Assembly.
    552,698   (49.7%)

Turnout: 50.1%

Greater London Authority referendum, 7 May 1998

Are you in favour of the government's proposals for a Greater London Authority, made up of an elected mayor and a separately elected assembly?
YES:	1,230,715	(72.0%)
NO:	478,413	(28.0%)

Turnout: 34%

Referendum in Northern Ireland, 22 May 1998

Q: Do you support the agreement reached in the multi-party talks on Northern Ireland and set out in Command Paper 3883?[4]
YES:	676,966	(71.12%)
NO:	274,879	(28.88%)

Turnout: 80.98%

One of the main difficulties in specifying a threshold, however, lies in determining what figure is sufficient to confer legitimacy – for example 60 per cent, 66.7 per cent or 75 per cent. A second is whether the threshold should relate to the total registered electorate or those who choose to vote. Thresholds related to a proportion of those eligible to vote raise the stakes even higher.

− INTERNATIONAL PRACTICE −

Internationally, thresholds have taken various forms. In Weimar Germany, a referendum had to receive the support of 50 per cent of the electorate to succeed. Abstention was equivalent to a 'No' vote. In one case a referendum drew 94.5 per cent support from those voting, but since the turnout was only 14.1 per cent it failed. In Denmark, 45 per cent of the electorate was once required for a referendum on a constitutional amendment to succeed. In 1939, a 92 per cent 'Yes' was nullified because the turnout was only 49 per cent, so the 'Yes' vote was 44 per cent of the electorate. In 1953, the threshold was changed to 40 per cent. Other countries have adopted diverse requirements:

- Australia requires a majority of voters nationally and in at least four of the six states.
- New Zealand once required a 60 per cent 'Yes' vote (1908–14).
- in Italy popular initiatives can only succeed if the turnout is over 50 per cent.
- in Gambia a new constitution failed in 1965 because it failed (by 1 per cent) to secure the two-thirds 'Yes' vote required.
- Uruguay requires the support of 35 per cent of registered votes.
- no country seems to have a double threshold – say of two-thirds in favour and a 50 per cent turnout, although Switzerland and Austria require a 'double majority', of individual cantons or states, for constitutional amendments.

There have been a number of referendums in Europe in relation to the European Union. No higher thresholds were in place even though the outcomes were invariably close. In France, the Maastricht Treaty was ratified with 51.4 per cent of ballots cast in 1991. In 1992, the same Treaty was accepted by 57.3 per cent of voters in Ireland but rejected by 50.7 per cent of voters in Denmark. That same year, 50.3 per cent of voters in Switzerland declined to join the European Economic Area. Sweden decided to become an EU Member State after 52.2 per cent of voters backed membership in the 1994 referendum, whereas the same percentage (52.2 per cent) of Norwegian voters chose to keep their country out of the EU in a referendum in the same year. On 4 March 2001, the Swiss stated their euro-scepticism once more, this time by rejecting membership of the European Union by 77 per cent to 23 per cent. On 7 June 2001 the Irish rejected the Nice Treaty in a referendum by 53.87 per cent to 46.13 per cent.

– UK EXPERIENCE –

The 1975 White Paper *Our Changing Democracy*, in which the Labour government proposed that both Scotland and Wales should enjoy extensive control over their own affairs by means of devolution, considered the arguments for a majority of a specified size, but concluded:

> The Government are concerned that the size of the poll should be adequate, and they are confident it will be so. They also consider it of great importance that the verdict of the poll should be clear and conclusive. In the circumstance, they consider that it will be best to follow the normal electoral practice and accept that the referendum result should rest on a simple majority – without qualifications or conditions of any kind.

As already noted, in 1979 the use of a threshold became the focus of Parliamentary opposition to the devolution bills. The 40 per cent threshold eventually adopted was the result of a backbench amendment and supported by those opposed to devolution. The subsequent devolution referendums in the 1990s, on the other hand, in London, Ireland and Northern Ireland, Scotland, and Wales did not have thresholds but applied the absolute majority rule of 50 per cent plus 1.

– THRESHOLDS IN CANADA –

The threshold debate has gained prominence in Canada since the Canadian Supreme Court examined Quebec's right to secession in domestic and international law in the *Quebec Secession Reference*. Even though there is no stipulation of a threshold in the Canadian Constitution, the Supreme Court held that the majority had to be 'clear'; a standard that was subsequently endorsed by the Canadian House of Commons in the Clarity Act.[5] The arguments for and against thresholds will be briefly rehearsed here as they are important and relevant for the referendums in Scotland.

– Pro –

The Canadian Government's position is that a 'clear majority' requires a higher threshold than a simple majority (50 per cent plus one). There is a certain finality about secession which, arguably, warrants the expression of consent from more than a mere plurality. Young points out that 'there has never been a reunification after a secession' (Young 1998: 132) so the assumption is that secession is an irrevocable act.

Empirical data from Quebec tends to boost the federal government's position. Asked whether 50 per cent plus 1 constitutes a 'clear majority' only 37 per cent of Quebecois said 'Yes' and 60 per cent said 'No'. The same CROP Opinion Poll found that a majority (70 per cent v. 27 per cent) thought that a referendum result of 60 per cent would represent a 'clear majority'.[6] The arguments in favour of a higher threshold than 50 per cent plus 1 that received the most support in the CROP Opinion Poll related to the importance of the referendum, and the potential for internal division after a close vote (65 per cent and 64 per cent respectively).

A final argument might be called the 'margin of error' argument, related to confused understanding of the question (considered below). In Quebec especially the sovereignty debate has over the years confronted voters with an array of concepts on 'sovereignty', 'sovereignty-association', 'economic and political partnership', and finally 'confederative union', which is the latest buzz word. One may reasonably doubt whether the nuances are appreciated by all political scientists and constitutional lawyers, let alone by ordinary citizens![7] And even if voters know, or think they know, what they are voting for the different concepts are all malleable and open to inter-pretation. For these reasons, the argument goes, a higher threshold is designed to reduce ambiguity of the referendum result and to take account of a margin of error by creating a 'buffer zone'.

– Contra –

Critics of a higher threshold point out that 'it is impossible to adopt different rules for joining or leaving a country unless this has been explicitly stated in the text of the Constitution' (Seymour 2000: 11). In the Canadian context it would mark a break with tradition where a simple majority has been the default decision rule in every national and provincial referendum. Newfoundland, for instance, entered the Confederation in 1949 on the basis of a referendum majority of 52.3 per cent. It is not clear to many people why Quebec should be not be allowed to withdraw on a similar result. The CROP Opinion Poll found that 35 per cent of Quebecois thought the Newfoundland precedent is the most important reason to use 50 per cent plus 1 as the decision rule.

In fact, in both Quebec sovereignty referendums held so far the federal government accepted that a simple majority would be decisive. Thomas Flanagan, a political scientist at the University of Calgary, frowns upon the Government's rather sudden change of heart, 'to announce unilaterally that the decision rule will be different in future looks suspiciously like bad faith' (Flanagan 1996: 130).

Dr Michel Seymour of the University of Montreal criticises the Court's ruling and the Clarity Act on the similar ground that:

it is inconsistent to adopt a rule requiring an absolute majority that is valid for all other questions but to propose a qualified majority rule when the question relates to the sovereignty of a province (2000: p. 12).

Opponents also argue that thresholds contravene basic assumptions about the equality and fairness of election and referendum results. A supermajority rule would be oil in the flames for separatists and, at least in Canada, may lead to a UDI. Flanagan illustrates this point vividly: 'if we set the bar so high that it is impossible to jump over it, the separatists might try to run under it instead' (Flanagan 1996: 130). On what grounds could any government reasonably ignore a 51 per cent–59 per cent majority in favour of independence? Flanagan goes on to ask: 'How strong would Canada's position look in the eyes of the other nations of the world, whose decision to grant or withhold recognition would ultimately determine the success of Quebec's UDI gambit?' (Ibid.).

– Relevance for Scotland –

Should thresholds be adopted in the two referendums needed to bring about Scottish independence? Since those referendums would in any case be advisory the issue of thresholds becomes in itself less significant. The first referendum is merely about assessing the public attitude towards Scottish independence which, if positive, would enable the Scottish Executive to enter into negotiations with the UK Government about Scotland's future in the United Kingdom. To impose a threshold in that referendum would be unnecessary, and would only serve to complicate and distract from its stated purpose – which is why opponents to independence might favour one. The imposition of a threshold would be completely unacceptable in Scotland (because of the Cunningham amendment in 1979). Any new attempt to insert a threshold would be seen likewise.

The second referendum is legally more important because it will determine the outcome. But legislation would still have to go before the Westminster Parliament. Parliament would take the referendum result and the margin of support into account, but would have the last word on whether and in what form the independence legislation is passed.

The need for thresholds is greatly reduced if, as we have argued, there are two referendums instead of just one. In place of a 'supermajority' we are proposing a double majority, one in each referendum. On the road we have here mapped out, Scottish independence would not hinge upon one vote in a non-binding referendum but upon two successful referendum results before and after the negotiations. In constitutional terms an Act of the UK Parliament would then be required to bring about and complete the process. Taking into account the double hurdle of two referendums, their advisory nature, the 1975 Government White Paper, UK practice in 1997, international practice, and the final check of the UK Parliament, the introduction of thresholds in referendums on Scottish independence is not recommended.

– THE QUESTION –

– Lessons from Quebec –

The Canadian Supreme Court in the *Quebec Secession Reference* case held that the question had to be 'clear', by which it meant that it was, at the very least, straightforward, comprehensible and reasonably short. The court could be seen as stating the obvious; but Quebec had had two sovereignty referendums in the space of fifteen years and, arguably, neither referendum question was 'clear'. In the Quebec referendum of 20 May 1980 the question was as follows:

> The Government of Quebec has made public its proposal to negotiate a new agreement with the rest of Canada based in the equality of nations; this agreement would enable Quebec to acquire the exclusive power to make its laws, levy its taxes and establish relations abroad – in other words, sovereignty – and at the same time to maintain with Canada an economic association including a common currency; no change in political status resulting from these negotiations will be effected without approval by the people through another referendum; on these terms do you give the Government of Quebec the mandate to negotiate the proposed agreement between Quebec and Canada? Yes/No.[8]

The most striking features about this question are its length (107 words) and its language which exposes the complexity of the subject matter. The objective of the referendum was to seek a mandate to negotiate 'sovereignty-association' and then put the outcome of these negotiations to another referendum. The PQ in 1980 wanted sovereignty only in connection with subsequent association with Canada. Both concepts were equally fundamental to the PQ's project. The mistake, however, was to link the two concepts as that enabled Canadian Prime Minister Trudeau to reject the possibility of association and thus kill the sovereignty debate with one stroke.

The second referendum – unrelated to the 1980 referendum – in October 1995 asked the following question:

Do you agree that Quebec should become sovereign, after having made a formal offer to Canada for a new economic and political partnership, within the scope of the bill respecting the future of Quebec and of the agreement signed on June 12, 1995? Yes/No.

This question improved on its word count (43 words). But the problem here lay not so much in conciseness but in clarity. It is not a self-contained question as it refers to two external documents with which voters would require some degree of familiarity before casting their vote. The Bill (Bill 1) referred to was framework legislation introduced in the Quebec legislature in September 1995 while the agreement of 12 June referred to a pact not between the Quebec and Canadian Governments, but between the provincial and federal wings of the sovereigntist movement. Moreover, this referendum too is unclear about what it is trying to achieve. As in 1980 the words 'independence', 'independent', 'state' and 'statehood' are conspicuous only by their absence.

The key difference to 1980 is the de-linking of sovereignty and partnership and the absence of a requirement for a second referendum after Quebec's negotiations with Canada. The referendum was seemingly on 'a new economic and political partnership' (which again guaranteed a higher 'Yes' vote than any of the other concepts). Partnership was an 'offer' the PQ would have made to Canada had it won the referendum. If after one year of negotiating the offer had been rejected by Canada, Quebec would have sought to become sovereign by issuing a unilateral declaration of independence (UDI) as set out in Bill 1 which is referred to in the referendum question. Whilst partnership was preferred, the prospect of independence was the PQ's threat should the negotiations fail. Many federalists regarded Quebec as thereby pointing a shotgun at Canada. Others point out that a UDI could not have been declared without prior approval by Quebec's National Assembly. In fact, no one knows what would have happened to Quebec had the PQ won the referendum and most commentators agree that Quebec's fate has not been decided conclusively by the very narrow 'No' vote.

Terminology is more of an issue in Quebec than in Scotland. Whereas it is the SNP's stated goal to attain 'Independence for Scotland', the term 'independence' carries negative connotations in Quebec. Polls have consistently shown that support for secession varies depending on the term that is used. According to the CROP Opinion Poll of August 1999, 38 per cent of Quebecois would vote 'Yes' to 'sovereignty-partnership' (a term similar to the one used in the 1995 referendum). But the 'Yes' vote decreases for questions clearly linked to secession: 35 per cent said they would vote 'Yes' to Quebec becoming an 'independent country'; 31 per cent to Quebec becoming an 'independent country separate from Canada'; and only 28 per cent would vote 'No' to Quebec remaining a province of Canada.[9]

Federalists argued that the close result was indicative, not of a strong desire for independence but, in part, of misunderstanding caused by asking a 'loaded' question. For example, asking whether Quebec should become sovereign rather than independent could be seen as misleading; and the reference to the June agreement may have been taken as implying that an agreement with Canada had already been reached, when in fact the agreement was one between different Quebecois parties on their negotiating stance. It is very unlikely that either question would pass the test of the Supreme Court that the referendum result be 'free of ambiguity both in terms of the question asked and in terms of the support it achieves'.[10]

– The Canadian Clarity Act –

The House of Commons in Canada responded to the Supreme Court's requirement for clarity in the *Quebec Secession Reference* case by passing the Clarity Act 2000. The Act is framework legislation that enables the government of the day to decide whether the majority is clear. It specifies an orderly process for achieving a political decision without substituting rules of law for that decision.[11] Under the Act, it is for the federal House of Commons (and not the Quebec Government or the National Assembly) to determine whether the question is clear: Section 1(1). The House of Commons will consider, 'whether the question would result in a clear expression of the will of the population of a province on whether the province should cease to be part of Canada and become an independent state': Section 1(3).

This provision tries to prevent the ambiguity in the previous two referendum questions. In future, referendums will have to be open and honest about what they are asking for. If it is secession then the referendum question must clearly say so. It should not couch its true intentions by referring to 'association' or 'partnership' as was previously the case. Section 4 of the Act states that in an independence referendum a clear expression of the will of the people could not result from

1. A referendum question that merely focuses on a mandate to negotiate without soliciting a direct expression of the will of the population of that province on whether the province should cease to be part of Canada; or
2. A referendum question that envisages other possibilities in addition to the secession of the province from Canada, such as economic or political arrangements with Canada, that obscure a direct expression of the will of the population of that province on whether the province should cease to be part of Canada.

The question would, therefore, not be clear (a) if it did not make clear that Quebec's ties with Canada would be severed upon independence, or (b) if it proposed that Quebec become a sovereign State and proposed to make an offer of economic and political partnership with the rest of Canada. The last requirement arguably goes beyond the standard the Supreme Court was trying to set. The Supreme Court envisaged a process in which the interests of both sides would be considered, and not necessarily a choice between two diametrically opposed options.

Patrick Monahan, who was the advisor to the Canadian Minister of Intergovernmental Affairs, Stéphane Dion, concedes that the federal government cannot prevent Quebec from asking a question which includes a reference to partnership.[12] According to him, a referendum question could provide for a political and economic partnership and still be clear.

This matter cannot be settled here. It also distracts from the justification for the Clarity Act, namely the desire to ensure that the next referendum on Quebec's independence reflects the settled will of the people. As Stéphane Dion said:

> You don't break your country with support of 50 per cent plus one. That's just never happened. On the contrary, outside the colonial context, referenda held as a part of a successful process of secession have always generated majorities of over 70 per cent. Separatist leaders around the world say: 'let my people vote under fair conditions and you'll see that they want to separate'. They are not saying: 'half my people want to separate'.[13]

The Quebec National Assembly responded to the Clarity Act with Bill 99.[14] Section 4 reiterates that the Quebec government will consider a 'Yes' vote legitimate if it receives 50 per cent plus one of valid votes cast.

– How should the question in Scotland be worded? –

There have been many debates about the wording of the question in an independence referendum. In these debates the assumption has been that one referendum would suffice. Opinion poll questions on independence ask only if independence is desired but not what it entails. This section will propose draft questions for both the referendums we have proposed: the referendum to trigger the negotiations, and the referendum to approve the terms of the independence settlement. But first, a few general points will be made.

No simple rules can be established for deciding on the wording of the referendum questions. What is important is establishing a process for reaching a decision. Key decisions must be made about the nature of any consultation on the wording and essential information associated with it, and about where responsibility lies for taking the final decision on the wording. This will normally rest with the government which drafts the referendum bill and the parliament which passes it.

The questions must be easy to understand and accessible. 'Reverse' wording, where the way in which the question is put makes it unclear what a particular answer means is to be avoided. The problem of reverse wording is difficult to eliminate entirely, and politicians may seek to manipulate wording to their advantage. California's 1976 vote on nuclear power is a good example. Most people believed that they were voting on whether to keep nuclear power, but there was confusion over whether a 'Yes' vote was one in favour of limiting future development (correct) or a vote to continue the development of nuclear power (incorrect).[15] Testing the ease with which the different wording of questions can be understood is now a task for the Electoral Commission.

It is trite to observe that the question one asks very much determines the answer one gets. As John Curtice, Professor of Politics at the University of Strathclyde, notes, 'words matter because not only do they convey meaning, they also convey symbolism and emotion'.[16] This is probably more important as regards the first referendum question where the once distant prospect of independence will be brought home to voters. The second referendum will be more 'technical' because people will be invited either to approve or reject the negotiated terms of independence; but the second referendum will also be surrounded by a great deal of emotion.

– Referendum 1 –

A number of options for Referendum 1 are available. The 'classic referendum' has one question and two possible answers – 'Yes' and 'No'. Former SNP National Convener Alex Salmond said that it had to be 'a straight question – do you want to see Scotland become an independent country – and that has to be a straight yes or no'.[17] Salmond also assumed that a simple majority would suffice to carry the referendum.

The alternative is a 'multi-option referendum', of which permutations can be described as the 'cafeteria' approach (where there is one question but several possible answers) and the 'supermarket' approach (where a series of questions, which may or may not be related, are put to the vote at the same time). The 1997 Scottish Referendum used this approach by asking two questions: whether there should be a Scottish Parliament, and whether that Parliament should have the power to vary income tax rates within Scotland. An example of the 'cafeteria' approach is found in Figure 3.3.

Figure 3.3. Public opinion on independence, devolution or rule from Westminster.

Thinking about the running of Scotland as a whole, which ONE of the following would you most like to see?

	Sept. 2000	Feb. 2001	May 2001
Scotland being independent of England & Wales, but part of the EU	24%	27%	25%
Scotland remaining part of the UK but with its own devolved parliament with taxation and spending powers	55%	53%	56%
Scotland remaining part of the UK but with no devolved parliament	18%	16%	17%
Don't know	3%	4%	2%

Source: *The Scotsman*/ICM Poll.[18]

In this poll, the respondents can choose from three different options: independence, devolution, or Westminster centralism. When given the three options, only a quarter of Scots would choose independence. However, in a binary question which puts to the electorate whether or not Scotland should become an independent country, the proportion supporting independence is much higher.

Figure 3.4. Public support for independence when asked a binary question.

Do you agree that Scotland should become an independent country?

	YES	NO	DON'T KNOW
March 2001	45%	49%	7%
January 2000	47%	43%	9%
May (2) 1999	38%	50%	12%
May (1) 1999	39%	48%	14%
April (3) 1999	41%	46%	12%
April (2) 1999	41%	48%	11%
April (1) 1999	47%	44%	9%
March 1999	42%	47%	11%
February 1999	44%	47%	9%
January 1999	49%	42%	9%
November 1998	49%	43%	8%
September (2) 1998	48%	37%	15%
September (1) 1998	51%	38%	10%
July 1998	49%	44%	7%
June (2) 1998	56%	35%	9%
June (1) 1998	52%	41%	7%

Source: ICM Research.[19]

If the alternatives to independence (devolution or Westminster centralism) are not included on the menu support for Scottish independence rises close to 50 per cent of the respondents. But even this question is not without problems. It does not define what 'an independent country' means. People may well have different opinions on the exact meaning of 'independence'. To one person, 'Independence in Europe', say, is a perfectly acceptable proposition whilst to another it is wholly unacceptable. And the poll does not distinguish between devolution and independence. The poll results prior to the first Scottish Parliament elections on 6 May 1999 may have included in the 'Yes' votes a number of voters who favoured devolution but not independence.

– Legal constraints on the wording of the Referendum 1 question –

There could be legal difficulties with a 'clear' or a 'straight' question ('Do you want Scotland to be independent? Yes/No?') because it would fall outside the powers of the Scottish Executive and Scottish Parliament defined in the Scotland Act. The question in the first referendum would have to bestow upon the Scottish Executive the power to enter into negotiations with Westminster. Professor Neil MacCormick suggests the following wording so as to stay clearly within the formal limitations of the Scotland Act and be expressly advisory:

> Do you advise and consent to the Executive opening conversations with the United Kingdom government to agree terms for Scottish independence on the basis of the constitution envisaged, or on such other basis as the people, by then, choose to put in place? (MacCormick 2000: 726).

This is an attempt to stay within the confines of the legislation. It anticipates having in place a draft constitution for an independent Scotland. If such a draft did not yet exist, the second part of MacCormick's question ('on the basis of . . .') could be omitted. For the Scottish Executive and the Scottish Parliament to stay *intra vires*, the question would have to be about commencing negotiations rather than a question about independence itself. As explained in Chapter 1, the UK constitution is a reserved matter under the Scotland Act and lies outside the powers of the Scottish Parliament.

The problem with the questions in the polls is that they would not meet the requirements as laid down by the Canadian Supreme Court and the Scotland Act. Multi-option referendums are not clear. And a clear question on independence is not within the powers of the Scottish Parliament. The requirements, then, are the following:

- The question is not about independence as such, but about authorising the Scottish Executive to negotiate the terms of independence with the UK Government.
- The question must be easy to understand and accessible.

The first referendum question might be:

> Do you authorise Scottish Ministers to negotiate terms for Scottish independence so that Scotland becomes a sovereign state separate from the United Kingdom? (23 words)

This question tries to bring home that independence does not merely mean greater autonomy, but would involve Scotland becoming a separate state. The inclusion of the word 'separate' is, however, unlikely to be acceptable to the SNP since it does not want to be branded as 'separatist'. The SNP say that 'separate' has acquired a specific meaning in Scottish political discourse, and is used pejoratively with negative connotations. An alternative variation of the question, more palatable to the SNP, might read:

> Do you authorise Scottish Ministers to negotiate terms for Scotland to be an independent state which is no longer part of the United Kingdom? (24 words)

– Referendum 2 –

The first referendum would authorise the negotiations; the second referendum would lead to independence. A positive outcome of Referendum 2 would lead to the implementation of the White Paper which embodies the negotiated terms of independence. Since the result of this referendum directly challenges the integrity of the United Kingdom, the Scottish Parliament would not have the competence under the Scotland Act to authorise it. Under UK law only the Westminster Parliament could authorise such a referendum. It could delegate the authority to the Scottish Parliament, but the ultimate authority lies with Westminster. In what follows we assume that the second referendum remains in the hands of Westminster. The wording would need to be settled by the UK Government and confirmed by Parliament (on the basis of the Government's proposal). The Government could seek the views of the Scottish Executive, but the final decision (subject to Parliament) would be that of the UK Government. This is inevitable in the UK context, given that only Westminster has the legal authority to change the constitution of the UK. But it might also command some support from the people of Scotland for the UK government to be involved in setting the question.

According to the CROP Opinion Poll the majority of Quebecois say the question should be set jointly with 'opposition parties in the National Assembly' (68 per cent v. 26 per cent), 'the Government of Canada' (58 per cent v. 37 per cent) or the 'rest of Canada' (56 per cent v. 40 per cent).[20] The Poll also suggests that a majority of Quebecois (51 per cent v. 41 per cent) agree that the Government of Canada 'has a role to play in establishing the rules of a future referendum'.

Another difference between first and second referendums is the involvement of the UK Electoral Commission. Under its governing statute the Electoral Commission only has authority over a referendum authorised by the Westminster Parliament. The referendum can be held in just one part of the UK; but it must be 'in pursuance of any provision made by or under an Act of Parliament' (Section 101 of the 2000 Act). This means that only the second referendum would fall to be supervised by the Electoral Commission. The conduct of the first referendum would be a matter for the Scottish Executive and Scottish Parliament, under rules of their own devising. There are three likely possibilities:

1. The Scottish Executive could invite the Electoral Commission to act on an agency basis;[21]
2. It could import into a Scotland Referendum Bill most of the UK rules on the conduct of referendums from the 2000 Act, but set up its own watchdog body;
3. It could import the referendum rules and watchdog body from the Scotland and Wales Referendums Act 1997. One of the biggest points of difficulty will be expenditure controls on the political parties and third parties (campaign organisations, CBI Scotland). The SNP complained that in the 1999 Scotland elections the political parties received a lot of funding from London and this issue would need to be addressed.

The first option would be sensible given that the Electoral Commission would be involved in the second referendum; and given the inevitable allegations of unfairness which surround any referendum. The best defence would be to invoke the assistance of the body specifically created to be the guardian of fairness in referendums. Such assistance could include advising on the wording of the question.

In the second referendum the Electoral Commission will be required to advise on the wording of the question proposed by the UK Government. Under section 104(4):

the Commission shall consider the wording of the referendum question, and shall publish a statement of any views of the Commission as to the intelligibility of that question (a) as soon as reasonably practicable after the Bill is introduced, and (b) in such manner as they may determine.

The second referendum invites acceptance or rejection of the terms of independence. The referendum question cannot be self-contained, but will have to refer to a separate document in which the terms of independence are set out. The question could be devised by the UK Government, or by the UK Government and Scottish Executive jointly, since it will present a document setting out the terms of independence which have been negotiated by the two governments jointly.

The second question might read:

Do you agree to the terms of independence as set out in the UK Government's and Scottish Executive's White Paper [title] [date]?

Or to make doubly sure that the Scots understand the consequences of the second referendum, the question could add at the beginning:

Do you agree to Scotland separating from the UK and becoming a sovereign state on the terms of independence set out in . . . [as above]?

If the second referendum asks the Scots to approve the terms of the White Paper, then free copies of the White Paper should be distributed to each household as happened with the Belfast Agreement in April 1998. Summaries of the Scottish devolution White Paper were also distributed before the referendum in September 1997.

– THE CAMPAIGN –

– Duration –

Election campaigns have no clearly defined duration. For UK general elections there is a statutory period of 23 days or so from dissolution to polling day; but usually the contest begins as soon as the date for dissolution is announced. For referendums a period of at least 23 days is necessary for administrative purposes. Postal and proxy votes need to be applied for 13 working days before the poll, and time is required to circulate the necessary information. The length of the campaign may also affect whether late additions can be made to the electoral register – supplementary claims cannot be accepted later than the 20th of the month to be effective on the first of the following month. Broadcasters would also be assisted by three weeks or more to allow for any referendum broadcasts and relevant programmes – though in practice informal campaigning and coverage in the media are likely to begin considerably earlier.

Provided that these administrative requirements were met, the need for a precise definition of a referendum campaign could arise only if particular restrictions were applied, for example limits on broadcasts or a requirement to account for expenditure. Statutory restrictions will apply to the second referendum, which will be subject to the full regulatory regime of the 2000 Act, and the supervision of the Electoral Commission. How much if any of this regime is applied to the first referendum is a matter for the Scottish Executive. In practice, those involved in campaigning may be happy to limit expenditure by confining the period of full scale campaigning to a minimum. Once the legislation is in place, the period of notice required to prepare for the referendum should not be long.

It might also be strategically wise to build momentum through a relatively short campaign, rather than let the issue of independence dominate Scottish politics for a number of years. The question is whether that would leave the SNP with enough time to turn public hostility around. Although it is a very big question for which the Scots need time to prepare and to absorb the implications, allowing too much time can be damaging to the economy (see Chapter 10) because of the uncertainty, and damaging to the rest of government and public policy because so much will be put on hold pending the outcome. For these reasons a short campaign seems preferable.

– Campaign organisation –

In the UK, the establishment of officially recognised 'umbrella' campaigning organisations for the purposes of referendum campaigns has happened only once. In 1975, two umbrella organisations were in existence as self-appointed campaign co-ordinators before they were given legal status under the Referendum Act. Thereafter they were unchallenged as the representatives of the two opposing views, although each had some difficulties in maintaining unity.

In the 1979 Scotland referendum there were a number of such groups. Aside from the party campaigns, support for a 'Yes' vote was garnered by 'Yes for Scotland' and 'Alliance for an Assembly'. The main anti-devolution campaign group was 'Scotland Says No'. In 1997 the campaign organisations were less fragmented, with 'Scotland Forward' pushing for devolution and 'Think Twice' opposing it (Denver et al. 1998: 215). Denver et al. point out that the reason the role of independent campaign groups was limited in 1997 was because of the strong position on devolution held by the political parties. This is *a fortiori* going to be the case in a referendum campaign on independence, which will probably be met with fierce resistance from all mainstream parties in Scotland (other than the SNP).

– Limits on expenditure –

No limits were placed on expenditure in the referendum campaigns of 1975, 1979 and 1997 since the Government took the view that there would be practical obstacles to enforcing statutory constraints as well as possible objections to restricting freedom of speech. In 1979 there were in any case no formally recognised campaign groups over which the Government could have exercised control. But in 1975 there was an evident problem of fairness as a result of the striking contrast between the resources of the two opposing campaign groups. The subsequent accounts of campaigning organisations showed Britain in Europe as having spent £1,481,583 against £133,630 spent by the National Referendum Campaign.[22] The two Scottish campaigns in 1997 spent the following amounts:

- Think Twice: £275,000
- Scotland Forward: £270,000[23]

In 1998 the Neill Committee argued that it would be 'futile and possibly wrong' to introduce limits on what parties and other organisations taking part in a referendum should be able to spend on their campaigns.[24] The Labour Government, however, believes that 'limits are desirable and practicable' and that:

> there is no reason in principle why spending limits should not operate, in a similar way as at elections, to discourage excessive spending by the political parties and others and to ensure that individual organisations do not obtain disproportionate attention for their views because of the wealth behind them.[25]

That is now the policy enshrined in the 2000 Act, which contains an elaborate regulatory regime to control expenditure on referendums by campaigning organisations, by the political parties and by individuals. Schedule 14 sets out limits on referendum expenses by permitted participants. Paragraph 2 provides that:

> The limit on referendum expenses incurred by or on behalf of a permitted participant during the referendum period in the case of such a referendum is such amount as the Secretary of State may by order prescribe.

This regulatory regime would apply to the second referendum, but not to the first. The Scottish Executive could seek to import this aspect of the Political Parties, Elections and Referendums Act 2000 along with other elements; but it might decide this was a regulatory step too far. Few other countries have attempted to limit the amount of money spent in referendum campaigns. The three states with most experience of referendums – Switzerland, California, and Australia – do not apply any limits to campaigning expenditure. The one exception lies in the Quebec Referendum Act. Quebec requires that referendum committees use a special fund to cover the expenses they incur during the referendum period. Each national committee may spend up to $Can1.00 per voter. The State contributes to the committees' funds an amount set by the National Assembly when it adopts the question – $Can0.50 at the last referendum. The committees may then raise other money up to the $Can1.00 per elector limit. Individuals may donate a maximum of $Can3,000 to each committee. Firms and 'legal persons' may not make any contribution.

By the time of any referendum on Scottish independence the UK may have held a referendum on entry into the Euro. That will be a major test of the new regulatory regime and of the feasibility of statutory expenditure controls. The Scottish Executive will take account of that experience in deciding whether to introduce spending limits for the first referendum. It will also have an eye to the balance of political advantage. Will the SNP and supporters of independence be heavily outspent by the major political parties and lobbies like big business which will favour the status quo? If the Scottish Executive decides to introduce spending limits it could seek to justify the decision on the basis that both referendums should be held under broadly the same set of rules. The UK government has no such latitude in relation to the second referendum: the full weight of the 2000 Act regime will apply. But the UK government will have discretion to prescribe the spending limits for the different participants in this particular campaign. It too will be mindful of any experience from the Euro referendum, and of how it perceives the balance of political advantage.

– CONCLUSION –

– The electorate –

- The UK precedents established in the 1970s and the 1990s, international practice and the principle of fairness all suggest that an independence referendum should be held in Scotland only.
- Both independence referendums in Scotland should use the electoral roll that is used in local elections. This was practised in 1997, and it also gives greater voice to those resident in Scotland (including EU nationals).

– Thresholds –

- There are strong arguments for and against the imposition of thresholds. The UK has not normally set a threshold requirement. In the two stage referendum process which we propose, the existence of the second referendum constitutes an alternative (and major) safeguard. Given that the Scots will be invited to vote twice, with a significant interval in between, before they can achieve independence, we do not believe that a threshold is required in either of the two referendums. A majority of those voting should suffice.

– The questions –

- The question of the first referendum – on the principle of independence – will be the harder one to draft. If it is authorised by the Scottish Parliament our suggestion is: 'do you authorise Scottish Ministers to negotiate terms for Scotland to be an independent state which is no longer part of the United Kingdom?'
- The second referendum question – on the terms of independence – will be more technical and hence easier. Our suggestion is: 'Do you agree to the terms of independence as set out in the UK Government's and Scottish Executive's White Paper?'

– Conduct of the referendum –

- The second referendum will need to be authorised by the Westminster Parliament, on a question presented by the UK government. It will be supervised by the Electoral Commission under the Political Parties, Elections and Referendums Act 2000. The first referendum will be initiated by the Scottish Executive, and subject to such rules as the Scottish Executive and Scottish Parliament decide. They may decide to import all or part of the regulatory framework created by the 2000 Act, to help ensure that the first referendum is perceived to be as fairly conducted as the second.

– The campaign –

- Financial and strategic considerations point to a relatively short campaign duration. Those involved in campaigning are usually anxious to limit expenditure by confining the period of full scale campaigning to a minimum. It might also be strategically wise to build momentum through a relatively short campaign, rather than let the debilitating issue of independence dominate Scottish politics for a number of years.

– NOTES –

1. *Electoral Studies*, ONS, 1999.
2. c. 61
3. This gives effect to a widely held (but not universal) view that those resident in a country, who contribute to the community by paying tax, should be given a political voice regardless of where they are from.
4. Command Paper 3883 is the technical parliamentary term for the Belfast Agreement.
5. Bill C–20, 2nd sess., 36th Parliament, 48 Elizabeth II, 1999 (as passed by the House of Commons 15 March 2000).
6. Available at: http://www.crop.ca/
7. For an overview of alternative models see Watts 1998.
8. On a turnout of 84 per cent, there were 2,171,913 'No' votes (59.5 per cent) and 1,478,200 'Yes' votes (40.5 per cent).
9. The Quebec debate about terminology is reminiscent of the sovereignty question that arose during the break-up of Czechoslovakia. The Premier of Slovakia Meciar sought 'sovereign Slovak statehood' but refrained from using the term 'independence' (Innes 1997: 419).
10. *Quebec Seccession Reference*, paragraph 87.
11. The debate about what constitutes a clear majority will continue in Canada. The PQ will argue for 50 per cent plus 1, the federalists for a higher threshold. The Supreme Court's opinion and the Clarity Act both leave this question open and for the government of the day to decide. In that respect a clear majority is a bit like an elephant: hard to define but easily recognised. The issue could be clarified by further litigation, but the Court seems to want to discourage that sort of litigation by characterising the issues as non-justiciable.
12. Monahan, P. J. (2000), *Doing the Rules – An Assessment of the Federal Clarity Act in Light of the Quebec Secession Reference*, CD Howe Institute (Commentary 135).
13. Notes for an address by Stéphane Dion on the Second Reading of the Clarity Bill C–20, House of Commons, Ottawa, Ontario, 14 December 1999.
14. *An Act respecting the exercise of the fundamental rights and prerogatives of the Québec people and the Québec State*, Quebec National Assembly, 1st sess., 36th leg. Bill 99 (assented to 13 December 2000).
15. See Prop 15 of 1976: website http://www.uchastings.edu/library/ballotprops.htm [visited 3 August 2001]. Technical laws such as this one go on for pages and pages. The actual ballot lists the title of the proposition – a one sentence précis – and 2 boxes (Yes and No). In other words, voters know what the question is – Yes or No. But they do not always understand the ins and outs of the proposal.
16. 'No surprise in scrabble of words', *The Scotsman*, 29 May 2001.
17. *The Scotsman*, 7 April 1999.
18. For the most recent result see website http://www.icmresearch.co.uk/reviews/2001/scotsman-may2001-poll.htm [visited 10 July 2001]
19. website http://www.icmresearch.co.uk/reviews/vote-intention-reports/scotsman-report.htm [visited 10 July 2001]
20. Available at: http://www.crop.ca/
21. Under section 10 of the 2000 Act the Electoral Commission has the power to provide 'any relevant body' (which could include the Scottish Executive) with advice and assistance.
22. *Referendum on United Kingdom Membership of the European Community*, Accounts of Campaigning Organisations, Cmnd. 6251, 7 October 1975.
23. See Denver et al. 2000: 59.

24. *Fifth Report of the Committee on Standards in Public Life*, Cm. 4057–I, paragraph 12.46.
25. *The Government's proposals for legislation in response to the Fifth Report of the Committee on Standards in Public Life*, Home Office, Cm. 4413, paragraph 1.14.

CHAPTER 4

The Negotiations

In the previous chapters we have outlined a process towards independence which involves two referendums: the first to authorise the Scottish Executive to enter into negotiations, the second to approve the terms of independence which result from those negotiations. This chapter will examine more closely the dynamics and the contents of the negotiation process that could take place between the first and the second referendum. More precisely it will examine which players might be involved, how long the negotiations would take, and what matters would be subject to negotiation.

It should be noted from the outset that the prime concern of any country negotiating a settlement, especially an independence settlement, is the protection of its national interest. However, the very nature of such negotiations can give rise to massive political disagreement. The experience of international relations ought to be borne in mind, which is that where there is conflict matters tend to be settled according to the relative power of the parties (Young 1994: 49). Ronald L. Watts, Professor of Political Studies at the Institute of Intergovernmental Relations at Queen's University, Canada, warns that:

> almost invariably the process of secession . . . has created a situation that has presented enormous barriers to the creation of a subsequent partnership, even when that was avowed as an objective at the time of separation . . . Whenever secession has occurred, it has inevitably been accompanied by sharp political controversies and acrimony which are not easily forgotten (Watts 1998: 387).

Watts points to the continued hostility between India and Pakistan since partition in 1947, and the difficulty or failure of developing alternative models of partnership in the Czech and Slovak Republics and Malaysia and

Singapore, as evidence of the impact secession and separation can have on public attitudes.

Robert Young, who is Professor of Political Science at the University of Western Ontario, Canada, has examined a number of cases of peaceful secession and argues that they are characterised by ten interconnected conditions (see Young: 1994; 1997; 1998):

1. Secessions usually follow protracted constitutional and political disputes;
2. The seceding state declares its intent to withdraw;
3. Secession is a momentous, galvanising event;
4. The predecessor state accepts the principle of secession: negotiations follow;
5. The government is broadened and strengthened on each side: there is a premium on solidarity;
6. The negotiations involve few participants;
7. The settlement is made quickly;
8. The settlement offers a short list of items;
9. Foreign powers play an important role;
10. Secession is accomplished constitutionally and is irreversible.

It is, therefore, imperative that the negotiations between Scotland and the United Kingdom are conducted in a spirit of co-operation and consent. The UK side ought to conduct negotiations '*strictly on the basis of what is good for us*, and most definitely *not* on the basis of what is bad for them' (Gibson 1994: 111 (original emphasis)). This chapter is mainly about the mechanics and the substance of the negotiations; but the spirit in which they are conducted is equally important. It is something which cannot be legislated for, but will be determined by the political context and attitude on both sides, and by the leadership shown by the main political actors.

– WHO NEGOTIATES FOR EACH SIDE? –

The parties involved in the secession process need not be large: the practice of successful negotiations suggests that the teams are small. The Singapore–Malaysia secession, for instance, was negotiated by the respective prime ministers and a few principal cabinet ministers. The break up of Czechoslovakia involved Vaclav Klaus (Civic Democratic Party, CDP) and Vladimir Meciar (Movement for a Democratic Slovakia, MDS), as well as a number of senior party members on either side. The full cabinet was brought into play once detailed treaties were being drafted. This section begins with the Czech–Slovak experience, before looking at the thought which has been given to the negotiation process in Quebec and Canada.

The members of the teams must also be seen as legitimate representatives, able to sell the deal to their respective sides. This requirement was totally absent in the Czechoslovak case as neither Klaus nor Meciar had a mandate to negotiate the break up of the State.

– The Czech–Slovak negotiations[1] –

The decisive talks were held in the immediate aftermath of the June 1992 elections, on 9, 11, 17 and 19–20 June, and involved principally Klaus and Meciar as well as the CDP and MDS. Eight MDS and nine CDP leaders were present at the final meeting in June. These few but high-profile meetings are but the tip of the iceberg when two countries so diverse and yet so closely linked decide to sever the State that unites them. But it was the meetings of the respective leaders that produced the agreement for the federal government and the timetable for settling the constitutional question that dogged earlier negotiations for so long. With the Declaration of Sovereignty and the resignation of President Havel, the next critical meeting between Klaus and Meciar was held on 22–23 July. Only four other CDP leaders and three from the MDS were present at this meeting which devised the procedural framework for the break-up and initiated thinking about post-independence relations. Once the negotiation process was in full swing it involved more participants on the political side. Basic agreements needed to be amended and were handled by officials. However, it was the principal coalition leaders on either side who handled the crucial issues.

– Lessons from Quebec –

In the Czech–Slovak split it was clear that the negotiating parties would be the two republics. In other countries, the relevant parties may be more numerous. For example, negotiations on independence for Quebec necessarily involve the other Canadian provinces. Under the Canadian Constitution changes to the constitution generally require the consent of the federal Parliament plus two-thirds of the provinces having 50 per cent of the population.[2]

Shortly before the 1995 referendum, the Parti Québécois (PQ) under Jacques Parizeau named five members of a committee that was to supervise negotiations with Canada about the partnership treaty. The committee comprised Jean Allaire, former Liberal and founder of *Action Démocratique du Québec*, Jacynthe Simard, head of the Union of Regional Municipalities and Counties, Denise Verreault, president of a shipyard firm, Serge Racine, president of a furniture company, and Arthur Tremblay, a former Progressive Conservative senator and constitutional adviser. The chief negotiator was to be Lucien Bouchard, who at the time was leader of the Bloc Québécois, the PQ's federal counterpart.[3]

The 1995 intentions have been overtaken by judicial intervention. Aside from federal and provincial governments, the Canadian Supreme Court in the *Quebec Secession Reference* also envisaged 'participants in' and 'parties to' confederation taking part (paragraph 88) in the negotiations. Their participation would help to address the interests of 'other participants, as well as the rights of all Canadians both within and outside Quebec' (paragraph 92)[4]. At the very least, the Federal Government, the Quebec Government and other provincial governments would have to appoint a negotiating team. The selection and appointment of the members of these teams would be entirely at the discretion of each government. It is fair to assume that the Intergovernmental Affairs Ministers would play a pivotal role, should the situation arise.

– Relevance for Scotland –

There are no set rules as far as the negotiating teams are concerned. A likely procedure would be preliminary negotiations between officials, acting under instructions, interspersed with direct negotiations at ministerial level. In practice everything would turn on the Prime Minister's wishes in terms of who represented the UK; and the Scottish delegation would need to be of equivalent size.

One question thrown up by the Canadian Supreme Court which has relevance also in the UK is whether the equivalent of the Canadian provinces, the nations and regions of the UK should be invited to participate as well. The governments of Wales and Northern Ireland (and the English regions, should devolution have progressed that far) might feel that they have a legitimate interest in the outcome of the negotiations. Some of the mechanisms that have been set up around devolution – the Joint Ministerial Committee or the Council of the Isles (see generally Hazell 1999: 139–40) – could provide fora in which their views are incorporated into the negotiations.

Negotiations on independence may also throw up a variant of the so-called West Lothian Question.[5] The UK Government may find it difficult to select its negotiating team without including representatives of Scotland. Could UK MPs or UK Cabinet Ministers representing Scottish constituencies (like Robin Cook and Gordon Brown) negotiate for the United Kingdom? Should they be excluded? If Gordon Brown was the Chancellor, could he be realistically entrusted with the financial negotiations given that his seat at Westminster would disappear and he might return to Scotland after independence? Similarly, the Scottish Executive would also technically lack competence to negotiate since it is formed under legislation which expressly excludes from its competence constitutional issues. There is no obvious precedent to turn to for a solution to this, and the same problem appears in Canada too. Would Prime Minister Jean Chrétien, who is from Quebec, be the best negotiator for (English) Canada? Would the rest of Canada accept him as chief negotiator for Canada?

There might also be a role for independent third parties to help facilitate the negotiation process. An independent chair, for instance, could impart a sense of objectivity and neutrality in what might be a bitter and politicised battle. Such a chair could be modelled on the role of the special US 'peace-making' envoy, former Senator George Mitchell, who from 1995 helped to chair the peace talks in Northern Ireland which led to the 1998 Belfast Agreement. One could also point to the UN/EC International Conference on Yugoslavia whose High Representative in March 1996 appointed Sir Arthur Watts as special negotiator for succession issues. His role was fundamentally that of a mediator during the succession negotiations. There could also be an observer role for EU officials and other external stake-holders as an independent Scotland would have to establish a new basis for membership of the European Union (see Chapter 6).

– THE CONTENTS OF NEGOTIATION –

Having considered the respective negotiating teams, the next question to be addressed is the substance of the negotiations. What are the main issues to be resolved, and the likely points of difficulty? The United Kingdom is a highly integrated political, economic and social union, and every aspect of government would need to be reviewed and divided up. Devolution will have helped – by dividing more sharply the institutions and public services devolved to Scotland. But many important public functions remain at the UK level. In addition, many of the issues to be negotiated are now subject to European law. This section will focus on the questions of defence, borders, national debt, assets, the currency and monetary policy, and commercial and economic relations. Issues such as citizenship, the provision of health services and social security are discussed in Chapter 14 on post-independence relations between Scotland and rUK.

Issues that need to be agreed range from the very large – how should the national debt be shared? – to the very small – how will the two countries co-operate on repairing cross-border roads? In the Scottish context some issues are predictably contentious – what will happen to the Faslane nuclear base?

– whilst others may flare up unexpectedly. Thus in Czechoslovakia there were arguments over the national flag (should the Union Jack be redesigned to remove the St Andrew's Cross?) and the fate of collections in the national museums.[6] This section starts by reviewing the main issues which were negotiated in Czechoslovakia in 1992, and in Ireland in 1920, before turning to specific issues, starting with defence.

The negotiations are likely to focus on a few central issues, even though (or because) the level of political, economic and social integration in the United Kingdom is very high. For a start, all legislation currently in force in Scotland will remain in force post-independence. It is standard practice for all successor States – after secession or decolonisation – to keep all prior legislation, unless it is incompatible with provisions of a new constitution/ bill of rights. To use an example, Irish law is based on Common Law and is enshrined in the Constitution of 1937. Statutes passed by the British Parliament before 1921 also have the force of law unless they have subsequently been repealed or have been found to be unconstitutional. Similarly, when the Scottish Parliament was opened on 1 July 1999 it did not start life with an empty statute book but with all existing laws in force. United Kingdom practice has been to keep a separate statute book for Scotland – as for Northern Ireland – so there will be minimal difficulty for the Scots after independence.

– Lessons from Czechoslovakia –

Czechoslovakia, although worlds apart from the United Kingdom, was also a highly centralised State. It may come as a surprise to learn that its break–up was achieved with very few formal agreements that were worked out between the two governments and ratified by the Federal Assembly. No precise official figure exists but a Canadian source lists a total of 31 agreements.[7]

Klaus for the Czechs and Meciar for the Slovaks agreed on the priorities and framework for the process in their meetings of 20 June and 23 July 1992. Initially, both had continuity of the federation in mind and set the deadline for 30 September by which to resolve their constitutional disagreements. However, in the event the decision to dissolve the federation was taken in July, as were the key principles to govern future relations. They agreed:

- in each republic, to protect equally the rights of the other's citizens, and to permit the free movement of people;
- to coordinate foreign policies and embassies, to have joint representation in the European Community, and to solve jointly the problem of succession to international treaties;

- to form a customs union, with free movement of goods, services, capital and labour;
- to continue a joint defence system for some time.

It should be noted that none of the above issues were to link the two states: Klaus expressly rejected that. All relations were to be on an interstate basis (Young 1994: 43). A draft treaty was produced and was approved by the federal government. It was put before the Federal Assembly on 27 October 1992. The various elements of this draft treaty will be examined in the ensuing paragraphs with a particular view to illustrate the kind of issues that require regulation after Scottish independence.

The Czech and Slovak Republics, not being members of the European Community at the time, negotiated a customs union to provide for the free movement of goods and services between the two states. If it was accepted in negotiations with the UK that Scotland would join the European Union after gaining independence, it would not have to seek agreement on a separate customs union with the remainder of the United Kingdom (rUK), because the free movement of goods and services would be required and regulated by EU law.

The agreements in the Czech–Slovak 1992 draft treaty were similar to ordinary international treaties. They are good illustrations of the everyday nature of matters that would require regulation after Scotland breaks away from the Union:

- a treaty on legal assistance to enable state agencies to take action at the request of the other country's authorities;
- a treaty to recognise marriages and inheritances;
- a border treaty to recognise the administrative border in place and the future international border;
- an agreement that no permit would be required to work in the other country. A treaty for paying social security and pension benefits to citizens of the other state.

Other issues in the Czech–Slovak draft treaty were:

- joint use of police and Ministry of Internal Affairs archives;
- co-operation in communications;
- health care services;
- co-operation in environmental protection;
- co-operation in education (see Young 1994: 46).

Although EU law provides for the free movement of persons and would make a treaty regarding the removal of work permits redundant, Scotland and rUK may agree to regulate over and above the European 'floor' and facilitate the paying of unemployment, social security and pension benefits. An indication of the scale but also of the rushed, ill-planned and often chaotic nature of the Czech–Slovak division is the large number of sub-agreements – over 2,000 – that followed the 31 blanket treaties negotiated prior to the dissolution.

– Lessons from Ireland –

In December 1920, the UK Parliament passed the Government of Ireland Act, which provided for two separate parliaments, one in six of the nine counties of Ulster (which became known as Northern Ireland) and one for the remainder of Ireland. The Act was not supported in its final form by any Irish MPs, nationalist or unionist.

In the Act the UK Government unilaterally partitioned Ireland – without any prior negotiations with Irish nationalists, or Sinn Fein, having taken place. In effect, it made concessions to Ulster Unionists first (in the shape of Northern Ireland) before opening negotiations with Sinn Fein, which represented an overwhelming majority outside of what became Northern Ireland.

The 1920 Act provided further that the United Kingdom was to keep hold of effective control of Irish affairs, especially in external relations. Sinn Fein did not accept the terms of the 1920 Act, which granted home rule for the two jurisdictions in Ireland rather than independence or sovereignty for either. The Irish war of independence and political protest against the British continued until 10 July 1921, when a truce was arranged. Subsequent negotiations between Sinn Fein, led by Arthur Griffith, and the UK coalition government, led by David Lloyd George, resulted in the agreement of the Anglo–Irish Treaty on 6 December 1921.

The United Kingdom wanted to avoid a break on the issue of Ulster. The Irish side, on the other hand, wanted to focus on achieving independence from the United Kingdom and from the Empire. In the end the United Kingdom, styling itself Great Britain, compelled the Irish negotiators to accept serious infringements on its sovereignty (which contributed to the eruption of civil war after the Treaty), while accepting that the Irish Free State should have dominion rather than home rule status. Under Article 1 of the Treaty, Ireland was to have the:

> same constitutional status in the Community of Nations known as the British Empire as the Dominion of Canada, the Commonwealth of Aus-

tralia, the Dominion of New Zealand, and the Union of South Africa, with a Parliament having powers to make laws for the peace, order and good government of Ireland and an Executive responsible to that Parliament, and shall be styled and known as the Irish Free State.

The opponents to the Treaty were led by De Valera who objected emphatically to Article 4 that required members of the Dáil to swear allegiance to the British sovereign, and Article 11 that virtually guaranteed a separate government in Northern Ireland. They also objected to the imposition of British requirements on the use of naval ports, and to the provisions made for Ireland's share of the UK's debt.

After extensive discussions the Treaty was ratified by the UK Parliament, and by the Irish Cabinet (in a split 4–3 decision) and by the Dáil on 15 January 1922, by a vote of 64 to 57. Ratification created the Irish Free State, with Arthur Griffith as president and Michael Collins, who was another prominent member of Sinn Fein, as chairman of the provisional government. The 1921 treaty was made under duress – aggravated when the UK subsequently placed restrictions on the Free State's first draft constitution. Lloyd George's threat of immediate and terrible war is hardly a model for future independence negotiations between the rest of the United Kingdom and Scotland.

In terms of the issues which were negotiated, the Irish example is interesting for three reasons:

• continued use of Irish naval ports;
• sharing of the national debt;
• Crown/Republic issues.

British insistence on continued use of British naval ports has a contemporary resonance in relation to the naval bases on the Clyde. The first two points, in relation to Scotland, are discussed below in this chapter. As regards the last point, the Irish wanted to avoid the suggestion that the UK Crown was sovereign. In their view, the Crown should not have had any continuing role in the government of Ireland. As a dominion Ireland had a Governor General who was responsible for the formation of the government. This meant that the Crown had a formal and symbolic role in domestic politics. The Irish Free State loosened its links with the Crown gradually, adopting a new constitution in 1937, passing the Republic of Ireland Act 1948, and withdrawing from the Commonwealth in 1949.

– Would Scotland retain the British monarchy? –

The ICM 'Scottish Poll' in September 1998 suggests that most Scots (56 per cent) would want to retain the monarchy if Scotland became independent. The SNP's policy for an independent Scotland is to keep the Queen and her successors as Head of State, 'as defined within the written constitution, subject to the democratic consent of the people in a referendum.'[8] In effect this would mean reverting to the situation in the seventeenth century, when Scotland and England were separate states but shared the same monarch. There was a Union of the two Crowns for the whole of the seventeenth century, after James VI became King of Scotland in 1567 and succeeded to the English throne in 1603 as James I of England. An independent Scotland could decide that the union of the two Crowns should continue, and Queen Elizabeth II could become Queen Elizabeth I of Scotland.

There would be nothing unusual about this. Queen Elizabeth is the Queen of Australia, and the Queen of Canada, and head of state of a dozen other independent Commonwealth countries (Bogdanor 1997). In each she reigns as a constitutional monarch subject to the constitution of that country. So in Scotland the Queen's powers and functions as Head of State would be defined in the constitution of an independent Scotland. Some of these are already defined in the Scotland Act 1998. They include the rules for the formation of a new government, dissolution of a government, the appointment of the most senior judges, and other key functions in which the Queen is involved.

It would be a matter of choice if Scotland wished to remain a monarchy, whether to codify all the powers and functions of the monarch, or whether to leave some of the prerogative powers defined at common law.[9] The likelihood is that all the important prerogative powers – to summon and dissolve parliament, to make treaties, to declare war and conduct foreign affairs – would be codified in the new constitution, and many of them made subject to parliamentary approval. This might revive the debate in rUK whether the remaining prerogative powers should be codified.[10] But the important point to emphasise is that it would be for an independent Scotland to decide what kind of monarchy to have. The powers and functions, and indeed the whole style of the monarchy, might be different north and south of the border. Part of the style would be set, in the Queen's absence, by the Governor General, who would be chosen by the Scottish Executive, although technically appointed by the Queen. As recent Governor Generals have shown in Canada and New Zealand, they can set a much less stuffy and informal style.

– Defence issues –

The questions of oil and defence are likely to be two of the most difficult issues of the negotiations. Oil is discussed in Chapter 10. They are two of Scotland's strongest bargaining chips. How the UK armed forces can be disentangled is not just a matter of political negotiation, because it also involves questions of international nuclear law which are considered below. It is beyond the scope of this work to examine the issues in detail and anticipate the likely outcome. The ensuing paragraphs will restrict themselves to making a few general observations.

For Scotland the main question is whether there should be an independent Scottish Defence Force (SDF). For the United Kingdom the question would be how to reconstitute the UK armed forces under two sovereign authorities. No serious studies have been done in this area – although a paper by Jack Hawthorne (1996) for the Scottish Centre for War Studies is a notable contribution. A starting point would be to examine the current Scottish contribution to the UK armed forces. What is located in Scotland? What do the regiments do? What would it take to disentangle the Scottish contributions?

This data is not readily available, nor is there much information about personnel in Scotland. However, at the beginning of 2001 the Defence Analytical Services Agency (DASA) of the Ministry of Defence (MOD) contributed data for an answer to a Parliamentary Question on 12 February 2001 about MOD related jobs in Scotland.[11] The DASA estimates of direct MOD related employment in Scottish local authorities areas are set out in Figure 4.1.

Figure 4.1. DASA estimates of direct MOD related employment in Scottish local authority areas.

Year	Employment
1995–96	8,000
1996–97	7,000
1997–98	6,000
1998–99	6,000

A month later, on 8 March 2001 DASA also contributed data for an answer to a Parliamentary Question about Scots serving in the armed forces.[12] The figures for Scots and non–Scots serving in the UK armed forces are set out in Figure 4.2.

Figure 4.2. Scots and non-Scots serving in the UK armed forces.

	Number
Scots	
Army[13]	12,956
RAF[14]	5,688
Non–Scots	
Army[15]	96,953
RAF	48,221

The new Scottish Defence Force

It is often argued by opponents of independence that a SDF would be very costly. However, the costs would very much depend on what the structure and tasks of the SDF were. On one end of the spectrum there could be a complete separation of Scottish defence capabilities from the UK. On the other end the Scottish capability could seek to continue as part of an integrated defence structure. It all hinges on the question what kind of defence capability Scotland thinks it needs.

What is clear is that Scotland needs some form of defence capability. It would need a force to protect the offshore oil installations, and Scotland's fishing fleet. It is doubtful whether oil companies would continue exploring in Scottish waters if there were no means of defending their investment against terrorist and other forms of attach. As Hawthorn puts it, 'only the foolhardy would adopt a position of unarmed neutrality and trust in the lack of aggression and political ambition in others towards a defenceless state' (Hawthorn 1996: 17).

Without an independent means of guaranteeing national security, Scotland's position in the world would be unusual. It would be a bold and unconventional move to leave a key state function like defence to other states. In Europe the move towards a common foreign and security policy under the Treaty of Amsterdam has led to talks of a European Rapid Reaction Force (ERRF). The SNP is committed to the ERRF. Its shadow defence minister Colin Campbell claims it, 'would make appropriate and proportionate contributions to such a force' and participate in, 'peace-keeping, humanitarian and disaster relief operations, which are the functions of the ERRF'.[16] Some, however, question the SNP's commitment to the ERRF when its formal policy on NATO is one of phased withdrawal from its military command structure.[17] Nevertheless, there would clearly be negotiations over the size of the SDF, its relationship to rUK armed forces, and the role it would play.

Excluding the question of nuclear weapons, the issues likely to feature in the negotiations would seem to be these:

1. An agreement which provides for continued UK armed forces defence cover of Scotland for a specific period (say, five to ten years), the nature and structure of political command over the Scottish element of these forces, and payment for this service;
2. An agreement for the recruitment , including from UK armed forces, of SDFG personnel, the transfer of equipment (such as ships and aircraft) and for joint operational command structures;
3. An agreement to govern the use of the SDF in the ERRF and (possibly) the SDF's role in NATO.

UK defence and the nuclear bases in Scotland

The hottest and most complicated issue on the negotiation agenda would be nuclear weapons. Trident is a submarine-launched ballistic missile system with a fleet of four submarines. The submarine fleet requires extensive facilities to support it. These have been constructed at the Naval Base at Faslane, which is the home of the UK strategic nuclear deterrent force, and the Royal Naval Armament Depot (RNAD) at Coulport on the Clyde. Sixteen atom bomb storage bunkers have been built in a ridge overlooking Loch Long. Trident missile warheads are stored at the RNAD Coulport weapons depot, where they are installed and removed from the submarine.

What would happen to Trident if Scotland became independent has been analysed in detail by Malcolm Chalmers, Professor of International Politics, Department of Peace Studies, University of Bradford, and William Walker, Professor of International Relations at the University of St Andrews: see Chalmers and Walker (2001). This section draws heavily on their work.

The general assumption is that an independent Scotland would be a non-nuclear weapon State, whereas rUK would continue to be a nuclear weapon State as defined in the Treaty on the Non-Proliferation of Nuclear Weapons, also referred to as the Nuclear Non-Proliferation Treaty of 1968.[18] This would be easy enough if it were not for the fact that the British nuclear force is located in Scotland. A political settlement would have to be struck between the two sides that would have to:

1. Serve Scotland and rUK's interests in conformity with international nuclear law;
2. Clarify Scotland and rUK's role within NATO;
3. Clarify Scotland and rUK's role within the European military arrangements in place.

A striking fact is that independence is almost bound to make Scotland a non-nuclear state. International law, and its application since the break-up of the Soviet Union, requires that either Scotland or rUK become a non-nuclear weapon state. Two (or more) states cannot succeed to the rights and obligations of the United Kingdom in international nuclear law. The most likely scenario is that Scotland disarms, and that rUK assumes the rank of nuclear weapon state as the successor to the United Kingdom. Its final status would be subject to acceptance by the international community.

The Non-Proliferation Treaty obligates the five acknowledged nuclear-weapon states (the United States, Russian Federation, United Kingdom, France, and China)[19], not to transfer nuclear weapons, other nuclear explosive devices, or their technology to any non nuclear weapon state (Article I). Non-nuclear weapon states undertake not to acquire or produce nuclear weapons or nuclear explosive devices (Article II). Yet crucially for the United Kingdom in an independence scenario, the Treaty does not prevent a nuclear weapon state from stationing nuclear weapons on non-nuclear weapon state territory, so long as the nuclear weapon state retains sole and total control over them. So rUK could keep Trident on Scottish territory, provided that Scotland itself disarms and that the Scottish Government is powerless over the use of the weapons. All in all there are three options:

1. Faslane and Coulport become Scottish territory upon independence and rUK has to withdraw the nuclear installations;
2. rUK is granted a lease over the bases for a specified period;
3. Faslane and Coulport become sovereign base areas that would fall under rUK's jurisdiction.

The first option would be the most expensive solution for the United Kingdom. Then Defence Secretary George Robertson warned in a lecture at Aberdeen University that Scotland could end up paying the United Kingdom huge sums of money in compensation.[20] But he did not explain on what basis in national or international law such a claim might be founded. The Scots might equally claim compensation for the rehabilitation and decontamination of the defence facilities. In truth this is just one of the many issues which will be bargained over on a political rather than a legal basis as part of the overall negotiations. Other defence facilities will also need to be relocated, such as the 25 Tornado F3 fighters based at RAF Leuchars in Scotland. What is different about Trident is the difficulty of finding somewhere else to put them. Aside from the immense cost involved, there are safety concerns. rUK would have to find a relatively isolated area (to build a depot for warheads and torpedoes). And even if it did find an alternative, maybe in Devonport or Milford Haven, rUK would have to overcome public hostility to having a nuclear base built in their neighbourhood.

The second option, whereby rUK's nuclear bases are kept in an independent Scotland, would be the United Kingdom's preferred outcome of the negotiation process. But it would also be a political hornet's nest. The Scots would not only have to continue to put up with Trident, but their government would also have no operational control over the nuclear armament. This would dilute Scottish sovereign powers considerably.

Keeping Trident in Scotland would bring some advantages as well as disadvantages for the new Scottish state. To begin with, it would keep many people in employment. As at 31 January 2000, the Clyde Naval Base had a directly employed work force of 3,300, comprising 2,550 at Faslane and 750 at Coulport.[21] Another advantage is that the nuclear base in Scotland could be counted towards Scotland's contribution to European and transatlantic defence. Given the USA's interest in Trident, it would aid the swift recognition by the international community of Scotland as a new state. On the other hand, the nuclear installations could only be run by rUK. Scottish regulatory bodies and governmental institutions would have no operational control but would still have to co-operate with their rUK counterparts regarding access rights, security services, and so on.

But can Scottish co-operation be taken for granted? Could rUK, for instance, rely on the Scottish police to protect effectively its nuclear bases? The Trident issue cannot be considered outside a broader political context. There would be international pressure (mainly from the USA) on Scotland to keep Faslane and Coulport up and running. But Scotland could demand something in return as the price of their co-operating.

Chalmers and Walker in Chapter 7 of their book spell out the magnitude of protecting and supplying the UK nuclear force. The nuclear navy may consist of 'only' four nuclear submarines but it requires a massive infrastructure (ranging from shore and seabed-based sensors, to the British Underwater Test and Evaluation Centre – BUTEC – and the participation of military, police and intelligence forces) in order to be maintained.

The third option, whereby rUK retains ownership of and sovereignty over the bases at Faslane and Coulport is a relic of the colonial age and unlikely to be acceptable to Scotland (see generally Woodliffe 1992). When the Irish Free State seceded from the United Kingdom in 1921, three British naval bases were retained in Ireland, coupled with other related defensive facilities, under the Anglo–Irish Treaty.[22] After Cyprus gained independence in 1960, the United Kingdom created sovereign base areas in Akrotiri and Dhekelia. But this approach is no longer practised and more recent instances of basing agreements have involved leases. Chalmers and Walker argue that any long-term arrangements for keeping Trident where it is would probably have to involve:

1. A political understanding between Scotland and rUK;
2. A framework treaty on nuclear weapons between Scotland and rUK;
3. A military base agreement covering Faslane and Coulport.

It seems probable that rUK would have to pay a large bounty to Scotland to facilitate such an agreement.

To conclude, the nuclear issue would require a high level of co-operation between Scotland and the United Kingdom. If the negotiating parties can solve this issue then they will have set a high benchmark for all other issues. The nuclear issue creates real opportunities and offers real bargaining power for Scotland, but it would be a reluctant beneficiary due to the history of anti-nuclear sentiment in Scotland. Scotland might ultimately be obliged to co-operate otherwise the United Kingdom could block their access to NATO and the European Union, and isolate Scotland completely.

– Borders –

The land border in the south of Scotland is uncontroversial. In the event of independence there are only two issues that would require negotiating:

1. The status of the Orkney and Shetland Islands;
2. The continental shelf delimitation lines.

It is an unlikely prospect that the Orkney and Shetland Islands would not be part of an independent Scotland. But both islands had home rule movements in the 1980s, and the idea of having a say over their own affairs is still very strong. The debate about greater autonomy for the islands would increase if Scotland negotiated independence with the United Kingdom. Shetlanders in particular do not see themselves as typically Scottish. Shetland has its own flag, a strong Nordic heritage, and a strong sense of distinctiveness. Because of historic tensions they might consider becoming autonomous, with a parliament each, like the Isle of Man, the Channel Islands or the Faeroe Islands. There might even be calls for the islands to join rUK, but this possibility is considered very remote.

A more pressing matter is continental shelf delimitation because the division of tax revenues from the North Sea oil depends upon them. A discussion of the maritime boundary issues has to begin with Article 6 of the 1958 Convention on the Continental Shelf, which states that:

> Where the same continental shelf is adjacent to the territories of two adjacent States, the boundary of the continental shelf shall be determined by agreement between them. In the absence of agreement, and unless another boundary line is justified by special circumstances, the boundary shall be determined by application of the principle of equidistance from the nearest point of the baselines from which the breadth of the territorial sea of each State is measured.

In other words, in the absence of agreement or special circumstances a boundary line shall be drawn in accordance with the equidistance principle. There is no absolute rule of international law which governs boundary delimitation of the continental shelf between adjacent or opposite States. Equidistance is a principle whereby a baseline is drawn around the coast to establish territorial waters, spanning bays and estuaries according to a set of detailed rules and conventions. A 'median' line is then drawn so as to be equidistant at every point from the nearest points on the baseline of the two states in question. While the equidistance principle results in a fair resolution of many boundary disputes, the presence of an irregular coastline or of islands can often prevent an equitable solution. The equidistance principle is thus a 'background rule' that can be replaced by a negotiated agreement, or modified by special circumstances. In fact, state practice shows that the principle is one method among many, and that is neither obligatory nor more or less important than the other methods in international law (Zahraa 2001: 82).

The other way to determine the boundary line is by resorting to a mass of case law and state practice, and in particular the International Court of Justice's (ICJ) authoritative statement on customary law in the *North Sea Continental Shelf Cases*[23] in 1969, which involved the delimitation between Denmark, Germany and the Netherlands. Although 'special [coastal configuration] circumstances' were mentioned in the 1958 Convention, it was not until the 1969 cases that they became part and parcel of the rules relating to continental shelf delimitation. On delimitation, the ICJ established that the over-riding principle should be equitable settlement rather than strict equidistance.

In the Anglo–Scottish case it is not so much the coastline that complicates matters as the presence of islands off the coast. Islands are important in the context of drawing the boundary line as they could result in one state being able to claim a disproportionate area of the sea. The 1982 Law of the Sea Convention states in Article 121(1):

> An island is a naturally formed area of land, surrounded by water, which is above water at high tide.

There are two schools of thought. The first school argues that all geophysical objects (that is, rocks, reefs, islets, isles, and islands) constitute a 'special circumstance'. The second school of thought ignores small islets or little rocks as legally irrelevant. The ICJ took a more restrictive approach in the 1969 cases when it found that:

> ignoring the presence of islets, rocks, and minor coastal projections, the disproportionally distorting effect of which can be eliminated by other means, such a line must effect an equal division of the particular area involved.[24]

This position is echoed in the 1982 Convention which states in Article 121 (3):

> Rocks which cannot sustain human habitation or economic life of their own shall have no exclusive economic zone or continental shelf.

The only islands in English–Scottish coastal waters are Holy Island and Farne Islands off the Northumberland coast. But they are, quite literally, borderline cases. They could arguably be ignored as their disproportionally distorting effect is negligible and could be eliminated by other means. On the other hand, rUK will almost certainly insist that the islands are legally relevant. In fact, the Farne Islands are capable of sustaining human habitation even though they are inhabited only by wildlife wardens. What is more, they have already been used as a basepoint for the calculation of the equidistance boundary line in the agreement between Norway and the United Kingdom in 1965.[25]

It is suggested that, because of the precedent and for reasons of legal certainty, the islands should be taken into consideration when drawing the boundary line between England and Scotland. The issue will probably have to be settled either by the International Court of Justice or, more likely, by an ad hoc arbitral tribunal.

– The national debt –

The national debt is money which has been borrowed by the government, mainly to finance capital expenditure and unexpected spending such as war costs. As the money has been spent for the benefit of all UK citizens, there is a compelling argument that Scottish citizens must take an equitable share of this debt and become responsible for meeting the interest and capital repayments should Scotland become independent. It amounts to a huge sum – £340.1bn in 1999–2000.[26] Interest payments on the debt are another huge sum – £25.6bn in 1999–2000.[27] Billions of pounds are at stake in this issue and resolving it will be contentious. In Quebec, tens of thousands of man–hours have been spent researching and debating it. It would be little different in Scotland.

The issue, and the Quebec experience, is discussed in more detail in Chapter 10. It is sufficient to say at this stage that it is the contention of the SNP that Scotland would not have to shoulder any of the debt. A rUK government would certainly say that Scotland should take a share. The conclusion of this report is that Scotland will have to take a share. Chapter 10 discusses how this share might be decided and the implications of various divisions.

An issue which also has to be considered in this context are the pension entitlements of civil servants. There will have to be negotiations between Scotland and the UK because it would not be clear at the outset which side public servants would work for, and on what basis. Civil servants are currently part of the British civil service. What would happen to their pensions upon Scottish independence? One option would be for rUK to pay standard pensions to all retirees in the period before independence, and to those civil servants who select UK citizenship afterwards. Scotland would pay pensions for their public servants for the period after independence. But those are the easy cases. What about a public servant who retains UK citizenship but chooses to work for the Scottish public service? Young's analysis of this issue suggests that pensions would be linked to citizenship so that, in this example, the UK would remain responsible for the civil servant. In contrast, those who choose Scottish citizenship and work for the Scottish public service would transfer to the Scottish authorities 'their full pension entitlements until the date of departure from the public service' (Young 1998: 211). But this analysis does not stand once citizenship is decoupled from public sector work. Under the European Communities (Employment in the Civil Service) Order 1991 nationals of Member States of the European Communities are permitted to take up civil employment under the Crown. Since nationality is no longer a criterion for selection each public service would be responsible for its incumbent public servants, regardless of nationality. (For a detailed discussion on citizenship and public sector restrictions see Chapter 14).

– Assets –

According to the National Asset Register (NAR), the United Kingdom possessed £274 billion worth of assets at the end of the 1999–2000. The road network is Britain's single most valuable asset and is valued at £62 billion. The NAR considers three categories of assets:

1. Tangible fixed assets (including military and heritage assets);
2. Intangible fixed assets (such as intellectual property rights);
3. Fixed asset investments (such as share holdings).

As a general rule, fixed assets are divided by geographic location (Brownlie 1995: 654). Examples of tangible fixed assets are all central government departments and their executive agencies, NHS bodies, and nationalised industries, and military bases. If Scotland becomes independent, Scotland would have the right to all public property on its territory. Conversely, the United Kingdom would be entitled to all financial and fixed assets on rUK territory. As far as liquid holdings are concerned they could be split on the same basis as the national debt is divided, as could fixed asset investments. Loans could be administered jointly, although loans to developing countries would be a tricky matter given the thrust of government policy towards writing them off.

However, there are assets where division is not at all straightforward. For example, the Bank of England, despite its name, is really the Bank of the United Kingdom. Is Scotland entitled to demand a share of the Bank of England? And what about the remnants of the British Empire, such as the Falkland Islands? If these are British assets, is Scotland not entitled to a share of them? Because resolution of these issues appears to have economic implications, this is considered in more detail in Chapter 10.

The NAR does not cover movable assets such as stocks and other current assets. The principles of division in the event of Scottish independence are far from being clear. There are three possible set of rules. First, the territorial principle governs the succession of movable assets. In other words, all movables in Scotland and rUK stay would where they are situated (see Shaw 1994: 90). Second, only those movable assets that can be identified with fixed assets situated in Scotland would pass to the new Scottish State, whereas other movables would remain the property of rUK (see O'Connell 1967: 204). Third, according to Articles 17(1)(c) and 18(1)(d) of the 1983 Convention movables would be allocated in 'equitable proportion' regardless of their location.

State practice in this area is inconsistent and does not support any of the above three possibilities. In the Czechoslovak case, the quotas (which affect the granting of credits) in the International Monetary Fund were divided in the ratio 2.29:1 (and not 2:1) between the Czech and Slovak Republics, which was in accordance with Articles 17 and 18 of the 1983 Convention (see Innes 2001: 206; Stanic 2001: 770). Moreover, according to the International Law Commission assets and debts should be divided consistent with the rule of equitable apportionment.[28]

If Scotland became independent assets and liabilities would probably be divided by acknowledging geographic location and population proportionality. However, even if it is agreed to divide assets and liabilities equitably the problem then lies in defining what is equitable. In past cases' this question has been 'a major stumbling block in succession negotiations' (Stanic 2001: 772), and the same is likely to be true for future cases.

– The currency and monetary policy –

Control of monetary policy, which determines the long-term rate of inflation, is regarded (at least in the United Kingdom) as a key function of an independent and sovereign state. Margaret Thatcher once remarked that it was the 'the core of the core' of national sovereignty (cited in Wallace 1997: 36). Likewise, the currency of a country is also a policy instrument because of how changes in the exchange rate affect internationally traded goods and services. The importance of these policies means that they would form a central part in the negotiation process.

The danger in the event of disagreement is a currency crisis. Investors could decide to withdraw assets from Scotland to rUK, or even out of rUK completely. Whereas there was no such crisis in the break-up of Czechoslovakia, that was mainly because (a) the currency was not freely convertible, and (b) because foreign debt was both small and held principally by international organisations and governments. The United Kingdom, however, has a free market economy, an open flotation of pound sterling, relatively large foreign debt, and international trading in securities.

In this respect, the UK economy is more akin to that of Quebec. During Quebec's 1995 sovereignty referendum, the kind of problems emerged which might manifest themselves during a move to Scottish independence. There was a fall in the Toronto Stock Exchange, falls in the value of the Canadian dollar, and rises in interest rates. Once it turned out that the Quebec electorate had voted against independence, stock exchange values, dollar values, and interest rates mostly returned to pre-referendum levels.

This problem is discussed in more detail in Chapter 10. Here, it can simply be noted that there is a clear lesson for the SNP and its negotiators. Since no UK government has shown itself to be even remotely sympathetic to the idea of Scottish independence, there would be no negotiations prior to a referendum. If the UK government was antagonistic to independence, it might allow the kind of turmoil that was evident in Quebec to occur in the UK, gambling that such upsets would increase the probability of a 'no' vote, whereupon the turmoil would rapidly dissipate. All that the SNP could do to mitigate this upheaval is to set out, in as much detail as possible, what its currency and monetary policy would be in the event of a 'Yes' vote. In that event, the balance would change, and it would be in both Scottish and rUK interests to sit down as soon as possible and hammer out an agreement fast.

One point can be made with complete certainty. If the SNP maintains and succeeds with its policy of seeking Scottish membership of the European Union, then the Euro will become the currency of Scotland. An 'opt-out' is not allowed to new applicants.

– Commercial and economic relations –

What will be the level of economic integration after Scottish independence? In other words, to what extent will the government of an independent Scotland want existing (banking, health and safety and so on) arrangements to continue? Industries and investors rely on a predictable environment within which to operate and the prime objective here is to minimise uncertainty. An economic standstill is entirely possible in the immediate aftermath of secession. In the long run the economic framework will range from the GATT floor (minimalist position) to full integration in the European Union (maximalist position).

Many UK businesses – manufacturers, retailers, the service sector, and some professionals – have plants and operations in England, Scotland and Wales. Banks in particular (the Royal Bank of Scotland, the Bank of Scotland) have many investments in England (including NatWest and Halifax). Co-operation between rUK and Scotland could be fostered by the use of concordats, that is non–statutory agreements.[29] Since concordats are 'not designed to create legal obligations or restrictions, but . . . act as the ground rules for administrative co-operation and exchange of information' (Gay 1999: 21) they are the perfect instrument with which to create a stable and predictable economic environment. It will be in both side's economic interests to create stability. The current economic union will undoubtedly be undermined by Scottish independence. While membership of the EU would ameliorate Scotland's economic position in relation to rUK the two sides could maintain integration above EU level simply by not changing commercial law (or by introducing identical legislation). It is perfectly conceivable that within the economic arrangement laws and regulations as well as taxes would be harmonised on a voluntary basis.

– Environmental issues –

Scotland and rUK will have many shared environmental interests, some of which already came up in devolution negotiations. From the Solway estuary and air pollution to control of foot and mouth disease, a mechanism for regulatory co-operation will be required since pollution and foot and mouth do not stop at national borders.

Environmental issues will be conditioned by Community law – should Scotland decide to join and be admitted to the EU. Included for the first time in the Single European Act 1986, the Maastricht Treaty (1993) extended the basis for EC environmental law by requiring that 'environmental protection requirements must be integrated into the definition and implementation of . . . Community policies and activities . . . in particular with a view to sustainable development' (Article 6 TEC; ex Article 3c EC). It is thus acknowledged that Member States cannot pursue economic growth without balancing the need for environmental protection.

– SPEED OF THE TRANSITION –

Negotiations can be swift. Once a clear will for separation has been expressed it will be in the interest of all sides to proceed as quickly as possible. As a report on the economics of Scottish independence noted, senior businessmen who are hostile to Scottish independence are:

> willing to admit that they could 'live with' independence, once achieved. What they fear most is the uncertainty which would accompany the transition to independence. In their view this could be extremely damaging. This damage would be worse if the transition period were prolonged.[30]

This must be of particular concern to all Scots, not just the business community. People in general do not like instability and support for independence might slump if the negotiations between the two sides ended in an impasse.

A paradigm case of a speedy break-up is provided by Czechoslovakia, which dissolved within six months. Within two weeks of the June 1992 elections, the critical decision to dissolve the federation had basically been taken and the 30 September deadline to resolve the constitutional deadlock had been set. The Czech and the Slovak Governments (neither of whom had been elected on a pro-independence platform) came to the conclusion separately that the country should be dissolved. Negotiations were held in October, which produced the formal decision that the republics should separate. On 11 November 1992, the Federal Assembly approved the dissolution of Czechoslovakia as a result of Parliament enacting the Constitutional Act of 1992. Arguably a secession referendum as provided for in a Constitutional Act of 1991 should have been held and in the opinion of some commentators the absence of a referendum made the dissolution illegal (Cox and Frankland 1995: 86). In any event, two new and independent States, the Czech Republic and Slovakia, were born on 1 January 1993.

The negotiation process that led to the 'velvet divorce' was rapid. Negotiating post-separation agreements as well as drafting and signing the new republic constitutions in the Czech and Slovak Republics took less than four months. Not all the details were dealt with in these few hectic months and it proved possible to take the fundamental decisions quickly whilst leaving the minutiae for later. However, while the adoption of a small number of draft treaties was good for speed it made for inadequate preparation for stable relations and administrative competence after the dissolution. Many of the treaties were vague and were subsequently reneged on (as for instance with the common currency agreement which was cancelled on 8 February 1993, or the Czech Republic's continued use of the flag and corporate names). The Czechoslovak case is characterised by an intrinsic level of inequality that threw the binding nature of treaties into doubt right from the outset.

In relation to Scotland, the challenge for the negotiating parties will be to make agreements binding. This is a question of partnership, and even though rUK would obviously wield much more clout Scotland does have assets (such as nuclear weapons on its territory) whose value to the rUK it could exploit to enforce agreements. The negotiation process would also need to make steady progress although that will not necessarily be easy. Both sides will have to concede ground and to accept compromises to maintain momentum. Too many compromises might diminish popular support for independence. How much autonomy to allow to the negotiators is hard to adjudge. On the one hand, the unprecedented nature of secession allows for considerable latitude to shape the agenda, in particular the early stages of it. However, as negotiations wear on national interests in the process will increase and both sides will have to take account of political and public opinion.

IMPLEMENTING THE TREATIES ONCE THEY HAVE BEEN NEGOTIATED

In Chapter 3 we suggested that once the independence negotiations had been concluded between the Scottish and British governments, the terms of independence should be put to the Scottish people in a second referendum. What happens after that? If the Scots approve the terms by voting Yes in the second referendum, legislation would be introduced in the Westminster parliament to grant independence to Scotland. But that would not be the end of the matter. The Scottish Parliament would want to legislate to create a constitution for Scotland (and for a time could sit as a constituent assembly for that purpose). And the Westminster legislation conferring Scottish independence would leave a host of further matters to be resolved in subsequent legislation after further negotiations.

Chapter 11, on the division of assets and liabilities, gives some indication of the complexities involved. In the Czech–Slovak case, division into the two separate states took effect just six months after the political decision to divide was made, but the subsequent division of assets took many years to sort out. Although most of this was achieved in the first couple of years, after five years assets which remained undivided included the state airline, the merchant shipping fleet, and the gold reserves. It was not until June 2000, seven and a half years after independence, that final resolution was achieved.

To negotiate the division of assets and liabilities, and shared use of other facilities (on an interim basis or permanently) the two governments will need to establish a Joint Commission, which will have a myriad of negotiating teams and other commissions reporting to it. The two governments would need to be granted considerable executive powers by their respective parliaments to divide assets and liabilities and to restructure government agencies without further primary legislation. Otherwise a huge amount of parliamentary time could be devoted to consequential legislation over several years, when both governments will have other legislative priorities. There will also need to be arbitration machinery to resolve disputes in cases where the two governments fail to agree. This could also be provided for in the independence legislation.

– CONCLUSION –

– The process of negotiations –

- The negotiating teams are likely to be kept small, and the negotiations may be swift. The Czech–Slovak negotiations took six months to agree 31 blanket treaties prior to dissolution. Some 2000 agreements were negotiated subsequently.
- Many of the issues to be resolved are now subject to European law. If Scotland remains or becomes a member of the EU (see Chapter 6), the EU will set the threshold requirements for the free movement of labour, goods and services: and for co-operation in justice and home affairs, and foreign and security policy. Scotland and the UK may agree higher levels of co-operation if they wish, but the EU will set the baseline

- If Scotland decides to retain the monarchy, it is a matter of choice for Scotland what powers and functions to confer on the monarch, and what style of monarch to have in Scotland. There could be a union of the two Crowns but a separation of the two States.

– The contents of negotiations –

- The main issues to be resolved are defence, borders, and division of assets and liabilities. The latter are considered in Chapter 10.
- The issue of defence in general, and of Trident in particular, will either make or break the negotiation process between Scotland and rUK. A Scottish Defence Force is both necessary and practicable, although the costs will depend on role, organisation and deployment of the SDF.
- The maritime boundary line will be drawn – at least initially – using the principle of equidistance and using the Farne Islands as a basepoint.
- Scotland will have to pay an equitable proportion of the national debt, which would currently come to about £30bn. There are no sound political, legal or economic arguments to suggest that Scotland would not be liable for its fair share.
- Fixed assets would be divided by geographic location, whereas moveable assets are divided on a proportional basis. If Scotland secedes from the United Kingdom, Scotland would have the right to all public property on its territory.
- Independence in Europe also means adoption of the single currency. The transfer of monetary policy to the European Central Bank in Frankfurt would be irrevocable and irreversible according to the Treaty of Rome (as amended). Scotland would not be allowed to become a new Member State of the EU but retain its own currency.

– The speed of negotiations –

- The break-up of Czechoslovakia was negotiated in half a year. Such speed may not be possible or indeed desirable in the case of Scotland. Separation, if done properly, will take time. Either national interest in the process will increase and both sides will have to take account of political and public opinion. Or support for independence decreases in Scotland, leaving the Scottish side in the difficult position of having to negotiate and then persuade the electorate to vote 'Yes' in the second referendum.

– NOTES –

1. For a more detailed discussion see Young 1994: Chapter 4, Innes 2001: Chapter 6.
2. There is some debate as to whether unanimity would, in fact, be required because

separation would require amending the office of the Queen, Governor General and Lieutenant Governor. See also Flanagan 1996: 131.

3. See the *Globe and Mail*, 7 October 1995. Cited in Young 1998: 433 n. 93.

4. The need to take account of the rights of Aboriginal nations is particular to Canada and has no equivalent in Scotland. Section 35.1 of the Constitution Act 1982 states that federal and provincial governments must hold a 'constitutional conference' with Aboriginal peoples before constitutional provisions affecting to their rights can be amended. See generally: Royal Commission on Aboriginal Peoples, *Canada's Fiduciary Obligations to Aboriginal peoples in the Context of Accession to Sovereignty by Quebec*, in Renée Dupuis and Kent McNeil (1995: 63–5).

5. This question arose for the first time during the devolution debates of the 1970s when Tam Dalyell, then Labour member for that Scottish constituency, highlighted the problem of English matters in a situation of asymmetrical devolution. In its simplest form the question is about whether Scottish MP's should be able to vote on English matters whilst English MP's do not have the equivalent power (see Russell and Hazell 2000: 202).

6. This illustrates the point made at the beginning of the chapter that often the relative power of the parties is determinative of the outcome. Even though the two sides had agreed in the Constitutional Bill on the Dissolution of the Federation of November 1992 not to use the symbols of the Czech and Slovak Federative Republics for the successor States, the Czechs subsequently decided to hang on to the federal flag without any change to the blue ('Slovak') wedge, thus breaking the agreement (Innes 2001: 202; 205).

7. 'The Dissolution of the Czech and Slovak Federal Republic', (1993, Canada: FPRO); cited in Young 1994: 42.

8. *Heart of the Manifesto*, 2001 General Election, SNP Publications, p. 3.

9. For further details see: Brazier (1999).

10. Liberal Democrat Manifesto, June 2001

11. House of Commons Hansard, Written Answers, 12 February 2001, Col. 54W.

12. Ibid. Col. 56W.

13. At 1 February 2001.

14. At 5 March 2001.

15. The non-Scots army figure includes 2,636 personnel with a recorded nationality at birth as 'British' with no further breakdown available.

16. 'Rapid reaction policy', Letters, *The Scotsman*, 4 December 2000.

17. The SNP's cornerstone anti-NATO policy looks set to change. According to *The Herald*, a working group under the chairmanship of deputy leader Roseanna Cunningham has drafted a review of SNP foreign policy, showing signs that the party's long-standing hostility towards NATO is fading ('SNP set to review stance on NATO', 15 January 2002).

18. UNTS No. 10485, vol. 729, pp. 169–75. The Treaty was adopted on 12 June 1968, and entered into force on 5 March 1970. The total number of parties in January 1999 was 186.

19. A NWS is defined as one, 'which has manufactured and exploded a nuclear weapon or other nuclear explosive device prior to January 1, 1967' (Article IX.3).

20. 'Closing Faslane "would cost billions"', *The Herald*, 2 March 1999.

21. See the statement by Minister of State for the Armed Forces, John Spellar, House of Commons Hansard, Written Answers, 21 February 2000, Col. 737W.

22. The agreement lasted until April 1938.

23. I. C. J. Reports (1969) 3.

24. Ibid. Paragraph 57.

25. Norway/United Kingdom Agreement of 10 March 1965.

26. HM Treasury, Budget: March 2001, Chapter C, Table C4.

27. HM Treasury, *Public Expenditure Statistical Analyses 2000–01*. Cmnd. 4601, April 2000, Table 4.5.
28. ILC Report, *ILC Yearbook*, Part 2, A/CN.4/SER.A/1981/Add.1 (Part 1) (1981), p. 4.
29. The term appeared for the first time in the Government's White Paper on devolution for Wales (see *A Voice for Wales*, Cm 3718, paragraphs 2.24 and 3.40). Concordats have since been used to guide relations between the Scottish Executive, the Welsh Assembly and the Northern Ireland Executive on the one hand, and UK Government departments on the other.
30. Simpson et al. 1999: 20 (original emphasis).

Part Two: Scotland in Europe and the World

Jo Eric Murkens

CHAPTER 5

What Confers Statehood?

– INTRODUCTION –

What would happen if Scotland were to leave the United Kingdom? Could Scotland remain a member of the European Union, or would the Scots have to apply for membership? Could Scotland remain a member of other international organisations, such as the UN? The interrelations of domestic constitutional law, European Union law and public international law are brought to the fore in what looks like a test case of legal hierarchies.

Constitutional law is relevant to identify the process by which Scotland can become independent – and this has been addressed in Chapters 1 and 2. European law and in particular two case studies will shed light on the question how the EU might react to Scotland breaking away from the United Kingdom whilst simultaneously asserting a wish to remain a Member State of the European Union. And finally, international law will be invoked when examining whether Scotland could automatically succeed to the United Kingdom's membership in international organisations (such as the United Nations and the EU).

Central to all the legal issues is the question of 'succession'. Would Scottish independence result in the creation of two entirely new States – England (plus Wales and Northern Ireland) on the one hand and Scotland on the other – both of equal international status? Or would it result in the rump United Kingdom (henceforth rUK, consisting of England, Wales and Northern Ireland) continuing the membership of the United Kingdom in international organisations? And crucially, who decides whether rUK may so continue? Would it be for Westminster to designate the continuing State in an Act of Dissolution? Or would it be for the international community to accept rUK as the continuing State of the United Kingdom and Scotland as a new State?

These questions underlie the ensuing chapters and they are interwoven with each other. This chapter will proceed to examine three forms of State succession. It will argue the importance of constitutional process but find that the international community will ultimately decide the matter of State recognition. The European Union will then be the chief focus of the debate. What will be the position of rUK once Scotland decides to leave? And under what conditions might it have to negotiate its re-entry? Conflicting arguments will be addressed and sifted through in order to find out what an independent Scotland's place would be in Europe and the wider world.

– STATE SUCCESSION –

State succession takes varied forms. Paul R. Williams, who was Attorney-Advisor at the Office of the Legal Adviser for European and Canadian Affairs at the US Department of State, narrows the possibilities down to three distinct forms: continuation, separation, or dissolution. Williams explains that:

> A continuation occurs when one or more sub-state entities breaks away from the predecessor state and forms an independent state. The remainder of the predecessor state is referred to as the continuing state (or continuity of the predecessor state). In general, this state retains the rights and obligations of the predecessor state. The break-away states are referred to as successor states.

> Separation refers to the break-up of independent states that previously joined together voluntarily to form a Union of states. In a separation all the states are considered successor states, and all resume their respective pre-union state personalities, rights and obligations. In addition, each state may assume some of the rights and obligations accrued during the life of the Union.

> In a dissolution, the predecessor state dissolves into a number of independent states, and none of these states is considered a continuing state. All the emerging states are successor states and are treated as equal heirs to the rights and obligations of the predecessor state (Williams 1994: 1–2).

The classic continuation cases are those resulting from the decolonisation process and those resulting from the secession of a sub-state entity other than a colony. Former colonies are generally not presumed to continue the treaty rights and obligations of the colonial power. They may, of course, freely choose to continue certain bilateral treaties, provided they obtain the consent of the other party. The cases that illustrate a sub-state entity seceding and a continuing state emerging are the secessions of:

- Belgium from the Netherlands in 1830;
- Panama from Colombia in 1903;
- Finland from Russia in 1917;
- Poland and Czechoslovakia from the Austro-Hungarian Empire in 1918;
- Ireland from the United Kingdom in 1922;
- Pakistan from India in 1947;
- Singapore from the Federation of Malaysia in 1965.

A prototype case for separation is the end of the Union of Norway and Sweden in 1905. Since both Norway and Sweden retained their distinct international personalities, the Government of the Union entered into treaties either on behalf of the Union or on behalf of one of the individual States. When Norway and Sweden separated, both States issued identical declarations asserting that, as far as they were concerned, each successor State would continue to be bound by the treaties of the Union as well as by the treaties concluded individually.[1] Other examples are the separations of:

- Greater Colombia between 1829 and 1831;
- the Austro-Hungarian Empire in 1918;
- the Union of Iceland and Denmark in 1944;
- the United Arab Republic in 1961;
- the Federation of Mali in 1961.

The two prime examples of dissolution are the break–ups of Yugoslavia and Czechoslovakia. Even though Serbia/Montenegro claimed to be the continuity of Yugoslavia it was not recognised as such by the other successor States. Moreover, the United States, the European Union and the United Nations all took the view that Yugoslavia had dissolved and that Serbia/Montenegro was not the continuing State. In contrast, after the State of Czechoslovakia ceased to exist on 1 January 1993, the European Community and the United States instantly recognised the Czech Republic and Slovakia as the successor States. According to Williams, dissolution lies between continuation and separation:

> As a result, the successor states arising from a dissolution of a predecessor state are more likely to be bound by the treaty rights and obligations of the predecessor state than in the case of continuation, but they are less likely to be bound than in the case of separation, where the successor states main-

tained some sort of international personality while members of the Union (Williams 1994: 16).

Of the above three forms, the first (continuation) and the last (dissolution) will be considered in greater detail – but in reverse order. It is important to understand the terminology used in these contexts. In the continuation case, rUK would be the 'continuing state' (or 'continuity of the predecessor State') and Scotland would be a 'successor state'. In the dissolution case, both rUK and Scotland would be regarded as 'successor states'. The 'separation' case, whereby the constituent states assume their pre-Union status is not a viable option for the almost 300 year old Union of Scotland with England and Wales. As Dr Robert Lane from the University of Edinburgh notes, 'there is no possibility of abrogation of the 1707 Treaty of Union because the parties to it have ceased to exist and could not, in any event, restore the *status quo ante*' (Lane 1991: 146–7). In other words, the repeal of the Acts of Union would not see the re-emergence of the old kingdoms of England and Scotland. Neither Scotland nor England enjoys international legal personality. In the UK/Scotland case the only alternative to continuation is dissolution.

– DISSOLUTION AND RECOGNITION OF STATEHOOD –

Consensual dissolution of the United Kingdom is favoured by some nationalist Scots as it places all constituent parts on an equal footing as far as Community and international rights and obligations are concerned. In so far as there may be legal or other qualms about breaking up a well-functioning State, not even opponents to a liberal interpretation of secession argue that dissolution by mutual negotiations or by constitutional right is illegitimate (see for example Buchanan 1998: 29).

But the dissolution option is not as clear-cut as Scottish nationalists would have it believe. It embodies more than formally according Scotland the same international status as England were the Union to be dissolved. Dissolution raises the question as to who or what would determine Scotland's statehood.

- is it the unilateral declaration of independence?
- is it a UK Act of Dissolution?
- is it recognition by third parties?

These questions will be addressed in turn.

– Unilateral declaration of independence –

For the reasons discussed in Chapter 1 a UDI is not an option for Scotland. The Scottish Parliament would have to secure consent from the United Kingdom first, otherwise the purported Act by the Scottish Parliament declaring the country's independence would be *ultra vires* and void. What is more, a UDI would have serious repercussions for Scotland's standing in Europe and the world. No State would be willing to recognise Scotland as an independent State if it attained independence through unconstitutional means and without the consent of the UK Government.

– An Act of Dissolution –

The Union of Scotland and England from 1707 (known as the United Kingdom of Great Britain) became in 1801 the United Kingdom of Great Britain and Ireland. Lane's argument is that Scottish withdrawal from the United Kingdom cannot be compared to the withdrawal of the Irish Free State in 1921–2, which led to the creation and recognition of two sovereign and independent States (the United Kingdom of Great Britain and Northern Ireland, and the Republic of Ireland in 1937). In contrast, Lane says, Scotland cannot break away like Ireland as it was 'one of the basic building blocks of "the United Kingdom of Great Britain"' (Lane 1991: 146). Without Scotland there is no 'Great Britain' and without Great Britain there is no 'United Kingdom'.

This position can be rebutted. Ireland's constitutional status in the United Kingdom post-1801 would appear to be the same as Scotland's from 1707 to 1801. This analysis may be controvertible but would require a very sound argument. The question then is not so much whether the United Kingdom could ever be dissolved – if Ireland seceded in 1922, why can Scotland not secede in 20XX? – but by what means it might be achieved. Unlike Germany, Britain has no concept of a constitution of eternal validity. Article 79(3) of the German Basic Law (*Grundgesetz*) embodies such an 'eternity clause' (*Ewigkeitsklausel*) by which the federal structure and the role of the *Länder* in the federal legislative process may not be abolished or even amended (subject only to Article 146: the termination of the Basic Law). Under its own constitution, Germany cannot abrogate the federation.

The closest Britain comes to having an eternity clause is, indeed, Article I of the 1706–7 Treaties of Union by which Scotland and England were united 'for ever after'. The clause was repeated in the 1800 Act of Union with Ireland. Yet that did not prevent the departure from the Union of the Irish Free State in 1922. If the SNP's reasoning were sound, the United

Kingdom should have come to an end upon the breach of a fundamental term of the 1800 Act of Union. The reason it did not is because the British constitution accepts no limitations on the legal sovereignty of Parliament. If two Acts of Parliament conflict, then the later Act prevails even if the earlier Act adopted an 'eternity clause'. British constitutional orthodoxy holds that Parliament cannot bind itself or its successor. Every Act of Parliament can be expressly amended or repealed at a later date, or, in cases of conflict, is implicitly repealed by the later Act.[2]

If it is agreed that there are no fundamental legal constraints on the sovereignty of Parliament and that Scotland could leave the Union by a simple Act of Parliament, the question is whether that Act can designate a successor state to the UK. Lane admits that 'it would not be constitutionally impossible for the Act to provide expressly for a new state of "Scotland" and another of "the United Kingdom of England and Northern Ireland"' (Lane 1991: 147), the latter of which would be the continuing state to all international rights and obligations currently vested in the UK, including membership to international organisations and the European Union.

However, were such an Act to lead to the dissolution of the United Kingdom and the subsequent creation of two sovereign states of equal status in international law the result would have implications for membership in international organisations such as the UN or the EU. The United Kingdom (which for present purposes is the country that is recognised by international organisations) would no longer exist. This view of dissolution is most eloquently expressed by the Scottish Centre for Economic and Social Research (SCESR) which asserts that:

> the successor states to the United Kingdom would then have equal claims to recognition as independent member states representing existing parts of the European Union. The claim by Scotland for recognition as an independent member state of the European Union would be no less substantial than the claim of any other successor state of the present United Kingdom (SCESR 1996: paragraph 22).

According to this view, if Scotland left the United Kingdom all constituent parts would be in the same boat. The dissolution of the United Kingdom would mean the effective end of membership to international organisations, and all constituent parts would start with a 'clean slate' in relation to international rights and obligations. Both England and Scotland would have to apply to join the EU, UN, NATO and so on, and the United Kingdom would also lose its permanent seat in the Security Council.

The difficulty with accepting this argument is that its attractive simplicity is not matched by corresponding legal rules or international practice. Whilst it is easy to imagine the creation of a Scottish state, it is harder to fathom the creation of an English state (with or without Wales). That is because the United Kingdom is a union state with a central and supreme Parliament in Westminster.[3] Scotland – even with a devolved Parliament – is a constituent part of that Union, with no special status in constitutional law and probably without the power to destroy the United Kingdom as a legal entity.

Moreover, arguing the dissolution case that Scotland and rUK would have equal claims to recognition as independent Member States of the EU and UN ignores the role and influence of the international community. It is one thing for the Act of Dissolution to designate the continuing state to the current UK but quite another for the continuing state to be recognised by the international community and, indeed, the European Union.

The role of the international community and the importance of state recognition is considered next.

– International recognition –

The alternative to dissolving the Union of 1707 and according its constituent parts equal status is for one part (usually the larger or politically dominant part) to continue in the footsteps of the predecessor state. Under this option, Scotland would break away from the United Kingdom, and rUK would continue its prior existence with one-third less territory and 5.1 million less population. The rUK would assert itself as the same state with identical international legal personality as the current United Kingdom. All international treaties, other than those referring solely or mainly to Scottish matters, would maintain their legal force as between the rUK and the other contracting parties. The rUK would also continue to be represented in those international organisations of which it is currently a member (such as the United Nations, the European Union, NATO, and the International Monetary Fund).

That said, the position of the rUK would not depend solely on what it claims to be itself (that is a new state like the Czech Republic or the continuing state of the United Kingdom) but it would also depend on how the international community responded to that claim. Lane, for instance, suggests that:

> there is no reason to believe that the international community would accept an English claim to succeed to all rights and obligations of the United Kingdom to the exclusion of a Scotland asserting a similar, if less exclusive and so more modest, claim (Lane 1991: 148).

Lane's reference to the international community is entirely correct.[4] Lane's conclusion, however, is misleading. Whilst he is correct in stating that the creation of a state has to be recognised by the international community in order to constitute a new state (or at least an effectively functioning new state), he is wrong to presume that the international community might not accept rUK's claim as the continuing state of the United Kingdom. The paramount interests of the UN have always been to maintain peace and prevent war, and it pursues those interests by advocating standards of state sovereignty. Accordingly, the UN will out of principle not accept any partial or total disruption of national unity and territorial integrity of a state (see for example Article 6 of the 1960 Colonial Declaration). As Anderson in his extensive book on borders points out:

> if every nation or ethnic group were to assert statehood, the international system would be destabilized. In practice, the international community of states has been hostile to secession (Anderson 1996: 44).

The international community would take sides with the United Kingdom. Authority for that statement is rooted in precedent, most notably after the Republics of Ukraine, Belarus, and Russia announced the dissolution of the Soviet Union and the creation of the Commonwealth of Independent States (CIS) on 8 December 1991. The Russian Federation then asserted itself as the continuation of the Soviet Union, which was accepted by the CIS as well as the international community at large. As in the case of rUK succeeding the United Kingdom, the nuclear issue was a key determining factor. Not only did Russia hold most of the nuclear assets of the former Soviet Union, it was also keen to remain a nuclear power as well as keep its seat in the UN Security Council and the veto.[5] The balance the international community had to strike was between rejecting Russia as the continuing state and watching a huge nuclear power emerge outside the Nuclear Non-Proliferation Treaty (1970), and accepting Russia's claims.

The international community would, for these reasons, recognise rUK as the continuing state to the United Kingdom in order to limit the disruption caused by Scotland's independence. For a relatively smooth and painless transition to independence it is imperative that Scotland is granted independence by the United Kingdom as that will set the benchmark for further international recognition. Recognition by the UN would be amongst the priorities for the new Scottish State. But as James Crawford notes, 'no new State formed since 1945 outside the colonial context has been admitted to the United Nations over the opposition of the predecessor State' (Crawford 1998: 113). UN membership is today recognised as presuming statehood. Whilst not being a member of the UN does not mean an entity is not a state – as was the case for Switzerland – the UN Charter does limit membership to 'peace-loving states' (Article 4), so that being a member clearly implies statehood. Membership of the United Nations is discussed at pp. 165–9.

– CONCLUSIONS –

- Under UK constitutional law, Scotland – even with a devolved Parliament – is a constituent part of that Union, with no special status in constitutional law and without the power to destroy the United Kingdom as a legal entity.
- Even though the Union between England and Scotland was entered into voluntarily by two parliaments on equal terms, Scottish independence would not result in the dissolution of the United Kingdom. Rather, Scotland would break away from the United Kingdom, and rUK would continue its prior existence with one-third less territory and 5.1 million less population. The rUK would assert itself as the same State with identical international legal personality as the current United Kingdom.
- The international community too would be likely to recognise the rUK as the continuation of the UK in order to maintain international stability.

– Notes –

1. Ibid. pp. 260–1.
2. See *Vauxhall Estates Ltd* v. *Liverpool Corpn* [1932] 1 K.B. 733; *Ellen St Estates* v. *Minister for Health* [1934] 1 K.B. 590.
3. Section 28(7) of the Scotland Act 1998.
4. Recent instances of state recognition indicate the dualism of a) the state's own claim, and b) the reaction by other states. For example, as a requirement for the recognition of the various successor states of Yugoslavia, the EC Member States demanded that the future status of the new Republics receive the support of the people. Referendums preceded recognition of statehood in all cases except Croatia, which joined Slovenia in their declaration of independence, and Serbia/Montenegro which has not been recognised by the EC or the USA.
5. For the evolving US approach to the successor states of the former Soviet Union see Williams 1994.

CHAPTER 6

Scotland in Europe

– INTRODUCTION –

The interplay and the tensions between the dissolution theory and the continuation theory are also illustrated in the important discussion of Scotland's place in the European Union. Would Scotland automatically be a member of the EU or would it have to renegotiate its entry (either alone or in the company of the rUK)?

The SNP's slogans 'Scotland in Europe' and 'Independence in Europe' are both catchy and complex. They act as a persuasive panacea for all who doubt that a small nation like Scotland would be able to stand on its own two feet in the big world. Moreover, they articulate that Scotland is not a parochial region of nationalist bigots but an open-minded and cosmopolitan one that embraces European integration. It is part of the same wider desire of European regions in general to be heard by the European Union, either in a 'Europe of the Regions' or as new Member States. The combined clout of the regions makes their wish to be heard one of the major challenges facing Europe.[1] As William Wallace, Professor in International Relations at the London School of Economics notes, 'the weakness of the European Community lies in the strength of national and sub-national identities' (Wallace 1997: 46).

But the two slogans are also complex statements in that they imply that an independent Scotland would have a natural right to be a player in the European Union. This is assumed and not established. There is also a paradox involved in that the SNP seeks sovereignty first and, having achieved it would then hand it over to the EU. It suggests that the alliance with Brussels is necessarily preferable to the alliance with Westminster. It also ignores the views of those nationalists in Scotland, 'who have opposed membership of the EU on the grounds that national independence would be sacrificed in a vast political organisation which is dominated by multinational economic interests and a remote bureaucracy . . .' (Kellas 1998: 204).

This chapter examines the issue of state succession to the European Union. Since the EC/EU Treaties themselves do not lay down rules on succession it is necessary to look at the rules governing succession to multilateral treaties in general and scrutinise individual examples of changes to the territorial application of the EC/EU Treaties. Finally, the chapter examines the effect an independent Scotland would have on the European Union.

The force of European law in the United Kingdom is based on the European Communities Act 1972 which accorded domestic legal effect to the Treaty of Accession by which the United Kingdom joined the European Communities (the European Economic Community, the European Coal and Steel Community, and Euratom). Were Scotland to withdraw from the United Kingdom, the consequences of an independent Scottish state would need to be addressed on European as well as on the domestic level.

– THE EUROPEAN UNION AND SUCCESSION –

There is no debate in principle about Scotland's entitlement to being a member of the EU. As an independent state, Scotland would instantly meet the (Copenhagen) criteria for membership, namely, 'democracy, the rule of law, human rights and respect for and, protection of minorities, the existence of a functioning market economy as well as the capacity to cope with competitive pressure and market forces within the Union.'[2] The debate in this and the following chapters is about the process. Could Scotland inherit the United Kingdom's membership? If not, what are the necessary steps to become a member?

The SNP makes two controversial claims: (a) that Scotland would enjoy the same rights and be bound by the same obligations currently in force for the United Kingdom; and (b) that membership to international organisations (including the EU) is governed by the same rules of succession. In 1997 and 1999 the SNP released dossiers on the legal basis for independence which endorsed statements made in 1989 by a number of lawyers. They argue that Scotland would naturally remain within the European Union. The legal and political opinion cited in the dossiers comes out in support of smooth and rapid accession to the EU. French Advocate Maitre Xavier de Roux summarises the argument in the following terms:

Scotland is part of the Common Market territory by virtue of the United Kingdom's accession to the Treaty of Rome and by application of the Treaty of Union 1707. If the Treaty of Union was revoked and if Scotland recovered its international sovereignty, it would be accepted within the Common Market without any formality.[3]

De Roux's argument assumes, or necessarily implies, that Scottish independence is the result of a revocation of the Treaty of Union. Does his argument still stand if Scottish independence is the result of a withdrawal from the Union, as this book argues?

As the EU includes Scotland within its remit and because Community law directly affects the Scots, de Roux concludes that Scotland is not a third party to the Treaty. On independence, it could not be regarded as a new applicant state as the United Kingdom acted on behalf of Scotland when it joined the European Communities in 1973. According to de Roux's argument, a change in Scotland's political status would have no bearing on the legal status of Scotland in Europe.

Professor Emile Noel, former Secretary General of the European Commission, and Lord Mackenzie-Stuart argued that Scottish independence would result in the creation of two Member States of equal status. The rUK would not be more powerful than Scotland. And without evidence to the contrary, Noel is certain that 'the will of the people would be interpreted as a desire to retain the European status quo'.[4]

Former Director General of the European Commission and former EC Ambassador to the United Nations Eamonn Gallagher sees 'no sustainable legal or political objection to separate Scottish membership of the European Community'. If Scotland is willing and able to meet the demands and requirements of Community membership, then the EU ought to be flexible enough to resolve any institutional matters arising in relation to, *inter alia*, weighted voting in the Council, the number of Members of the European Parliament (MEP), and number of Commissioners.

With such heavyweight opinion to back up their claim, as well as various statements by European and foreign officials, Ministers, Ambassadors and politicians of Member States who cannot conceive of Scotland being excluded from membership, the sentiment that Scotland might not be admitted to the EU does seem 'specious and [without] constitutional or legal credibility'.[5]

BACKGROUND OF THE VIENNA CONVENTION ON STATE SUCCESSION IN RESPECT OF TREATIES

The SNP's claim to succession to rights and obligations arising from EU membership stands or falls on the application of the Vienna Convention on

State Succession in Respect of Treaties (henceforth the Convention).[6] Their claim will be examined in greater detail below. A closer look at the Convention, however, is required beforehand.

The Convention is concerned mainly with the position of the 'newly independent state', which Article 2(1)(f) defines as 'a successor state the territory of which immediately before the date of the succession of states was a dependent territory for the international relations of which the predecessor state was responsible'. The focus on colonies is not coincidental. The Convention is concerned with state creations in the post–colonial context which is important when thinking about its relevance for Scotland.

Newly independent and other successor states are treated differently under the Convention. Controversially, the former are presumed to begin life unencumbered with a clean slate ('negative' theory), whereas other successor states are presumed to continue automatically the treaty obligations of the predecessor state ('universal succession'). Article 2(1)(b) of the Convention defines the succession of states as the 'replacement of one state by another in the responsibility for the international relations of territory'. Does the SNP hope that Scotland would fall into the latter category and be the 'successor state' in international law to the United Kingdom? Would Scotland be resurrecting its historic claim to statehood rather than establishing a brand new one? According to international practice, rUK rather than Scotland would be the successor state (or better: the continuing state). Continuity is presumed for the sake of legal certainty (Articles 34 and 35 of the Convention).

The Convention targets only the above two scenarios of state succession (neither of which applies to Scotland) and does not consider the various routes succession can take (continuation, separation, dissolution, merger, cession and so on). Under the two available definitions Scotland would have to be squeezed into the category of a newly independent state within the colonial context. What the framers of the Convention had in mind, however, were in the first instance colonial territories that were granted independence and could not be expected to continue the bilateral treaty obligations of their colonial ruler (Article 16 of the Convention).[7] Ideally there should have been included a third category of '"quasi-newly independent states" which would have included States emerging outside a colonial context but in circumstances resembling the emergence of a newly independent State' (Kamminga 1996: 471). Indeed, the International Law Commission had proposed such a category for cases like the partition of Pakistan (East and West) from India in 1947.[8] However, France and Switzerland objected to this category, apparently because they did not want to undermine the territorial integrity of their unitary state by inadvertently promoting separatist movements (Ibid.).

In sum, the situation the Convention envisages does not fit squarely with the situation Scotland's independence would create.

– Relevance to the European Union –

Since the SNP believes that it nonetheless has an arguable case for establishing that the Convention would govern Scotland's succession to the EU's rights and obligations, their claim needs to be addressed in more detail. The case of separation of states is covered by the Convention, which emphasises continuity of treaty relations. In relation specifically to the EU, the SNP relies heavily on Article 34(1) of the Convention which provides:

> When a part or parts of a territory of a state separate to form one or more states, whether or not the predecessor state continues to exist:
>
> a) any treaty in force at the date of the succession of states in respect of the entire territory of the predecessor state continues in force in respect of each successor state so formed . . .

On the face of it, Article 34(1) of the Convention would seem to support automatic continuation of the EC/EU Treaties in an independent Scotland, and it would apply regardless of whether the United Kingdom continued to exist. Relying only on this provision, French Advocate de Roux argues (for the SNP) that 'the simple acceptance by the successor state [an independent Scotland] of the obligations contracted on its behalf by its predecessor [the United Kingdom] is equivalent to an accession by that successor state'.[9]

However, there are numerous and severe difficulties relating to the assumption that the EC/EU Treaties will continue to apply by virtue of Article 34(1).

First, the Treaty of Rome established its own legal regime and created an international organisation that is fundamental to the substantive legal regime established. The general rules of succession in international law do not apply to this case. Rather, Article 4 of the same Convention governs treaties establishing international organisations to which the predecessor state was a party. It provides that:

> The present Convention applies to the effects of a succession of states in respect of:

a) any treaty which is the constituent instrument of an international organization *without prejudice to the rules concerning acquisition of membership and without prejudice to any other relevant rules of the organization*;

b) any treaty adopted within an international organization without prejudice to any relevant rules of the organization (emphasis added).

The Convention in one of its very early provisions places paramount emphasis on the rules of accession and the rules of the international organisation in question. In other words, the Convention does not override the regime set up by the Treaty of Rome.

Second, paragraph (1) of Article 34 of the Convention on which de Roux relies has to be read in conjunction with paragraph (2) of the same provision which states that the former paragraph does not apply if:

b) it appears from the treaty or is otherwise established that the application of the treaty in respect of the successor State would be *incompatible with the object and purpose of the treaty* or would *radically change the conditions for its operation* (emphasis added).

The object and purpose of the European Union can be found in the preamble as well as in Articles 2 and 3 TEC. The creation of a new Scottish state would – if only formally – change the conditions for operation and application of the institutional and financial provisions of the European Union. This cannot be over–emphasised: independence would be adding a new Member State to the EU and this would require formal treaty changes according to the specific rules of EU accession rather than the general and vague rules of international law on succession to multilateral treaties. Negotiations would not be about the principle of membership but about the practicalities and details involved. To illustrate, the European Union is premised upon the existence of a particular number of Member States. Voting rights are weighted and numbers of representatives are allocated on the basis of the size of the state. Amendments to those provisions require negotiation of an amending treaty and its subsequent ratification by all the existing Member States and by the newly acceding state.

Third, the rule enshrined in Article 34(1) is widely believed to be 'too rigid and simplistic and [not to] correspond . . . to international practice: therefore it cannot be considered a customary norm' (Mullerson 1993: 488). For instance, bilateral treaties and multilateral treaties with limited participation concluded by the Soviet Union passed over only to Russia. The other successor states had to discontinue their participation or renegotiate the treaty in question. Former Deputy Foreign Minister of Estonia Rein Mullerson goes on to argue that, as far as international practice is concerned, it is the proviso in Article 34(2) that best encapsulates the general rule that the tenor of the treaty in question is to be respected above all else.

Fourth, the Convention is of only limited value to the present discussion. Although it has been open for signature since 1978 and in force since 1996, the United Kingdom is not a party to the Convention; nor is any other EU Member State. Whereas the Legal Advisor to the US State Department expressed the view in 1980 that the rules of the Convention were 'generally regarded as declarative of existing customary law by the United States',[10] a majority within the Committee of Legal Advisors for the Council of Europe agreed that the Convention did not so reflect customary law.[11] But even if doubts regarding the Convention as a whole persist, there seems widespread consensus that 'the formulation in Article 34 cannot be taken as reflective of customary law' (Shaw 1997: 690). There is, therefore, no general rule which would permit a seceding entity (like Scotland) to succeed to a treaty (like the EC/EU Treaties) if such succession would upset the treaty regime.

Fifth, the International Law Commission has also asserted that, where membership is on account of a formal process of admission (such as is the case with the EU):

> a new State is not entitled automatically to become a party to the constituent treaty and a member of the organisation as a successor State simply by reason of the fact that at the date of the succession its territory was subject to the treaty and within the ambit of the organisation.[12]

As with other international organisations, a new state can only become a member if the existing members agree to admit it. The EC/EU Treaties would require alteration to make room for Scotland's representation and this in turn would require the consent of all Member States. There is no automatic right of entry and no precedent for such a proposition. As Happold concludes, 'the structure of the EU's constituent treaties themselves does not permit a state to succeed to membership of the Union' (Happold 2000: 31). Scotland cannot claim membership to the EU as of right. This conclusion is also supported by the practice of other international organisations to which new states cannot succeed automatically but have to apply to join.

The above analysis rebuts the SNP's claim that Article 34 (1) would govern automatic membership to the EU.

Application of Community law in an independent Scotland without succession

Even though Community law would not continue to apply by virtue of Article 34(1) of the Convention, that is not to say that Scottish membership of the EU would never be automatic. Much would depend on the overall political context, on the attitudes taken by the (rump) UK and on relations between the UK and the EU. The EU has at least three options:

- it could decide that a newly independent part of an existing Member State is automatically a member of the EU;
- the EU could give the new state expedited membership;
- the EU could insist that the new state is to be treated like an applicant state and has to apply for admission.

But importantly, in none of these three cases is it for Scotland to decide which possible route is chosen. The EU chooses whom it lets in and it does so rigorously: all membership applications require unanimity among the Member States negotiating accession, assent by the European Parliament, and ratification by all the national parliaments. Thus, it ought to be borne in mind that the rUK would have a veto with respect to Scottish membership (although it is doubtful on what grounds it might be exercised), so it is imperative that the internal negotiations are sorted out amicably and prior to an Intergovernmental Conference which recognises Scotland (either as a new or as a successor state).

Realistically, Scotland can expect – more or less automatically – negotiations for EU membership to begin before independence is gained. In the event that the negotiations are not completed at the date of independence there would be a continuation of the imposition of the *acquis communautaire* on an agreed basis until negotiations are completed and all sides ratify the agreement. If Scotland maintains its legal framework, save as varied by the Scottish Parliament, this would in effect happen automatically.

Scotland's options are two-fold and subject to external pressure. It can keep a low profile and go for smooth and rapid acceptance by the EU. By conforming to the UK's terms of membership and adopting the *acquis* in its entirety, Scotland would continue its place in Europe in a spirit of co-operation and continuation that is unlikely to raise objections from other Member States.

Alternatively, Scotland could decide to make use of its newly gained independence and re-negotiate the terms of membership. It might, for instance, try and secure a better deal on fisheries than the United Kingdom did or demand more money for the Highlands and Islands out of the Structural Funds. Once Scotland starts cherry picking, adopting the legislation it likes and rejecting the legislation it does not, it will meet with resistance from and tough negotiations with other Members. The question then becomes how much time and resources the other Member States and the Commission want to invest if Scotland enters negotiations in a spirit of confrontation and conflict. Scotland's strategy could easily backfire and it may end up having to relinquish access to fishing grounds, for instance, in order to 'buy off' some Member States.

– WORST CASE SCENARIO –

The worst case scenario is that both law and politics fail Scotland's independence. On the legal plane, the Vienna Convention on Succession of States in Respect of Treaties is somewhat doubtful evidence of customary international law and Scotland does not have a right under the Treaty to succeed to the United Kingdom's EU rights and obligations. On the political plane, negotiations with the other Member States could run into difficulties and Scotland could then find itself outside the EU. But even then it still seems hard to accept that all the substantive law that has emanated from Brussels since 1958 and has applied in the United Kingdom since 1973 would cease to have effect overnight in Scotland at the date of its independence. Due to the long-standing object and purpose of the European Union, the profound impact of European law, and the evolving nature of the Union as a whole, integration – of the kind Scotland has mastered – cannot be revoked with the stroke of a pen.

What would happen if Scotland became independent but did not – for whatever reason – negotiate with the EU? If Scotland failed to negotiate the status of Community law would be ambivalent. That ambivalence is best borne out by the following, extremely unlikely, scenario. Say Scotland issued a unilateral declaration of independence and then relied totally on automatic membership and did not engage in any negotiations with the European Union. Even then Community law would continue to apply, as it is part of Scots law by virtue of the European Communities Act 1972 as amended. So EC Regulations and domestic laws applying EC Directives on fishing or the environment would remain law until an independent Scotland changed them – which it could do if it wanted.

However, Scotland would be under no legal obligation to adopt any pending or future EC legislation or follow any decisions of the ECJ.[13] Moreover, the whole Treaty insofar as it gives rights, gives them to Member States and their nationals. So Scottish individuals could not claim Treaty rights (for example to free movement or non-discrimination) because Scots would no longer be treated as EU nationals would as they would no longer be 'UK nationals'.[14] The Treaty provisions would not apply unless Scotland became a member. Scotland could also not be taken to the ECJ under Article 226 TEC (ex Article 169 EC), Article 228 TEC (ex Article 171 EC), or bring an action under Article 232 TEC (ex Article 175 EC) or seek its guidance under Article 234 TEC (ex Article 177 EC).

− THE POLITICAL KNOCK-ON EFFECTS −

The above scenario is unrealistic but it illustrates the crucial link between membership and the application of Community law. In a real-life case, continued membership in the EU depends as much on political negotiations as on European law. Politics may or may not work in Scotland's favour. Where there is political will within the EU there is without doubt a way in for Scotland. Without such a will, however, Scotland may find itself staring in the face of politics. Accession to the EU requires unanimity. Germany, France, Italy and Spain are the big boys of Europe and are anxious to avoid splintering their states. Some commentators cannot imagine that they would watch Scottish independence without any form of resistance. According to Professor Clive Archer from the University Association for Contemporary European Studies, such idleness would 'defy both logic and politics'. The implication is that the six other signatories of the 'Flanders Declaration', namely, Bavaria, Catalonia, North–Rhine–West-phalia, Salzburg, Wallonia and Flanders, as well as other regions such as Lombardy, Corsica, and Brittany, would be casting a keen eye on Scotland, acutely observing the follow-on improvements and drawbacks that are significant not least for their own regions. This was the position held by Robin Cook, former UK Foreign Secretary. In November 1998 he suggested that EU Member States, many of whom have secessionist movements of their own which their central governments are not keen to encourage, would veto Scottish membership.[15]

Others, however, do not share these worries. Secessions and the break-up of states happen all over the world. Would the mere fact that Scottish independence took place in the context of the EU set a dangerous precedent for other Member States? Would the same not be true for all other separatist movements the world over? Arguably, so long as Scottish independence is the expression of the democratic will of the people and provided the United Kingdom resolves the matter in a democratic and civilised manner, no Member State would have the right or interest to block Scottish member-ship. It is an internal affair of the United Kingdom. Robin Cook's current position has become more closely aligned with this view. In July 2000 he said, 'Europe is not going to throw Scotland out. It's in the nature of the European Union, it welcomes all-comers and Scotland would be a member'. He added, however, that membership itself was not the issue, 'the issue is what is the price at which Scotland becomes a member of the European Union, and renegotiation would not work in Scotland's favour.[16] (Renegotiation of Scottish membership is discussed below).

Is Scottish independence a political movement that European states would want to stop in its tracks? One school of thought tells us that a move towards Scottish independence would first and foremost be an internal affair of the United Kingdom, and that other states would not interfere in the matter. Experience, however, indicates that the international community does show an interest in the activities of states, especially in the case of a secession or dissolution. In the aftermath of the dissolution of Czechoslovakia in 1993, the Czech Republic emerged as one of the leading lights in the former Eastern bloc, whereas Slovakia lagged behind. Robin Shepherd notes that one reason why Slovakia's progress was hindered was because of 'a clear tendency among foreign journalists and politicians to see the entire move to independence as the work of troublemakers' (Shepherd 2000: 127). US Vice-President Dan Quayle, who visited Slovakia in 1991, believed that maintaining the federation was in the best interest of both Slovakia and the region as a whole. Influential journalists too expressed their bitterness about the split:

> The break-up of the Czechoslovak federation is a sad unnecessary event that in the long run may benefit some sectional interests of the Czech economy and the irrational fantasies of some Slovak nationalists but is of little value to Central Europe (Glenny 1993: 246).

The response to Scottish independence by other European states and the rest of the international community can only be mooted. Of course an independent Scotland will not be shunned as a pariah. But, below the surface, there will be ill will to the very idea of secession and an independent Scottish State, and a lingering question what good will have been achieved by breaking away from the United Kingdom.

Finally, the notion that Scottish independence is primarily an internal affair is thrown into doubt by its current membership of the European Union. Independence would not happen in isolation from the EU. On the contrary, the SNP consistently seeks to strengthen Scotland's links with the EU and expressly demands increased European participation. By the same token, however, one consideration for a hostile UK Government would be to rally round its counterparts in Germany, France, Italy and Spain and block entry of Scotland to the EU. Lane brings out the domestic/European nature of independence. He concludes that:

> Independence in Europe for Scotland (and for England) can be brought about only if action at the national level proceeds concurrently with action at the Community level, thus producing, at the end of the day, an agreed result which necessarily includes the concurrence of the Community institutions and all member states. A Scotland bent upon independence grounded in the clear democratic support of the Scottish people would create a moral and, given the international law principle of self-determination, probably a legal obligation for all member states to negotiate in good faith in order to produce such a result, *but this solution lies essentially within the domain of politics, not law* (Lane 1991: 154–5; emphasis added).

Lane here acknowledges that Scottish independence would not be a purely internal affair for the United Kingdom but would involve parallel negotiations with the European partners. He also argues that independence is primarily a political rather than a legal process. In the interaction of law and politics, the law is, however, a serious constraint and whoever leads Scotland into independence would be wise to move within the parameters of the legal framework.

– Scotland and EEA/EFTA –

The SNP's 'Scotland in Europe' mantra was identified early on as complex. It creates a dilemma for certain voters, namely those who favour independence but outside the EU. It would be wrong to assume that the Scots are generally more EU-friendly than the English or Welsh. They may conclude, for example, that the EU does not offer their fishermen the best deal and that Scotland should not seek to be a Member State.

Scotland as a whole may find that its fortunes lie outside the EU and that it is better off within the European Economic Area (EEA). The EEA widens the net of the EU's Single Market to cover three of four European Free Trade Association (EFTA) countries: Norway, Iceland and Liechtenstein. Switzerland is a member of EFTA but voted against EEA membership in 1992. The analogies with Iceland and Norway are close – one is a fish producing country and the other a fish and oil producing country like Scotland.

The EEA brings together the 15 EU Member States with the three EFTA EEA States. Together they form a huge single market that is governed by a common set of rules to which the EFTA EEA countries (at least in theory) are able to contribute.

The benefits for Scotland would be real. It would have access to the Internal Market on a reciprocal basis. The four freedoms (of goods, services, capital and persons) are guaranteed within the EEA. That means that, subject to a few exceptions in certain areas, the citizens of 18 states have the right to move freely throughout the EEA in order to live, work, set up business, invest or buy real estate. Crucially, the EEA Agreement does not cover the EU's Common Agricultural Policy or the Common Fisheries Policy. It is limited to certain provisions governing various aspects of trade in agricultural and fish products.

EEA membership would also make life 'easier' for the other EU Member States. The institutional consequences an independent Scotland would have on the EU (votes in the Council, a Commissioner, a judge, MEP's and so on) need no longer be accommodated. It is easier to imagine EEA membership being accorded without the other EEA Members taking advantage of Scotland and demanding something in return.

– Practical difficulties –

That said, there are a number of difficulties with the EEA. The EU reserves the right to discontinue the whole EEA agreement if any EEA member fails to adopt and implement all Community legislation. That places an onerous obligation on the EEA States when they do not take part in the elaboration and adoption of Community legislation. It is a common complaint, especially from Iceland, that EEA countries have none of the rights but all of the obligations.

Moreover, the EEA grants access only to the Internal Market. But the most important Community developments are currently taking place outside the Internal Market. Economic and Monetary Union, enlargement, asylum, justice and foreign affairs, common foreign and security policy are areas that do not bear on EEA countries at all.

The final question is whether the EEA would at all be open for new members. One could certainly not count on any goodwill from the EU to re-invigorate the EEA. There would be a great reluctance to open it up for new membership. For these reasons Scotland's future lies either within the EU or outside it.

– Conclusions –

● The Vienna Convention on State Succession in Respect of Treaties was drawn up against a colonial background and lays down the rules relating to newly independent states (which are given a clean slate) and other successor states (which are presumed to succeed automatically to the treaty heritage of their predecessors). The rules do not accurately reflect customary law and have not proved generally acceptable.

- There is no automatic right to membership of the European Union. State succession to treaties has to be governed by the nature of the treaty. Continued cover by the EC/EU Treaties of the Scottish territory would thus only be possible with the approval of all Member States.

- Realistically, Scotland can expect – more or less automatically – negotiations for EU membership to begin before independence is gained. In the event that the negotiations are not completed at the date of independence there would probably be a continuation of the imposition of the *acquis* on an agreed basis until negotiations are completed and all sides ratify the agreement.

- Should all negotiations fail, Community regulations and directives would continue to apply in Scotland as they are part of Scots law by virtue of the European Communities Act 1972 as amended. Scottish nationals and companies would, however, lose the EU rights elsewhere in Europe (including the rUK).

- However, Scotland would be under no legal obligation to adopt any future EC legislation or follow any decisions of the ECJ. Moreover, the provisions of the EC Treaty would cease to be binding on Scotland and its citizens.

– NOTES –

1. See, for example, the *Political declaration by the constitutional regions of Bavaria, Catalonia, North Rhine–Westphalia, Salzburg, Scotland, Wallonia and Flanders*, 26 April 2001. See http://europa.eu.int/futurum/documents/contrib/dec280501__en.htm [visited 7 August 2001].
2. European Council in Copenhagen, 21–23 June 1993, *Conclusions of the Presidency*, SN 180/93.
3. SNP Press Office, *Independence in Europe Dossier*, 28 May 1999.
4. Ibid.
5. *The Herald*, 7 November 1998.
6. Adopted 22 August 1978; see 17 *International Legal Materials* (1978) 1488, or http://www.un.org/law/ilc/texts/treasucc.htm (visited 7 August 2001). The Convention has been ratified by more than the necessary fifteen States and entered into force on 6 November 1996 in accordance with Article 49(1). By the end of 1999 it had twenty signatories and seventeen parties, namely Bosnia-Herzegovina, Croatia, Czech Republic, Dominica, Egypt, Estonia, Ethiopia, Iraq, Morocco, St Vincent and the Grenadines, Seychelles, Slovakia, Slovenia, the Former Yugoslav Republic of Macedonia, Tunisia, Ukraine, and Yugoslavia. Source: 'Multilateral Treaties Deposited with the Secretary General: Status as at 31 December 1999' Vol. II at 277, (United Nations Publication). It can thus be seen that the Convention took a very long time to attract even fifteen

ratifications (out of nearly 200 potential parties), and that the states which have ratified are to a disproportionate degree small states recently involved in questions of state succession. The United Kingdom has not ratified the Convention, nor has any other major state.

7. The principle of non-succession is also echoed in Articles 17 and 24 of the Vienna Convention on the Law of Treaties whereby a new state is under no obligation to succeed to a treaty.

8. Yearbook of the ILC (1974) II, Part One, 260–6.

9. SNP Press Office, *Independence in Europe Dossier*, 28 May 1999.

10. 1980 Digest of United States Practice in International Law 1041 n.43 (quoting memorandum of Roberts Owen, U.S. State Department Legal Advisor).

11. Committee of Legal Advisors on Public International Law for the Council of Europe, Extraordinary Meeting (16 January 1992), at 3.

12. (1974) Y.B.I.L.C., Vol.II, pt.1, p. 177–8.

13. The Scottish Government may, as a matter of politics, choose to adopt such legislation and follow such rulings, as do a number of Eastern European candidate States.

14. This term is defined by a unilateral declaration by the United Kingdom which was last amended in 1981 to take account of the British Nationalities Act 1981. The rUK would no doubt ensure that it was amended to take account of Scotland's independence.

15. 'EU rebuffs Cook claim in attack on SNP', *The Guardian*, 21 November 1998.

16. http://news.bbc.co.uk/hi/english/uk/scotland/newsid_845000/845039.stm [visited 7 August 2001].

CHAPTER 7

Greenland and Germany: Lessons for Scotland?

There is no direct precedent for part of a Member State breaking away to form a separate, independent state which either remains in or accedes to the EU. But a few indications of what might or might not happen regarding the European Union in the event of Scotland leaving the United Kingdom can be gleaned from the Greenland case and the continuation of the Federal Republic of Germany in the EC after reunification.

The SNP's main claim is that if Scotland breaks away from the United Kingdom it does not automatically leave the European Union. There are at best a handful of cases from which the status of an independent Scotland can be deduced. Two of these cases will be addressed in greater detail below. The Scottish Centre for Economic and Social Research (1996: paragraph 24f; henceforth the SCESR Report) and MacCormick (1999: 203; 2000: 734) frequently cite the Greenland case as an example that unilateral withdrawal from the European Community is not possible but has to be negotiated with all parties to the Treaty. How much credence is there to the claim that the mere fact of Scottish independence would not suffice to propel Scotland from the protective reach of the European Union? Denmark had to negotiate Greenland's exit from the European Community. Why should Scotland upon independence automatically find itself outside the Community?

This chapter seeks to throw light on the Greenland case. It will then proceed to analyse the event of German reunification, its impact on the European Communities, and the reaction of the Member States and the Community institutions.

– THE GREENLAND CASE[1] –

After 600 years of colonial occupation, Greenland was granted internal autonomy (home rule) on 1 May 1979. With the introduction of home rule came the devolution of local legislative and executive powers from Danish to Greenland authorities. The unity of the Kingdom of Denmark, however, was not undermined, and the traditional sovereign powers in international affairs, constitutional affairs, defence of the realm, and the treasury were left untouched.

However, internal autonomy also meant a reappraisal of Greenland's place in the European Community for two principal reasons. First, under the common fisheries policy Greenland was not entitled to exclusive fishing rights within its own coastal waters. And second, its local fishermen were interested only in exploiting Greenland's own coastal waters and not foreign waters. In short, Greenland neither wanted nor needed membership of the European Community.

Unlike the Faeroe Islands, which acquired Home Rule in 1948 and had rejected membership of the EEC, Greenland started out with full member status on exactly the same conditions as continental Denmark. When Greenland acquired Home Rule in 1979 it was informed by Denmark and by the Community that, if it wanted to withdraw, it would have to select one of three arrangements in existence for third parties.

1. OCT (Overseas Countries and Territories) association according to Articles 131–6 EEC (now Articles 182–7 TEC);
2. The same status as the Faeroe Islands which had a trade and fishing arrangement with the EU based on two Council Regulations;[2]
3. The same status of the Isle of Man and the Channel Islands which have reduced member status.[3]

On 23 February 1982, 52 per cent of the Greenland electorate chose for their territory to leave the European Community and adopt OCT status.[4] In spite of 240 EC (now Article 312 TEC), which lays down that the Treaty is concluded for an unlimited period, the principle of Greenland's withdrawal was never subject to serious dispute. UK Government minister Malcolm Rifkind explained the consequences of Greenland's decision to the House of Commons:

> As the treaties contain no provision for withdrawal of a member state, or part of one, the precise terms of Greenland's change in status had to be negotiated within the Community to provide appropriate amendments to the Treaties.[5]

Although some Danish lawyers voiced constitutional concerns they were marginalised as the decision to withdraw received the support of the Danish government and was accepted by the bodies of the European Community, albeit 'with regret', according to one spokesperson (cited in Nash 1996: 1019). The Treaties would have had to be amended whatever option Greenland selected because of the reduction of the territorial application of the Treaties. A negotiated settlement among the Member States was finalised on 1 February 1985 and Greenland formally departed from the Community territories while retaining the special privileges enjoyed under the EEC Treaty by the OCT.

Whereas the reasons for Greenland's departure were mainly economic (Greenlanders wanted autonomous control over the fisheries policy), there is also a geographical and sociological dimension to the decision. Dr Harhoff was Associate Professor in International and European law at the University of Copenhagen, and Legal Advisor to the Greenland Home Rule authorities when he explored this matter in 1983. Greenland cannot strictly speaking be regarded as core European territory or be compared with any other European region. Greenland's geographic location makes it part of the North American continent. Moreover, it is an Inuit[6] society, ethnically identical to native inhabitants of arctic Canada, Alaska and the extreme north-eastern Siberia; its language, culture, climate, social structure and economy are particular to Greenland and cannot be assimilated even with Denmark, let alone the European Community. Since the working population is heavily reliant on fishing and hunting, obtaining full control of its fisheries policy was a vital consideration. By changing its status under the Treaty, Greenland received all the benefits of OCT treatment but none of the burdens of sharing the fishing quotas.

Moreover, the granting of home rule to a former colony is consistent with the right to self-determination that is recognised in all major UN documents.[7] Whilst home rule in this case did not equate to independence or national sovereignty, it did buttress and enhance Greenland's unconstrained responsibility and, by extension, its identity. Harhoff adds the crucial observation that

> Greenland's withdrawal from the EC is not directed towards the Community for any hostile reasons [but] only reflects the simple need of preserving and concentrating the political and legislative powers within a new system which is still in the making (Harhoff 1983: 23).

Two possible conclusions follow from the above. On the one hand one can take the Greenland case as an illustration that when a part of a state attains internal autonomy it does not automatically leave the European Union even if it expressly requests to leave. This is the view adopted in the SCESR Report and by Professor Neil MacCormick (SNP MEP) who maintain that

Scotland's inclusion in the EU would continue post–independence. In a letter to the *Glasgow Herald* (1 June 1999) MacCormick wrote:

> The Greenland precedent is of decisive importance, for it shows that as a matter of European law a territory cannot sever itself unilaterally from the constitutional jurisdiction of the European Communities (or, now, European Union) simply by means of a change of the constitutional relationships within a member state.

According to his analysis, the Denmark–Greenland negotiations demonstrate that a part of the EU can move outside or cease to be subject to European law only through a negotiated settlement. It is thus plausible that the whole body of European law would continue to apply unless and until a decision is reached to end it. There would have to be a negotiated exit of Scotland, as with Greenland.

MacCormick's conclusion, however, is itself contestable. That Greenland's exit from the EC had to be negotiated cannot be taken as evidence that an independent Scotland would remain in the EU unless it specifically negotiated an exit. In 1979 Greenland did not become independent of Denmark, and the referendum held in 1982 was simply a vote to leave the EC by a portion of a continuing state. The situation is analogous to a vote by Scotland to seek to leave the EU whilst remaining part of the United Kingdom. Furthermore, the negotiations were not simply about Greenland leaving but about the terms on which it could transfer to Overseas Countries and Territories (OCT) status.

The SCESR and MacCormick interpret the case to signify that negotiations must precede withdrawal and assume that by analogy the same would apply to Scotland's withdrawal. Upon Scottish independence, representation and voting rights in Community institutions as specified in the Treaty would be redistributed and the Treaty amended. On the other hand, one can confine the Greenland case to its specific facts and not interpret it broadly. According to Harhoff, only a territory that is:

- overseas and non-European;
- a former colony of a Member State;
- a developing area.[8]

can be compared to the Greenland case. The only other possible candidates would be the French overseas departments like St Pierre and Miquelon (Harhoff 1983: 31), which are islands off the south coast of Newfoundland. They had enjoyed OCT status until 1976 when France changed their status under the constitution to overseas departments, thereby bringing them under Article 227(2) EEC (now Article 299 (2) TEC). When the islands expressed their wish to return to OCT status, modification of the Treaty of Rome was not an issue. The upshot of the Greenland case is that it is up to each Member State to determine the status of its overseas territories when it accedes to the Treaty and that (within reasonable limits) this status may subsequently be modified. So when Denmark joined the EEC in 1973, Greenland was treated with full member status as a constituent part of the Kingdom of Denmark – unlike the Faeroe Islands which had been granted Home Rule in 1948 and opted out of the European Communities upon Denmark's accession. According to Pieter Jan Kuyper, who was a Legal Advisor to the European Commission, the cases of St Pierre and Miquelon and Greenland:

> had always been regarded and treated as relatively simple cases of moveable treaty boundaries, that is to say that the boundaries within which the EC treaties applied were simply seen as contracting so as to exclude, for instance, Greenland from this area (Kuyper 1994: 623).

If the Greenland case is essentially about changing the boundaries within which the EC Treaties apply, then what is its significance for Scotland?

– Significance for Scotland –

Harhoff denies the Greenland case any major precedent value. The status Greenland acquired is crucial in that respect. Greenland's transition was from being part of the territory of a full member to being an OCT territory, on which Harhoff comments that, 'granting OCT status to Greenland is also an important part of the Danish endeavour *to limit the precedent impact of Greenland's withdrawal*' (Harhoff 1983: 31; emphasis added).

To recap, the SCESR claims that unilateral departure from the European Union is not permissible and that a state can withdraw only by negotiation and with the consent of all other Member States. But the real negotiations over Greenland were neither about the reduction in Denmark's territory, nor over the principle of withdrawal by a territory of a Member State. They were about the wish of Greenland to be given OCT status rather than full membership.

The differences between Greenland and Scotland are crucial here. In the former case, Denmark negotiated on behalf of Greenland the removal of part of its national territory from the ambit of the European Community treaty. As Happold puts it succinctly, 'it was not an example of a member state (still less a state that had seceded from a member state) being unable to withdraw from the EC without the consent of the other members' (Happold 2000: 32).

The upshot of the Greenland example is that that since Greenland did not secede from Denmark, but only chose to withdraw from the European Community, it was necessary to negotiate terms.[9] The Scottish scenario is the inverse. Whereas Greenland wanted to break away from the European Community but remain part of its parent state (Denmark), Scotland wants to break away from its parent state but remain part of the European Union. Even if Greenland had wanted to secede from Denmark it would not have meant the end of Community membership for Denmark. This construction turns the tables on the interpretation by Scottish nationalists. If the Greenland example shows anything it is that Scotland could leave the United Kingdom without destroying continued membership of the United Kingdom (with reduced territory) in the European Union.

In conclusion, the precedent of Greenland is a complex one. On the one hand, it shows that the Commission can respond pragmatically – 'its approach has been one of adapting EC legal theory to the economic and geographic realities of Greenland, rather than rigidly applying various treaty provisions' (Mason 1983: 874). The Member States accepted Greenland's modified status despite the fact that the EC Treaties did not really make provision for such a change in status. On the other hand, there can be no guarantee that a claim by a newly independent Scotland would be met with the same flexibility. Scottish independence is implicit in the following assertion:

> It is indeed ironic that a case such as Greenland's can do such violence to the Community legal order and yet go through, as it were, 'on the nod'. If it came, however, to a matter of raising a nationality to 'equal partnership' within the EC, to integrating it more directly in the fate of the Community in response to the aspirations of its people – legally, a far less traumatic event than withdrawal – it would, no doubt, be opposed vehemently and obdurately by more than one 'master of the treaty' (Thomas 1991).

If the chances of an independent Scotland remaining within the EU are to be predicted, it is not Greenland that matters, but the likely attitude of the other Member States to the issues of regionalism and nationality. Geopolitical reasons indeed underpinned the EC's response to German reunification in 1990, which is the next case study.

– GERMAN REUNIFICATION –

The historically significant event of German reunification raises similar issues for Scottish independence. Enlargement of its territory could have had ramifications for Germany's EC membership. However, the combination of constitutional process and Community pragmatism was finely balanced in this case and the question is whether Scotland could achieve the same feat.

Constitutionally, there were two possible options – which are not discussed in detail here – by which the German Democratic Republic (GDR) and the Federal Republic of Germany (FRG) could have been unified. The GDR could either have acceded to the FRG by virtue of Article 23 of the Basic Law (*Grundgesetz*) of the FRG, or it could have been incorporated in a new constitution by virtue of Article 146 of the Basic Law.[10] In the end accession proceeded pursuant to Article 23.

Externally, and of central interest to the present discussion, the big question was whether the territorial application of the EC Treaty could be extended to cover an enlarged FRG. This question is of the utmost relevance for nationalists in Scotland for whom the question is (a) whether the EU can be 'extended' to cover a new Member State comprised of existing Community territory; and (b) whether the EC/EU Treaties require amending before or after the date of independence.

Scottish prospects of a smooth transition into Member State status start to look very good if one assumes that the EU would embrace Scotland in the same way it embraced the former GDR. German reunification is a crystal clear illustration of how, in spite of some legal wrangling, politics can gain the upper hand when it is opportune and it did so in the process of integrating the two Germanys. David Spence, who at the time acted as Secretary of the European Commission's Task Force for German unification, notes that:

> integrating the new German Länder into the Community in the space of three months at the end of 1990 . . . was a fascinating example of the Community's ability to act effectively and rapidly, provided that the political will to do so exists (Spence 1991: 1).

Although there were both legal and political doubts as to the correct procedure to be followed, all Member States agreed not to make Treaty amendment a condition so that the process of reunification could be swiftly completed. The five new *Länder* acceded to the FRG by virtue of Article 23 of the Basic Law. Article 227 EC (now Article 299 TEC), which lists the

Member States including the FRG, did not have to be changed as the legal identity of the German state remained the same as before; the state had only increased in size. Non-amendment meant that Germany had to accept – at least in the short run – the existing institutions and structures, and in particular the (unchanged) Treaty rules relating to the institutions, the weighting of Council votes, and the allocation of seats in the European Parliament.[11]

At the end of the day, by 'softening' the moving treaty frontier rule, politics triumphed and the EC Treaties were extended without further ado. This in itself is legally debatable. Whereas the much maligned Vienna Convention on Succession of States in Respect of Treaties includes this rule in Article 15 (under the heading 'succession in respect of part of territory'), the commentary of the International Law Commission to the Convention denies its application in the case of total absorption of one state by another.[12] Instead, Article 31 et seq. ('effects of a uniting of states') should have applied, which places great value on continuity of all existing treaty obligations by both states.[13] The informality that accompanied the 'moving treaty frontier rule' did not cause major upset in the constituent states.[14]

The Inter-German Treaty on Economic, Monetary and Social Union (*Staatsvertrag*) and the Unification Treaty (*Einigungsvertrag*) met the requirements of legal certainty. A large number of Council regulations and other instruments required technical modification, which were agreed in considerable haste by the Commission and the Council. Institutional matters, such as representation of the East German population in the European Parliament, were deliberately left unresolved *pro tempore*. They did not reappear until the Nice Summit in December 2000 when France and Germany clashed over figures and the balance of power in the EU.

But is it realistic to assume that the EU will repeat its generosity of 1990? Is the Scotland case a straight analogy to the East Germany case? The key fact with Germany was that, as a matter of politics, the United Kingdom, France, the USA and West Germany had recognised the link between unification and European integration in the preamble to the Bonn Convention of 26 May 1952, which stated:

> Whereas the Three Powers and the Federal Republic recognize that both the new relationship to be established between them by the present Convention and its related Conventions and the Treaties for the creation of an integrated European Community, in particular the Treaty on the Establishment of the European Coal and Steel Community and the Treaty on the Establishment of the European Defence Community, are essential steps to the achievement

of their common aim for a unified Germany integrated within the European Community.[15]

In the event, France did not ratify the declaration and it never entered into force. But it is nonetheless evidence that the EEC members were aware of the possibility of reunification and without doubt favoured the participation of a united rather than a divided Germany in Europe (see Jacqué 1991: 4).

Scotland faces a number of hurdles in a different context and (possibly) with differing outcomes. First, Scotland would have to win over all Member States. If Scotland failed to achieve a political settlement beforehand then accession to the EU could easily become a long and drawn-out process. This is all the more so if one or more Member States expresses discomfort. Accession to the EU requires unanimity. And there are good reasons why a Member State may be uncomfortable with either Scottish secession and/or continued membership in the EU. Indeed France had initially been in favour of full admission of the former GDR to the European Community but later gave in and accepted that the negotiation process would not involve the GDR itself. German reunification took place at a time when the Community consisted of twelve Member States and was not in the process of eastward enlargement – in fact unification initiated expansion to the east.

By the time Scotland joined the EU as an independent State the EU may well consist of 21 or more states with veto rights that could be exercised in theory – especially if Scotland sought to re–negotiate the terms of membership. As Heather Grabbe from the Centre for European Reform put it in an interview, the terms of membership may be 'demand-led' from Scotland rather than 'supply-led' by the EU and this may not find favour with other Member States.[16]

That said, it is not obvious on what grounds a Member State might wish to veto Scotland's accession. There is no provision in the Treaty on that matter. And there are no fundamental concerns (relating to human rights, for instance) which would warrant use of the veto right.[17] An oft-cited reason against Scottish independence is the wariness of some Member States to encourage separatist movements within their own territory. But those states may use the negotiations to gain non-related benefits elsewhere. Bargaining lies at the heart of the EU. Some states may relinquish their veto right if they get something in return.

– How close is the analogy? –

Scotland differs from Germany in one crucial respect – and this is why the analogy does not work. Scotland cannot become a Member State without Treaty amendment. Whereas German representation at EU level continued to be secure after reunification, Scotland would not be represented at all.

Relying as the SCESR, MacCormick and, by implication, the SNP do, on a legal right to automatic succession is entirely academic. Even though this position has received the backing of some international and European lawyers and diplomats, it runs counter to established doctrine and practice, and to the realities of how change within the European Union must be accommodated.

O'Connell has argued persuasively that abstract and general rules of international law are positively unhelpful when it comes to illuminating an area such as state succession to treaties. He proposes an approach that looks at each treaty individually and tailors the rules to the specifics of the case (O'Connell 1979: 738). In context it is easily argued that the inclusion of the former GDR or an independent Scotland in the territorial span of the NATO Treaty cannot be governed by abstract and general rules of international law as it requires the careful balancing of political and security interests and hence universal consent by all signatories to the Treaty.

In the German reunification process Europe ignored conflicting and confusing legal arguments and pursued an intergovernmental course and let all the Member States decide the fate of Germany unanimously. Thus Article 227 EEC (now Article 299 TEC), which lists the Member States, was not revised; assent from the European Parliament, ratification by all national parliaments, and formal negotiations between the Community and the GDR was not required. Spence points out that whilst any Member State could have requested Treaty amendment:

> no state saw a need to do so, but the important point here is that *political* consensus on the issue was reached at the Dublin European Council in April 1990. The German case was clearly *sui generis* (Spence 1991: 11; original emphasis).

Political consensus, rather than legalistic and formalistic disputes, did justice to the momentous achievement of unification. Tomuschat makes the interesting point that if automatic extension of the EC Treaty had been denied the FRG would have had to tolerate an economic frontier within its territory. But the Community wanted to avoid this at all cost as 'it is axiomatic for the EC Treaties to treat Member States as legal and economic units' (Tomuschat 1990: 423).[18]

So whatever position the Community adopted regarding the swift unification of the two German states it cannot be concluded that the Community would adopt the same position regarding the recognition of

Scotland as a new member. To all intents and purposes, Germany remained the same state with identical international legal personality. In other words the end result here is diametrically opposed to the desired end result of Scottish independence, which is to create a new state with distinct international legal personality to the United Kingdom.

There remains a further distinction between the Scotland and the Germany cases. German reunification had been a constitutional goal from the moment of partition. The 1952 Treaty between the Allies and the FRG proclaims that the ultimate objective is reunification and the 1955 Treaty between the USSR and the GDR also refers to Germany as a whole. According to Timmermans, the reason integration of a reunified Germany into the European Community caused no legal upsets and received the backing of all Member States was because:

> German reunification cannot be considered as a real novum, it is an intrinsic heritage of the accession of the Federal Republic of Germany to the Communities, of which the other Member States have been fully aware from the beginning (Timmermans 1990: 440).

The efficiency of the Community's reaction to unification and the institutional flexibility that marked the process of integrating the former GDR was premised upon an overall political agreement as to what was at stake and what was desired. If Scottish independence had been the acclaimed political goal of the United Kingdom for a certain length of time then the Member States might show at least a modicum of understanding. But if Scottish independence emerges as a surprise development or late entry on the European stage, rather than a longstanding political goal shared by the United Kingdom, the EU has no incentive to support the act of dissolution or secession. It risks weakening the infrastructure of the EU if dissolution/secession is not wholeheartedly supported by each and every Member State. The EU has demonstrated to most commentators' surprise and satisfaction that integration and fusing aspects of national sovereignty can lead to peace and prosperity. Scottish independence may jeopardise the European economic and political agenda, especially if Scotland finds itself outside the EU. Spence concludes that 'the political will and the flexibility present for German unification were quite unique – and probably not to be repeated' (Spence 1991: 47). Although the SNP emphasises both integration and national sovereignty (summed up in their 'Scotland in Europe' slogan) this looks to be very much a case of the SNP wanting their cake and eating it.

– Notes –

1. For an in depth discussion see Harhoff (1983), Mason (1983), Weiss (1985), Nash (1996).
2. Council Reg. No. 2051/74 of 1 August 1974 on a customs arrangement for certain goods, and Council Reg. No.2211/70 of 27 June 1980 on the conclusion of a fishing arrangement between the EC and the Faeroe Islands.
3. See Article 227(5)(c) EEC (now Article 299 (6)(c) TEC).
4. The OCT status is primarily designed for the non-European colonial possessions of Member States, allowing duty free entry of goods from the OCT into the Community in return for partial reciprocity from the OCT.
5. House of Commons Hansard, 31 October 1984; cited in SCESR Report at paragraph 24.
6. The term 'Inuit' here is used in preference to 'Eskimo' as appears in the original text.
7. See Chapter 1 at n. 1.
8. Harhoff treats Greenland as a developing area, not within the conventional under-standing of the term, but because its heavy reliance on mono-production, the lack of infrastructure, and the receipt of financial support from Denmark are features characteristic of other developing areas (1983: 24).
9. See *Treaty amending, with regard to Greenland, the Treaties establishing the European Communities* (Brussels, 13 March 1984), Cmnd. 9490.
10. For an in-depth discussion see Frowein (1991); Jacqué (1991); Oeter (1991); Spence (1991); Timmermans (1990); Tomuschat (1990).
11. See Article 11 of the Unification Treaty: 'The Contracting Parties [the FRG and the GDR] proceed on the understanding that *international treaties and agreements* to which the Federal Republic of Germany is a contracting party, *including treaties establishing membership in international organisations or institutions, shall retain their validity* and that the rights and obligations arising therefrom . . . shall also relate to the territory specified in Article 3 of this treaty' (emphasis added).
12. Yb. ILC 1974, Vol II, Part 1, p. 253; cited in Kuyper (1984: 621).
13. The applicability of this provision is hampered by the fact that the GDR was not regarded as a state by the other members of the EC. Under all post-war agreements 'Germany' continued to exist as a state, albeit a temporarily divided one (Hendry and Wood 1987).
14. Whether the 'moving treaty frontier rule' applies in relation to the EU is subject of some dispute. Lane (1991: 152) believes that it does not, whereas Malanczuk (1997: 168) argues that it does. The response by the Community to German reunification is a *de facto* recognition of that rule.
15. Cited in Jacqué (1991: 3–4).
16. The desire to re–negotiate terms might, of course, also be true for a UK Government pursuing a 'eurosceptic' line of policy.
17. The Treaty on European Union (as amended by the Treaty of Amsterdam) now provides for suspension of rights of membership if the Council, following the criteria and processes laid down in Articles 6 and 7, finds that human rights or other fundamental values of the EU have been flagrantly violated by a Member State.
18. Tomuschat here refers to the memorandum *The Community and German Unification: communication from the Commission to the Special Session of the European Council in Dublin, 20 April 1990*, (SEC/90/751), Brussels, point 4.

CHAPTER 8

Accession to the European Union

In the case where Scotland secedes from the United Kingdom and finds itself outside the European Union, whilst rUK continues in the footsteps of the United Kingdom, the Scottish Government would have to decide whether or not to apply for EU membership. If Scotland desires to be a Member State then, alongside negotiations with the UK Government, the Scottish negotiating team would have to consider an independent Scotland's relationship with the EU. These negotiations would have to be handled in tandem. The events of German reunification and Greenland's withdrawal from the EC illustrate that such major issues arising today have to be, 'treated as a Community issue rather than in terms of traditional nation-state perspectives' (Spence 1991: 47).

– REQUIREMENTS –

The current applicant states are expected by the EU to satisfy the so-called 'Copenhagen criteria' for EU membership which stipulate the following:

> Membership requires that the candidate country has achieved stability of institutions guaranteeing democracy, the rule of law, human rights and respect for and, protection of minorities, the existence of a functioning market economy as well as the capacity to cope with competitive pressure and market forces within the Union. Membership presupposes the candidate's ability to take on the obligations of membership including adherence to the aims of political, economic and monetary union.[1]

These criteria go beyond the formal requirements in the Treaty on European Union as amended by the Treaty of Amsterdam, which are limited to being a 'European State' (Article 49 TEU) that respects those fundamental values enumerated in Article 6 TEU (liberty, democracy, respect for human rights and fundamental freedoms, and the rule of law). The Copenhagen criteria are, however, largely declaratory of the political values which have been applied to other candidate states in the past. These criteria will be dissected and addressed in turn.

– Political criteria –

Article 6 TEU (ex Article F EU) designates that 'the Union is founded on the principles of liberty, democracy, respect for human rights and fundamental freedoms and the rules of law'. Scotland would not have any difficulty in meeting these criteria. In its strategy paper on enlargement, the Commission looked at issues such as public administration, the judiciary, corruption, childcare institutions, gender equality and minority protection.[2]

– Economic criteria –

The two fundamental economic criteria are (a) the existence of a functioning market economy and (b) the capacity to withstand competitive pressure and market forces within the Union. The Commission Communication on 'Agenda 2000: For a Stronger and Wider Union', which was submitted to Council and Parliament on 15 July 1997, elaborated on these criteria.

The existence of a functioning market economy presupposes the liberalisation of prices and trade as well as the existence of an enforceable legal system and property rights. The emphasis is on performance of the economy (through macroeconomic stability and consensus about economic policy) and efficiency of the economy (through a strong financial sector and the absence of barriers to trade). In EU terms the efficient running of a market economy is required so that common policies such as the Single Market and the four freedoms of goods, persons, capital and services can be implemented smoothly and given full effect.

The capacity to withstand competitive pressure and market forces within the Union requires a stable market economy as well as a propensity to permit economic agents to make decisions in 'a climate of predictability'. Nationalised industries must be privatised and investment is seen as the key to improved efficiency.

– Other obligations of membership –
The acquis communautaire

The final point in the Copenhagen criteria is that membership requires, 'the candidate's ability to take on the obligations of membership including adherence to the aims of political, economic and monetary union.'

Accordingly, Scotland would have to adopt, implement and enforce the *acquis communautaire* (to the extent that it has not already done so), by which is meant the commonality of rights and obligations that bind the Member States together. This body amounts to some 80,000 pages and includes not just the successive treaties but also all secondary legislation (such as regulations and directives, as well as the jurisprudence of the European Court of Justice) that stems from the European Union.

There is no principled reason why Scotland should not be able to meet the *acquis*. Rather, the hurdles it needs to surmount are practical. Many of the physical structures like a Scottish Central Bank, whose role would be to inform the European Central Bank of monetary conditions in Scotland and convey Scotland's standpoint on monetary policy, tax collection structures and securities regulators have yet to be set up and implemented. The same can be said for customs, free movement of capital and other institutions.[3] But such difficulties are neither new nor insoluble. According to Elizabeth Holt at the European Commission Representation in Scotland, the system that had been in place to communicate the adoption of national legislation emanating from EU legislation has already had to adapt to the requirements of devolution. Under Schedule 5 to the Scotland Act, the Scottish Executive may select its own implementation methods for EU Directives covering a devolved matter. Linkage mechanisms are certainly in place in Scotland but they would take a considerable amount of money and time to improve were Scotland to become independent, thus adding to the transition costs.

Moreover, respecting and recognising the *acquis* takes place not just at the level of government and administration but also at the level of businesses, regional and local bodies, and professional organisations. The European Parliament, the Economic and Social Committee, and the Committee of the Regions wish for deeper involvement of civic society in the *acquis*. Scotland's authorities would need to improve communication with the Scottish parliament to clarify the *acquis* and to foster nationwide adoption and implementation.

EMU *and the* euro

Adopting Economic and Monetary Union (EMU) and the convergence criteria are a further part of the *acquis* which new Member States have to sign up to. However, achieving convergence is not part of it. Since the United Kingdom has opted out of EMU the question is whether Scotland would inherit the benefit of the United Kingdom opt-out if it wanted to? This is not an offer made to current applicants. Member States would have to decide but would not allow Scotland to opt-out. Adopting the euro is very much seen as the crowning of what will have been a long process of economic integration in the EU.

The process of adopting the euro is divided into three stages:

1. The pre–accession phase: focus is on functioning market economy and macroeconomic stability;
2. The intermediary phase: the new member has acceded to the EU and participates fully in the Single Market whilst progressively integrating its monetary policy with the euro zone and participating in the exchange rate mechanism;
3. And finally, participation in the euro zone.

– Conclusion –

There is nothing to suggest that Scotland would not be able to meet the criteria set out above. But meeting the accession criteria is not the be-all and end-all for applicant states. There will still be plenty to quarrel over, ranging from the number of votes in the Council to financial contributions and such like. There will in practice have to be a whole raft of negotiations with the Commission in the preparatory stage and the EU members in the negotiation of an accession treaty. The process of negotiation is discussed in Chapter 6 in the context of deciding whether continued membership in the EU would be prompt or problematic. The next section will continue examining the case where Scotland has to apply to join like any applicant state.

– THE PROCESS –

Scotland cannot be compared to the other applicant countries currently queuing to be admitted to the EU. Crucially, the Scots have enjoyed EU rights and obligations for almost 30 years. The following will provide an indication of the laboriousness of the process although it is extremely probable that most of this process will be side-stepped for Scotland unless Member States seriously want to make an awful example of Scotland for their own reasons.

– Negotiations –

The guidelines for the negotiations approved by the Luxembourg European Council (1997) and the Helsinki European Council (1999) provide that each applicant country proceeds at its own pace. The level of preparedness is a crucial factor. Applicants are assessed on their own merits and join the EU when they are found ready to meet the Copenhagen criteria. This is not anticipated to be problematic for Scotland.

Negotiations are generally carried out in bilateral accession conferences (that is between the existing Member States and Scotland). They are conducted by the presidency of the EU on behalf of the Member States with the support of the Commission. The Commission draws up common positions for all Member States as a basis for negotiations in each sector. With respect to the dozen or so applicant countries currently waiting to 'sail' into the EU under the 'regatta principle' or 'flotilla system' as adopted by the European Council in Helsinki in December 1999,[4] the *acquis* was divided into 31 chapters. At the date of the EU's enlargement report in 8 November 2000 negotiations with the six first countries had taken place in all but two chapters (on 'institutional questions' and 'other questions') and 11 to 16 chapters had been provisionally closed, meaning that credible commitments as regards the harmonisation of laws plus administrative enforcement had been given. The Commission monitors those commitments.

The duration of accession negotiations is difficult to predict and depends on the complexity of the issues. In the case of Austria, Sweden and Finland, they were completed in thirteen months, whereas with Spain and Portugal they lasted for nearly seven years.

– Changes for the EU –

Assuming that an independent Scotland can meet the Copenhagen criteria, it would then need formally to accede to the EU whilst the EC/EU Treaties would have to be amended to cover Scotland. The process of accession is laid out in Article 49 TEU (ex Article O EU) and requires an application to the Council which, having consulted the Commission, must act unanimously. An absolute majority in the European Parliament must also agree to the new accession.

But it is the second paragraph of Article 49 TEC that causes much difficulty and confusion. According to this sub-clause,

> The conditions of admission and the adjustments to the treaties on which the Union is founded, which such admission entails, shall be the subject of an agreement between the Member States and the applicant state. This shall be submitted for ratification by all the contracting states in accordance with their respective constitutional requirements.

Different international organisations deal with accession and succession in different ways. Whereas the UN Charter, for instance, does not require amendment the European Treaty does. Some of the reasons for amendment are:

- to name the Member States of the Union;
- to define the territorial application of the Treaty;
- to stipulate the number of Members of the European Parliament (Article 190 TEC (ex Article 138 EC));
- to state the number of weighted votes held by each Member State when the Council is required to act by a qualified majority (Art 205 TEC (ex Article 148 EC));
- to nominate a member of the Commission (Article 213 TEC (ex Article 157 EC));
- to nominate judges in the European Court of Justice (Article 221 TEC (ex Article 165 EC));
- to place a member in the Court of Auditors (Article 247 TEC (ex Article 188b EC));
- to increase representation in the Economic and Social Committee (Article 258 TEC (ex Article 194 EC));
- to increase representation in the Committee of the Regions (Article 263 TEC (ex Article 198a EC)).

The SNP has called for Treaty amendment, among other reasons because of what they call the 'West Luxembourg' question. Whereas Luxembourg (with 360,000 inhabitants) currently has six members on the Committee of the Regions, Scotland has only four. Scotland has eight Members of the European Parliament (MEPs) compared to Denmark's 16, although both have similar populations. According to calculations by the SNP, an amended Treaty after the Nice summit in December 2000 would give rise to the changes outlined in Figure 8.1.

Even if the SNP's predictions were correct this would make the continued inclusion of Scotland in the European Union more problematic than automatic. Figure 8.1 lists the numerous necessary changes to be made to the EC/EU Treaties in order to give full effect to Scottish membership. As discussed above, there can be no question of Scotland demanding that such changes be made as of right. They have to be negotiated and discussed at an Intergovernmental Conference.

Furthermore, the SNP's predictions are very generous. They assume, for instance, that Scotland would have a right to nominate a Commissioner. Whilst this would be true if Scotland were independent now, it might not be true in the long run. The Nice summit suggested that as from 1 January 2005 the five big states give up their second commissioner in order to reduce the size of the Commission. Each Member State will have one Commissioner until the EU has 27 members, after which the Council will unanimously decide the size of the Commission. The Commission will then consist of fewer members than there are Member States and commissioners will be appointed by rotation among Member States on the basis of equality. As Scotland would be one of the small states, it would probably have to join the rotating system. The details have yet to be worked out but it cannot be taken for granted that Scotland will have the right to nominate a commissioner.

Figure 8.1: SNP forecasts of Scottish representation within the EU.

- *Commission*: Within the UK, Scotland has no right to nominate a Commissioner but would acquire that right as an independent Member State.
- *Council of Ministers*: Within the UK, Scotland has no guaranteed right to attend, lead or vote in national or European interest. As a Member State, Scotland would have a guaranteed seat as well as speaking rights and 7 votes (equal with Denmark, Finland and Ireland) which is roughly a quarter of the current UK total (29 votes).
- *European Parliament*: Within the UK, Scotland will lose seats down from 8 to 6 or 7. As an independent Member State Scotland would have 13 MEPs (matching its comparator countries Denmark and Finland in terms of population).[5]

Other changes, according to the SNP, would be as follows:[6]

	Scotland Now	Scotland as Full Member of the European Union
Economic and Social Committee Seats	2	9
Committee of the Region Seats	4	9
Able to take a turn as President of the Council?	No	Yes
Able to nominate member of the European Court of Justice?	No	Yes
Member of the Court of First Instance?	No	Yes
Member of the European Court of Auditors?	No	Yes
Member of the European Investment Bank?	No	Yes
Member of the Committee of Representatives COREPER?	No	Yes
Beneficiary of balance in the 28,000 civil service jobs among nationalities?	No	Yes

Another instance where the SNP's calculations are optimistic is with their estimation that an independent Scotland would have more MEPs than it currently has. To be sure, the previous cap of 700 for the number of MEPs was set aside and increased to 732 at the Nice summit. But Scotland cannot necessarily rely on the figures for its comparator countries. The exact allocation of seats was not systematic but was an impromptu decision to compensate for the weighting of votes in the Council. The examples of the Czech Republic and Hungary illustrate that the present allocation of seats is contrary to the principle of equality, as the number of seats allocated to those countries is smaller than the number assigned to Member States with smaller populations. So enlargement means a reduction of MEPs per state to accommodate the newcomers. If Scotland became independent at a time when the EU had 21 Member States, it would force a further reduction of MEPs per state or an increase in the overall number of MEPs.

– EFFECTIVENESS OF SCOTTISH REPRESENTATION –

The SNP's slogan 'Independence in Europe' once more brushes over the specific issues and the nuts and bolts of EU membership. From a dispassionate Scottish perspective the question is not so much whether Scotland could be an independent player in Europe (for there can be no doubt that it could) but whether independent Scottish representation in the EU would be more effective than its current representation via the United Kingdom.[7] This section considers the SNP's drive for better representation and examines the way Scottish representation has been handled since the creation of the Scottish Parliament. Finally, it raises questions as to the efficiency of an independent Scotland's representation.

Devolution has not led to any increase in attendance by Scottish ministers at meetings of the Council of Ministers in the European Union. Although they may attend all meetings that concern devolved matters (such as justice, transport, health, agriculture and fisheries), research done by the SNP in December 2000 showed that Scottish ministers had attended only eleven out of 120 Council sessions since the creation of the Scottish Parliament. In comparison, all 15 EU Member States (including Scotland's comparator countries Ireland, Denmark and Finland) had a 100 per cent attendance record. For the SNP the 9 per cent attendance record of Scottish Ministers flags up the underlying compromise of Scottish devolution. Scotland may enjoy certain devolved powers but it does not have a regular voice in Europe. Since the Scotland Act stipulates that Scottish ministers may attend EU meetings the SNP is determined that, 'under an SNP government, there will be a Scottish Ministerial or official representation at every Council of Ministers meeting'.[8]

The trouble with the SNP's determination to attend each and every EU forum is that it ignores the reality of the devolution settlement. Most of the devolved areas (agriculture, economic development, industry, transport, and the environment) also form part of the EU policy agenda – and so one might have expected more Scottish direct participation. But when negotiating at EU level (a non-devolved matter of foreign policy), it is the UK Government which represents the interests of Scotland, Wales and Northern Ireland. The United Kingdom representatives have to speak in unison at those meetings. There is no room for dissent from the devolved administrations before the EU. It is thus not for the SNP to determine that they will attend each EU formal meeting once they make up the Scottish Executive; it is for the United Kingdom government to invite Scottish Ministers to attend such meetings.

The Scottish Office recognised these difficulties early on and helped draft a Concordat on Co-ordination of European Union Policy Issues[9] which guarantees a consultative role for the devolved administrations. Whilst the EU remains the responsibility of the United Kingdom Government:

> the UK Government wishes to involve the Scottish Executive as directly and fully as possible in decision making on EU matters which touch on devolved areas (including non-devolved matters which impact on devolved areas and non-devolved matters which will have a distinctive impact of importance in Scotland). In general, it is expected that consultation, the exchange of information and the conventions on notifications to EU bodies will continue in similar circumstances to the arrangements in place prior to devolution.

> Participation will be subject to mutual respect for the confidentiality of discussions and adherence by the Scottish Executive to the resulting UK line without which it would be impossible to maintain such close working relationships. This line will reflect the interests of the UK as a whole. In accordance with these general principles, the co-ordination mechanisms should achieve three core objectives:

> - they should provide for full and continuing involvement of Ministers and officials of the Scottish Executive in the process of policy formulation, negotiation and implementation, for issues which touch on devolved matters;

> - they should ensure that the UK can negotiate effectively, in pursuit of a single UK policy line, but with the flexibility that fast-moving negotiations require; and

> - they should ensure EU obligations are implemented with consistency of effect and where appropriate of timing.[10]

The current position is that the influence of the Scottish Executive on EU policy making is only indirect via the UK Government. The Scottish Executive must respect confidentiality as well as the UK Government's position.

It is therefore not surprising that the SNP sees material benefits for an independent Scotland at EU level. Scotland's view is currently merged into the United Kingdom's view. The unionist position plays into the hands of the SNP who can exploit the weaknesses of the Scotland Act. The political compromise at national level fails, in practice, at supranational level.

Nonetheless, the perceived benefits of having an independent Scotland negotiate at EU level, and 'punching above its weight' as it is commonly said, are misleading. On the one hand, Scotland would be better represented numerically at EU level. Just looking at the weighted votes in the Council it appears that an independent Scotland might get seven votes, whilst rUK would either keep its current 29 or face a reduction but to no fewer than 27 votes (equal with Spain). The joint force of those votes would be a remarkable 34–6 votes – provided that Scotland and rUK vote together. But the conclusion that Scottish interests are therefore better or more effectively represented is mistaken. As of now the Scottish voice is heard in Europe via United Kingdom representation. If Scotland needed to pursue a policy of its own, it would be more effective if it received the backing of the UK Government. The guarding of national interests by small states, on the other hand, is particularly difficult in the EU. Whilst small countries will continue to enjoy disproportionately large voting power (compared to the size of their population) in the Council, the Nice Summit did weaken their future position. The Summit also extended Qualified Majority Voting (QMV) to a number of areas so that small states will find it increasingly hard to secure exceptional arrangements for themselves.

The questions that will remain unanswered are to do with the political line taken by a future Scottish Government. In which policy areas would Scotland adopt the same or different policies to the United Kingdom? There are conceivable 'grey' areas, such as food standards, employment, and the adoption of the Euro currency, over which an independent Scotland and rUK could clash. But those are not the only conflict areas. According to Sloat:

1. Over 60 per cent of the fishing industry is in Scotland;
2. Scottish agriculture is based on sheep and hill-farming on less–favoured land, while England has more prairie farms suited to beef and dairy;
3. Scotland has more peripheral areas than England, creating a greater need for Structural Funds (Sloat 2000:104).

The difference here appears to be in the emphasis placed on different policy sectors (hill-farming vs. sheep farming) rather than different policy areas. That said, those differences may become substantial rather than subtle. Some have suggested that the BSE crisis should have been treated as an 'English' – as opposed to 'British' crisis – because Scotland and Northern

Ireland had different regulatory practices (Ibid.). So if Scotland wanted to choose a line of policy distinct from rUK, where would it find allies? Would Scotland gang up with other small countries (like Ireland, the Nordic Countries, or Benelux) to form a powerful voice that may be – in political terms – stronger than the sum of its parts? Or would it follow the lead of small countries and look to either Germany or France to safeguard its interests?[11] Scotland would not have a stronger voice in the EU if it found no allies and was constantly outvoted. If it ended up voting with its natural ally – the United Kingdom – the gains of independence in Europe would be apparent rather than real.

– TERMS OF ADMISSION –

If it were the case that an independent Scotland found itself outside the European Union and had to negotiate its re-admittance into the EU it is worth considering on what terms it might be re-admitted. Scotland would most likely lose its allocation of the budget rebate. In 1984, the then Prime Minister Margaret Thatcher negotiated a special discount on budget contribution worth £2bn a year and the United Kingdom has defended the rebate ever since. In July 2000, the Foreign Secretary Robin Cook told business leaders in Edinburgh that he did, 'not for one moment believe that other countries of the European Union would allow [an independent] Scotland to retain the budget rebate from which taxpayers in Scotland benefit'.[12] At the Berlin summit in March 1999 the Labour Government refused to negotiate the rebate even though the planned changes in contributions would have given the United Kingdom a windfall.

– THE EUROPEAN STRUCTURAL FUNDS –

The SNP has claimed that Scotland does not receive the amount of EU funds from the UK Government which is its due.[13] The question is whether Scotland currently receives an appropriate share of the Structural Funds allocated to the United Kingdom by the EU, or whether Scotland would be better off as an independent country. The European Committee of the Scottish Parliament considered the matter in 2000[14] and its findings are considered below.

The Structural Funds are a cornerstone of EU support for those areas suffering from high unemployment figures and undergoing economic regeneration. The Structural Funds are made up of four separate parts:

- the European Regional Development Fund (ERDF);
- the European Social Fund (ESF);
- the European Agricultural Guidance and Guarantee Fund (EAGGF);
- the Financial Instrument for Fisheries Guidance (FIFG).

Scotland has been in receipt of EU funding ever since the Structural Funds were set up in 1975. Until 1988, no specific funds were set aside for Scotland. The European Commission approved individual projects on a case by case basis, as and when they were submitted within the quotas of the ERDF allocated to each Member State. The Structural Funds were re-formed in 1988 and eligible regions (such as the Highlands and Islands) received allocations for multi-annual development programmes covering the 1989–92, 1992–3 and 1994–9 programme periods.

The Structural Funds are generally implemented through regional development programmes. It is for the most part up to the Member States and regions to define their priorities for development. But since the programmes are part–financed by the EU, the Member States and regions also have to take Community priorities into account so as to further the stated objective of economic and social cohesion.

Prospective EU enlargement has necessitated a re-evaluation of the Structural Funds. Continuous operation of the Funds would not be possible without reform as EU expansion invariably places increased demands on resources. For the period 2000–6 the previous six objectives have been streamlined and divided into three objectives:[15]

- **Objective 1**: Assistance will still be targeted at (i) areas with a GDP per capita of less than 75 per cent of the EU average, (ii) former Objective 6 areas, and (iii) certain remote regions. Coverage will be reduced from 25 per cent to 20 per cent of the EU population. There will be at least four Objective 1 areas in the UK: Cornwall and the Isles of Scilly, Merseyside, South Yorkshire, and West Wales and the Valleys.

Since 1999 the GDP per capita in the Highlands and Islands has risen above 75 per cent of the EU average, which means that they no longer have Objective 1 status. It was only due to the special characteristics of the region (in particular peripherality and low population density) that the Berlin summit in March 1999 agreed to a further cash injection of €300 million (£194 million at 1999 prices) under the Special Transitional Objective 1 Programme. The programme is targeted at the Highlands and Islands from 2000 until 2005 and the Islands only in 2006.

- **Objective 2**: The new Objective 2 supports the economic and social conversion of areas facing structural difficulties, particularly socio-economic problems in areas of industrial decline, rural areas, urban areas and fishery-dependent areas. It brings together Objectives 2 and 5 (b) of the current programming period and extends them to cover other areas. Three programmes are devoted to Western, Eastern and Southern Scotland with a total allocation of €807 million (or £521 million).

- **Objective 3**: The new programme amalgamates the previous Objectives 3 and 4 and provides funding from the European Social Fund to support the adaptation and modernisation of policies and systems of education, training and employment. It will fund assistance outside the areas covered by Objective 1 and 2, which will receive ESF allocations as part of their programmes, and provide a framework for all measures to promote human resources in each Member State. The UK's total allocation is €4,568 million (£2,947 million), of which 10.5 per cent, or €481 million (£310 million), has been allocated to Scotland.

For the 2000–6 period, Scotland has been allocated Structural Funds of £1,094 million (10.8 per cent of the total UK allocation). There has thus been a marked drop in Scotland's share from 24.9 per cent of the UK total in 1975–88 to 10.8 per cent in 2000–6. The question the European Committee of the Scottish Parliament sought to answer was whether the UK Government has allocated Scotland sums under the Structural Funds of a similar value to those the EU would expect Scotland to receive.[16]

The European Committee of the Scottish Parliament concluded that the allocation process by the United Kingdom is 'relatively transparent and objective', and that (as far as it can tell) Scotland receives, 'an appropriate share of the Structural Funds allocated to the United Kingdom by the EU'.[17] There is also no evidence to suggest that over the 2000–6 period 'Scotland is losing out in the allocation for Structural Funds in the Assigned Budget'. The Committee acknowledged that the converse had been argued but stated that, 'in the absence of the relevant information, this cannot be confirmed'.[18]

As can be seen from the above, the allocation of Structural Funds to any Member State depends on a number of factors: the indicators selected to measure relative disparities in income per head, unemployment, population and so on, among the regions of the EU; the relative disadvantage of regions relative to EU averages; and the political influence of Member States on the allocation of EU funds (the designation of eligible areas and the allocation of finance to those eligible areas). Scotland has historically benefited from the Structural Funds due to its disadvantage in relation to the rest of the EU. This is unaffected whether Scotland is part of the United Kingdom or an independent state.

But at least two factors have to be borne in mind. First, the EU is in the process of enlargement and the streamlining of the Objectives means that existing beneficiary states will lose much if not all of their funding. According to EU Commission figures, Scotland's annual receipts for Objectives 1, 2 and 3 will drop by 4 per cent from €244 million between 1994–9 to around €234 million between 2000–6. That may not seem like much of a reduction. But looking only at Objective 2, eligibility will drop from €170 million a year in 1994–9 to around €87 million a year in 2000–6 – roughly speaking a 50 per cent drop that corresponds to population reduction. The eligible population for Objective 2 and 5(b) in 1994–9 was 3,704,000, whereas now it is 2,029,000. The difference of 1,675,000 will receive transitional support of almost €200 million.

The second factor is that the United Kingdom has been able to negotiate special deals on behalf of Scotland, for instance the Special Transitional Objective 1 Programme for the Highlands and Islands at the Berlin Council in March 1999. It can be argued that Scotland, negotiating as an independent state without the weight of the United Kingdom, would not have been able to negotiate such an arrangement against all the odds. On the other hand, agreement on Structural Funds at the time of the Berlin Council required unanimity among the Member States and that might well have allowed Scotland to secure the special deal for itself anyway. Unanimity would have allowed Scotland to argue its own interests resulting in at least the same deal for the Highlands and Islands.

In conclusion, Scottish independence will largely leave untouched the issue of the Structural Funds. EU enlargement changes the map of disadvantaged regions, boosting the position of Scotland relative to new EU averages and making it harder for Scotland to qualify for additional funds.

Moreover, at the Nice summit in December 2000 it was decided that the Structural Funds will be subject to QMV as from 2007. QMV reduces the ability of states to secure special deals for themselves – which is why Spain, Greece and Portugal, who have always done well out of the Fund, were so unwilling to give up their veto rights. Arguably, Scotland would be better off as part of the United Kingdom regarding its negotiating position, especially if the United Kingdom makes the Highlands and Islands a priority. Alternatively, it is also quite possible that an independent Scotland could ally itself with the Nordic countries and negotiate 'en bloc' a favourable settlement for sparsely populated areas.[19]

– Conclusion –

The route from application to accession is mapped out below. This is standard process which will most likely be followed in the event of Scottish independence.

1. Scotland would submit an application for membership to the Council of the European Union.
2. The Council asks the Commission to deliver an Opinion on the application.
3. The Commission delivers its Opinion on the application to the Council.
4. The Council decides (unanimously) to open negotiations for accession.
5. Negotiations are opened between the Member States on the one hand, and Scotland on the other hand.
6. The Commission proposes, and the Council adopts (unanimously), positions to be taken by the Union vis à vis Scotland in accession negotiations.
7. Agreement reached between Union and Scotland on a Draft Treaty of Accession.
8. Accession Treaty submitted to the Council and the European Parliament.
9. The Commission delivers another Opinion, on the Accession Treaty.
10. European Parliament delivers its assent to the Accession Treaty (by an absolute majority).
11. The Council approves the Accession Treaty (unanimously).
12. Member States and Scotland formally sign the Accession Treaty.
13. Member States and Scotland ratify the Accession Treaty.
14. After ratification, the Treaty comes into effect on the day of accession: the applicants become Member States.

It is virtually impossible to predict the duration of negotiations. It took almost 11 years for the United Kingdom, Denmark, and Ireland to join the Communities (starting with their first application in 1961), more than eight years for Spain, but only three years for Finland. The exceptional case of German unification was dealt with rapidly within three months. Graham Avery, who is Chief Advisor, and Fraser Cameron, who is Advisor at the European Commission, suggest that, 'a year would seem to be the minimum time required to complete the procedures' (Avery and Cameron 1998: 28).

If Scotland were to apply to become a member timing would matter because the EU is in a process of enlargement and the terms that an independent Scotland could negotiate would differ if the EU had 28 rather than the current 15 Member States. The first intake of new members will probably take place from the end of 2002. But the possibility of transition periods should be noted. The accession treaties will include transitional measures on the free movement of persons to quell fears of cheap migrant labour from the Eastern bloc flooding the EU. Full membership of Poland, Hungary and Estonia, the applicant states with the best credentials, is not expected to be granted until 2005–6.

The process of negotiation is unlikely to be easy even for Scotland. Evidence from other candidate countries suggests that the EU uses its pre-accession bargaining strength to extract the maximum concessions from acceding parties. Member States are obviously aware that once candidates have joined, existing Member States will never have such an advantage again. Moreover, all new accession treaties have to be ratified by all national parliaments, a process which takes a minimum of twelve months and may take much longer if (as with the Treaty of Maastricht) major issues are at stake, or the treaty is rejected by a national parliament or in a referendum.

– NOTES –

1. European Council in Copenhagen, 21–3 June 1993, *Conclusions of the Presidency*, SN 180/93.
2. EU Commission Strategy Paper: *Regular Reports from the Commission on Progress towards Accession by each of the candidate countries*, 8 November 2000, p. 14. *http://www. europa.eu.int/comm/enlargement/report__11__00/index.htm* (visited 8 February 2001).
3. For a list of the *acquis* chapter headings used in the screening of applicant States see *http://www.europa.eu.int/comm/enlargement/negotiations/screen__en.htm* [visited 8 February 2001].
4. Six countries (Cyprus, Estonia, Hungary, the Czech Republic, Poland and Slovenia) began negotiations on 31 March 1998 and are hoping to be admitted as soon as possible. Six other countries have been negotiating since 15 February 2000. Latvia, Malta and Slovakia are the strongest candidates, followed by Lithuania, whilst Bulgaria and Rumania are lagging behind. A thirteenth possibility is Turkey which has so far not taken up detailed negotiations.
5. SNP Scottish Parliamentary Group, 11 December 2000.
6. SNP Manifesto for the European Parliament Elections 1999.
7. See generally Clark (1999), Happold (2000), Jeffery (2000).
8. Address by the leader of the SNP John Swinney to the Scottish European Association in Brussels, entitled 'Independent Scotland in EU Partnership', 6 November 2000.
9. In 'Memorandum of Understanding and supplementary agreements', Cm. 4444, October 1999; superseded by Cm. 4806, July 2000.
10. Paragraphs B1.3–B1.4.
11. 'Nice Uncle Gerhard and the little "uns"', *The Economist*, 3 February 2001, p. 44.
12. *http://news.bbc.co.uk/hi/english/uk/scotland/newsid__845000/845039.stm* [visited 2 February 2001].
13. 'EU aid for Scotland "goes astray"', *The Independent*, 2 June 1999.

14. European Committee, 6th Report (2000), *Report of the Inquiry into European Structural Funds and their Implementation in Scotland*, Scottish Parliament, Edinburgh.
15. Various figures are found in the literature on Structural Funding. The divergences stem mainly from converting euros (which is the default currency for Structural Funds) into pound sterling. The figures used here stem from the *Scotland in Europe* brochure by the European Commission and from the European Commission's *Highlands and Islands Special Transitional Objective 1 Programme 2000–2006* (June 2000).
16. Ibid. Paragraph 43.
17. Ibid. Paragraph 45.
18. Ibid. Paragraph 52.
19. This in turn assumes the existence of a homogenous 'Nordic bloc'. In fact, the Nordic countries often compete for national interests amongst themselves. The common (outside) perception of a Nordic community is seen as a myth and an illusion.

CHAPTER 9

Scotland in the World

– INTRODUCTION –

An independent Scotland will not just be part of Europe but will also play a part in the world. It is unlikely to be an isolationist state. It will want to play an active part in international organisations and be party to many multilateral treaties. It is worth recalling what the main international organisations are. Other than the European Union, the most important ones are:

- the United Nations;
- the Council of Europe;
- the North Atlantic Treaty Organisation;
- the Commonwealth;
- the World Trade Organisation;
- the Organisation for Security and Co-operation in Europe;
- the Organisation for Economic Co-operation and Development; and
- the International Monetary Fund and the World Bank.

The question is whether Scotland will automatically be a member of all the above organisations and a party to the multilateral treaties to which the United Kingdom is bound, or whether it will need to apply for membership of the organisations and take steps to become party to the multilateral treaties. It should be noted that bilateral treaties raise different questions and will be dealt with separately.

But first, any question of treaty succession must take account of the historical and geographical facts. The Union has lasted for nigh on 300 years and although Scotland has retained its own legal system the ties with the rest of the United Kingdom are very strong and close. It is hard to conceive of treaty succession being a particularly difficult task when both nations have belonged to the same state for such a long period of time and have helped shape a highly developed Union. The international community has no incentive to create difficulties with respect to state succession to treaties. Even in the case of a much younger state such as Czechoslovakia that was founded in 1918, when it dissolved treaty succession was not particularly difficult or contentious. All parties involved wanted the process to be as smooth and as speedy as possible.

– The rules for state succession to treaties –

For the reasons discussed in Chapter 6 the Vienna Convention on State Succession in Respect of Treaties (1978; henceforth the Convention) cannot be relied upon as a statement of the law on this subject. The Convention binds only its 17 parties (out of some 190 possible parties). Although some states have relied upon some of its provisions in recent years, it is going too far to suggest that the Convention reflects customary law. More important is the practice since 1978, particularly with the break-up of states of central and eastern Europe. Only a few general principles can be identified with reasonable certainty, and they will be discussed below in the context of Scotland's secession.

Problems arise in practice because the birth and death of states is not a regular occurrence and takes several quite different forms. It is nearly always the result of events which are politically sensitive at the least. The founding of new states was seen in Latin America in the early nineteenth century, in Eastern Europe after the First World War, during the decolonisation process of the 1960s and 1970s and, finally, after the dismemberment of the USSR and Yugoslavia. The law surrounding these new states evolved on a case by case basis. The states created were marked by their distinctive historical and geo-political context and attracted inconsistent state practices.

It is therefore difficult in the extreme, some say impossible, to formulate abstract and universal rules governing state succession (O'Connell 1979). State practice confirms that there is no singular approach with respect to treaty succession. Edwin D. Williamson and John E. Osborn, former Legal Advisor and former Special Assistant to the Legal Advisor respectively at the US Department of State, contend that:

at one end of the continuum, where a portion of the state breaks away from the primary, predecessor state, the practice tends to support a 'clean slate' approach. At the other extreme, where a state divides into its constituent parts, the practice supports continuity of existing treaty rights and obligations (Williamson and Osborn 1993: 263).

There are various ways of analysing state succession: either one approaches the issue by examining general practice (as Williamson and

Osborn propose), or by analysing the nature of the individual treaty in question, or one does both.

– General practice –

Williamson and Osborn (Ibid. pp. 263–4) list examples where treaty obligations were either continued by the successor state or renounced ('clean slate'). The examples are quite old and are of historical interest only, particularly given the much more recent practice of the 1990s. The newly emerging states were treated as bound by their predecessor's treaty obligations after the following the break–ups:

- the Greater Colombian union, formed between 1820 and 1830, which later dissolved into Colombia, Ecuador and Venezuela;
- the Union of Norway and Sweden (dissolved in 1905);
- the separation of Austria and Hungary in connection with the dissolution of the Austro-Hungarian Empire after World War I;
- the separation of Syria from Egypt in connection with the dissolution of the United Arab Republic.

However, in the case of secessions, the general practice has been to grant the newly emerging state a 'clean slate' to enable a fresh start. Some examples are:

- the secession of Panama from Colombia in 1903 (unlike the USA and the United Kingdom, France was not prepared to grant a 'clean slate' to Panama);
- the secession of Finland from the Soviet Union after World War I;
- the separation of Poland and Czechoslovakia from the Austro-Hungarian Empire after World War I (though the 'core' states of Austria and Hungary were deemed to succeed to the existing rights and obligations);
- the secession of Pakistan from India in 1947 (though it was held to certain treaty terms under a devolution agreement).

As can be seen, state practice reveals divergent approaches and is therefore inconclusive. The first set of cases tends to suggest that, in the unlikely event that the United Kingdom were to dissolve upon Scottish independence, then both countries (Scotland and rUK) would succeed to the United Kingdom's treaty obligations. It was argued in Chapter 5 that, notwithstanding the loss of about 5 million people and some territory, the United Kingdom would continue as a state. The situation is analogous with that of the Soviet Union. Although it lost proportionally more territory and more population, the international community nonetheless regarded Russia as the continuation of the Soviet Union. In other words, the state remained the same even though the name changed. The United Kingdom of Great Britain and Northern Ireland stems from the union of Great Britain (England, Wales, and Scotland) with Ireland following the 1801 Act of Union – not the previous Act of Union with Scotland which produced Great Britain.

The second set of cases tends to suggest that, if Scotland were to secede, then Scotland would not be bound by any treaties which currently affect its territory – it would start independence with a 'clean slate'.

Neither approach seems to be satisfactory. For a start neither approach distinguishes multilateral from bilateral treaties. Moreover, the all or nothing method fails to take account of the nature of treaties. Some bilateral treaties which the United Kingdom has concluded affect only (or primarily) Scotland – such as oil exploration treaties with Norway. Why should they not continue? Other treaties do not directly affect Scotland at all. Why should they continue? Moreover, treaties establishing membership of international organisations cannot be governed by abstract and general rules of treaty succession. It is thus imperative to look at the nature of treaties in order to understand their fate if and when Scotland becomes independent. This is discussed in the following section.

– Nature of the treaty –

The second way to ascertain the fate of a treaty is by classifying it. The rules of succession differ depending on whether the treaty is bilateral, multilateral or whether it establishes an international organisation.

Bilateral treaties

A bilateral treaty has only two parties – in this case the United Kingdom and a foreign state. Upon Scottish independence, the question in respect of each of such treaties would be not only whether Scotland would remain or wish to be bound by the treaty, but whether the foreign state would be bound or wish to be bound. Recent practice suggests that this is essentially a matter for agreement between the new state and each foreign state. This could potentially be done on an ad hoc basis as and when the problem arises. A more systematic but time-consuming way would be to comb through all the bilateral treaties and agreeing which should continue to bind the new state and the foreign state. Within the bilateral category of treaties it is necessary to establish whether the treaty in question is:

- purely political: the treaty will terminate upon the demise of the state;
- 'localised' or 'dispositive': the treaty will remain in force; or
- a bilateral trade agreement: the treaty has to be modified through negotiations by the parties to meet changed circumstances.

It is acknowledged that these three categories cover only a fraction of the normal range but they are most relevant for an independent Scotland. (For a more detailed analysis of the various options see: Aust 2000: Chapter 22.) The three different kinds of treaties will be addressed in turn.

1. *Political treaties*: Political treaties govern the political and economic status of the individual state and include alliances, military pacts, treaties of friendship, treaties of union, and treaties of economic integration. These are treaties that are rooted in the distinctiveness of the political and economic order of the state at the time of conclusion and are not presumed to continue upon the demise of the state. This category of treaty is relatively uncontroversial. As Anthony Aust, who is Deputy Legal Adviser at the Foreign and Commonwealth Office in London, states:

   > A new state does not succeed automatically to a treaty if the subject matter is closely linked to the relations of the predecessor state with the other party (it will usually, but not always, be a bilateral treaty) (Aust 2000: 307).

   Extradition and mutual legal assistance treaties are the sort of treaties which a new state and a third state would wish to continue. They are examples of technical treaties which are not usually subject to the political relations with the third state. Particularly in the case of Scotland, the other parties would probably want these sort of treaties to continue in force.

2. *Localised or Dispositive treaties*: Some treaties are called 'localised' or 'dispositive' because they run with the land and are unaffected by changes of sovereignty. Examples of such treaties are those that create international servitudes (like navigation rights on rivers), and boundaries.[1] These treaties create real rights of an *erga omnes* character. Aust makes the following assertion, although he adds that the exact extent of the principle is not as well established as the principle itself:

   > A new state will succeed, without any action by it, to treaties (or at least to the legal situation created by them) relating to matters such as the status of territory, boundaries or the navigation of rivers (Aust 2000: 307).

3. *Commercial treaties*: Commercial treaties and other trade agreements are generally entered into over a substantial period of time and involve long-term investment and calculations. These generate certain expectations between the parties which cannot be ignored when the question of state succession is being dealt with. It is very questionable whether the other party would wish these to continue without at least some renegotiations.

Multilateral treaties

In comparison, multilateral treaties are easier since, in most cases, the other parties will have no objection to the new state becoming a party. The main exceptions are treaties establishing international organisations, when a new state in the position of Scotland would have to apply for membership.

With respect to multilateral treaties, succession by the new state will generally not be automatic. But it will not be particularly difficult either. The recent case of Slovenia illustrates this well. On 6 July 1992 Slovenia informed the UN Secretariat that it was a successor state and considered itself bound by the international human rights treaties of the former Yugoslavia. It thus became a party to the treaties from the date of its recognition as an independent state and not, as the treaties provide, several months after deposit of an instrument of accession (see generally Aust 2000: 321).

The important point to note is that succession to treaties was not automatic in this case or with regard to other multilateral treaties. According to the UN Office of Legal Affairs the Secretary General, in exercising depositary functions for the 517 multilateral treaties that are deposited with him, would not automatically list Scotland as being party to a treaty which the United Kingdom was a party to. Entries for Scotland would be included in 'Multilateral Treaties Deposited with the Secretary General' (a publication known internally as 'the Bible') as and when Scotland performs its own treaty actions.

Among other active steps, Scotland could deposit notifications of succession in respect of treaties which the United Kingdom had ratified (or by which it had otherwise consented to be bound) before the date of Scottish independence. If such notifications passed without objection from the United Kingdom or from other contracting parties, this would ensure its continued entitlement to existing treaty rights and obligations. Such notifications have to be made specifically for each treaty. A Scottish Government would, therefore, have to notify the UN Secretariat (or other depositary) of its intention to succeed to those treaties. Often notification is forgotten because of other priorities for a newly independent state.

We argue in this book that an independent Scotland would emerge, not from secession, but from a grant of independence by the United Kingdom. Whether an international treaty would bind Scotland is a complex matter. One has to distinguish between (a) the new state being bound because the treaty in question has become customary law, and (b) Scotland being bound as a treaty matter. Typical examples of treaties that are generally regarded as being already binding on new states as a matter of customary law are:

- the Vienna Convention on Diplomatic Relations;[2]
- the Vienna Convention on Consular Relations;[3]
- the Genocide Convention;[4]
- the Geneva Conventions of 1949; and
- the Vienna Convention on the Law of Treaties 1969.

A list of the parties to the Vienna Convention on Diplomatic Relations can be found in Denza 1998: Appendix 2, which is based upon the UN Secretary General 'Bible'. If a state has seceded from a state which is a party to the Vienna Convention, the new state is not listed by the Secretary General unless he receives a declaration of secession. Then again, that Convention has become customary law (Ibid. p. 6) and so would be binding on Scotland in any event. There are important practical consequences resulting from this. As Aust points out:

> even if the new state is bound by customary rules reflected in a human rights treaty rather than the treaty itself . . . [t]he state will not have the right to attend meetings of the states parties. Nor will it be under any obligation to report to any monitoring body established by the treaty (Aust 2000: 308).

The point that Aust makes here is that although the new state is bound by customary international law, it will not benefit from certain treaty rights. However, it will also not be under an obligation to, for example, report to a monitoring body established by the treaty. The latter would for some new states be a distinct benefit, though not in the case of Scotland. In order to benefit fully from an international treaty regime, Scotland would have formally to become a party to it.

The European Convention on Human Rights

A special case amongst treaties is the European Convention on Human Rights (ECHR). Aside from containing reciprocal arrangements between states, it also grants rights and freedoms to individuals under its jurisdiction. Scotland's position would be uncertain unless it became a member of the

Council of Europe. By the passing of the Scotland Act, the ECHR was incorporated into Scottish law in the areas of devolved powers. It became binding on the Scottish Executive on 1 July 1999, that is 15 months before the Human Rights Act 1998 came into force in England and Wales. There can be no question that Scotland would wish to be, and would have no problem in being, admitted to the Council of Europe, and therefore becoming a party to the ECHR in its own right.

– Conclusion –

Scottish succession to treaties will not be extraordinarily complicated or contentious. Scotland's ties with England and Wales are so strong and close, having formed a Union for almost 300 years, that it would not be a 'rogue state' in the eyes of the international community were it to become independent. However, the subject of state succession is notoriously complex and the rules are very uncertain. Any problems that arise are likely to be of a practical nature. For a start, there will be an extensive body of treaty law in the event of independence. Scotland would have to decide which treaties it might wish to succeed to from the outset; which treaties it might first want to review before it succeeds or accedes to them; and finally it would have to make sure that the foreign state wants to become or remain a party as well. Depending on the timescale allowed for independence, the task of deciding how to deal with the treaty corpus might not be capable of being completed before independence. In that case, some form of declaration might be a useful holding device.

– INTERNATIONAL ORGANISATIONS –

Membership by a new state to international organisations is generally straightforward: it has to apply to join. A new state cannot simply be added or removed from the list of member states. It will not succeed to membership of an international organisation if the predecessor state continues to exist (Aust 2000: 309). This section will look at two international organisations in order to illustrate Scotland's position post-independence.

– The United Nations –
Membership
The United Nations has a formal admission procedure which is outlined below. Membership of many of the UN specialised agencies requires UN membership.[5]

After the India/Pakistan partition of 1947, the General Assembly's Sixth

(Legal) Committee considered the question what rules should apply to new states that are created by the partition of a state that had been a member of the UN. It concluded:

1. That as a general rule, it is in conformity with legal principles to presume that a state which is a Member of the organization of the United Nations does not cease to be a Member simply because its constitution or its frontier have been subjected to changes, and that the extinction of the state as a legal personality recognised in the international order must be shown before its rights and obligations can be considered thereby to have ceased to exist.
2. That when a new state is created, whatever may be the territory and the populations which it comprises and whether or not they formed part of a state Member of the United Nations, it cannot under the system of the Charter claim the status of a Member of the United Nations unless it has been formally admitted as such in conformity with the provisions of the Charter.

Beyond that, each case must be judged according to its merits.[6]

Two issues are made clear:

- membership to the UN does not cease on grounds of constitutional alterations;
- succession to membership of international organisations is not possible (see also Mullerson 1993: 477–8).

New states formed from the territory of existing members have to apply. The normal procedure for admission to membership in the United Nations is set out in Article 4 of the UN Charter which states:

1. Membership in the United Nations is open to all other peace-loving states which accept the obligations contained in the present Charter and, in the judgement of the organisation, are able and willing to carry out these obligations.
2. The admission of any such state to membership in the United Nations will be effected by a decision of the General Assembly upon the recommendation of the Security Council.

As regards UN membership, international practice too underlines the assertion that it would not be automatic for Scotland. On consensual separation from Singapore from Malaysia in 1965, Malaysia remained within the UN whilst Singapore had to apply for membership. When Pakistan separated from India in 1947, India retained UN membership whilst Pakistan had to apply; and when Bangladesh seceded from Pakistan it was Bangladesh that had to apply whilst Pakistan's membership continued. Likewise, after the dissolution of the USSR, Russia continued to represent the other republics (with their consent) in the UN. The other successor states (not including Belarus and the Ukraine who had been members of the UN from the beginning)[7] had to apply for membership. In 1993 Eritrea seceded from Ethiopia and had to apply for UN membership whereas Ethiopia remained a member.

Practice differs where a state fragments in such a way that none of the new states has a clear claim, either on the basis of territory or of population, to be the 'continuation' of the fragmented state. For example, on the dissolution of Czechoslovakia in 1992 which resulted in the creation of two new sovereign states (the Czech Republic and Slovakia) both states applied to the UN and were admitted as new members on 19 January 1993. After Yugoslavia broke up, Serbia and Montenegro had claimed to be the successor state of Yugoslavia and that membership was theirs by right but this claim was considered spurious by the international community. The Yugoslav situation was radically different from the break-up of the Soviet Union, largely because of widespread and serious acts of aggression in violation of the UN Charter. With the passing of Resolution 777 of 19 December 1992,[8] Serbia/Montenegro were in effect excluded from partaking in the United Nations as the continuation of Yugoslavia. The Socialist Federal Republic of Yugoslavia had dissolved and the Federal Republic of Yugoslavia (Serbia and Montenegro) was not its successor for the purposes of UN membership. The other successor states (Slovenia, Croatia, Bosnia-Herzegovina and Macedonia) applied and were accepted for membership. After eight years of diplomatic impasse the Federal Republic of Yugoslavia was accepted as a new member of the UN as one of Yugoslavia's successor states by a General Assembly resolution of 1 November 2000.[9]

The above is relevant as regards the United Kingdom post Scottish independence and Scotland's position in Europe. It suggests that the United Kingdom of Great Britain and Northern Ireland (without Scotland) would be regarded as the continuing state, with the same international legal personality as the current United Kingdom, for the purposes of membership to UN. To elaborate on the Russia example: when Russia succeeded the USSR it was recognised by other states as the continuation of the former Soviet Union. This was due to political reasons that were related to the stability of the world order and the importance of guaranteed continuity of the Soviet Union's treaty obligations. The other permanent members of the Security Council did not want to question its permanent membership. The international community chose to accept that Russia formally continued the international rights and obligations of the USSR. This is likely to be the case with respect to the rUK too, partly but not solely because rUK would still be a nuclear power.

But, like Russia, the rUK's rights and obligations will be affected despite continuation. Russia is not able to meet the treaty obligations of the USSR with respect to the Baltic Sea as it has lost much of the coastline (Mullerson 1993: 478). The rUK may lose considerable amount of power over the North Sea. Absorption or secession of territory does not in itself determine the continuity of the state, but may well affect its power to perform its treaty obligations.

The Security Council

As was seen above, most of the time membership of international organisations entails rights and duties, and sometimes even special privileges such as permanent membership in the UN Security Council. Upon the demise of the USSR it was not assumed that Russia alone would inherit the seat (Blum 1992). The reason it did is due to a number of sound factors, part objective and part subjective in nature:

1. Russia is substantially bigger than any of the other successor states of the USSR. Both in terms of landmass and population, it remains one of the largest states in the world.
2. Russia's continuation received the formal backing of the other successor states. In a letter of 24 December 1991 to the Secretary-General of the United Nations, President Yeltsin wrote that, 'membership of the Union of Soviet Socialist Republics in the United Nations, including the Security Council and all other organs and organisations of the United Nations system, is being continued by the Russian Federation (RSFSR) with the support of the Commonwealth of Independent States (CIS)'.[10]
3. There was political agreement amongst the international community that Russia should be in charge of the USSR's rights and obligations.

It is suggested that, for these reasons, the pattern would be repeated in the case of Scottish independence. Since England, Wales and Northern Ireland (and even just England, for that matter) are politically, geographically and demographically dominant, they would continue the international rights and obligations of the United Kingdom on all levels, including the Security Council.

– The International Monetary Fund and the World Bank[11] –

Membership in the IMF is a prerequisite for membership in the World Bank but in practice new applications for membership are generally processed concurrently.[12] From the World Bank's perspective membership is necessary to combine finance with ideas in an effort to raise living standards, alleviate the worst forms of poverty and spread the benefits of economic globalisation to the poor. The first thing to note is that Scotland would be a donor country to and not a receiving country. The countries Scotland most likes to compare itself with (Ireland and Denmark) are both members of the World Bank.

What would be Scotland's incentive to join? Article 1 of the Articles of Agreement of the International Monetary Fund (IMF) sets out its purposes:

1. To promote international monetary cooperation through a permanent institution which provides the machinery for consultation and collaboration on international and monetary problems.
2. To facilitate the expansion and balanced growth of international trade, and to contribute thereby to the promotion and maintenance of high levels of employment and real income and to the development of the productive resources of all members as primary objectives of economic policy.
3. To promote exchange stability, to maintain orderly exchange arrangements among members, and to avoid competitive exchange depreciation.
4. To assist in the establishment of a multilateral system of payments in respect of current transactions between members and in the elimination of foreign exchange restrictions which hamper the growth of world trade.
5. To give confidence to members by making the general resources of the Fund temporarily available to them under adequate safeguards, thus providing them with opportunity to correct maladjustments in their balance of payments without resorting to measures destructive of national or international prosperity.
6. In accordance with the above, to shorten the duration and lessen the degree of disequilibrium in the international balances of payments of members.

The structure of the Bank
The World Bank Group is made up of five organisations:[13]

1. The International Bank for Reconstruction and Development (IBRD), which provides, 'loans and development assistance to middle-income countries and creditworthy poorer countries. Voting power is linked to members' capital subscriptions, which in turn are based on each country's relative economic strength. The IBRD is not a profit-maximising organisation but has earned a net income every year since 1948.'
2. The International Finance Corporation (IFC); whose mission is, 'to promote private sector investment in developing countries, which will reduce poverty and improve people's lives.'[14]
3. The International Development Association (IDA), whose goal is to provide, 'long-term loans at zero interest to the poorest of the developing countries. The mission of IDA is to support efficient and effective programs to reduce poverty and improve the quality of life in its poorest member countries.'
4. The Multilateral Investment Guarantee Agency (MIGA); their mission is, 'to enhance the flow to developing countries of capital and technology for productive purposes under conditions consistent with their developmental needs, policies and objectives, on the basis of fair and stable standards for the treatment of foreign investment.'[15]
5. The International Centre for the Settlement of Disputes (ICSID). 'The Bank's overriding consideration in creating ICSID was the belief that an institution specially designed to facilitate the settlement of investment disputes between governments and foreign investors could help to promote increased flows of international investment.'

In March 2001, the IBRD had 182 members, IDA had 161, the IFC had 174, MIGA had 154 and ICSID had 133.[16] The main co-ordinating body for membership issues is the Membership and Capital Subscriptions Unit of the Corporate Secretariat (henceforth the Unit), and would thus be the first port of call for an independent Scotland. The Unit is responsible for communications to and from the applicant country regarding membership formalities, for example amounts of proposed capital subscriptions and required payments and documentation. It prepares a draft membership resolution and a report recommending adoption of the resolution which contains the terms and conditions of the applicant country's membership to the Executive Board, and with the Board's approval, to the Board of Governors for a vote.

Procedure

According to the Fund's Articles of Agreement, admission to membership in the Fund requires an application for membership, as well as two decisions by the Board of Governors: one on membership and another on the country's quota in the Fund. In practice, only one resolution is presented covering the two points. The same also holds true in the Bank. The powers to admit new members and to determine the quotas of these new members are bestowed directly on the Board of Governors and cannot be delegated.[17]

When a member of an international financial organisation breaks up, the two key questions are: what becomes of the membership of the predecessor state, and what becomes of the assets and debts of the predecessor State (see Williams 1994: 784)?

Continuation

In a continuation case the general rule is that the part that secedes from a Member State has to apply for membership in the IMF (and the World Bank) as a new member – provided it wants to be a member. The original member, on the other hand, maintains its subscriptions to shares of the Bank's capital. It should be noted that the Bank does not have the power to reduce a member's share unilaterally, that is without the state's consent.

The continuing state (rUK) thus remains a member with its subscription to shares of the Bank's capital intact. The Board of Governors decides on membership applications by simple majority of votes cast. The rUK would be held liable for the debt obligations of the predecessor state, and Scotland would be held liable for territorial debt, if the United Kingdom was a debtor to the bank – which it is not.[18] This is a straightforward application of the principles that apply in continuation cases, which are exemplified by the separation of Pakistan from India in 1947 and of Bangladesh from Pakistan in 1971.

Political criteria

The cases of Yugoslavia and Czechoslovakia are interesting and intricate. They saw the introduction of political criteria by the IMF in addition to the legal hurdles set by international law. The IMF agreed to a form of 'conditional succession', which was not followed in the case of the World Bank. In essence:

> The succession aspect of the approach was born out of the desire to preserve the assets of successor states, while the conditional aspect was born out of the political desire to exclude the participation of Serbia/Montenegro, and the financial desire to provide for complete assumption of debt obligations by the predecessor states (Williams 1994: 807).

The successor states of federations were permitted to succeed to membership of the IMF, provided that they met certain conditions. The important point to note is that succession to membership was not automatic. It was permitted in these instances because the respective predecessor state had ceased to exist for the purposes of membership. It is clear that dissolution cases would be treated differently from the case of secession of one or more states from the predecessor state. Were Scotland to withdraw from the United Kingdom it could not succeed to membership of the IMF but would have to apply.

What worries Williams is not so much the introduction of political conditions but, 'the arbitrary and inconsistent approach taken by the IMF and World Bank with regard to the imposition of those conditions' (Ibid.). The conditions were designed to exclude Serbia/Montenegro and were not applied even-handedly to all Yugoslav successor states. This case by case approach has potential ramifications for an independent Scotland. As Williams concludes:

> The dangers involved with this approach are that Serbia/Montenegro, or any future successor state faced with similarly inconsistent conditions, might successfully contend before an arbitration tribunal that it has been unjustly precluded from the right to succeed to the membership and assets of the predecessor state, and therefore should not be deemed liable for any portion of the debts of the predecessor state (1994: 808).

Besides the division of assets and liabilities a further question for Scotland is whether it could be kept out of the World Bank Group. Unanimity is normally required – including here the consent of rUK. But the inconsistent approach of the IMF makes predictions problematic. Might a sizeable majority also be sufficient to accept a new member?

In practice, if a major existing shareholder raises objections with respect to the applicant state, it is doubtful that the other members will pursue the application regardless. If the objecting state manages to win over other members, then according to insiders at the World Bank, a forced vote would be ineffective.

– Conclusion –

The general consensus is that if Scotland were to secede rUK would continue in its current form, albeit with reduced territory and population. The situation is similar to Bangladesh splitting from Pakistan: the parent state continues its existence as well as the rights and obligations in force except for localised/dispositive rights that run with the seceded land (see generally Shaw 1997: 677).

General theory of state succession is positively unhelpful. There is no clear winner in the contest between the 'clean slate' theory and the 'automatic succession' theory. The general 'clean slate' principle enunciated in Article 34 of the Vienna Convention is not supported by state practice and should not be regarded as evidence of customary international law on succession to treaties. As for automatic succession:

> the practice of state succession has confirmed that the automatic acceptance of obligations of predecessor states (except perhaps universal treaties) is often impossible (Mullerson 1993: 493).

With respect to local border treaties, for instance, Scotland will not have a choice but to take on United Kingdom's existing rights and obligations. But Scotland could enter into new treaties on taxation, aviation and a host of other issues.

Aside from the EU, the UN and the IMF there are numerous other bodies and treaties that an independent Scotland might wish to join – the United Kingdom itself is party to almost 13,000 treaties.[19] The treaties which Scotland would automatically be bound by and those where there would be an element of choice depend either on Scotland's decision whether to accept the obligations, or on the other parties as to whether they should accept Scotland. The former Director of the United Nations Legal Department Oscar Schachter suggests that there be a presumption in favour of succession to treaties:

> A presumption of continuity would enable [new States] to maintain rights and obligations generally. In the absence of that presumption, they may forego their rights and be heedless of obligations that call for action. For this reason, among others, it makes good sense for states to accept prima facie continuity as a basic premise, leaving room for adjustment or exceptions when they appear necessary or desirable in a particular case (Schachter 1993: 260).

Since international stability is the key, it seems likely that Scotland will accept the United Kingdom's responsibilities, at least on a temporary basis, until it has decided which treaties to continue. This process too will require time and effort.

- Treaty succession will not be a particularly difficult task. But the rules of succession differ depending on whether the treaty is bilateral, multilateral or whether it establishes an international organisation.
- Membership to the UN does not cease on grounds of constitutional alterations. The rUK will continue to be a member of the UN and will retain its seat in the Security Council.
- Succession to membership of international organisations is not possible. It is imperative to look at the organisation–specific rules and conditions of membership. An independent Scotland will have to apply to join the UN.
- An independent Scotland would neither begin its life without any treaty obligations nor will it be bound by *all* the obligations of the United Kingdom.

– NOTES –

1. The ICJ recognised automatic succession to boundary treaties in the territorial dispute between Burkina Faso and Mali, where it held that, 'there is no doubt that the obligation to respect pre-existing international frontiers in the event of a State Succession derives from a general rule of international law whether or not the formula is expressed in the formula of *uti possidetis*'. Judgement of 22 December 1986, ICJ Reports 1986, *Case Concerning the Frontier Dispute (Burkina Faso/Republic of Mali)* at 556.
2. 18 April 1961, 23 U.S.T. 3227, T.I.A.S. No. 7502, 500 U.N.T.S. 95.
3. 24 April 1963, 21 U.S.T. 77, T.I.A.S. No. 6820, 596 U.N.T.S. 261.
4. Convention on the Prevention and Punishment of the Crime of Genocide, 9 December 1948, 78 U.N.T.S 277.
5. See for instance United Nations Educational, Scientific and Cultural Organisation (UNESCO) Article II (1); International Labour Organisation (ILO) Chapter I, Article 1(3) of their respective Constitutions.
6. See (1947–8) U.N.Y.B. pp. 39–40.
7. At the Crimean Conference (February 1945) the Heads of the Governments of Great Britain, USA and USSR there was agreed that the USSR would be represented in the international security organisation by two more of sixteen Soviet Republics: Belarusia and the Ukraine. The Resolution of the Constituent Conference (San Francisco, April–June 1945) about the inclusion of the Ukrainian SSR and the Belarus SSR as original members of the United Nations became a decisive factor for the Republics to enter the international scene as a subject of international law.
8. UN Doc. S/RES/777 (1992).
9. Resolution A/RES/55/12.
10. (1992) 31 I.L.M. 138; cited in Mullerson (1993: 477).
11. See generally Williams (1994), Shihata (1999) and
    http://www.worldbank.org/html/extdr/about/members/unit.htm
    http://www.worldbank.org/html/extdr/about/members/generalinfo.htm [visited 12 February 2001].
12. World Bank Articles of Agreement, Article II(1)(b).
13. See generally *http://www.worldbank.org* [visited 6 March 2001]; unless otherwise stated.
14. *http://www.ifc.org/* [visited 6 March 2001].
15. *http://www.miga.org/* [visited 6 March 2001].

16. *http://www.worldbank.org/html/extdr/about/members/* [visited 6 March 2001].
17. Articles II(2), III(1) and XII(2)(b).
18. The United Kingdom had no outstanding borrowings as of 31 December 2001: *http://www.imf.org/np/tre/tad/exfin2.cfm?memberKey1 = 1010* [visited 12 February 2001].
19. According to Foreign and Commonwealth Office figures, the UK was party to approximately 10,005 bilateral and 2,812 multilateral treaties in January 2001.

Part Three: The Economics of Independence

Peter Jones

CHAPTER 10

Scotland at the Starting Line

– INTRODUCTION –

It may seem absurd to start with a statement of the glaringly obvious: an independent Scotland does not exist. But the obvious may at times be a little obscure, especially as such things as Scottish politics, the Scottish economy, and the Scottish nation are commonly discussed. In dealing with the economics of independence, the starting point has to be that the existing Scotland is a Scotland within the United Kingdom of Great Britain and Northern Ireland. Politically and economically, this Scotland is highly integrated within the UK. While much political decision-making has been devolved to the Scottish Parliament since 1999, economic decision-making is not devolved. A description can be made of something which may be called the Scottish economy, but economic Scotland is still part of an economic unitary state. Economic activity in Scotland is governed by the same monetary, fiscal and regulatory regimes as is the rest of the UK.

The point of independence, of course, is to change this. Independence would have little meaning if it were not. There are, however, constraints on how much might be changed. Mobility of people and capital constrains all governments' abilities to operate economic policies which differ markedly from their trading partners. The global trend at the start of the twenty-first century towards economic liberalisation and openness encourages convergence, and is in complete contrast to early twentieth century trends towards protectionism and economic divergence. The existence of such institutions as the EU, of which an independent Scotland might be a member, further constrains differentiation. For example, corporate taxation rates in the EU have tended to both fall and converge in recent decades (KPMG 2001).

Nevertheless, the EU does tolerate some fiscal variation: low corporate taxation in Ireland, high indirect taxation in Scandinavia, a range of fuel and alcohol duties, and so on. There are different business regulatory regimes within the EU single market. Thus an independent Scotland could be a different Scotland, different from the rest of the UK (rUK) and the EU.

Whether this different Scotland would be an economic success or failure is outwith the scope of this study. The aim of this study is to draw together what is known about the economics of the existing Scotland and to point out obvious gaps in that knowledge. It is also to note what economic information might be inferred about an independent Scotland and the limits of such an extrapolation. The main limitation is, of course, the fact that the existing Scotland cannot be assumed to be similar to an independent Scotland.

– Is Scotland a viable country? –

Working out whether an independent Scotland would be rich or poor in comparison to its current economic condition as part of the UK is an extremely hazardous, if not impossible, task. Such a calculation has four main elements.

1. An assessment has to be made of current assets and liabilities, both in capital and revenue terms, covering both the public and private sectors. A public sector which was too large to be sustained by current tax revenues from the private sector would present problems. It would necessitate either privatisation of public assets or cuts in the public sector, and/or increases in private sector taxation, in order to produce a sustainable economy. Conversely, if private sector tax revenues were larger than those currently consumed by the public sector, there would be scope to cut taxes or to increase the size of the public sector.

2. An assessment of the costs and benefits likely to be incurred by the process of moving to independence. Two main types of costs would affect the public sector: those incurred by the need to add on functions, such as defence, which Scotland does not have at the moment; and those incurred by the need to disentangle the Scottish element of such UK-wide bodies such as the Inland Revenue. There will be off-setting benefits, of which the most obvious is obtaining control of offshore oil and gas resources. Similarly there will be costs and benefits affecting the private sector. Even without any change being made to the taxation system, companies which operate across the Scottish–rUK border would have to adjust their structures to cope with the fact that there would be a new government to deal with on such matters as company law.

3. An assessment of whether Scottish standards of living would be better or worse than at present. Much of this evaluation would be built on the previous two assessments. It is, in many ways, the acid economic test of independence, as individuals are likely to form their own opinion on the merits or otherwise of independence from the available evidence on how their own economic circumstances would be affected.

4. An assessment of the dynamic effect that independence might have. The economic position that an independent Scotland might be in at Day One is only part of the equation. This static position says little about what the economy might look like at Day 100 or Day 1,000. It is beyond the scope of this study to recommend particular policy actions. All it sets out to do is to indicate the elbow room that a Scottish government might have and hence the scope for deploying various policy instruments.

Making these calculations with any precision gets progressively more difficult as one moves to the third and fourth assessments. The quality of available information declines markedly, raising the risk of minor errors compounding each other, leading to major errors in the final calculation. A further problem is that any such calculation will be affected by highly variable factors whose precise effects cannot be forecast.

One such factor is whether the independence negotiations are conducted with goodwill or on an antagonistic basis. With goodwill, negotiations could be fairly short and, if an amicable outcome was the stated aim of both parties, uncertainty would be minimised. The degree of uncertainty has economic importance, for the greater it is, the more it affects such things as business confidence and investment. Because the Scottish economy is much smaller than the rUK economy, a prolonged period of uncertainty which reduces investment would be much more against Scotland's than rUK's economic interest. Knowing this, a rUK government could choose to prolong the negotiations and suggest that there are many difficulties. This would apply pressure to the Scottish negotiators, strengthening the rUK government's hand in trying to secure the best deal possible for rUK taxpayers. Against such a threat, the Scottish negotiators' hand would not be entirely empty. Major international businesses with substantial existing investment in Scotland, such as the major oil companies, would not wish the new Scottish economic and political environment to be much worse than the old UK environment, and might therefore be expected to apply pressure aimed at encouraging a swift outcome.

Another factor, which is entirely outwith political control, is whether the general economic environment is good or bad. If the negotiations were held during a global economic boom, international companies with Scottish interests would be more likely to be relaxed about independence. Scottish-based companies could also be expected to be less nervous. A further consideration is that the new Scottish government, like all governments, would have to borrow money. The better the economic wind, the lower the interest rates that it would have to pay although, compared to the rates the UK government pays, Scotland would have to pay a small risk premium in the initial years at least. This premium, the cost of which would fall on taxpayers, would vary according to the policies adopted. Setting up a separate currency would push the risk premium up; joining the euro would pull it down. It would also vary according to the global economic climate. In adverse times, business would be extremely nervous about independence as would the international money markets. Then, the price of independence could be quite high.

– SCOTLAND'S WEALTH –

The unpredictability of these factors means that the assessment of the economics of independence cannot be precise. A range of possible outcomes, from best case to worst case, is all that can be produced. How wide is that range? It need not be excessively wide. In European terms, Scotland is neither as poor as Greece or Portugal, nor as rich as Switzerland. By world standards, Scotland has a well-educated population, a respected legal system, is richly endowed with excellent universities and many other civic institutions, has a strong financial industry, and has a long democratic tradition with an uncorrupted political class.

It also has substantial natural resources. Chief among these are offshore oil and gas resources. No British government has ever sought to argue that these assets would not be part of an independent Scotland's inheritance. There might be an argument about where the marine boundary lies, and perhaps even a question mark over whether Shetland and the oil and gas in its offshore waters (a large part of offshore production) would be a part of an independent Scotland. But in the absence of a principled argument, this analysis assumes that Scotland would gain control of most of Britain's current offshore resources.

Indeed, the SNP repeatedly assert that Scotland would be among the world's richest countries. 'Overall, Scotland's balance sheet as a percentage of GDP – wealth created per head – is the healthiest in the EU, and across Europe as a whole second only to Norway' (SNP 2001a: 13). The claim stems from a reply to a question asked by the SNP of the House of Commons Library.[1]

The SNP asked where Scotland would appear in a list of OECD countries ranked by GDP per capita; in other words, how wealthy an independent Scotland would be in comparison to other economically developed countries. The answer was that Scotland would be ranked seventh in the world league of rich countries behind (in order of wealth) Luxembourg, the United States, Switzerland, Norway, Japan, and Iceland. It would also be some 20 per cent richer than rUK.

There are some problems with this finding. As the researcher pointed out, it is 'only possible to place Scotland in the list on a rough-and-ready basis' as the GDP data for Scotland are not directly comparable with those used for OECD rankings.[2] The research was also conducted on assumptions supplied by the SNP, a main one being that 90 per cent of North Sea profits should be allocated to Scotland. The reasoning was relatively simple: profits made by companies are one component of GDP but profits from offshore oil and gas activities are presently deemed to accrue to a UK region known as the Continental Shelf (UKCS) and not to any part of the UK mainland. Since most commentators accepted at the time that it was reasonable to consider that 90 per cent of North Sea operations would fall under Scottish authority, the SNP assumption seemed reasonable.

However, subsequent research has shown that this assumption is invalid. The Scottish share of UK oil tax revenues between 1979–98 would have varied from as low as 61 per cent to as high as 98 per cent (Kemp and Stephen 1999). Since much of these tax revenues flow from corporation tax which is levied on profits, it is reasonable to assume that Scotland's share of North Sea profits and thus of North Sea GDP would not be a constant 90 per cent, but would vary similarly. Unfortunately the research did not calculate a theoretical Scottish share of these profits so it is not possible to calculate precisely what an independent Scotland's GDP would be with North Sea oil wealth added in. A precise calculation matters because adding a slightly smaller percentage radically affects the outcome. One independent study found that adding 80 per cent of North Sea wealth would put Scottish per capita GDP ahead of rUK per capita GDP, but moves Scotland only slightly up the international rankings of national per capita GDP (Peat and Boyle 1999: 12).

A further flaw in the GDP question asked by the SNP is that it contained no estimate of the costs of independence noted above. These costs would depress the GDP figure, but again it is not possible to say by how much.

More generally, this GDP calculation is mainly statistical. Even if the SNP were right, and Scottish per capita GDP jumped by 20 per cent on the achievement of independence, individual Scots would not be immediately 20 per cent wealthier. No individual would suddenly have a bigger income or find that their existing income suddenly bought more goods. One reason for this is that the additional GDP is the profit made by oil companies offshore. These profits are mostly repatriated outside the UK, and still would be under independence.

In this respect, Scottish economic statistics would come to resemble those of Ireland, the recent economic performance of which is enviable. In most countries, the outflow of profits repatriated by foreign-owned firms is usually balanced by the inflow of profits from the overseas operations of indigenous firms. Ireland is unusual in that the outflow is much greater than the inflow. If the net flow of profits is added to GDP, the resulting figure is called Gross National Product (GNP). In 1997, Irish GDP was £45.9 billion, but its GNP was £5.6 billion less at £40.3 billion (Sweeney 1998: 46). Arguably, the GNP statistic is a truer representation of Irish economic wealth and indeed the Irish Government has argued that the EU should be using this figure when assessing Ireland's need for European regional aid.

There are no statistics for Scottish GNP. But where independence could eventually make a difference to Scotland would be the diversion of a share of North Sea tax revenues from the UK Treasury to a Scottish treasury. If these were large, it would give a Scottish chancellor scope to consider tax cuts or public spending increases.

– THE ROOM FOR FISCAL MANOEUVRE –

The state of public finances in Scotland – whether public spending is greater or less than the amount of tax revenues raised – has been a hot political topic since 1992 when the Scottish Office (the Scottish Executive since September 1999) published estimates of tax revenues and spending in Scotland for 1990–1 (Scottish Office 1992). The statistics it contained were said by the Conservative Government to be fair and impartial, but were denounced by opposition politicians as suffering from political bias. The figures were produced by government statisticians and the main valid criticism of them, accepted by the statisticians, is that they are estimates rather than collected data. While the Scottish National Party routinely refers to them as 'discredited' (SNP December 2000), the statistics have been produced annually ever since. They have become known as GERS and are accepted by most independent commentators as the best available approximation to Scotland's public sector accounts.

Over the years, the quality of material available to the statisticians has improved. They have also taken account of criticisms of some of their calculations. For example, early GERS publications were said to under-estimate Scottish receipts from the EU because they simply apportioned a pro–rata share of the UK's net contribution to the EU.[3] In the later publications, this underestimate has been corrected (Scottish Executive 2000). The figures for 1998–9 are shown in Figure 10.1.

Figure 10.1. Government expenditure and revenues in Scotland 1998–9.

	SCOTLAND		UNITED KINGDOM		
EXPENDITURE/ REVENUES	£ bn	% share of aggregate expenditure/ revenues	£ bn	% share of aggregate expenditure/ revenues	Scotland as a % share of UK
EXPENDITURE					
1. Identifiable	25.7	77.7	253.2	76.5	10.2
Of which:					
Scottish Executive	15.6	–	–	–	–
Social Security	9.2	–	–	–	–
2. Non-identifiable (est.)	3.2	9.8	37.8	11.4	8.6
3. Other (est.)	4.3	13.1	40.9	12.4	10.6
Of which:					
Debt interest	2.5	–	29.5	–	–
4. Reconciliation	0.1	0.2	–0.9	–0.3	
5. EU Adjustment	–0.27	–0.8	–	–	
Aggregate Expenditure	**33.1**	**100.0**	**331.0**	**100.0**	**10.0**
REVENUES					
Income tax	6.4	22.6	86.4	25.9	7.4
Social Security contribs.	4.7	16.6	55.1	16.5	8.6
Value added tax	4.3	15.2	52.3	15.7	8.2
Local authority revenues	2.5	8.9	27.5	8.2	9.2
All other revenues	10.3	36.5	112.3	33.7	9.1
Aggregate Revenues	**28.2**	**100**	**333.5**	**100**	**8.4**
NET BORROWING	**4.9**	**–**	**–2.5**	**–**	**–**
N.B. as % of GDP	**–**	**7.0**	**–**	**–0.3**	**–**
Note: Population 1998					8.6
GDP 1998					8.3

[Handwritten margin notes: "– srvp would dispute this.", "– higher pay gives SE", "– hits lower paid more", "– company HQ lots in London"]

Source: Scottish Executive, December 2000, 'Government Expenditure and Revenues in Scotland 1998–99', Edinburgh. Taken from Tables 8, 9 and 12.

The headline to be drawn from this Figure is that in 1998–9, a year when the UK as a whole had a fiscal surplus, Scotland had a fiscal deficit. Total public spending in Scotland exceeded Scottish tax revenues by £4.9bn. As this was a year in which the UK had a small fiscal surplus (£2.5bn), it can be assumed that when UK public finances are in balance, Scotland has a fiscal deficit of just over £5.0bn. The main flaw in this analysis is that North Sea oil revenues (and privatisation proceeds) are not included. This is simply because the GERS figures reflect the fact of Scotland's current condition within the UK. But if Scotland were independent, most of the oil revenues would accrue to Scotland. The figures can be adjusted to deal with this, but other criticisms of the GERS figures need to be examined first.

– CRITICISMS OF THE OFFICIAL BALANCE SHEET –

The most sustained critique has come from the SNP. It maintains that the GERS figures, apart from ignoring oil revenues, underestimate revenues and overestimate expenditure. For example, GERS 1995–6 estimates that in that year, Scottish revenues were £23.5bn, spending £30.9bn, giving a fiscal deficit of £7.4bn (Scottish Office 1997: 24). The SNP produced their own figures for 1995–6: revenues of £24.9bn (excluding oil revenues), spending of £28.9bn, giving a deficit of £4.0bn (SNP 1995). A more recent critique (SNP 2000) contends that in the two years 2000–02, Scotland will generate a surplus of £7.7bn of revenues over expenditure. In political terms, Nationalists feel it is important to demonstrate that Scotland does have a fiscal surplus since that is likely to help convince voters that independence is viable, while non-Nationalists feel it is important to show that Scotland gets a good deal within the Union. Where does the balance of the debate lie?

The SNP have a number of criticisms of the GERS figures (SNP 2000). On the revenue side, three of the most important are:

1. EU payments to Scotland are under-estimated. As detailed above, this has been corrected in the most recent GERS reports, so this criticism can be discounted.[4]
2. Income tax receipts are under-estimated. The GERS estimate of income tax raised in Scotland is drawn from the Inland Revenue's Survey of Personal Incomes (SPI) which is a sample of tax liabilities rather than actual tax payments. Because the Scottish part of the sample is small, it produces variable estimates for the Scottish percentage of UK income tax liabilities (from 8.5 per cent in 1995–6 to 9.2 per cent in 1994–5). There is an alternative source: the National Income Statistics survey (NIS). This has a bigger sample and gives less variation in the Scottish share of income tax revenues, but it only measures income from employment and not income, for example, from savings. The SNP compared the PAYE elements of both surveys and noted that the NIS-derived percentage is 0.4 points higher than the SPI-derived percentage. So they contend that the GERS percentage used to estimate Scottish income tax revenue in 1998–9 (7.9 per cent) should be 8.3 per cent. But it appears that the difference noted by the SNP comes from one year only, and that in other years the NIS-derived percentage can be 0.4 per

cent lower than the SPI-derived percentage.[5] The SNP's criticisms gained some force with the publication of GERS 1999–2000 which showed that the Scottish share of income tax receipts had fallen to 7.0 per cent from 8.0 per cent in 1996–7, a surprisingly big reduction. The accompanying text said that economic factors could explain some of the reduction, but the possibility of sampling error could not be discounted.[6] The variability of both the SPI and NIS–derived percentages suggests that neither gives an accurate estimate of income tax receipts, but the SNP version is not robust enough for it to be preferred over the GERS version. Moreover when comparing Scotland to the UK as a whole, it can be noted that in Scotland unemployment rates tend to be higher, average earnings are lower, and the proportion of high rate paying taxpayers is lower. Thus it seems probable that Scotland's percentage share of income tax receipts will be significantly lower than Scotland's 8.6 per cent share of UK population. If it is assumed that Scotlands share of income tax should be 8 per cent, this would add about £500m to the revenue side. Scotland's net borrowing would be cut to £4.4bn or 6.3 per cent of GDP. However, there is no way of knowing if this adjustment is justifiable or not. Better data is needed to produce a more accurate percentage share but until that becomes available, the GERS estimate is the best available.

3. Social security contributions are under-estimated. GERS uses Regional Accounts data to estimate the Scottish share of these as 8.6 per cent of UK revenues. The SNP avers that the NIS survey indicates that the Scottish share should be 9.0 per cent. But the unemployment and earnings factors noted above make this improbable and suggests that even the GERS estimate is too high.

On the expenditure side of the balance sheet, the SNP has two main criticisms to make:

1. Defence spending is over-estimated. GERS allocates a population share (8.6 per cent) of UK defence spending to Scotland. This is done on the premise that Scots receive the same security benefit from defence spending as does every UK citizen. The SNP argues that what matters is actual defence spending in Scotland which they estimate is only 8.0 per cent of the UK total. The argument is irrelevant, as the GERS estimate deals with Scotland as a part of the UK. Even if there were zero actual defence spending in Scotland, Scots would still receive the benefit of being defended by UK armed forces. Under these hypothetical circumstances, an independent Scotland would need to spend

more on defence (and by implication, less on other public services) in order to provide adequate defences. The GERS estimate therefore provides a reasonable proxy figure for what that defence spending might be.

2. National debt interest payments should be excluded. The GERS figures assume that the national debt has been incurred for the benefit of all UK citizens and that therefore Scotland must take a share of it. The SNP argue that this is not the case and that Scotland would take no share of the debt. For reasons set out below (see pp. 204–9), this analysis rejects the SNP argument and accepts the GERS figures.

In summary, neither the GERS figures nor the SNP figures present a totally accurate picture of the current Scottish fiscal balance. The expenditure figures, which are mostly based on actual spending, are more robust than the revenue figures, which are estimates. But on balance the GERS figures appear to be a closer approximation and the SNP figures to be overly optimistic. With the exception of earlier GERS treatment of EU expenditure, neither the SNP nor other commentators have made out a case which would lead to rejection of the GERS figures in favour of other numbers. Broadly speaking, most commentators conclude that GERS 'does provide a very rough indication of the current state of the fiscal balance' (Simpson et al. 1999: 11). One says that 'the GERS figures have not been fiddled, and the judgements made are defensible. The SNP's criticism over income tax receipts and EC funding are subject to the very imprecision they attributed to the report itself' (Midwinter 1998). Therefore, in order to produce a rough indication of the likely fiscal balance in an independent Scotland, the next step would be to add oil revenues to the GERS picture of non–independent Scotland.

– SCOTLAND WITH OIL –

Recent research (Kemp and Stephen 1999) has made the task of adding in oil revenues much easier. They divided the North Sea into Scottish and rUK territories in accordance with international law using the principle of equidistance, that is, that all points on the line are at the same distance from the Scottish and rUK coastline. A case for other lines can be made, but this line 'has much merit on grounds of equity, legality, and precedence' (Kemp and Stephen 1999: 3). Drawing a boundary line under the most favourable circumstances to Scotland makes little difference to the revenue outcomes for Scotland as the oilfields affected have either been exhausted or are close to exhaustion.[7]

The findings were surprising. While, since 1977, more than 90 per cent of offshore production has taken place in Scottish waters, the Scottish share of tax revenues varied from as low as 61 per cent in 1977 to as high as 98 per cent in 1982. This, in essence, is because revenues vary according to the price of oil. When prices are low, taxable profits are low, especially in Scottish waters where the costs of exploration and development (which are offset against tax liabilities) are high. The calculations allow very precise estimates of the Scottish share of North Sea revenues to be added.

Figure 10.2. UK and Scottish fiscal balances, 1979–99 (£bn at 1998–9 prices).

	UK surplus/ Deficit (–) excl. privatisation proceeds and NS revenues	Scottish surplus/ Deficit (–) excl. privatisation proceeds and NS revenues	Total North Sea revenues	Scottish North Sea revenues	Scottish surplus/ Deficit (–) including privatisation proceeds and NS revenues
1979–80	–13.84	–5.41	6.34	5.79	0.61
1980–81	–18.35	–6.87	9.15	8.67	1.90
1981–82	–14.16	–3.42	13.72	13.45	10.22
1982–83	–16.68	–5.33	15.52	15.23	10.06
1983–84	–20.77	–5.60	16.63	16.16	10.90
1984–85	–24.44	–5.43	21.83	20.57	15.69
1985–86	–21.92	–4.98	19.36	18.00	13.67
1986–87	–14.79	–4.89	7.93	7.50	3.61
1987–88	–8.18	–6.11	7.28	6.59	1.51
1988–89	1.57	–4.25	4.69	4.20	1.18
1989–90	0.0	–4.40	3.29	2.81	–0.96
1990–91	–7.45	–5.17	2.99	2.22	–2.24
1991–92	–23.91	–6.00	1.22	0.77	–4.31
1992–93	–49.61	–8.96	1.54	0.99	–7.10
1993–94	–56.11	–9.71	1.38	0.89	–8.25
1994–95	–48.03	–9.13	1.87	1.53	–6.95
1995–96	–42.00	–8.34	2.62	2.08	–6.03
1996–97	–34.19	–7.45	3.79	3.11	–3.94
1997–98	–8.16	–5.20	3.52	2.65	–2.39
1998–99	2.50	–4.90	2.60	1.72	–3.18

Sources: House of Commons Hansard, Written Answers, 25 November 25 1996, Col. 67; Scottish Executive 2000, Table 19; House of Commons Hansard, Written Answers, 8 July 1996; National Statistics Office, June 2001, 'Public Sector Finances', Table PSF4; National Statistics, 2000, 'Inland Revenue Statistics 2000'; Figures for 1979–80 – 1987–8, 1990–1, 1991–2 derived from applying ratios given in House of Commons Hansard, Written Answers, March 21, 1997, Col. 969 to UK GGBR figures, figures for 1992–3 – 1998–9 from GERS series, figures for 1988–90, 1990–1 derived from regression analysis of 1992–3 – 1998–9 UK GGBR/NB and Scottish GGBR/NB figures.

Apart from oil revenues, it is also necessary to add in privatisation proceeds. By convention, these are excluded from calculations of government borrowing requirements. Nonetheless, they are a source of revenue. No precise figures are available of the value of government-owned assets that could be described as Scottish and which have been privatised are available. The convention, used by both GERS and the SNP, is that Scotland's share of UK GDP is used to derive a share of annual privatisation proceeds.

These calculations have been done for the 20 years between 1979–80 and 1998–9. The GERS series cover the years since 1992–3. No similar data is available before that, but a Treasury answer to a parliamentary question provided enough information to enable estimates of the Scottish fiscal balance (excluding privatisation proceeds and North Sea revenues) to be calculated for the years 1979–80 to 1991–2.[8] A note to this answer warns that the estimates prior to 1990–1 are very approximate. For arithmetic reasons, data for 1988–9 and 1989–90 was not published, so estimates for these two years were calculated by regression analysis of the GERS series data. Figure 10.2 shows the results.

The figures show that when oil revenues and privatisation proceeds are excluded, Scotland's public finances have been in deficit over the 20 year period. The biggest deficit is £9.7bn in 1993–4 and the smallest is £3.4bn in 1981–2. But on the same basis, the UK has also been in deficit for all but three of those years. Adding in the oil revenues and privatisation proceeds produces a different picture. On this basis, Scotland had a quite large surplus throughout the 1980s, falling into a deficit in the 1990s.

– THE BALANCE SHEET AND THE ECONOMY –

Assessing how important this is requires converting these cash figures into percentages of national wealth or GDP. This presents difficulties. The GDP arising from offshore oil and gas production is listed separately in government statistics as UK Continental Shelf (UKCS) GDP. Only a rough estimate can be made of the proportion of UKCS GDP that would accrue to an independent Scotland under the North Sea division described above. Much, if not all, of this GDP arises from the profits made by oil companies from their North Sea operations. And as much of the government's oil tax revenues comprise corporation tax on these revenues, the Kemp and Stephen division of these revenues provides a very rough approximation of the division of GDP.

A second difficulty is that when presenting data of this sort, the convention is to use a measure of GDP defined as GDP at market prices. This measure values output at its price including expenditure taxes minus any subsidies. It is usually higher than GDP measured at factor cost, which excludes taxes and subsidies. GDP market price figures are only available for the UK as a whole. Scottish and other regional GDP data are GDP factor cost figures. To get round this problem for this analysis, Scottish and UKCS GDP market price data was derived by applying the Scottish and UKCS proportions of UK factor cost GDP in each year studied to UK GDP market price data. Figure 10.3 shows the results.

Figure 10.3. UK and Scottish net borrowing as percentages of GDP at market prices, 1998–9 prices.

	UK Net Borrowing (–) /surplus, £bn	UK Net Borrowing (–) /surplus as % of UK GDP at Market Prices	Scottish Net Borrowing (–) /surplus, £bn	Scottish Net Borrowing (–) /surplus as % of Scottish GDP at Market Prices
1979–80	–4.79	–0.85	0.61	1.29
1980–81	–8.12	–1.47	1.90	4.16
1981–82	1.67	0.31	10.22	22.43
1982–83	0.54	0.10	10.06	21.57
1983–84	–0.24	–0.04	10.90	22.60
1984–85	3.73	0.63	15.69	32.79
1985–86	4.98	0.81	13.67	27.29
1986–87	4.83	0.76	3.61	6.81
1987–88	11.25	1.69	1.51	2.75
1988–89	20.93	2.99	1.18	2.05
1989–90	10.94	1.53	–0.96	–1.63
1990–91	4.20	0.58	–2.24	–3.70
1991–92	–11.77	–1.66	–4.31	–7.14
1992–93	–37.67	–5.31	–7.10	–11.62
1993–94	–48.10	–6.62	–8.25	–13.28
1994–95	–38.60	–5.09	–6.95	–10.70
1995–96	–36.69	–4.71	–6.03	–8.95
1996–97	–25.75	–3.22	–3.94	–5.84
1997–98	–2.83	–0.34	–2.39	–3.49
1998–99	5.17	0.61	–3.18	–4.51

Sources: UK data supplied by HM Treasury; Scottish data supplied by Royal Bank of Scotland and from Figure 10.2

The results are remarkable. With the addition of oil revenues, Scotland enjoyed an enormous surplus in the 1980s, peaking at £15.7bn, or nearly a third of GDP, in 1984–5. But in the 1990s, declines in oil prices and an easing of the North Sea tax regime means that even oil revenues did not prevent the public sector account from plunging into deficit, bottoming out at £8.25bn, or 13.3 per cent of GDP, in 1993–94. By comparison, the UK public sector account has fluctuated much less wildly, from a surplus of 3 per cent of GDP to a deficit of 6.6 per cent of GDP.

These figures illustrate why, although it seems counter-intuitive to a layman, having large reserves of oil is not necessarily a good thing. The problem is that the value of these reserves is determined by outside influences, mainly the ability (or inability) of the Organisation of Petroleum Export Countries (OPEC) to control prices. Although Scotland could be an OPEC member, its ability to influence OPEC decisions would be minimal. If Scotland had been independent since 1979, the large surpluses in the 1980s would have exerted strong inflationary pressure. They might also have been used in ways which would have stored up problems when the surplus turned into deficit in the 1990s. For example, the political weight in Scotland in the 1980s was against privatisation and even pro-nationalisation. It is quite realistic to argue that an independent Scotland would not have privatised the gas and electricity utilities and would have continued to subsidise, rather than close, industries such as coal mining, shipbuilding and steel production. Even if that had not happened, few politicians could have resisted the temptation to cut taxes and increase public spending. Either strategy would have run into terrible trouble in 1986–7 when public revenues crashed by £10bn.

Conversely, it could be argued that the early surpluses would have easily paid for the initial costs of independence, such as establishing a defence force. They could have also paid for one-off infrastructure improvements such as motorways, rail electrification, hospitals, schools and so on, which, although there would have been an inflationary effect, would not have led to the same revenue problems when the money dried up. And perhaps an independent Scotland would not have made the same reductions in the offshore tax regime that the UK Government did, thereby reducing the revenue problem in the 1990s.

Both arguments underline the fact that the figures produced here show only what would have happened in an independent Scotland since 1979 if it had pursued exactly that same policies that the UK Government has done. Of course, from the principle noted at the start of this chapter, this would not have been the case.

One item which would change on the Scottish balance sheet with independence (provided Scotland was accepted into EU membership) is the Scottish contribution to the EU. Scotland is estimated to have paid £667m in taxes to the EU in 1998–9 and to have received agricultural and structural fund payments worth £600m, a net contribution of £67m (Scottish Executive 2000: 21–2). However, these figures include a Scottish share of the reduction in UK contributions to the EU of about £2bn a year negotiated in the Fontainebleau agreement (McCrone 1999: 152). It is almost certain that an independent Scotland would not enjoy this abatement, especially given the SNP's claims of Scotland's relative wealth. On a pro-rata basis, Scotland's contribution to the EU would rise by about £200m.

Nonetheless, the data is useful. It shows the kind of fiscal position from which an independent Scotland is likely to start. The recent pattern from the 1990s is that when the UK public finances are in balance, Scottish public finances are in deficit. In order to maintain present spending and taxation patterns, an independent Scotland would be heavily dependent on not just buoyant oil prices but also a relatively low value of the US dollar against the £ sterling. This is because crude oil and gas sales are denominated in US dollars, and if the value of the US dollar falls in relation to the £ sterling, the value of North Sea production rises.

Calculations have been made of the kind of price and currency values that would bring the Scottish public account into balance or a small surplus (Fitzpatrick 2001). At current offshore production levels and an oil price of $22 per barrel, Scotland would have a revenue surplus only at an exchange rate where £1 buys less than $1.40. At an oil price of $25 a barrel, Scotland would be in revenue surplus when £1 buys $1.60 or less.

There is plenty of oil and gas left in the North Sea, at least as much as has already been extracted. However, production volumes are unlikely to increase much beyond present levels. Since the usual £/$ trading range is between 1.40–1.60, Scotland would need oil prices that are higher than recent historic levels to balance the books. Between 1990–2000, the average oil price was just under $18 a barrel. Such higher prices are not implausible; the average price in 2000 was nearly $29 a barrel and in 2001, it was just over $24 a barrel.[9] But the volatile history of oil prices strongly suggests that it would be foolish to expect such high prices. The prudent course would be to emulate the strategy of oil companies by planning for unfavourable oil prices and currency values, hoping that events will prove this strategy to have been too pessimistic.

– PUBLIC AND PRIVATE SECTORS –

The data shown above enables an assessment to be made of whether the economy of an independent Scotland is large enough to sustain the current volume of public spending. The standard measure used by the OECD for international comparisons is to express total public spending as a percentage of GDP at market prices. Broadly speaking, the lower this percentage, the more dynamic an economy is judged to be by free-market economists. On another, social market, yardstick, the higher the percentage, the more generously funded will be public services.

Figure 10.4 sets out the public spending percentages for Scotland for the years for which figures on aggregate Scottish public spending are available. It shows the percentages for firstly, the Scottish economy without North Sea oil GDP, and secondly, with North Sea oil GDP.

Figure 10.4. Scottish public spending as a percentage of Scottish GDP 1992–9.

	Aggregate Scottish public spending, £m at 1998–99 prices	Agg. Sc. Spending as percentage of GDP (mkt prices) excl. NSea GDP	Agg. Sc. spending as percentage of GDP (mkt prices) incl. NSea GDP
1992–93	32,035	52.4	48.0
1993–94	32,574	52.4	47.4
1994–95	33,918	52.2	45.3
1995–96	34,172	50.8	43.9
1996–97	33,635	49.9	41.3
1997–98	33,017	48.1	41.4
1998–99	33,100	47.0	43.3

Sources: Scottish Office, 1998, Table 18; Scottish Executive, 1999, Table 8; Scottish Executive, 2000, Table 8; ONS; HM Treasury; Author's calculations.

The figures show that adding North Sea GDP reduces the public spending percentage by between four and nine percentage points. They also show that public spending as a percentage of the Scottish economy has been steadily reducing, partly because of real terms public spending reductions and partly because of economic growth. It will be noted that in the years 1996–9, the public spending percentage behaves differently depending on whether North Sea GDP is excluded or included. This is because North Sea GDP is much more volatile, as it depends on the price of crude oil, than the Scottish mainland economy. North Sea GDP fell sharply between 1997–8 and 1998–9, causing the public spending percentage to rise.

The figure for Scotland (including North Sea GDP) can be set in an international context, shown in Figure 10.5. The comparisons made are with selected smaller European countries plus the UK.

Figure 10.5. Public spending as percentage of GDP for selected countries in 1998.

	Population (millions)	Public Spending as % of GDP
Sweden	8.85	56.2
Denmark	5.30	53.6
Austria	8.07	50.1
Belgium	10.21	48.2
Finland	5.15	48.1
Norway	4.43	46.4
Scotland	5.12	43.3
Netherlands	15.69	43.3
Greece	10.51	42.6
Portugal	9.87	40.2
United Kingdom	59.24	39.7
Ireland	3.71	31.8

Sources: OECD, December 2000, Annexe Table 28; Table 10.4 above. Note: figures for Scotland are fiscal year 1998–9, figures for all other countries are for calendar year 1998.

On this basis, Scotland would occupy a mid–table position in a public spending league, neither with an excessively large or small percentage of its economy being consumed by public spending. It would have a larger percentage public spend than the UK, but it is not unmanageably larger. It does imply however that the public sector is larger in Scotland than in the UK as a whole. The point is confirmed when looking at other estimates of the size of public services in the Scottish economy; they are about 22 per cent of the Scottish economy compared to about 18 per cent of the UK economy (Peat and Boyle 1999: 15).

– IMPORTS AND EXPORTS –

The balance of trade – whether the value of exports is greater or less than the value of imports – used to matter a great deal. Monthly trade statistics were headline news eagerly seized upon by politicians and economic analysts. Depending on the verdict, the value of currencies would rise and fall. A lot less significance is placed upon such figures these days, but they still matter. This is because the balance of trade is a guide to the overall health of an economy. If a country exports more than it imports, it is generating wealth and its citizens, assuming that they all share in the wealth creation, will prosper as a general rule. If it imports more than it exports, it is not generating wealth, but consuming it. If such a feature is perpetuated over a long period, the country would have an economic problem.

In a system where countries have currencies which are freely exchanged, exchange rates offer a method of correcting imbalances. A country which exports more than it imports will see its currency rise in value, making imports cheaper and its exports more expensive. A net importer's currency would fall in value, making imports more costly and exports cheaper. This should enable to net importer to export more and curb its imports, bringing its economy back into balance.

Because Scotland is currently part of the UK, the Scottish balance of trade matters only as a contribution to the UK balance of trade. But under independence, the Scottish balance would matter a great deal more. Working out with precision what this Scottish balance of trade would look like is difficult because there is a shortage of accurate data. But there is enough to make some general observations.

A good deal of information exists about exports. Data has been collected by the Scottish Council Development and Industry (SCDI) for a number of years. A summary is presented in Figure 10.6.

Figure 10.6. Scottish exports outside the UK in 1999.

	Value of Scottish exports to non–UK destinations, £m	Sector as percentage of total Scottish exports	Scottish exports as percentage of comparable UK sector
Primary	5,542	22.2	55.0
Manufacturing	19,234	77.2	12.4
Services	3,015	12.1	4.7

Sources: SCDI, April 2001. A note in the text explains that the nature of the primary sector makes it difficult to calculate an exact share of UK totals although available information does suggest that Scotland's primary exports account for between 50 per cent and 60 per cent of the UK total.

The performance of Scottish manufacturing is, rightly, a source of considerable pride. Manufacturing accounts for more than three-quarters of exports, a much higher proportion than in the UK as a whole. Scotland exports about 40 per cent more of UK manufactured exports than might be expected for Scotland's share of UK population and GDP. Exports per manufacturing employee are also about 40 per cent higher than in the UK as a whole, which is partly accounted for by the fact that just under 30 per cent of manufacturing employees work for subsidiaries and associates of overseas-owned companies. In economic terms, it means that Scotland is an open economy, open to trade and investment, which is normally considered to be an asset in an increasingly open world economy (Hood 1999). Scotland's impressively large share of UK primary sector exports arises because 95 per cent of Scottish primary exports stem from UK offshore oil and gas production, much of which is landed and refined in Scotland before being exported.

This is, however, only part of the story. Scotland also exports to the rest of the UK. It also imports from rUK and the rest of the world. Data on imports is not collected with the same zeal as export data. An estimate of the balance of trade is however available from the Scottish Input–Output tables produced by the Scottish Executive (and previously by the Scottish Office. These tables are designed to give a picture of the flows of products and services between producers and consumers, and to give an indication of what might happen to the economy if the demand for a particular product or service increased or decreased. They are not built with the aim of producing balance of trade figures, although that is a by-product. Figures for 1998 are shown in Figure 10.7.

It turns out that Scotland has a hefty trade deficit with rUK and that the trade surplus with the rest of the world is not enough to bring the account into balance. For 1998, Scotland had an overall trade deficit, estimated to be £3.9bn. Moreover, this deficit figure is not unusual. A run of these figures was compiled for the years 1951–95, and it turns out that Scotland had a trade deficit for all these years except 1952 (Gibson, 1997).

Figure 10.7. Scotland's balance of trade, 1998.

	Scotland's trade with rest of UK £m	Scotland's trade with rest of world £m	Scotland's total trade £m
Imports	30,953	17,439	48,392
Exports	22,774	21,677	44,451
Balance	–8,179	4,238	–3,941

Source: Scottish Executive, 2001. Note: These figures are compiled at basic prices, i.e. excluding taxes less subsidies, and are therefore not comparable with the figures in Figure 10.6.

However, this is still not the full story. The Input–Output tables follow UK national accounting convention, classifying offshore oil and gas production as belonging to the UK continental shelf which is, statistically at least, another UK region. So machinery and materials which is made onshore in Scotland and then shipped out to North Sea platforms is classified as an export to rUK. The crude oil and gas production which is landed in Scotland, then refined and consumed in Scotland, is classified as an import from rUK. But in an independent Scotland, much of this trade would become internal to Scotland and would therefore disappear from the balance of trade figures.

Two additions then need to be made. First, oil and gas landed in Scotland and then transferred by pipeline to rUK does not appear in the Input–Output tables in the same way as a lorry load of goods from Northern Ireland which arrives off a ferry and then is driven directly to England does not appear. These raw oil and gas products would count as an export under independence.

A second addition would need to be made of the value of oil and gas which is produced in Scottish waters but which is exported directly to destinations outside Scotland. In 1998, for example, 29 per cent of oil was loaded directly from platforms to tankers which could be routed to any destination (SCDI 1999). Some may have landed in Scotland, but no figures giving a breakdown of destinations are available. Similarly, gas from Scottish fields can be landed through an interconnecting pipeline system either at the St Fergus Terminal in North East Scotland or at Teesside or Bacton in England. Again, no data on these flows originating in the Scottish part of the UKCS but making landfall outwith Scotland are available.

These and other data shortcomings make it impossible to calculate a robust balance of trade figure for Scotland under independence. It is only possible to make a rough estimate.[10] On the export side, the Kemp and Stephen figures provide good estimates of the proportion of UKCS oil and gas production that can be attributed to Scotland. An estimate of the amount of this production consumed in Scotland can then be deducted. For 1998, this yields an export value of about £9bn.[11]

On the import side, no breakdown of offshore industry expenses (which totalled £5.75bn in 1998)[12] is available which would allow a figure for the cost of imported materials to be estimated. But if even half of this cost was due to imports, then in 1998 the Scottish part of the UKCS would have produced a trade surplus of about £6bn. This is more than enough to turn the trade deficit noted in Figure 10.7 into a trade surplus.

It can also be noted that 1998 was a year of exceptionally low oil prices, averaging $13.2 per barrel. In 1999, the oil price rose to $16.9 per barrel and in 2000 to $28.8 per barrel). Additionally in 1998, the US$ was low in value in relation to the £ (£1 = $1.66). Since then, it has risen in value (£1 = $1.44 in 2001), meaning that the value of North Sea production has risen. So, given that 1998 was a poor year for the North Sea and that an independent Scotland would still have had a trade surplus, it can be inferred that an independent Scotland would have a trade surplus under almost all conceivable conditions.

– CONCLUSIONS –

- Forecasting the economic outcome of independence with any precision is impossible. The outcome depends on too many variables, some of which are not under Scottish political control.
- Scotland has higher public spending and lower tax revenues per head than does the UK average implying that when UK tax revenues and public expenditure are in balance, Scotland is in deficit. This excludes oil revenues which, when included, do not necessarily bring Scotland into balance. Relatively high oil prices and low US dollar values are required to bring present Scottish tax and spending patterns into balance.
- The existing pattern of tax revenues and expenditure in Scotland cannot be assumed to be the same pattern that would apply under independence.
- Fluctuating oil prices and dollar values could cause enormous variations in Scottish tax revenues which would pose problems for the economic management of an independent Scotland.
- The overall level of public spending in Scotland, especially when the Scottish part of the North Sea is included as part of the Scottish

economy, is neither excessively high nor low when compared with other European countries of comparable size.

- An independent Scotland which controlled a due share of offshore oil and gas production would have a balance of trade surplus.

– NOTES –

1. Letter to Alex Salmond MP, 21 August 1998, from Robert Twigger, Economic Policy and Statistics Section, House of Commons Library (Copy supplied by the SNP).
2. Ibid.
3. 'Economics of Independence', *The Economist*, 21 November 1998, p. 33.
4. For a full explanation, see Scottish Executive 2000, pp. 61–2.
5. For a full explanation, see Scottish Executive 2000, p. 36.
6. For a full discussion, see Scottish Executive 2001, pp. 33–5.
7. Personal conversation with Professor Alex Kemp.
8. House of Commons Written Answers, 21 March 1997, Col. 969W.
9. Information supplied by Royal Bank of Scotland.
10. The author is indebted to Hervey Gibson, chairman of Cogent Strategies International Ltd and visiting Professor of Economics at Glasgow Caledonian University, for advice on this.
11. Derived from DTI, 2001. Appendix 7.
12. Ibid. Appendix 7.

CHAPTER 11

Breaking Up is Hard to Do

In considering the question of how Scottish independence might affect the UK's public infrastructure and its resource base, the political debate has tended to concentrate on North Sea oil. That question has already been dealt with, but there are many other matters to be considered. They range from division of the national debt to ownership of the BBC.

— LIABILITY FOR THE NATIONAL DEBT —

The national debt is money borrowed by the government in order to help finance its spending programmes. It comprises government stocks (gilts), national savings securities (bonds, savings certificates), various Treasury instruments (such as temporary deposits), and foreign loans (war debts). At the end of March 2001 the amount of public sector net debt (the debt of the whole public sector, less its liquid financial assets, such as foreign exchange reserves) outstanding is estimated to have been £313.4 billion, equivalent to 31.8 per cent of GDP. The general government gross debt at end March 2001 (excludes assets and is the measure used to define fulfilment of Treaty of Maastricht criteria) was £383.7bn or 40.6 per cent of GDP.[1] By contrast, in 1922 the National Debt was £7.6 billion, equivalent to 150.3 per cent of GDP. The question is how the national debt would be divided upon independence.

The Vienna Convention on Succession of States in Respect of State Property, Archives and Debts 1983[2] (henceforth the 1983 Convention) is background legislation that is intended to apply where the parties cannot agree. It establishes principles in this area of law, for example by imposing on the seceding part an obligation to assume an 'equitable proportion' of the national debt: Article 17(1)(c). However, the 1983 Convention is not yet in force. It will enter into force once 15 States have ratified or acceded to it. At the end of December 2000, it only had six signatories and five parties.[3] The Convention does not, or only partially, reflect customary international law.

On the principle that the national debt has been incurred raising money to be spent for the benefit of all UK citizens, GERS assumes that Scotland must take a share of this expenditure on servicing the national debt. This, it contends, should be done on the basis of Scotland's share of national wealth (8.3 per cent of GDP) rather than population.

However, the simple division of the debt is unacceptable to the SNP. In a document that sets out the economic strategy for an independent Scotland the SNP argues that two-thirds of the current UK national debt was accumulated between 1979 and 1995 – during which period Scotland accumulated an absolute surplus of over £34bn.[4] In 1978–9 Scotland's population share of the national debt amounted to £13bn. According to the SNP the revenues gained from oil since 1979 mean that Scotland has paid off its share of the national debt more than twice over. Therefore, the SNP contends, an independent Scotland would not take any share of the national debt and would leave it all to rUK.

This calculation is, however, deeply flawed. First of all, the national debt is United Kingdom debt and no specific proportion is attributed to Scotland. Secondly, the choice of 1978–9 is an arbitrary one. There is no accounting convention that considers only the last 20 years or so when sharing the national debt. Thirdly, it assumes that, during any independence negotiations, rUK would accept that 90 per cent of the oil-producing UK Continental Shelf should have been treated as being part of Scotland since 1979. This assumption would have some force if, say, Scotland had staked a legitimate claim to independence in 1979 but this had been unreasonably refused. But this is not the case.

– The Irish example –

These two positions are analogous to the initial positions of the British and Irish representatives in the Irish independence negotiations in the 1920s. In the Treaty between the two sides signed on 6 December 1921 there were two financial articles. The first of these, Article 5, stated that:

> The Irish Free State shall assume liability for the service of the Public Debt of the United Kingdom as existing at the date hereof and towards the payment of war pensions as existing at that date in such proportion as may be fair and equitable, having regard to any just claims on the part of Ireland by way of set-off or counter-claim, the amount of such sums being determined in default of agreement by the arbitration of one or more independent persons being citizens of the British Empire.[5]

The British Treasury eventually calculated the sum owed by Ireland to the UK under this article as a liability of £117.5m in respect of the public debt; £12.75m in respect of war pensions; and £27.5m in interest payments from the date of the Treaty to the date of the assumption of liability, a four-year period.[6]

The Irish had different ideas. They argued that Britain had over-taxed the Irish, drained the country of capital, destroyed flourishing industries, banished millions of Irish people, and thus owed Ireland a large fortune. The exchange between the Irish negotiators (led by Michael Collins and Erskine Childers) and the British representatives (led by Sir Robert Horne, Chancellor of the Exchequer, and Sir Laming Worthington-Evans, Secretary of State for War), putting a monetary value on the Irish claims, is worth quoting. The two sides met in October 1921:

> **Mr Collins**: I will put some arguments that may surprise you.
> **Sir Laming Worthington-Evans**: Mr Collins will never surprise me again. We would like to have a statement of your counter-claims. Could you put these in now? It need not wait for our memorandum.
> **Mr Collins**: According to my figures our counter-claim works out at £3,490,000,000.
> **Sir Robert Horne**: I suppose that dates from the time of Brian Boru. How much did we owe you then?
> **Mr Collins**: Oh no, it is the capital sum since the Act of Union.[7]

Given the enormous gulf between the initial two positions, it might be presumed that this was the cause of the delay in reaching a final settlement, achieved in March 1926. In fact, Irish instability and civil war was the main cause. The financial negotiations focused on a number of issues which, in hindsight, seem relatively minor. These were: Irish payment for munitions supplied by the British; British and Irish liability to compensation for personal and property damage during the Anglo–Irish war of 1919–21; Irish payment for railway assets in the Free State; Irish liability for pensions due to members of the Royal Irish Constabulary and Irish members of the British armed forces; resolution of a problem of double income tax levied on Irish holders of British Government stock; and Irish liability for annuities being collected by the British Government from Free State tenants under land purchase agreements.

Once these matters had been settled, the British Government waived Irish liability to a share of the UK national debt. This was more a matter of politics than accounting. Stanley Baldwin, the Prime Minister, and Winston Churchill, Chancellor of the Exchequer, argued it would be against

Britain's interest to further impoverish an already poor country. A poor Ireland would mean a flow of immigrants to Britain, exacerbating Britain's unemployment problems, whereas a prosperous Ireland would be a market for British manufacturers.[8] The young Republic did not escape free of any burden. In its initial years, it had to pay £3.13m a year in respect of land annuities, £1.75m a year in respect of RIC pensions and £250,000 a year compensation for damage to British government property. The total sum was reduced in initial years by off-setting British payments to Ireland, but even so the liability was stiff given that the new state's revenues in 1926-7 totalled £24m.[9]

Three broad points emerge from this:

1. A legal precedent that a new state arising by secession from Great Britain should shoulder a portion of the predecessor state's national debt was set and accepted by the successor states through Article 5 of the 1921 Treaty;
2. A political precedent that liability for a due portion of the national debt by the seceding state can be waived by the other state if doing so suits its interests was also set;
3. The relative poverty of the seceding state, while a factor in the financial negotiations, did not extinguish all its liabilities to make payments to the richer state.

The first point reinforces the view that an independent Scotland would have to accept a share of the UK national debt. The second point does not negate that view since the waiver was made with regard to Ireland's relative poverty. These circumstances do not apply in Scotland's case; indeed the SNP argue that Scotland is richer than rUK. The SNP's proposition that rUK would shoulder 100 per cent of the national debt as a goodwill dowry to Scotland is rather unlikely as it would set a precedent which might encourage the people of Wales to seek independence or the people of Northern Ireland to vote to join the Irish Republic. Moreover, any rUK government which did accept this SNP proposition would certainly face a backlash from the rUK electorate, especially if Scotland was seen to be walking away with most of the UK's offshore oil and gas assets.

– OTHER PARTIES AT THE TABLE –

One other factor makes the assumption of some of the debt by an independent Scotland a certainty. This is that in any negotiation between Scotland and rUK, third parties would be involved, if not actually in a seat at the table. The third parties are the creditors. They have loaned money to the UK Government in the expectation of being re-paid and of earning interest payments on the loan.

More importantly, the creditors have the means to enforce their will. They have three levers: reducing the availability of future credit through rationing; increasing the price of future credit through increased interest rates; and using the influence of international institutions such as the G7 or the EU to impose a particular division. For example, the G7 used its influence to impose a division of the Soviet Union's debt on the successor states. The EU would have obvious leverage over Scotland if it wished to join, while the G7 would have leverage over rUK. What creditors will seek to ensure is observance of what might be called an ability-to-pay rule:

> From the creditors' perspective, the optimal division of a country's debt is one that maximises the expected debt-related repayments. In deciding what this optimal division will be, creditors will consider both the capacity of each state to make payments, as well as their own ability to enforce the debt contracts (Rowlands 1997: 45).

Thus while there is no legal means of enforcing a particular debt division, there is a real practical means. This is both a protection and a hindrance for Scottish independence. It protects Scotland from rUK trying to impose an overly burdensome division of the debt on Scotland. But equally, it also militates against Scotland escaping from assuming some share of the debt.

One further point needs to be made. The agreement in which all the Soviet Union's successor states accepted a share of the USSR debt was eventually abandoned because of various problems, including a lack of accurate economic data. Russia took on all the USSR's debts, except for the Ukraine's 16.4 per cent share. 'The government of Ukraine actually desired its own debt in order to demonstrate its sovereignty in the area of international finance' (Rowlands 1997: 42). In other words, it may be in Scotland's advantage to accept a share of the UK national debt in order to prove its credentials as a new and credit-worthy state.

– SHARING THE DEBT –

Historical examples of debt division are relatively rare. But from the available examples, two categories of division emerge: the simple and the complex.[10]

Simple divisions:

1. Population: the successor countries take a share of the debt according to their share of the predecessor state's population. This was used in the break-up of Great Columbia with the secession of Venezuela in 1829 and Ecuador in 1830 from Columbia, in the collapse of the Central American Federation (a grouping of Costa Rica, Nicaragua, Honduras, El Salvador and Guatemala) in 1838, and in the division of Czechoslovakia in 1993.

2. Fiscal: the successor countries take a share of the debt according to their contribution to the gross revenues of the predecessor country. This method was applied in the break-up of the Austro-Hungarian Empire (dissolved by the Versailles Treaty in 1919) and the break-up of the Ottoman Empire (1922).

3. Wealth: the successor countries take a share of the debt according to their capacity to generate wealth measured by their share of the predecessor state's GDP. This criterion was used in the dissolution of the Central African Federation, a British construct which brought together the colonial administrations in 1953 of what are now the countries of Zambia, Zimbabwe and Malawi and which was wound up in 1963.

Complex divisions:

1. Joint-and-several formulae: the initial formula used to determine shares of the USSR debt was based on four factors: GDP, imports, exports, and population. This was an attempt to modify a basic GDP/population division to take account of the fact that the USSR was a centralised command economy. For example, some new countries had apparently low GDP levels despite being oil producers because oil production was centrally controlled. Adding in exports and imports factors dealt with these anomalies. Shares on this basis were agreed remarkably quickly but, as recounted about, this formula was eventually abandoned.[11]

2. Liability-and-asset formulae: these have been proposed in Quebec but not, obviously, implemented. Two reports, the Le Hir Report and the Bélanger–Campeau Commission, which were sponsored by the Quebec provincial government, argued that liability for a share of the Canadian debt could not be separated from questions of ownership of Canadian national assets which the debt had financed. Both reports contended that Quebec had a disproportionately low share of federal assets which should be taken into account. In essence, the effect of the proposals would be to establish a wealth share of the debt (as defined above) which would be reduced to compensate for the low asset share. The

Bélanger–Campeau approach calculated the division of assets and liabilities simultaneously, and applied different rules to different categories of assets and liabilities.[12]

3. Historical Benefits: this method, conceived in Canada, contends that the debt was incurred through the provision of goods and services by the Canadian government. So over a time period, say 25 years, all such spending by the federal government in Quebec should be balanced against federal tax revenues on Quebec. The implication is that larger beneficiaries should pay more (Boothe et al. 1991).[13]

One further method has been called the zero–option rule. This is where one successor state takes no share of the debt. Panama, when it broke with Great Columbia in 1903 took no share of Great Columbia's debt, and Bangladesh, when it broke from Pakistan in 1971, took no share of Pakistan's debt (Rowland 1997: 42). The zero-option rule is, in effect, the SNP's position, but, as argued above, will not apply in Scotland's case.

The various methods produce different results. In Quebec's case, the percentage share of the Canadian debt would vary quite widely: from 17.4 per cent (Liability-and-asset formula – Le Hir), 18.5 per cent (Liability-and-asset formula – Bélanger–Campeau), 22.3 per cent (Wealth share), 24.8 per cent (Population share), to 32 per cent (Historical benefits share).

These methods could be applied in Scotland's case. But there are three reasons to think that a simple rather than a complex division would be used. First, calculating shares under the complex divisions is enormously difficult. The methodology is often subjective rather than objective and therefore open to challenge. Jacques Parizeau, the PQ leader at the time of the 1995 referendum, appeared to accepted that a population formula would be used in the event of Quebec secession when he said: 'We will, I suppose, haggle for a few weeks before we come to something like a quarter.'[14] Second, the near-certain application of the ability-to-pay rule by creditors, points to simple divisions, particularly fiscal or wealth shares. Third, the division which may be agreed by the Scottish and rUK negotiators would become an issue in an independence referendum and, arguably, in subsequent elections in both successor states. A simple division, particularly a population share, has the virtue of being easily understood by voters and would be less open to subsequent arguments that it is unfair to either side.

From the 1998–9 figures in Figure 10.1, it appears that the share of the national debt that Scotland is likely to shoulder is within a fairly narrow range: from 8.3 per cent (Wealth or GDP share), 8.4 per cent (Fiscal share), to 8.6 per cent (Population share). But these figures are for a non-independent Scotland. Independent Scotland would gain control of most of the oil and gas revenues. Following the ability-to-pay rule, figures which took account of this change to Scotland's balance sheet would be the basis for agreement on debt sharing. Figure 11.1 sets out some figures for 1992–9 calculated on this basis, an analysis which also indicates some further problems which would have to be resolved in negotiation.

Figure 11.1. Base figures for debt–sharing, 1992–9.[15]

	Scotland's population as % of UK population	Scottish tax revenues as % of UK tax revenues	Scottish GDP as % of UK GDP (at market prices)
1992–93	8.8	9.5	9.5
1993–94	8.8	9.4	9.6
1994–95	8.8	9.6	10.0
1995–96	8.8	9.6	10.1
1996–97	8.7	10.0	10.4
1997–98	8.7	9.7	9.8
1998–99	8.6	9.2	9.1

As might be expected, inclusion of a Scottish share of offshore revenues increases the Scottish share of the debt. Generally, a population-based share is most advantageous to Scotland, a fiscal- or wealth-based share most advantageous to rUK. A problem with the population share is that Scotland's population, relative to that of rUK is in slow decline. By 2006, Scotland's share of UK population is projected to be 8.4 per cent and by 2011, it is projected to be 8.2 per cent.[16] Thus any fixed percentage which might be agreed to be paid over a period of years will gradually become disadvantageous to Scotland as its percentage share of UK population falls below the share fixed at the time of independence. A further (and incalculable) variable factor is the effect that independence might have on population. If people were optimistic about prospects, the population might increase through immigration. If people were pessimistic, the decline in population share might accelerate.

The same risks are apparent in using a fiscal- or revenue-based share. If Scotland had become independent in 1996–7, then its revenue-earning and wealth-creating capacity would have fallen in the subsequent two years. The reverse would have been true if 1993–4 had been the base year for determining a fiscal- or wealth-based share for dividing debt. A further, and again incalculable, variable factor is the effect that independence would have on the economy. Clearly, there are risks in setting a share of the debt, but the interests of Scotland, rUK and the creditors, lie in having a solution which minimises the risk.

One problem would present a particular difficulty for Scottish negotiators. On the ability-to–pay rule, a fiscal- or wealth-based division is preferable. But this would worsen Scotland's fiscal deficit. This can be illustrated with figures from 1998–9. In that year, the GERS report estimated Scotland's share of central government debt interest to be £2.4bn, based on Scotland's 8.3 per cent share of UK GDP.[17] Calculated on an independence basis (that is, including Scotland's share of offshore revenues), Scotland's share of debt interest would rise by £230m to 9.1 per cent (fiscal share) or by £260m to 9.2 per cent (wealth share). If the higher revenues from 1996–7 applied in that year, the Scottish share of debt interest would increase by almost £500m to 10 per cent (fiscal share) or by just under £600m to 10.4 per cent (wealth share).[18] In this last scenario, Scotland's fiscal deficit for 1998–9 would have gone up from £4.9bn to £5.5bn, or from 7 per cent to 7.8 per cent of GDP.

This implies two things. First, Scottish negotiators could argue that using a fiscal or a wealth basis for debt division would harm Scotland's ability to pay debt interest, a good card to have in negotiations. But second, if the SNP contention that the GERS reports under-estimate Scotland's tax revenues is correct, that increases the likelihood that a fiscal or wealth division would be used. Better information about revenue could, paradoxically, harm Scotland's case in negotiations.

Evidently, the use of simple methods to resolve the question of dividing the national debt does not sweep away all complexity. The issue is important, for hundreds of millions of pounds are at stake. Even more ticklish than the question of dividing the debt are the mechanics of actually sharing it. The UK Government cannot simply transfer lumps of its debt to Scotland without the agreement of the creditors which might not be granted. There are several possibilities – guaranteeing to pay a due share of interest and capital, issuing new securities to cover a due share, issuing bonds to guarantee a cash flow to rUK – but none of these can extinguish the added risk created by splitting one debtor country into two.

A particular problem would be the division of National Savings – money which has been borrowed by the Government from a few million UK citizens. In March 2000, this amounted to £63.6bn.[19] Since the UK Government would be ceasing to exist, some people might want to redeem their savings, others might be happy for their savings to be maintained with one or other of the successor governments. Sorting this out, and avoiding a run on national savings with consequent problems for government cash flows, would be difficult.

International creditors would seek a risk premium which would apply to both Scottish and rUK debt, more so to Scotland because it would be the more unknown quantity. And for any new loans which Scotland sought to finance additional expenditure, a risk premium would also have to be paid until creditors were satisfied that Scotland was a reliable re-payer.[20] Scotland's choice of currency would also affect creditors' calculations, a question discussed later (see pp. 236–45).

Two further issues could also impinge on the question of debt division: the division of assets, and the uncertainty caused by a move to independence.

– DIVISION OF ASSETS –

If Scotland has to shoulder a share of the national debt, it is both logical and reasonable to accept that Scotland must also acquire a due share of the assets which have been built up through use of the money borrowed by the UK. The point is reinforced by the fact that taxes paid by Scots have always been pooled by the UK Treasury and spent on a UK basis. All public assets, whether they are in the Shetland or the Scilly Isles, are UK assets. It is logical that whatever figure is used to divide the national debt should also be used to divide national assets.

Until recently, the SNP has not given this issue much attention. This is strange, for the SNP has always argued that Scotland has not received a fair share of public spending. An example of this argument came in a 1990 television programme. Discussing 'non-identified public spending', that is government spending which is not attributed to any UK region, the presenter asserted: 'The spending now amounts to £31bn a year and it's estimated that half of that goes into London and the South-East.'[21] The assumption appears to be that Scotland and rUK would take control of all assets on their sides of the border and, apart for a small financial adjustment to deal with the fact the rUK would inherit most of the UK's overseas embassies, that would be that.[22] It is not so simple.

– THE CZECH–SLOVAK EXAMPLE –

The break-up of Czechoslovakia in 1993 provides the nearest example of what might happen to UK assets (Innes 2001). By 1990, a year after the 'velvet revolution' had deposed Communist rule, Czechoslovakia had become a federal state. Institutionally, there was a federal assembly, with semi-autonomous legislatures in the Slovak National Council in Bratislava, and the Czech National Council in Prague. Alongside these legislatures, separate political parties had grown up:

[In 1992] diverse political parties, including the offspring of the Czech and Slovak revolutionary movements, submit themselves to an election; every party (excepting a small Slovak National Party) declares itself in favour of a common state. Barely two weeks later the victors, the Czech leader Václav Klaus and the Slovak leader Vladimir Mečiar – both professedly pro-federal before the election – announce that Czechoslovakia is to be broken apart. Within seven months they dissolve the Czechoslovak state and launch the independent republics of Czechia and Slovakia (Innes 2001: 39).

There were two rules used to divide federal assets. First, immovable property, such as bridges, airports, and buildings, was allocated to the successor state in which it was situated. Second, movable property, such as railway vehicles, aircraft, and military equipment, was allocated to the Czech Republic and Slovakia according to their share of the population of Czechoslovakia. This was set at a 2:1 ratio (Klima 1994). This was a little odd, as it was slightly advantageous to the Czech Republic (the actual population ratio was 1.95:1). The Slovaks had long argued, with some justification, that the Czechs had benefited from a disproportionately high share of federal spending (Innes 2001: 164).

Division began before the date of the split, 1 January 1993. By mid-1994, about 95 per cent of the assets had been divided according to a Czech–Slovak committee set up to determine the division. By November 1997, assets which remained undivided and required a prime ministerial negotiation to resolve included the state airline, the merchant shipping fleet, fuel reserves, a market regulation fund, and some federal asset funds.[23] Final resolution did not occur until June 2000 and after Vladimir Mečiar, the Slovak Prime Minister, had been voted out of office. At issue were four tonnes of Slovakian gold kept in the Czech national bank in Prague, a Czech demand for 26 billion crowns (about £500 million) said to be owed by the Slovaks from the division of the former State Bank of Czechoslovakia, and a Slovakian claim for compensation for federal 'know-how' said to have been taken over by the Czechs. In the event, Slovakia got its gold, plus 1 crown in settlement of all other claims.[24]

The simplicity of the division and its relative speed derive from two things. First, there were no reliable economic statistics available for a serious discussion of dividing assets in any way other than by a 'rough justice' method. Second, the leaderships of both countries could not get away from each other fast enough. Delays in settling the last few remaining matters were more due to posturing for populist political reasons than anything else. The leaders also had the historical legacy of centralised power in order to achieve break-up. Even though the evidence suggests the people of both countries were opposed to division, the new democratic institutions were too fragile to stand in the leaders' way (Innes 2001: 163–5; 115–46).

The lessons from this are, firstly, that even where there is the political will and the means to divide up state assets, it still takes time – from eighteen months to two years. Secondly, that some matters where quite large amounts are at stake can take much longer to resolve; seven years in the Czechoslovak case. And thirdly, that political personalities can cause major difficulties.

– SCOTTISH–rUK ASSETS –

This analysis does not attempt to make an exhaustive examination of all assets. Rather, it classifies the various types of asset and then uses examples to illustrate some of the problems involved in tackling a division of the assets. Developing a classification used by the SNP, four types of asset can be distinguished (SCESR 1996: 25):

1. *Territorial assets*: land and property situated in one or other of the successor states used in connection with the delivery of services within and to that area. This is the easiest issue to resolve. It would encompass things like *roads, bridges, hospitals, health services, the property and buildings of the Scottish Executive*, and so on. A distinction might be made between those assets which have common equivalence in each of the successor states, and those which do not. For example, roads exist in each state and can be assumed to be equitably shared between the states. But some items have no common equivalence. An example is *water and sewerage infrastructure*, which is publicly-owned by the Scottish Executive but privatised south of the border. The rUK negotiators might argue that rUK tax-payers have contributed to the construction of these assets and are therefore entitled to compensation. An rUK claim to a share of the proceeds should they be privatised might also be staked. Similar questions might be raised over some movable assets, such as the ships of the state–owned *Caledonian MacBrayne shipping company*. Since they are already under the authority of the Scottish Executive, they should stay in Scotland but there might be compensation issues.

2. *UK-wide assets*: land and property situated in both of the successor states and which is used for the delivery of services to the whole of the UK. The most obvious example is *land and property used for defence*. An airfield such as RAF Leuchars is in Scotland. Its runway and other facilities are obviously immovable but they are used for the defence of

the whole of the UK. A policy aim of both parties would have to be that neither the defence of rUK and Scotland nor overseas obligations requiring a military presence should be imperilled by division. If the policy objective of a Scottish government is, as has been stated by the SNP, the creation of a Scottish defence force, then eventually Scotland would inherit the immovable assets and would seek a share of the movable assets – ships, tanks, aircraft, and so on. But an interim measure which would permit defensive continuity would be to maintain the present UK structure of the armed forces. Scotland could pay its share of defence costs and have an appropriate presence in political command structures. This would allow time for negotiation on future divisions and defence structures if that was the policy goal. Less significant policy issues and more straightforward negotiations would be involved with matters like the *employment, social security and pensions* services infrastructure. While there are offices dealing with the local delivery of these services throughout the UK, most of the headquarters assets would be in rUK. The rUK government could reasonably demand payment for the use of headquarters services until such time as Scotland built, equipped and staffed its own head offices. Equally, the Scottish government might reasonably claim a share of the capital value of the existing UK headquarters. Similar questions would surround the fate of the *Inland Revenue* and *Customs and Excise*. The same considerations, but in reverse, would apply to the *Forestry Commission* and its commercial arm, *Forest Enterprise*, which are headquartered in Scotland. A review of forestry policy announced in 2002 involved the Scottish Executive, the Northern Ireland Executive, the National Assembly for Wales, the Forestry Commission, and three UK Government departments – the Department of Environment, Food, and Rural Affairs; the Cabinet Office; and the Treasury.[25] Clearly, the number of parties that would be involved in the division of UK-wide assets would make these very complex negotiations.

3. *Territorial UK assets*: land and property situated only in one of the successor states and which is used for the delivery of services to the whole of the UK. These would include such things as the *Bank of England*, actually the central bank of the UK, and the *National Statistics Office*. Scotland could reasonably lay claim to a share of the value of such assets and perhaps a share of the knowledge amassed by the national statistical service. An extremely difficult claim to contend with would be one on the *Security Services*, not just the capital value of the buildings it occupies, but the also the value of the intelligence information it has gathered. Scotland would wish its own security service; could

it lay claim to information about potential threats to its own domestic security? A more practical problem is posed by such institutions as the *Driver and Vehicle Licensing Agency*. Scotland could continue to let the DVLA licence and tax vehicles, remitting the revenue collected to a Scottish treasury which would pay for this service. It could also lay claim to a share in the *British Library*, the *British Museum*, the *Victoria and Albert Museum*, and other UK cultural collections which would be all situated in rUK, on the grounds that Scottish taxes have helped to amass and maintain these collections. Such a claim would be hotly disputed. How it might be settled is hard to foresee, as valuing all the collections would be a difficult and laborious task. Scotland might want to claim particular items for Scottish museums, such as the Lewis chessmen, originally found in Scotland but most of which are kept in the British Museum to the chagrin of some Scots.

4. *Overseas assets*: land and property situated outwith the UK and used by the UK Government. The most obvious items are the embassies and consulates of the *diplomatic service*, and *overseas defence installations*. Scotland might be able to negotiate temporary rents of some diplomatic facilities, while laying claim to a share of their capital value. This could be a large sum, as some of the embassies, for example those in Paris, Washington and Tokyo, are extremely valuable real estate. A much thornier question would be whether a claim could be made by Scotland on the UK's remaining *overseas territories*. Some of these last outposts of empire (in which the Scots were enthusiastic participants), such as South Georgia or the Pitcairn Islands, have little value. But Gibraltar, the Falkland Islands, and Diego Garcia (an important strategic military base) clearly do have value. How would this value be measured? Or shared?

Resolving the division of assets would present a difficult dilemma for Scotland. On the one hand, it is a fair guess that totting up the value of UK assets according to their location would reveal that Scotland has somewhat less than a wealth or even a population share of these assets within its territory. The value of the shortfall, it is also fair to guess, would run into billions. Resolution of this issue would therefore radically affect the resources available to Scotland for construction of the new state. On the other hand, agreeing an asset division and a valuation of all assets could be extremely time-consuming. The list of agencies, other quangos, and natio-nalised corporations which would have to be scrutinised is extremely long. The list of parties that may be involved in considering some assets is also long. The longer the duration of negotiations, the longer and the more debilitating would be the period of uncertainty until the outcome was settled. Finally, an exhaustive scrutiny of every item would use an enormous amount of civil service manpower.

The SNP has recently made an assessment of the National Register of Assets 2001, a list and valuation of all the UK government's assets which was first drawn up in 1997.[26] It is remarkably comprehensive, covering all the central government departments and the devolved governments, executive agencies and other public bodies, NHS bodies, and other public corporations and nationalised industries. The valuation encompasses tangible fixed assets (including military and heritage assets), intangible fixed assets (such as intellectual property rights) and fixed asset investments (such as shareholdings). It does not include art and museum collections, nor stocks of materials.

The register states that the total value of all UK Government assets at March 2000 was £273.9bn. The SNP examined this list and discovered that the assets of the Scottish Executive (the devolved government of Scotland) were valued at £15.6bn and those of the Scotland Office (the central government's department in Scotland) at £1.1bn. In general terms, these assets can be defined as Territorial Assets in Scotland. The value of assets of other Government departments' properties in Scotland, such as the local offices of the Department of Work and Pensions, was £2.1bn.[27] This can be defined as the value of UK-wide Assets located in Scotland. These two categories total £18.85bn, or 6.88 per cent of the UK total.

The SNP calculate that if a population share (8.6 per cent) is used to divide UK assets, Scotland would be entitled to receive £23.5bn. On this population basis, Scotland would be entitled to receive £4.7bn to cover the shortfall between the value of assets located in Scotland and the population share entitlement to asset value. But if a revenue or a wealth rule was being applied equally to assets and liabilities, the shortfall would be larger. If such a sum were negotiated, Scotland could use it to offset its debt liability. Figure 11.2 sets out the amounts involved in the various share scenarios used in Figure 11.1.

Figure 11.2. Scottish shares of UK debt and assets (£bn).[28]

Percentage share	Share of Gross Debt	Share of Net Debt	Share of Assets	Shortfall on Asset share
Population – 8.6	33.0	26.4	23.5	4.7
Low wealth – 9.1	34.9	28.0	24.9	6.1
Revenue – 9.2	35.3	28.3	25.2	6.3
High wealth – 10.0	38.4	30.8	27.4	8.5

In net debt terms (share of net debt less shortfall on asset share), Scotland's liability ranges from £21.7bn to £22.3bn. In gross debt terms (share of gross debt less shortfall on assets), Scotland's liability ranges from £28.3bn to £29.9bn. If Scotland was able to make out a claim on the value of national museum and art collections, and on overseas territories, these amounts might reduce yet further.

These are, however, purely indicative figures. They also represent a 'best case' settlement of the assets and liabilities question from Scotland's point of view. Actual negotiations could well throw up all sorts of difficulties and problems which would affect a final settlement figure. For example, the difficulties surrounding National Savings have already been mentioned. An rUK government could reasonably argue that the considerable cost of sorting this out should be borne entirely by Scotland since it was Scotland's wish to be independent that was causing the problem. Similar arguments might apply in a lot of other areas, such as the division of Royal Mail, the Government-owned company which runs the Post Office. But it does seem clear that the division of UK assets could yield a sum which could be used, either to offset Scotland's debt liability or as a capital sum to finance the construction of the additional public sector infrastructure which an independent Scotland would need.

– THE PROCESS OF NEGOTIATION –

As has already been indicated, actual negotiations would be complex. A probable course can only be sketched out.

1. The broad parameters of what would be at stake would have to be established. This would cover all the assets and liabilities which need to be divided and the dates on which the successor states would come into existence. At this stage, it would also be important to establish the principles to be applied: whether Territorial Assets and immovable UK-wide assets should be assigned to the successor state in which they are located, and what share proportion should be used in division of the debt and other assets. As is shown in Chapter 13, it is important for Scotland that this share should be established and agreed as early as possible, particularly in relation to the debt.

2. Scotland would need to establish its policy priorities. There may be areas where it would want an early division, such as North Sea oil assets, the Inland Revenue, and Customs and Excise. There may be areas where it would be content to agree to the continuation of UK arrangements under a joint Scottish/rUK authority, perhaps for a

defined period, such as defence forces. Appropriate payment agreements for these things would have to be made. Some matters might be relatively simple to resolve. For example, the division of Government-owned corporations such as Royal Mail could be effected by Scotland taking a due shareholding stake in the company with a view to later de-merging of the Scottish operations. Others might be more complex, such as the division of the Driver and Vehicle Licensing Agency, where payments for processing of Scottish licensing may be necessary prior to establishment of a Scottish DVLA and could become quite high if Scotland wished to alter the rates applicable to Scottish residents.

3. Legislation would be required before Scotland could take ownership of any asset. This includes all Territorial Assets such as the buildings and property of the Scottish Executive which are presently occupied and used under the authority of the UK Crown exercised through the Westminster Parliament. This legislation would need to be passed by both the Westminster Parliament (to pass the property on) and by the Scottish Parliament (to establish lawful authority to use it). The simplest procedure would be to pass an enabling Act to give the respective governments executive authority to implement such agreements. In current times, which demand much greater parliamentary scrutiny and accountability, giving such wide authority to a government could well be resisted, both at Westminster and in the Scottish Parliament. But there are arguments against legislation which listed every single item to be transferred. One is that the negotiations are likely to be so lengthy that such legislation could only come in a number of tranches. This would crowd out other legislation which the two governments wished to pass in order to deal with routine issues in education, health, law and order, and so on. Problems that might occur here include the possibility that one parliament might operate at a faster pace than the other, so causing political frustration, or that political opponents of Scottish independence could use line-by-line scrutiny of legislation to delay, or even frustrate entirely, the object of securing independence. Evidently, much thought and care would need to be given to the legislative process.

– CONCLUSIONS –

- International law regarding the division of a predecessor state's assets and liabilities is, as yet, of no assistance to the Scottish–rUK case because the relevant UN convention has not entered force.
- A British legal precedent that both successor states should accept liability for the predecessor state's debts was set by the 1921 British–Irish Treaty.

The Irish share of this liability was only waived by the British side because it was in the British interest to do so.

- The SNP's case that Scotland is not liable for a share of the UK national debt does not stand up to examination. The interests of the creditors alone would ensure that Scotland would take a share.

- While there is no international law which can be used to enforce a share of the debt, there are international institutions such as the EU which have the political clout to ensure an equitable share.

- Simple rather than complex formulae are much more likely to be used to decide the apportionment of the debt. The interests of creditors point to a GDP-based or wealth share being the likely basis for division. In such a division, Scotland's post-independence GDP which includes the GDP created by the Scottish part of the North Sea, rather than pre-independence GDP, would be used.

- The same share formula used to divide the national debt should also be used to divide national assets. Assets are likely to be shared in two ways: firstly, immovable assets located within the territories of the successor states would accrue to these states; and secondly, assets which are shared between the two states would be divided according to a formula.

- The valuations set out in the UK National Register of Assets appear to indicate that there is a shortfall between the value of UK assets located in Scotland and the share of asset value to which Scotland would be entitled.

- While this shortfall appears to entitle Scotland to a large sum, which may be paid either by reducing its liability to the national debt or by payment, negotiations may throw up problems which reduce Scotland's entitlement to an asset shortfall payment.

- The process of dividing assets is immensely complicated and likely to take many years, in some cases, to resolve. Interim mechanisms would need to be devised so that assets can continue to be used for the benefit of the citizens of both states.

– NOTES –

1. The latest published figures at the time of writing were for 1999–2000 when the public sector net debt amounted to £340.1 billion: HM Treasury, Budget: March 2001, Chapter C, Table C4.
2. 22 I.L.M. 306 (1983); for a detailed analysis of the 1983 Convention see Streinz (1983).
3. The signatories were Algeria, Argentina, Egypt, Niger, Peru, and Yugoslavia. The parties were Croatia, Estonia, Georgia, the Former Yugoslav Republic of Macedonia, and Ukraine. See *Multilateral Treaties Deposited with the Secretary General-status as at 31 December 2000*, UN Publications.
4. SNP (1999), *Taking Scotland into the 21st Century*, SNP Publications.

5. Cited in Fanning, R. (1978), *The Irish Department of Finance 1922–58*, Dublin: Institute of Public Administration.
6. Ibid. p. 162.
7. Cited in Ibid. p. 121.
8. Ibid. p. 167.
9. Ibid. pp 164–6, and Lee, J. J. (1989), *Ireland 1912–1985; Politics and Society*,Cambridge: Cambridge University Press. 1989, pp. 109–110.
10. For a review of many of these cases, see Armendariz de Aghion, B. and Williamson, J. (1993) 'The G7's Joint and Several Blunder', *Essays in International Finance*, No. 189, International Finance Section, Department of Economics, Princeton University.
11. Ibid. p. 12.
12. Quebec, Government of (March, 1991), *Commission sur l'avenir politique et constitutionnel du Québec*, (Bélanger–Campeau Commission) Quebec. (Text available at http://www.uni.ca/belangercampeau.html) Quebec, Government of (1995), *La partage des actifs et des passifs du gouvernement du Canada la souverainété du Québec* (Le Hir report).
13. A useful summary, apart from spelling mistakes, of the various approaches to dividing Canadian debt is available at http://www.uni.ca/archive3.html
14. Quoted in Young (1998: 184).
15. Sources: ONS, Population Trends 106, Winter 2001; GERS 1992-3 – 1998-9; HM Treasury; Author's calculations.
16. ONS. Population Trends 106, Winter 2001.
17. Scottish Executive. GERS 1998-9. December 2000. Table 7.
18. From Figure 10.6.
19. HM Treasury (2001), 'Debt Management Report 2000–2001' , London: The Stationery Office.
20. For a discussion of this topic in relation to Quebec and further references, see Young (1998: 185–6).
21. Scottish Television. *Scotching the Myth*. 1990. Published by the Scottish Centre for Economic and Social Research as: Rosie, G. *Scotching the Myth*. Calton Series No 4. February 1992.
22. Scottish Centre for Economic and Social Research. *Scotland's Government: The Transition to Independence*. August 1996, pp. 25–26.
23. *The Warsaw Voice*, 'Czech–Slovak breakthrough', 16 November 1997.
24. *The Warsaw Voice*, 'Tying up loose ends', 4 June 2000.
25. Scottish Executive Press Release, 'Forestry Policy Review', SE199/2002, 22 January 2002.
26. HM Treasury (2000), 'National Register of Assets 2001', London: The Stationery Office; SNP Westminster Parliamentary Group (2001), 'An analysis of the National Asset Register 2001 and the missing billions that Scotland has contributed to the UK', SNP Publications.
27. These figures have been checked and appear to be accurate.
28. Derived from: HM Treasury (2000), 'National Register of Assets 2001', London: The Stationery Office; HM Treasury (2001), 'Debt Management Report 2000–2001', London: The Stationery Office.

CHAPTER 12

A State of Uncertainty

Any major constitutional change involves a move from one familiar economic environment to an unfamiliar one, creating uncertainty about whether the new environment will be good or bad. The creation of the Scottish parliament in 1999 caused some uncertainty amongst Scottish businesses, but not enough to cause any discernible effects. This is mainly because the matters which concerned business most – taxation and regulation – remained in the familiar political environs of Westminster. Independence however would be a much greater change with control of taxation and regulation moving to Edinburgh. There would therefore be a great deal of uncertainty until the new political framework became clear.

This would have a range of possible economic effects. At one end of the spectrum, if individuals and businesses concluded that there are considerable benefits from independence, there would be a positive economic effect. People and companies would tend to increase their activities in order to take advantage of expected benefits. At the other end, activities would be decreased and companies might even move out of Scotland entirely in order to escape an expected poorer economic climate. In the middle, individuals and businesses might simply postpone spending or investment plans until they saw the outcome and its implications.

– THE QUEBEC EXPERIENCE –

In the developed democratic world, the closest parallel to Scotland seeking independence from the UK is Quebec and Canada. After the Parti Québécois (PQ) failed to persuade Quebecers to vote for sovereignty (that is independence) in a 1980 referendum, the question did not assume significance again until 1994. Following the failure of attempts to re-engineer the Canadian constitution to suit Quebec sensibilities in the Meech Lake and Charlottetown Accords, the PQ won the Quebec provincial elections in September 1994. The new provincial government, led by Jacques Parizeau, had promised to hold a sovereignty referendum within six months of the election.

The referendum campaign began in earnest with the recall of Quebec's National Assembly on 7 September 1995 to consider a bill introduced that day which set out a declaration of sovereignty. The poll was held on 30 October 1995. A remarkable 93.52 per cent of eligible voters cast ballots: 2,362,648 voted no to independence and 2,308,360 voted yes. The independence proposal was thus defeated by a wafer-thin margin: 54,288 votes or by 50.58 per cent to 49.42 per cent.[1]

As might be expected, what independence would mean for the Quebec economy played a large part in the campaign debate. Historically, the Quebec economy has under-performed relative to the economy of Canada. But there is debate about whether Quebec has under-performed or over-performed relative to Ontario, its neighbouring province.[2] The causes of variable economic performance are even more hotly debated. There is neither a consensus on likely causes, nor on the extent to which Quebec's uneasy constitutional position within Canada contributes to any under-performance.

One study does identify constitutional uncertainty as a problem which has handicapped the Quebec economy (Bennett 1998). But it was unable to distinguish the contribution of that factor to under-performance from others. These included the restructuring of the Quebec economy which reduced dependence on agriculture and some mineral resource-based industries; the impact of increasing free trade and globalisation which saw a shift in financial service activity from Montreal to Toronto; French language laws which inhibited the ability of Quebec to attract strategic economic activities; and the disproportionate effect of North American recessions of 1980–2 and 1990–2.

What is reasonably clear however, is that the 1995 referendum did have short-term economic effects. These were discernable from the outset of the campaign, becoming more pronounced when opinion polls indicated that the 'Yes' side might win. The impact was visible in four ways: Canadian stock market values, the value of the Canadian dollar, flight of capital, and in interest rates.

– The Canadian stock market –

Movements in the Toronto Stock Exchange index (TSE), especially when compared to movements in the Dow Jones Industrial Average (DJIA), show how investors viewed the prospect of Quebec independence. It is evident that the two indices generally move in the same direction, but from 17

October to 30 October 1995, there is a sharp decline in the TSE. In this period, the market fell by 200 points, losing 4.5 per cent in its value. There was then an equally rapid recovery. This can only be attributable to the effect of the referendum (see Figure 12.1).[3] The longer term divergence between the TSE and the DJIA and, in particular, the relative poor performance of the TSE, are attributable to longer term factors affecting investors' confidence in the Canadian economy at that time. These include the TSE's heavier weighting in natural resource-based industries such as metal production at a time when metal prices were falling, and more general worries about the Canadian government's strategy for reducing the country's fiscal deficit.[4]

Figure 12.1 TSE and DJIA Q4 1995 performance.

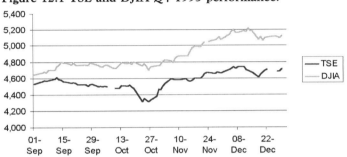

Press reports at the time make it abundantly clear that investors' overriding short-term concern was with the outcome of the referendum. Contemporary comments by analysts underline the nervousness that the referendum induced in the stock markets. 'The political climate in Quebec is now being monitored heartbeat by heartbeat', said Dunnery Best, vice-president of Canadian equities for Richardson Greenshields of Canada.[5] 'Markets will be watching each and every poll, even every rumour of a poll', said Craig Wright, Assistant Chief Economist at the Royal Bank of Canada.[6]

Opinion polls seem to have been the main driver behind investors' behaviour. Up to early October, polls showed that the 'No' campaign was ahead. In this period, investors tended not to sell their stock holdings, but held back from making new investments, preferring to hold any new funds in cash in money markets.[7] But by 20 October, polls started to show the 'Yes' campaign was in the lead and stock selling gathered pace.[8] Selling occurred right across all sectors; shares in banking, forestry, media, and industrial conglomerates all took losses. Some sectors rose – utilities, gold, and other precious metals – but this was the result of investors seeking safe havens.[9] On 23 October, a poll appeared to confirm that the 'Yes' campaign had taken the lead and the TSE plunged 122 points, a 2.7 per cent fall and the biggest one-day decline in the exchange for six years.[10] The plunge was cushioned to some extent by investors buying, gambling that there would be a 'No' vote and that therefore Canadian stocks were under-valued, but there were comparatively few such risk-takers.[11]

After the 'No' vote was declared on 30 October, the stock market rallied sharply. The TSE shot up 3 per cent when it opened on 1 November, ending the day 1.8 per cent higher, the biggest one-day rise in eight years.[12] The narrowness of the 'No' victory meant that some uncertainty remained. Political events, such as the resignation of Jacques Parizeau as Quebec's Premier and PQ leader on 31 October, persuaded some investors to remain cautious.[13] But as it became apparent that Quebec was not about to secede from Canada, confidence returned.[14] By the close of trading on 3 November, the TSE had recovered to where it was when the slide started on 17 October.

– Canadian dollar values –

The currency markets also appeared to be strongly influenced by political events and opinion polls. In the week after the PQ presented its sovereignty bill to the Quebec national assembly, the Canadian dollar ($Can) slid from a value of about 0.745 US dollars ($US) to about 0.73 $US. The Bank of Canada intervened in the markets to support the $Can, and as polls indicated that the 'No' campaign was ahead, the $Can rose again (Young 1998: 285). But further uncertainty ensured that the $Can was in for a rough ride during September and October (Figure 12.2).[15]

Figure 12.2 $Can v $US, 1 Sep–29 Dec 1995 futures performance.

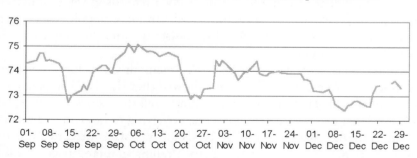

After a poll published on 2 October gave the 'No' campaign a nine-point lead, the Canadian dollar ($Can) rose sharply to stand at a value of 0.75 US dollars ($US). 'The only uncertainty that seems to be left is the margin of victory for the "No" side,' said Andrew Spence, chief economist with Citibank Canada. The Bank of Canada was able to sell $Can.[16] But as the 'No' campaign's margin over the 'Yes' campaign dwindled, the $Can started to slide. It was down to 0.74 US$ by 19 October, when traders reported that there was heavy buying of 'put' options on the futures market, a means whereby holders of $Can insured themselves against further falls in the currency's value.[17] A poll published late on 19 October which gave the 'Yes' campaign a 2 per cent lead, prompted further selling of $Can on 20 October and buying by the Bank of Canada in order to hold the price of $Can just below 0.74 $US.[18]

In the week beginning 23 October, the last week before the referendum, the currency markets showed extreme nervousness. The $Can hovered around 0.73 $US all week, prevented from falling further by some patchy intervention by the Bank of Canada and varying opinion on what the referendum outcome would be.[19] Paul Martin, the Canadian finance minister, felt the need to pledge that Canada would meet all its financial obligations whatever the outcome, while simultaneously warning that the consequences of a 'Yes' vote would be dire.[20] Worries about the effect of a 'Yes' vote were sufficiently great for the Canadian government to make it known that it would, if necessary, borrow money from the International Monetary Fund.[21] The Quebec provincial government was even rumoured to be buying $Can to help stop the currency's decline in value. True or not, the rumours helped produce some stability.[22]

As polling day approached, nerves continued to shred. On 26 October, the $Can lost a third of a cent in selling within minutes of a poll being announced which put the 'Yes' side ahead.[23] On polling day itself, a Monday, the $Can ended the day a little down on the previous week's closing price, although during the day it leaped up and down, rising and falling a full cent within one 15-minute period.[24] Overnight, the Bank of Canada kept its exchange desk staffed in case immediate action was needed in response to the vote.[25] Analysts forecast panic and steep falls in the $Can if there was a 'Yes' vote. 'Everyone is panicking,' said Jodi Schenck, a dealer at Toronto Dominion Bank in New York. 'Spreads in Canadian dollars and bonds are so wide you can drive a truck through them. Volatility is wild.'[26]

Waves of relief washed through the currency markets when the narrow 'No' victory was announced. The $Can surged sharply, gaining a full cent on the previous day's close to move up to 0.744 $US. At one point in the European markets, it gained nearly two cents.[27] The result did not, however, see the $Can regain the vibrancy of early October when the markets were convinced there would be a 'No' vote. The referendum left a bit of a hangover. There were two concerns. First, there was a worry that the narrowness of the result would sap the Canadian government's will to reduce its public spending deficit, which stood at $Can35.7 billion in 1994–5. Cutting the deficit meant cutting federal government transfers to Quebec which might re-ignite the independence debate.[28] And second, there was an underlying fear that another referendum might not be far away. As *The Economist* commented: 'Unless hearts change all across the country on a huge scale, Canada has been spared break-up on this occasion only to prepare for it on the next.'[29]

– Flight of capital –

The fall in the TSE came about because investors, who were mainly large financial firms handling large sums of money for clients such as pension funds, decided that the possibility of Quebec secession from Canada made holding shares in Canadian companies too risky. The extent of capital flight that occurred does not appear to have been quantified, but one report talks of 'hundreds of millions' of $Can flowing back after the referendum.[30] This may seem a large sum, but compared to the total value of the TSE, more than $Can300 billion in 1995, it is very small fraction.

Most of the capital which did flee appears to have been moved as a precautionary measure more than anything else. It went into cash (in money-market funds) or short-term government bonds. The investors who did this made a loss, as they had to buy back into the equity market at higher prices than when they sold. There are some signs that some money may have moved permanently. One fund manager is reported as saying that there had been a 'paradigm shift' from Canadian to international investment markets, particularly of money linked to long-term retirement savings.[31]

In the other direction, some investment managers saw the opportunity to make gains. One view was that Canadian equities were under–valued as the long–term trends were for interest rates to come down and for the Canadian public sector deficit to be reduced. High interest rates, relative to the United States, and high levels of public sector debt were factors felt to be contributing towards private sector inefficiency. Resolving these problems would therefore make companies more efficient, hence the investment opportunity.[32] The evidence suggests, however, that this was a minority view.

The uncertainty did not just affect bond and equity holders. Both the Royal Bank of Canada and the Bank of Montreal reported that some account holders moved their bank accounts out of Quebec to branches in Ontario, presumably out of fear that their cash and deposit accounts would be devalued. Again, these movements do not seem to have been quantified.

While the banks said the movement was sizeable, they also said they were not concerned about it.[33]

– Interest rates –

As might be expected, the financial turmoil affected interest rates. The effect, shown in Figure 12.3,[34] was of a sharp upward spike in interest rates during October 1995, after which interest rates resumed their longer-term downward trend. The chart shows the Bank Rate set by the Bank of Canada, which determines a range of other interest rates, including the mortgage rate.

Figure 12.3. Bank of Canada daily bank rate, Jan 1995–June 1996.

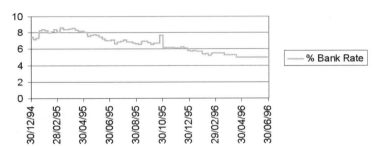

Canadian interest rates in the early 1990s were high, particularly in comparison to the other G7 developed nations. Three factors contributing to this were economic: rapid growth in government debt, restructuring in the public and private sectors which undermined the confidence of investors and consumers, and the chronic inflation of the previous two decades. A fourth was political: the uncertainty over Quebec's position in Canada (Clinton and Zelma 1997). It is not possible to quantify the extent to which each of these factors contributed to increasing interest rates.

However, volatility caused by the political uncertainty in the run-up to the referendum was blamed by various bank spokespeople for a July increase in mortgage interest rates (Young 1998: 285). These rates declined a little at the beginning of October following a cut in the Bank Rate of 0.21 per cent to 6.5 per cent on 3 October. These rates were cut because of increasing confidence that the 'No' campaign was going to win.[35] But as the 'No' lead began to fall, the Bank Rate edged up again, to 6.63 per cent on 10 October, and 6.67 per cent on 17 October.[36]

As polls from 20 October onwards indicated that a 'Yes' vote was a strong possibility, interest rates came under further pressure amidst the selling of equities and the $Can.[37] On 24 October, the Bank of Canada put the Bank

Rate up by nearly 1 per cent to 7.65 per cent. Parallel increases in government bond rates put pressure on mortgage lenders to increase their rates.[38]

Once the referendum result was declared, the pressure on interest rates eased sharply. The bank rate was slashed on 31 October by 1.47 per cent to 6.18 per cent and the major banks cut their prime lending rates from 8 per cent to 7.75 per cent.[39] But the narrowness of the result meant that continued uncertainty about Quebec's position in Canada and the effect that that might have on the federal government's economic policies helped to keep Canadian interest rates above US rates. Commenting on the gap, Gordon Thiessen, Governor of the Bank of Canada said a week after the vote: 'The gap is still fairly significant – about 170 basis points [1.7 per cent] – and that's still a very large gap. The uncertainty hasn't disappeared entirely.'[40]

_ THE QUEBEC REFERENDUM AND THE ECONOMY _
– LONGER-TERM PERSPECTIVES

The available research evidence suggests that the market volatility really only hit in the last two weeks of the referendum campaign. An analysis has been conducted of stock options – trades in which dealers estimate the likely value of a stock at some point in the future and strike a bargain to buy or sell at that estimated price (Poole et al. 1996). The volatility of these options – the spread between low and high forward prices on the same stock – provides a measure of market uncertainty. The normal volatility on TSE300 options in 1994–5 was around 10.5 per cent.

Despite a couple of polls on 12 and 14 October showing the 'Yes' side in front, there was little market reaction, probably because the polls had little credibility (one was published by the PQ's pollster). But when a third poll putting the 'Yes' campaign ahead was published by a pollster with considerable credibility on 23 October, volatility increased sharply. On 25 October, it increased to 21.1 per cent and by 30 October, it was up to 30 per cent (Poole et al. 1996: 13). The day after the vote, volatility fell to 13.1 per cent, indicating that despite the narrowness of the result, the markets believed the instability was over.

In Canadian dollar options, the normal volatility range in 1995 was between 4 and 8 per cent. Volatility started to climb around 17 October when it went up to 9.6 per cent and it thereafter rose steadily to 25.9 per cent on 30 October, thereafter falling back rapidly to normal levels. The analysts attribute the earlier rise in dollar option volatility to the probability that international investors were more nervous than Canadian investors (Poole et al. 1996: 16).

Because this volatility analysis is an analysis of forecasts of future prices, it enables an assessment to be made of what the markets predicted would happen if there had been a 'Yes' vote. The prediction was that the TSE would fall between 7 and 10 per cent in value to around 4000 points (the lowest value in the last three months of 1995 was 4700) which would have been the biggest crash since 1987. The $Can was similarly expected to fall to $US0.67, an all-time low.

Looking beyond the day-to-day volatility of equity sales and currency movements, the strong impression gained from studying press reports during and immediately after the sovereignty referendum is that business activity stalled until the result was known. Executives of big companies, including francophones such as Laurent Beaudoin, chairman of Bombardier, were overwhelmingly opposed to Quebec independence, and owners of small businesses were only slightly less hostile. A survey of the Quebec members of the Canadian Federation of Independent Business found that 65 per cent intended to vote 'No'. [41]

Those most deeply concerned were people with businesses based in Quebec with large exports to the rest of Canada and the USA. For example, Quebec's clothing industry employed 150,000 in the province in 1995 and accounted for 60 per cent of clothing sales in Canada with sales outside Quebec valued at $Can10 billion. They worried that trade barriers might be raised around Quebec and that they might have to include 'made in Quebec' rather than 'made in Canada' labels on their products. Bert Lafford, President of the National Apparel Bureau, which represented 500 companies, said: 'There is concern that if Quebec separates, there will be a backlash in the rest of Canada and they will not want to buy Montreal clothing.'[42]

Apart from worries about sales, companies were also concerned that capital for future expansion would become more expensive and harder to get. That caused a number of firms to put expansion plans on hold until after the referendum. For example, Paul Penna, chairman of Agnico-Eagle Mines Ltd, said US investors in his company had been nervous because all of the firm's gold production was in Quebec, where the company was planning to invest $Can100 million. John Hooper, chairman of Pheonix International Life Sciences, a Quebec-based biotechnology firm, said: 'I'm assuming things will work out. We have a huge installation here and long-term leases and properties. It's real tough for us to leave Quebec. On the other hand, if things get bad here, I wouldn't see us expanding any further in Quebec. We're not likely to spend any further here, if there were no prospects for reconciliation between the federal government and Quebec.'[43]

A post-referendum general survey of Montreal business leaders reported the same disquiet: 'Business leaders regard political uncertainty as yet another business risk. They fear that their assets will generally lose value in the event of a difficult transition to the sovereignty of Quebec and, as a result, they tend to postpone decisions which would have the effect of tying up their assets in Quebec.'[44]

Big American companies with operations in Quebec could afford to be a little more sanguine. General Motors was quoted as saying it would reassess its investment in Canada only after the referendum result. A spokesman for IBM Canada, which had 3,000 employees in Quebec, said: 'Given the closeness of the vote, I think people are going to be watching to see what happens next and so will we.'[45]

The uncertainty lasted into 1996. One report asserted that many of Montreal's garment-makers had kept the investment plans on hold for several months after the referendum. It quoted Jack Kivenko, chairman of Jack Spratt Manufacturing, a maker of jeans as saying: 'There's so much political uncertainty, that I can't imagine anyone investing long-term dollars.' Gordon Ritchie, chief executive of Strategico Inc, an Ottawa-based trade consultancy, said: 'You name me a company with pan-Canadian or North American interests now headquartered in Montreal, and you've named me a company looking at moving out.'[46]

The collective result of this waiting and watching appears to have been a stalling of economic growth, particularly within Quebec and less so in the rest of Canada. Figure 12.4 shows the quarterly economic growth in Quebec, the rest of Canada, and the USA for the three years around the 1995 referendum. These figures have to be set in the context of the fact that within North America, Canada has tended to grow more slowly than the USA; and within Canada, Quebec has grown more slowly than the rest of the country.

Figure 12.4. Quarterly change in GDP in Quebec, Canada, and USA, 1994–6.[47]

	Quebec %	Rest of Canada %	USA %
1994 Q1	1.60	1.41	0.84
Q2	0.80	1.87	1.38
Q3	0.90	1.49	0.54
Q4	0.78	0.96	1.22
1995 Q1	0.72	0.85	0.37
Q2	–0.11	–0.13	0.19
Q3	–0.22	0.31	0.77
Q4	0.22	0.54	0.79
1996 Q1	0.88	–0.06	0.71
Q2	0.06	0.36	1.62
Q3	0.38	1.09	0.50
Q4	0.82	1.12	1.13
Average Quarterly GDP Change 1981–2000	0.58	0.71	0.77

Because the USA is the biggest single export destination for both Canadian and Quebec products, a slowdown in the US economy hits all of the Canadian economy. So the 1995 second quarter negative growth in Quebec and Canada is attributable to poor growth in the USA. But despite a marked US acceleration in the third quarter of 1995, Quebec's economy continued to record negative growth while the rest of Canada picked up speed. The fourth quarter, the three–month period of the referendum, also shows sluggish growth in Quebec while the rest of Canada continues to move ahead. But in the first quarter of 1996, the activity which was stalled in Quebec appears to kick back in as the province's economy gets back into gear.

This analysis is open to criticism. The Canadian and the Quebec economy are also sensitive to factors which are not affected by localised political uncertainty such as the price of oil and other raw materials such as metals and wood. But the picture of business activity suffering a big hiccup because of political uncertainty appears to be confirmed when looking at the detail behind the GDP figures. Items that would be expected to be most affected by uncertainty were so affected. For example, business gross fixed capital formation (that is investment in buildings and equipment) fell by 8.4 per cent in Quebec in 1995.[48] Housing starts in Quebec in 1995 fell by 43 per cent from the previous year to 8,000, the lowest level since record-keeping began in 1965.[49]

_ Lessons from Quebec and Canada _ for Scotland and the UK

It is not possible to read the economic history of Quebec and Canada directly into an independence scenario for Scotland and the UK. Quebec is a very much larger part of Canada (it has a quarter of the population and a fifth of economic output) than Scotland is of the UK (it has less than a tenth of the population and just over a tenth, including oil, of economic output). Geographically, an independent Quebec would have split Canada in two whereas an independent Scotland would leave the rest of the UK intact. Politically, an underlying fear in Canada was that Quebec independence would have led to the break–up of the Canadian federation, but this is a much more remote possibility in the UK.

These factors tend to suggest that the economic volatility experienced by Canada during the Quebec referendum would be much less pronounced in the UK. All the same, because the UK is a big economy in world terms, being, like Canada, a G7 member, it is naïve to think that nothing would happen. The economic effects noted above mainly occurred in a two-week period when opinion polls showed that a 'Yes' vote to Quebec independence was a real possibility. They rapidly diminished after the 'No' campaign won. Had the 'Yes' campaign won, the uncertainty would have continued and volatility would have increased.

So, depending on the perceptions of the likelihood of Scots voting for independence, there could be pre-referendum falls in UK stock market values. Companies with particular exposure to Scotland, such as the Royal Bank of Scotland/NatWest bank or Stagecoach, could experience share sales and see their share value decline. There could be a reduction in the value of sterling. Interest rates might well have to go up. Some companies and individuals might well move their bank accounts from Scotland, either south of the border or into the Eurozone. Investment in new buildings, both residential and commercial, could be put on hold. If the result was a 'Yes' vote, these effects would worsen and continue until people became certain of the economic effect of independence.

Forecasting the extent to which this would happen is hazardous in the extreme. In a 1992 report on the economic consequences of Quebec independence, the Royal Bank of Canada commented: 'The things that cannot be measured accurately in the current debate, are the things which will have the most important influence on the economic consequences of disunity.'[50] It is possible, however, to learn four main lessons from the Quebec experience.

First, the extent to which there will be economic turmoil and costs created by uncertainty depends on how many unknowns there are. For example, one factor which was unknown during the Quebec referendum was how the Canadian federal government debt would be divided. It was accepted by PQ leaders that Quebec would take some share of the debt, but the proportion was never defined. This question was highly significant to overseas investors, particularly holders of Canadian securities, because Canada's debt was enormous. By 1996, Canada's gross government debt, federal and provincial, approached 100 per cent of GDP. Quebec provincial debt was 98 per cent of Quebec GDP (Clinton and Zelma 1997: 7). Worries about how this debt was to be divided and serviced played a large part in currency and stock market fluctuations.

This issue would have less salience in the event of Scottish independence because the UK's gross government debt was down below 40 per cent of GDP in 2001 and forecast to decline further to around 36 per cent of GDP.[51] Scotland also has the advantage that its devolved government does not borrow money, so there would be no pre-existing Scottish national debt. But, if the SNP maintains its current stance of insisting that Scotland would not take a share of the debt, there would be uncertainty about how the UK debt would be serviced given that the UK would be losing about 10 per cent of its taxable capacity. The only way of minimising uncertainty would be for a Scottish government to agree in advance that it would shoulder an acceptable and equitable share of the debt burden.

Another unknown in the Quebec referendum was what the economic relationship between an independent Quebec and the rest of Canada would be. An agreement between the various branches of the sovereigntist movement on 12 June 1995 set out that there would be a formal Treaty of economic and political partnership. Apart from dividing assets and common debt (without specifying actual shares), it said that the political partnership would act to provide a customs union allowing the free movement of goods, people, services and capital, a monetary policy, labour mobility and citizenship, trade, transport, financial institutions, fiscal and budgetary policies, and all sorts of other matters (Young 1998: 273).

This was seen as so important that it was enshrined in the referendum question: 'Do you agree that Quebec should become sovereign, after having made a formal offer to Canada for a new Economic and Political Partnership, within the scope of the Bill respecting the future of Quebec and of the agreement signed on June 12, 1995. YES or NO?' (Young 1998: 278).

The problem was that this was a one-sided agreement. There was no indication from either any of the other provincial leaderships or from the federal government that such an offer would be accepted. Ontario's Premier, Mike Harris, repudiated the notion, asserting that Ontario would treat an independent Quebec like any other foreign government (Young 1998: 282). Jean Chrétien, the Canadian prime minister, said in a televised 'address to the nation': 'A "Yes" vote means the destruction of the economic and political union we already enjoy' (McRoberts 1997: 230).

This points to a second lesson, that however much a Scottish government tried to reassure that independence would not be economically disruptive, the UK government and its supporters would probably assert the opposite. Although this would tend to increase uncertainty, a Scottish government would have a number of means of reducing it:

1. An early declaration of intentions to maintain all economic links would allow time for debate on the proposals to move beyond the politicians into commercial and industrial spheres of interest. This debate, provided the proposals looked like common sense, might conclude that disruption would be minimal.

2. Insistence that Scottish membership of the EU is an essential part of independence would allay many fears since EU membership would ensure as much free movement of goods, services, people and capital as exists already. As was argued in Chapter 6, Scottish EU membership

cannot be assumed to be automatic. But the Scottish government could also state that regardless of the outcome of EU negotiations, it would maintain the existing EU rulebook and even continue to incorporate new EU law into Scottish law for a minimum period of, say, five years.

3. A Scottish government could similarly state that it intended to maintain the body of UK law and regulation governing companies and commercial activity, and even to update it as it was updated by the rUK government, for a defined period.

4. Arguing that independence would cause massive disruption carries the risk that if there was a 'Yes' vote to independence, the financial markets might take the argument literally and panic. While this would be against Scotland's interests, it would also be against rUK's interests. At the point when independence looks unstoppable, it would be in the interests of both the Scottish and rUK governments to work with the common aim of minimising disruption.

A third lesson is that the economic turmoil which would be created by uncertainty would affect the whole of the UK and not just Scotland. While Scotland, as much the smaller economic unit, would suffer most, the UK could not escape the effects of currency and stock market fluctuations or interest rate rises. Overseas holders of UK equities, bonds, and currency would be entitled to ask themselves just how well the UK government was running the country if things had got to the point where the Scots wanted to depart. In such circumstances, there is not much a Scottish government could do, except to say that Scotland wished to leave the union, not because the UK government was bad, but simply because independence offered a better future. Such rhetoric, however, runs counter to much of what the SNP argues, that the UK government mistreats Scotland.

This third lesson is important because it has a direct bearing on the fourth: that uncertainty and consequent economic turmoil would increase as the degree of acrimony between the governments north and south of the border increases. If the people of rUK felt that they were suffering because of the Scottish desire for independence, this could have severe consequences for the post-independence Scottish economy.

For example, around 90 per cent of the market for the Scottish life assurance and pensions industry, on which tens of thousands of jobs depend, is in England and Wales. Holders of these policies might decide that they no longer wished to have their future financial security entrusted to a country which was about to become foreign and was already causing a great deal of trouble. Again, the bulk of the Scottish tourist industry's income, on which some 180,000 jobs depend, comes from visitors from south of the border. These tourists might decide it would be prudent to avoid visiting Scotland until the situation had calmed down.

To raise such potential problems runs the risk of being accused of scaremongering. But the evidence from Quebec, particularly of people moving their bank accounts out of the province in the weeks before the referendum, shows that these might become real problems. There were similar flows of money from Slovakia to the Czech Republic before the split of Czechoslovakia on 1 January 1993 (Fidrmuc and Horvath 1998). The careful use of language in political rhetoric, for example, to insist that it is not the people of England, but their government that is the problem, might go some way to diminish such difficulties. But the real problem of uncertainty remains that its effects are unforecastable.

– Conclusions –

- The best available evidence of the kind of economic uncertainty that would be caused by Scottish independence is from Quebec. No firm conclusion can be drawn about whether Quebec's uncertain constitutional future has had long-term deleterious effects on Quebec's economy. It has probably had some undesirable but unquantifiable effect.
- The 1995 Quebec independence referendum did have measurable short-term effects. All of them – on stock market values, the value of the Canadian dollar, capital movements, interest rates – were to the economic disadvantage of both Quebec and Canada.
- The economic manifestation of uncertainty happened only in the last two weeks of the Quebec referendum campaign, and only when opinion polls indicated there was a growing possibility that Quebec would vote for independence. Once the vote was revealed and accepted as a 'No' to independence, economic turbulence disappeared.
- The evidence suggests that the Scottish economy would be more adversely affected by uncertainty than would the rUK economy, but there would still be effects felt throughout the UK.
- Clarity about economic policies to be pursued under independence and about such matters as division of the national debt would help to reduce uncertainty and the economic problems it would cause.
- Business activity would be affected by uncertainty. This is basically caused by worry about the extent to which hitherto known factors such as the existence or lack of barriers to trade would become unknown. Policies could be pursued which aim to maintain continuity, at least for a definable period, but this has the effect of reducing the freedom of political action which is the object of independence.

– Notes –

1. For accounts of the campaign, see Young (1998); McRoberts (1997).
2. See for example: Fortin, Pierre (2001).
3. Source: Bloomberg Financial Statistics.
4. *National Post*, 'The TSE as an under–achiever and Debt debate will hit again after vote', 7 October 1995.
5. Reuters News Service Canada, 'Canada: Toronto stocks end mixed as weak gold trims gains', 17 October 1995.
6. *National Post*, 'Canada: Quebecers told of Yes consequences', 24 October 1995.
7. *National Post*, 'Canada: referendum tremors lift money market funds', 20 October 1995.
8. Reuters News Service Canada, 'Canada: Markets worry as poll shows separatists in the lead', 20 October 1995.
9. Reuters News Service Canada, 'Canada: Toronto stocks spiral down as Quebec vote looms', 20 October 1995.
10. Reuters News Service Canada, 'Canada: Toronto stocks plummet as Quebec vote looms', 23 October 1995.
11. *National Post*, 'Canada: This may be just the time to vote Yes to stocks', 20 October 1995.
12. *Los Angeles Times*, 'Canada: Markets surge in Canada after defeat of separatists,' 1 November 1995.
13. Reuters News Service Canada, 'Canada: Toronto stocks end mixed amid profit-taking', 1 November 1995.
14. *National Post*, 'Mutual Fund investors flock back to equities and bonds', 2 November 1995.
15. Source: Bloomberg Financial Statistics.
16. Reuters News Service Canada, 'Canada: Canadian Dollar rallies after Quebec poll results', 3 October 1995.
17. Reuters News Service Canada, 'Canada: Canada DLR futures trade booms on Quebec poll talk', 19 October 1995
18. Reuters News Service Canada, 'Canada: Markets worry as poll shows separatists in the lead', 20 October 1995.
19. Reuters News Service USA, 'IMM currencies end mixed, Marks up, Can dollars *fall*', 23 October 1995.
20. *National Post*, 'Quebecers told of Yes consequences', 24 October 1995.
21. Reuters News Service Canada, 'Canada says following finance market nervousness', 24 October 1995.
22. Reuters News Service Canada, 'Canada dollar closes firm on Quebec rumours', 25 October 1995.
23. *National Post*, 'New poll boosts Yes, hits $C', 27 October 1995.
24. Reuters News Service USA, 'Stocks, dollar rise on Quebec vote, bonds edge higher', 30 October 1995; *Evening Standard*, 'Poll puts Canadian dollar on see-saw', 30 October 1995.
25. Reuters News Service Canada, 'Bank of Canada to staff exchange desk for vote', 30 October 1995.
26. *The Times*, 'Canadian Markets go on panic alert – Quebec referendum', 30 October 1995.
27. Reuters News Service Canada, 'Canada dollar soars on separatist defeat in Quebec', 31 October 1995; Reuters News Service UK, 'Canada dollar revives, European stocks gain', 31 October 31 1995.
28. *National Post*, 'Don't lose sight of the need to reduce the deficit', 3 November 1995.
29. *The Economist*, 'Break-up postponed', 4 November 1995.

30. *National Post*, 'Mutual Fund investors flock back to equities and bonds', 2 November 1995.
31. Ibid.
32. *National Post*, 'Five experts share their investing strategies', 25 October 1995.
33. Reuters News Service Canada, 'Canada dollars flowing out of Quebec ahead of vote', 27 October 1995.
34. Source: Bank of Canada.
35. Reuters News Service Canada, 'Canada Bonds close slightly up after dollar rally', 3 October 1995.
36. *National Post*, 'Bank rate edges up on mixed poll results', 18 October 1995.
37. Reuters News Service Canada, 'Markets worry as polls show separatists in lead', 20 October 1995.
38. *National Post*, 'Mortgage rates under pressure', 24 October 1995
39. Reuters News Service Canada, 'Canada stocks jump in post-referendum buying spree', 31 October 1995.
40. *National Post*, 'Separatists push up interest rates', 8 November 1995.
41. Young 1998, p. 281; and *National Post*, 'Focus separation debate on the costs of sovereignty', 24 October 1995.
42. *National Post*, 'Apparel industry fears backlash if Quebec votes yes', 27 October 1995.
43. *National Post*, 'Corporate leaders breathe sigh of relief after no vote', 1 November 1995.
44. Task Force on the Revitalisation of the Montreal Region, 1996, 'Montreal, a North American City: the views of business leaders', Montreal, The Task Force. pp. 13–14. Cited in Bennett (1998).
45. Ibid; and *National Post*, 'US shelves trade dispute until Quebec votes', 26 October 1995.
46. *Business Week*, 'Business in Quebec is voting with its feet', 5 February 1996
47. Source: Statistics Canada.
48. Statistics Canada.
49. *Business Week*, 'Business in Quebec is voting with its feet', 5 February 1996
50. Royal Bank of Canada (1992), *Unity or disunity: an economic analysis of the benefits and the costs*. Montreal. Cited in Young (1998), p. 97.
51. HM Treasury (2001), *Pre-Budget Report 2001*, London, Table 2.6.

CHAPTER 13

Building the New Scotland

Scotland at the start of the twenty–first century already has a lot of the institutions that an independent country would need. Quite apart from its devolved Parliament, executive government and civil service which could easily evolve into something more powerful, it has a big range of civic institutions which pre-date legislative devolution. It has its own legal and justice system which is quite capable of moving smoothly into an independence era. It has its own education system, health service and system of local government. It has a lot of the agencies which would be important under independence, such as those dealing with economic development, natural heritage, culture, and tourism.

Independence would still require a lot more institutional architecture. This chapter does not purport to offer a detailed design brief. It aims to look at the main areas where additional structures would need to be built, drawing on the lessons of the preceding chapters. The question of the currency and related economic management institutions is examined first, and then other additional institutions. It also offers an indicative guide to the sort of costs involved and goes on to estimate how much economic freedom an independent Scotland has to be different.

– SCOTLAND'S CURRENCY OPTIONS –

Although Scotland was joined in political union with England and Wales in 1707, a full currency union was not established until 1805. In 1707, the rate of exchange between the two currencies was fixed at 12 Scottish pounds to one English pound. In 1805, the rate of exchange was fixed at par and transaction costs were abolished. The legacy of this union is visible today in Scottish banknotes, issued by the Scottish clearing banks and fully interchangeable with Bank of England notes, by which the Scottish notes have to be fully backed (Johnson 1996: 24–5). The benefits of this union are also visible in Scotland's trade account. Just over 50 per cent of Scotland's non-oil exports are with the rest of the UK, the origin of over 60 per cent of imports. In large part, this volume of trade is due to the UK single market with its lack of currency transaction and fluctuation costs. Indeed, this currency union success is sometimes cited as an example which ought to encourage supporters of European monetary union.

In the context of this analysis, the trade pattern is a powerful reminder that decisions about the currency of an independent Scotland are hugely important with potentially very significant economic effects. There is, in theory at least, a range of options. One set assumes that at the date of independence, Scotland is still part of the present sterling currency zone:

1. Adopt a new currency which floats against the pound and other currencies;
2. Adopt a new currency whose value is tied to sterling;
3. Adopt sterling unilaterally;
4. Remain part of the sterling zone by agreement;
5. Join the euro with EU membership while sterling remains outside.

A second set assumes that at the date of independence, the UK is already inside the euro, but there is doubt about Scottish EU and euro membership:

6. Disengage from the euro, adopt a new currency and float;
7. Disengage from the euro and adopt a new currency tied in value to some other currency;
8. Adopt a new currency tied in value to the euro;
9. Adopt the euro unilaterally.

The final option assumes that the UK is in the euro at the point of independence and there is no doubt about Scottish EU and euro membership:

10. Remain part of the eurozone.

– Scotland and the euro –

Political and economic realities, however, severely constrain this theoretical freedom. A major political reality is that if Scotland decides to become a Member State of the European Union then the currency question will be taken out of its hands. Agreeing to EMU is part of the *acquis communautaire* and opt-outs are not offered to current applicants. The transfer of monetary policy to the European Central Bank in Frankfurt would be irrevocable and irreversible according to the Treaty of Rome (as amended). Scotland would not be allowed to be an independent state in Europe with a currency other than the euro (options 5 and 10).

However, past SNP manifestos have not indicated an awareness that membership of the European Union – to which the SNP is committed – would not be granted without a declaration of intent to adopt the single currency. The SNP's position in 2001 in that respect was identical to that of the post-1997 Labour Government. The Nationalists saw '. . . advantages in Scottish membership of the single currency, but this can only be achieved when the economic conditions are correct, when an acceptable exchange rate is delivered and where public consent has been given in a referendum' (SNP 2001a: 7).

The currency issue would be least problematic if the UK was already part of the euro by the time independence occurred and Scottish EU membership is agreed: option 10. All the conversion costs would have been already incurred. There would be no uncertainty arising from questions about monetary policy since that would be in the hands of the European Central Bank. Even without or before EU membership was granted, Scotland could continue in the eurozone simply by opting for and continuing with the euro: option 9. This would incur little cost and much continuing benefit.

If the UK is not in the euro, Scottish euro membership under option 5 becomes more difficult. Weighing the costs and benefits becomes more complex because a currency border would have to be created between Scotland and rUK. This would not affect trade in oil, as this is denominated in US dollars, as is quite a large part of trade in Scottish electronic products. But all other trade over this border, crossed by more than half of all Scottish non–oil trade, would become burdened by transaction and currency fluctuation costs. These costs might not be as large as is implied by this trade fraction as many rUK companies will have euro accounts through which transactions could be conducted. However, it seems safe to say that the costs side of the cost/benefit analysis under option 10 would rise.

Option 5 might also encourage capital flight, threatening Scotland's financial industry. Much of this business is based around fund management. At the end of March 2001, Scottish funds managed £326bn of assets.[1] Much of this money is invested on behalf of pension funds, many of whose pensioners are in the rest of the UK. Managers and their customers like their funds and their payments to be denominated in the same currency because that reduces the risks caused by currency fluctuation. Creating a currency border between Scotland and rUK would increase this risk. Thus there would be a tendency for funds managed in Scotland to move across the border. Eventually the jobs associated with fund management would go with them.

Another consideration which arises under option 5 but not under option 10, is the exchange rate at which Scotland enters the euro. EU entry terms require that a country should demonstrate stability in its currency for two years and that it should not have devalued its currency. The entry rate is fixed somewhere within the value range against the euro that the currency has fluctuated during the two years. This rate has to be unanimously agreed by all the eurozone countries. Scotland's problem is that these conditions rather assume that an entrant country has its own currency. But Scotland does not. Unless some special conditions of entry can be negotiated, Scotland would be stuck with the fate of sterling during the two year pre-entry period as the determinant for the value at which a 'Scottish' pound would join the euro.

This presents some obvious problems. The future of Scotland's currency would be in the hands of the rUK government, whose interests would lie solely with the currency of rUK. This government might not wish to enter the euro, so the direction its currency policy took might be entirely at odds with the direction that Scotland's economy required in order to enter the eurozone at a satisfactory exchange rate. For example, throughout 2001 manufacturing industry complained that that the prevailing euro/sterling exchange rate at around €1.60 to £1 was too high and making their goods uncompetitive against European goods. Since the Scottish economy is more dependent on manufacturing than the rUK economy, this kind of 'wrong' rate would have more severe effects on Scotland than rUK.

Under the current constitutional arrangements, the Bank of England is obliged to have some regard to the effects of its monetary policies towards Scotland. But under independence, that obligation would cease. Therefore, pursuing option 5 would entail some risk for Scotland. Current euro entry terms imply that achieving option 10 would require Scotland to spend a minimum two-year period still bound to sterling. It may be possible to reduce to a minimum the risk implied by this period of having to use a currency which would be no longer managed with the interests of Scotland at least partly in mind. This is because the date of independence would not arrive without notice.

Under the schedule proposed in Chapter 4, there would have to an election which produced a pro-independence government, then a referendum followed by a period of negotiation, and then a second confirmatory referendum. Even without the second referendum, this process would still take time. A Scottish government might be able to use this time to negotiate a provisional deal on euro-entry, including a deal on an entry date and the rate of exchange, with the EU. This might coincide with the date of independence, but it does assume a great deal of goodwill on the part of the EU euro-zone members.

– Meeting the Maastricht criteria –

Like any other entrant country, Scotland would have to meet the criteria for euro-membership. There are five main tests laid out in the Treaty of Maastricht (Pitchford and Cox 1997: 80).[2] The first requires price stability: an average rate of consumer price inflation that does not exceed by more than 1.5 per cent the average inflation of the three states with the lowest inflation. Assuming that the Bank of England maintains its policy of keeping inflation within a range of 1.5–2.5 per cent, this criterion should be met. The second requires budget deficits not to exceed more than 3 per cent of GDP. Figure 10.3 shows that since 1996–7, Scotland has been close to meeting this criterion. Looking at the overall spending trend in the last decade, unless oil revenues are particularly buoyant, the odds appear to favour the necessity of making some public spending cuts to bring the deficit down to 3 per cent. However, the cuts need not necessarily be large.

The third criterion requires general government gross debt to be less than 60 per cent of GDP. Assuming that Scotland assumes a share of the UK debt, following the figures given in Figure 11.2, its initial debt to GDP ratio would range from 48 per cent (population share) to 50 per cent (revenue share). All governments need to borrow to finance their expenditure, and Scotland would be no exception. These figures suggest Scotland would have some room to make additional borrowings while still staying within the Maastricht debt limit. The elbow room is not massive – the additional borrowing power could range between £7bn and £8.5bn – but neither is it enormously constricting.

The fourth criterion – the currency exchange rate stability requirement – runs into the problem of a lack of a Scottish currency discussed above. Again, unless some special entry terms could be negotiated to take account of this special circumstance, Scotland would have to hope that sterling would meet this requirement.

Fulfilling the fifth criterion, however, would be more in Scotland's hands. This is of interest rate convergence – that entrant countries' long-term government bonds should have a nominal interest rate no more than two percentage points above the rates applicable in the three best-performing member states. These interest rates, generally speaking, are dependent on market perceptions of long-term financial stability. A problem for Scotland would be that as a new country, its borrowings would carry a risk premium that might push its long-term rates outside the criterion. Mitigating this effect would entail proving that the Scottish government intended to maintain very strict financial discipline. It would be a hard task, but not impossible.

Apart from these considerations, pursuing option 5 would also entail the Scottish government having to do great deal of work domestically to overcome a serious technical problem. Changing a currency requires a lot of work. Banks, businesses, shops and the population have all to be prepared, and to prepare, for the changeover. The manufacture of notes and coins, the conversion of tills and the preparation of the necessary financial systems all takes time. The evidence from the process of EU monetary integration is that this kind of preparatory work is not earnestly undertaken until it becomes obvious that the changeover is going to happen. This was why the EU allowed three years from the date of locking national currencies together to the introduction of euro notes and coins (De Grauwe 1997: 161). In the absence of goodwill, or even the absence of agreement by the EU to admit Scotland, the other options come into play.

– Non-euro currency options –

If the UK was in the euro at the point of independence, and Scotland was not to be admitted to the EU, it could just carry on using the euro by recognising it as legal tender – option 9. In 1944, the west African country of Liberia unilaterally adopted the US dollar as its currency by making US banknotes legal tender and fixing the Liberian dollar at parity with the US dollar. Panama did the same with the US dollar in 1904. Closer to home, sterling, which had been used in Ireland since 1846, continued as Ireland's currency after Irish independence in 1922 until 1928 (Bordo and Jonung 2000: 32). Luxembourg's pre-euro use of the Belgian franc is another example. The same arrangement could be made with sterling if that was the UK currency at the point of independence, either unilaterally (option 3) or by agreement (option 4).

Using sterling by agreement would be the preferable option. An elegant solution could follow from the principles set out in Chapter 11 for the division of UK assets and liabilities. If agreement was reached that Scotland took on an equitable share of these assets and liabilities, this principle could be applied to the Bank of England, a UK Government asset. Scotland could assume the same equitable share in the ownership of the bank. The rUK government would have the majority holding. Both governments would become joint guarantors, in the same proportion, of UK debt existing at the time of independence. This solution would have the appeal, to both governments, that it would remove much uncertainty about the security of existing debt.

Other uncertainties would also be removed as the bank would retain its position at the apex of the financial regulation system. The arrangement would also be a clear signal that Scottish independence was not intended to disrupt financial and trade linkages within the UK. Under this sort of arrangement, Scotland would have the right to appoint a minority of the bank's board and to the monetary policy committee. It would also receive a minority shareholder's share of profits and seignorage (earnings from the right to issue currency). The arrangement would not be ideal from Scotland's point of view; practical experience of these sort of joint monetary arrangements tends to suggest that decisions eventually tend to suit the interests of the majority interest and the minority interest gets ignored (de Grauwe 1997: 95–7). But it would certainly be in Scotland's short- and medium-term interest.

If agreement to this effect was not possible, Scotland could unilaterally adopt sterling as its currency. The rUK government and the Bank of England might object, but in practice there is not a lot they could do to prevent it. The measures required to stop Scotland from taking such a course – strict exchange controls – would be so draconian that rUK companies and individuals would not tolerate them. Neither would they work.

The disadvantage of unilateral adoption of the euro or sterling is that Scotland would have no representation or involvement within the monetary authority, either the European Central Bank or the Bank of England. The virtue of these arrangements is that they are simple and cheap to implement. They would not expose Scotland to the costs of having to manage a Scottish currency or to the risks of fluctuating exchange rates that a Scottish currency would entail.

– A Scottish currency –

Establishing a Scottish currency, which might be called the Scottish pound (Sc£), invokes risk, even if it were pegged in value to either sterling (option 2) or the euro (option 8). In essence, pegging the value of the Sc£ would be a promise to manage the supply of money, interest rates, and tax policies so that the value of the Sc£ exactly matches the value of the currency to which it is pegged. Managing a currency under these conditions requires extreme discipline and the establishment of credibility in the money markets. Under these circumstances, it is hard to see what gain there is for Scotland.

Indeed, credibility is the gold standard for such arrangements. In an attempt to mitigate the effects of the Czech/Slovak break-up in 1993, the two countries kept a common currency, a customs union and a common labour market. The currency union was intended to be a temporary measure to last at least six months with the possibility of extending it (Fidrmuc and Horvath 1998). In trade terms, 50 per cent of Slovak exports went to the Czech Republic and 30 per cent of Czech exports went to Slovakia, figures which many economists would argue made the two countries an optimum currency area.

In the event, the currency union lasted just six weeks. The flight of capital from Slovakia, caused by expectations of a Slovak devaluation (which eventually occurred in July 1993) became too large for the central banks and the government to handle. The Irish had similar credibility problems, albeit to a lesser degree and with less dramatic consequences, when they broke the sterling link and joined the European exchange rate mechanism in 1979 (Leddin and Walsh 1998: 503). The outflow of capital from Slovakia and Ireland that occurred suggest that it is not just international credibility which needs to be established, but also credibility with Scottish firms and individuals as well.

The classical free market answer to this credibility problem is to allow a currency to float to that the markets can determine its value. The major problem of having a 'sovereign' Scottish currency (options 1 and 6), for example, is the importance of oil to the Scottish economy. If the price of oil was to rise sharply, or the value of the US dollar to fall, the value of oil output would increase markedly. This would cause the value of the Scottish currency to rise as well, putting pressure on other sectors of the economy, such as manufacturing industry. Manufacturers would see the price of their exports rise, making it more difficult to sell them. This is what happened to sterling in the 1980s, with devastating consequences for manufacturing industry and unemployment.

Underneath these options of a floating Sc£ and a pegged Sc£ are a whole sub-set of other questions. In what currency would Scotland's share of the UK debt be denominated in? And would new borrowings be denominated in Sc£s, sterling, or the euro? A different set of questions would arise from the extent to which the highly integrated UK financial system would be put under strain by the existence of a Sc£. Retail banking transactions (cheques, direct debits, and so on) are processed through the computerised Bankers' Automated Clearing Services system. Wholesale banking transactions are processed through a similar system which the Bank of England supervises. Regulation of banking and other financial activity is managed through the Financial Services Authority, along with other regulators such as the Personal Investment Authority.

Arguably, this UK financial system ought to be able to cope with a Sc£ and Scottish banks based on a Sc£ in much the same way as it has coped with the penetration of overseas banks into the UK financial market. By

1996, overseas banks accounted for 26 per cent of total sterling lending to the UK private sector (Buckle and Thompson 1998: 72). But a Sc£ would generate additional transaction costs within the UK system. This would put Scottish financial institutions with large volumes of business in Sc£s at a competitive disadvantage.

The only circumstances under which a Scottish currency is worth considering are if a major policy goal necessitated having such a currency, or if some major external event forced it to happen. In this case, the easiest route to follow is that of Ireland. It introduced its own currency, the Irish punt, in 1928. This was valued at parity with sterling and every IR£ had to be backed by £1 sterling, either in gold or sterling assets.

In the 1960s and 70s, the Irish started to debate the wisdom of maintaining the sterling link. It was argued that Ireland was importing British inflation and was tied to a currency falling in value (Leddin and Walsh 1998: 493). The chance to break the link came in 1978 when the European Monetary System (EMS) was proposed. Once the UK announced it would not participate in the exchange rate mechanism (ERM) of the EMS, the Irish rapidly decided to take part. It joined on 13 March 1979 and broke the sterling link, which became impossible to maintain alongside ERM membership, on 30 March. In effect, the Irish started with option 4, shifted to option 2, moved to a form of option 8, and since 1999, have been operating option 10.

This Irish process took the best part of 80 years. It would be possible to move more directly to a free-floating Scottish currency: options 1 and 6. This would be desirable only if the risks of not doing so were greater than the risks of setting up such a currency. This circumstance arose in the former USSR in the early 1990s when Russia began to experience currency instability and hyperinflation. The new independent states risked importing hyperinflation if they remained in the rouble zone. By 1994, Azerbaijan, Estonia, Georgia, Kyrgyz Republic, Latvia, Lithuania, Moldova, Turkmenistan, and Ukraine had all established their own currencies (De Grauwe 1997: 101–2). The policy was more successful where central banks were given independence from political control. But there were risks of failure – the Ukraine experienced worse monetary instability than Russia did.

Pegging a Scottish currency to another carries only slightly less risk than a floating currency, but can have economic benefits. These most obviously occur where the lion's share of a small country's trade is with a larger country. Trade and the economy gains because the uncertainties associated with currency fluctuations are removed. This was why Ireland tied its currency to sterling, and partly why the Netherlands and Austria tied their currencies to the German mark pre-ERM. In Scotland's case, about 50 per cent of its exports (including oil) are to rUK and about 30 per cent to EU countries. Thus while sterling remains outside the euro, sterling would be the most beneficial link. If sterling joins the euro, the attractions of the euro to Scotland (80 per cent of exports going to the same currency area) become rather obvious.

– Scotland's best currency option –

The general rule which emerges from this discussion is that a Scottish government's currency policy would be well advised to follow the path of least risk and least cost. While sterling is outside the euro, remaining with sterling is the least risky path. If sterling goes into the euro, Scotland should go with it, again the least risky path. That still leaves the tricky problem of what to do about a Scottish wish to enter the euro before sterling does. This could only be resolved by the negotiation of some special entry terms which took account of the fact that Scotland does not have its own currency.

If these options are, or become, impossible, a separate Scottish currency pegged to another currency is the next best option. A separate Scottish currency with a floating exchange rate is the worst option.

The conclusion that Scotland's interests would be best served by denying the presumed benefits of Scottish independence and opting for currency arrangements which gave minimum and even no autonomy to Scotland looks rather controversial. But it is also a conclusion which others have reached in examining the similar problems of Quebec independence and Canada. One such conclusion says:

> The economic benefits that currently accrue from the existence of a common Canadian market, even the present imperfect one, and from the Canadian monetary union that goes with it, are large and worth preserving. Their loss would be serious, not only for Quebec, but for all of Canada. If . . . the political federation disintegrates, a straightforward economic analysis suggests that the benefits of a continued monetary union are still there to be preserved (Laidler and Robson 1991: 37).

Importantly, this conclusion was also accepted by the PQ in the terms of Quebec independence which it wished to negotiate with Canada. These terms included that 'Quebec would have the Canadian dollar as its legal currency' (Young 1998: 278).

– A central bank –

Central banking in the form of a state-owned bank which handles the government's finances and regulates private sector banking is such a normal feature in developed countries that it is often assumed to be a necessary feature of nation–state architecture. History suggests that need not be the case. The Bank of England has only been state-owned since 1946. Prior to the Bank of England Act 1946, when it was nationalised, it was a private bank which carried out the functions of a central bank (Buckle and Thompson 1998: 350). The Central Bank of Ireland did not come into being until 1943. Prior to that, a Currency Commission, a government agency, had issued Irish notes and coins since 1927. A central bank for Scotland could evolve in the same gradual way.

There are a lot of advantages in having a central bank. One is that they usually make profits for governments. The Central Bank of Ireland, for example, made a net profit in 2000 of about £830m, of which about £720m was paid to the government.[3] Norway's central bank, Norges Bank, made a profit of just over £1bn in 2000, but a loss of about £250m in 1999.[4] However, such a Scottish bank could not leap readily into being. While there is considerable banking expertise in Scotland, it is in commercial and retail banking. Central banking skills are in the operation of monetary policy and regulation, quite different areas of expertise.

The Central Bank of Ireland provides a model to which Scotland could aspire. It is agent for, and banker to, the Irish government and has the task of ensuring price stability. It supervises most of the country's financial institutions. It also prints banknotes, mints coins and issues them. These, since 2002, have been euro notes and coins. It is a member of the European System of Central Banks (ESCB); the bank's governor sits on the 18-member Governing Council of the European Central Bank. The ECB defines and implements the single European monetary policy, conducts foreign exchange operations, holds and manages the official foreign reserves of member states and promotes the smooth operation of the payments system.

From the discussion of currency above, it is apparent that there are a variety of monetary circumstances in which an independent Scotland could find itself. Membership of the euro is only one scenario. The Irish model shows what would be the minimum requirements whatever the circumstances were. These are:

1. Banking services: this could be provided by the private sector initially. Eventually, the portion of the bank conducting this business could be bought by the government and become a central bank.
2. The ability to borrow: governments, even those in surplus, need to borrow money. This is because the inflows of money from taxation do not match the outflows of money on public expenditure. The UK

Government does this by selling bonds, known as gilt-edged securities or gilts, which pay interest until the end of the bond's life; by selling National Savings products; and by selling Treasury bills, which are a form of short-term bonds of less than 12 months' life. The sum total of money owed is the National Debt which Chapter 11 showed that a Scottish government would have to continue paying off its share. This payment would gradually reduce until 32 years after independence when the longest-life bonds existing at the date of independence were re-paid. In the meantime, the Scottish government would start accumulating its own debt in much the same way as the UK Government now does. This borrowing may have to be quite large, for two reasons. First, Chapter 10 showed that on existing tax and spending patterns, it is probable that a Scottish government would start life with a deficit. This deficit could be reduced or eventually eliminated, but it could not be done immediately, so borrowing would have to fill the gap. Second, Chapter 12 showed that a great deal of economic uncertainty would probably be caused by independence. This would reduce tax revenues, but public spending requirements would remain steady at least, and might even rise if the uncertainty caused unemployment. So borrowing would be needed. It is not possible to offer an estimate of how much a Scottish government would need to borrow, nor how much it would cost. Interest rates on bonds are determined by the market. These can vary quite widely. In 1998–9, a year when interest rates were at a particularly low level, rates payable on 10-year UK bonds varied between 4.2 per cent and 6.0 per cent.[5] A Scottish government, because it was a new issuer, would have to pay a risk premium above these rates. If a Scottish government required to borrow £5bn in its first year, and the average rate payable was 7 per cent, the cost would be £350m. This is only an indicative figure, not an estimate. A year of high oil prices could reduce it, a year of high interest rates could increase it. But it would be prudent to budget for such a payment of perhaps between £300m and £400m. The mechanics of creating an office to do the borrowing would not be arduous. Since 1998, the UK debt has been handled by the Debt Management Office, an executive agency of the Treasury. In 2000, it employed 50 people and cost £6.7m to run.[6] Setting up a smaller version in Scotland should not be too expensive.

3. Currency issuing: if independence occurred while Scotland was still in the sterling zone and intended to stay there, note issue would remain with the Bank of England. If it occurred after the UK had entered the euro, the Scottish government would become responsible for Scottish euro note issue. This could be done initially via a Currency Commis-

sion and then by a central bank should that be set up. Being in the euro zone would probably accelerate the formation of a central bank as there might be problems with Scottish representation on the Governors' Council of the ECB without such a bank. Under unilateral adoption of either sterling or the euro, note issuing would remain the responsibility of either the Bank of England or the ECB. Scottish banks could only continue to issue notes by agreement and by depositing the relevant sterling or euro assets with either bank. Other currency options would entail the Scottish government taking responsibility for note issuing and increase the need for a central bank. Printing of notes and minting of coins could be done under contract at the Royal Mint.

4. Price stability: good economic practice and the dictates of euro-entry terms point to the necessity of a Scottish government having to ensure that price stability is independently controlled. Within the sterling area, either under agreement or unilaterally, this task would continue to be handled by the Bank of England. Within the euro zone, the task could be handled initially by a Currency Commission, but a fully-equipped and independent central bank would generate more confidence that the job was being done satisfactorily. Under other currency options, the need for an independent central bank would become yet more urgent.

5. Financial regulation: the importance of maintaining the highly integrated UK financial market was noted in Chapter 12. Whatever the currency arrangements were, regulation of financial affairs in Scotland could continue to be handled by the Financial Services Authority and other regulators. Payment for these services would be necessary but it should not amount to more than a few million pounds per year. As the rUK parliament passed new financial regulations, the Scottish Parliament would need to pass mirror-image legislation, much as the Parliaments of the Isle of Man and the Channel Islands do now.

The general conclusion to be drawn is that the need for a Scottish central bank depends on the currency which would be used. Under sterling, there is no urgent necessity and a central bank could gradually evolve. Under the euro, it would become more of a priority, and under other currency options, it would become a necessity.

Establishing such a bank would be expensive. It would require a prestigious looking building and a lot of expensive IT equipment. Recruitment of financial specialists, many of who would be highly paid, would be required. Because the functions it would house are difficult to define, these set up costs are impossible to establish. In early years, they would exceed earnings.

– Other new Scottish institutions –

As has already been noted, Scotland already has a range of institutions necessary for the government of Scotland. Many more, however, would be needed. They range from the large, such as defence forces, to the small, such as a driver and vehicle licensing agency. This would be costly. The administrative cost of the devolved Scottish Executive in 2000–1 was £200m.[7] It is inconceivable that an independent government could deliver its services for this cost. Apart from the annual running costs, there are also the initial costs of setting up the infrastructure for these new institutions.

There is an allowance for the running costs of these services under the label 'non-identifiable expenditure' in the Scottish budget set out in Figure 10.1. This item covers all spending by the UK Government which benefits all UK citizens but cannot be allocated to particular parts of the UK unlike, say, social security spending. The UK amount under this heading was £37.75bn in 1998–9, of which £3.2bn is said to have been spent on behalf of Scots, in line with Scotland's 8.6 per cent share of UK population.[8] It may also be possible for some or all of the set-up costs to be financed if the division of UK assets results in the kind of sums set out in the final column of Figure 11.2 becoming payable to Scotland.

Apart from the uncertainty of the negotiations outcome, there are two further problems. First, the additional institutions required are currently established as UK institutions. Running these institutions on a UK basis creates economies of scale – administrative costs, for example, become a progressively smaller percentage of the total spending as the size of the institution increases. Thus one cannot take, say, the cost of running the UK social security system and divide it by Scotland's share of UK population in order to get the cost of running an independent Scottish social security system. This is, however, the method used by statisticians to derive Scotland's share of the costs of various UK institutions in the non-identifiable expenditure category. It seems likely, therefore, that providing the institutions that would be needed by an independent Scotland would be more expensive than is suggested by these statistics. For this reason, comparisons with the comparable institutions of other countries of a similar size to Scotland are used.

The second problem is the hazard of estimation. Devolution of power to Scotland in 1999 involved costs, the most obvious of which were the annual running costs of a parliament and the construction of a building to house it. The history of the devolved Scottish Parliament graphically illustrates the hazards of trying to estimate the costs of constitutional change. In 1997, the government estimated the likely parliament construction costs as between £10m and £40m and probable annual running costs as between £20m and £30m (Scottish Office 1997: 32–3). By 2001, construction costs had risen to an estimated £241m and annual running costs to £47m.[9] In considering the costs of independence, this cautionary history of the difference between theory and reality needs to be borne in mind.

If independence has any purpose, it ought to be that there would be benefits from bringing such functions as macro-economic management, control of foreign affairs, policy management of social security, and so on, to Scotland. These services could then be tailored more precisely to suit Scottish circumstances. This side of the equation is extremely hard to estimate. No independent study has been made of this question and this analysis will not attempt it. However, it is fair to note that such benefits could only begin to accrue a couple of years after independence. The costs would have to be borne first.

This study does not attempt an exhaustive analysis of every single institution that might conceivably be needed in an independent Scotland. What follows is a look at some of the principal areas: macro-economic management, defence, foreign affairs, and social security.

– Treasury –

The devolved Scottish Executive has a finance department. It also manages the central services of the Executive, such as personnel management and legal services. The finance function is solely concerned with managing devolved Scottish expenditure (£15.6bn in 1998–9). A Treasury of an independent Scottish government would obviously have to be much bigger as it would be also concerned with tax receipts and the management of revenue flows. Another additional function would be economic modelling and forecasting. There is a small such office within the Scottish Executive run by the Executive's chief economic advisor, but a Treasury-style function would be much bigger.

The core of the UK Treasury is surprisingly small. In 1999–2000 it cost £64m to run and had about 1000 staff.[10] A Scottish Treasury would not need to be so large, but it would cost more than Scotland's share of Treasury costs – £5.5m. Ireland's finance department cost £29m and had 530 staff in 2000 (GoI 2000).[11] Norway's finance ministry had about 300 staff and cost about £15m to run.[12] Allowing for Scotland's share of UK Treasury costs and existing Scottish Executive resources, it still seems likely that Scotland would have to spend an additional £10m–20m on a Treasury.

– National statistics –

Much of the discussion in this section of the book has been hampered by the lack of adequate statistical information. Chapter 10 noted that there was good information about public expenditure, but there were only estimates about tax revenues. Information about imports and exports is poor. Requirements for price stability in the discussion above about the role of a central bank could not be met initially because there is no Scottish Retail Price Index. There is therefore a pressing need for a Scottish national statistics office.

The UK National Statistics Office cost £93.5m in 1998–9.[13] On the principles used in the GERS reports, Scotland's share of this cost is £7.76m. This is the notional sum available in existing spending patterns for a national statistics office. Additionally, there are also the statisticians already working for the Scottish Executive. No estimate of the cost of this has been obtained, but it is unlikely to bring the total of existing spending on statistical services up to more than £10m.

This would not be enough to meet the full cost of a national statistical office. Ireland, for example, spent £16.5m on its central statistical office which in 2000 employed more than 500 people (GoI 2000). It seems likely therefore that Scotland would have to spend an additional £5m–£10m annually on statistics office running costs. Further, the National Statistics Office has offices in England and Wales, but none in Scotland. Capital costs would therefore be incurred on a building and equipment.

– Defence –

The issue of the defence forces of an independent Scotland is not addressed in detail by the SNP. One possible solution to deal with the matter of maintaining continuity with the existing defences of the UK would be to strike a deal with rUK whereby Scotland pays a proportion towards maintaining existing defence forces. On the GERS figures, this would have amounted to £1.96bn in 1998–9.

But SNP manifestos make it clear that this could only be an interim solution. It thinks Scotland should have its own Scottish defence force (SDF). The SDF would be 'an all–professional force supported by part-time volunteers' which 'will be initially equipped with Scotland's negotiated share of UK defence resources (SNP 2001a: 7).' Scotland's comparator countries in terms of population, Denmark (5.3 million), Norway (4.3 million), and Ireland (3.6 million), all have armies. Size and expenditure varies as can be seen in Figure 13.1, figures from which are from 2000.

Figure 13.1. Defence expenditure in Denmark, Norway, Ireland and the UK (2000).

Country	NATO Member	Defence Expenditure (in million)	Defence Expenditure as % of GDP	Annual Average Strength of armed forces
Denmark	Yes	DKK19,349 (Approx. £1.6bn)	1.5	25,000
Norway	Yes	NKK25,675 (Approx. £2bn)	1.9	32,000
Ireland	No	IEP600 (Approx. £463m)	0.7	10,500
UK	Yes	£22,823	2.4	218,000

Source: http://www.nato.int/docu/pr/2000/p00-107e.htm[14] Department of Defence, Dublin, Ireland.

How much is spent on defence is a decision for national governments. The decisive factor is what the individual nation wants its defence force to be capable of. Irish defence spending falls short of that of countries of a similar size because of its historic neutrality and its geographic position. Irish defence spending might well have to increase if Ireland became a NATO member since NATO encourages its members to spend well on defence. On the other hand, Iceland is a member of NATO but does not have armed forces, which suggests that defence policy is ultimately determined by the individual state and not by NATO.

The SNP claims it could operate a defence force – outside NATO – on an annual defence budget of £1.7bn, which is roughly what Denmark spends each year. The cost of a defence force per taxpayer would be less than now, the SNP claims, as Scotland would not be paying for the Trident nuclear submarines. On the SNP defence budget, there would be a saving of £260m.

The SNP further hopes to obtain its fair share of UK defence equipment. After the Czech/Slovak split, both republics set up a Ministry of Defence, and each received military assets on a 2:1 ratio. This was beneficial for Slovakia, which received a great number of weapons and aircraft from the Czech Republic. But military equipment is not always divided along equitable lines. When the Irish Free State broke away from the United Kingdom in 1921 it did not get any UK military equipment.

The SNP's defence ambitions are quite large. Apart from safeguarding 'the land, sea and airspace of Scotland', the SDP would also be equipped for 'rapid deployment overseas' and 'humanitarian and disaster relief operations (SNP 2001a: 7)'. Thus the SDF might still be in need of expensive air transport, anti-submarine ships and planes, and anti-tank helicopters. However no study has been undertaken of whether these ambitions can be fulfilled with an annual budget of £1.7bn and it is outwith the scope of this study to assess whether or not these plans are realistic.

– Overseas services –

Two matters come under this heading: a diplomatic service and overseas aid to less developed countries. On the first function, the SNP has said that it would have 'a commercially focussed presence for Scotland in the major commercial and population centres of the world.' This would be achieved by amalgamating the foreign representation of Locate in Scotland, Scottish Trade International (combined into Scottish Development International in 2001) and VisitScotland (formerly the Scottish Tourist Board) into external affairs offices of the Scottish government. This department 'would operate on a budget no greater than the current spending by the Scottish Executive and its agencies on overseas representation and our population share of Foreign and Commonwealth Office (FCO) spending' (SNP 2001a: 8).

The FCO budget in 1998–9 was £1.1bn. Of this, £758m was spent on the diplomatic service including the maintenance of 223 overseas embassies and consulates. The remainder was spent on items including subscriptions to international organisations such as the UN, support for the BBC World Service, and maintenance of the British Council.[15] Assuming that Scotland would wish to maintain its share of these obligations, Scotland's population share of the diplomatic service costs is £65m.

When added to what is already spent by the Scottish Executive on external relations, this would pay for a respectable diplomatic service. By comparison, Ireland spent £55m in 2000 on its foreign service (GoI 2000). Scotland might even be able to make a saving on present spending of about £15m, although it should be noted that Denmark's foreign service is rather more expensive – £153m in 2001, excluding development aid spending.[16] A reasonable course of action towards setting up a diplomatic service post-independence would be to negotiate an agreement with rUK whereby Scotland could make a payment for the use of existing buildings and overseas staff until it eventually secured its own overseas premises and staff. Such a course would be necessary because, for example, the Scottish Executive has no offices or staff in any of the EU country capitals with the exception of Brussels. Of course, Scotland could not hope to match the global coverage of the UK FCO, but there is no reason to suppose that it could not have broadly the same diplomatic coverage of other similar small European countries.

On the second function, the SNP says it 'has a long-standing commitment to raise Scotland's international aid budget to UN recommended levels' (SNP 2001a: 8). This recommended level is that developed countries should spent 0.7 per cent of their gross national product (GNP) on development aid.[17] There are no GNP figures for Scotland, although such a figure is likely to be a little below the GDP figure (see p. 184). Using 1998–9 figures, if Scottish GNP turned out to be 95 per cent of Scottish GDP, then a Scottish aid budget of about £470m would be need to fulfil the UN target figure. The Department for International Development spent £2.2bn on international aid in 1998–9.[18] Scotland's population share of this was £192m. A Scottish government would therefore need to find about another £280m in order to meet the SNP target. There would also be the administrative costs of supervising the spending of this budget.

– Social security system –

The SNP clearly envisages taking control of social security. It plans to examine 'the structure for social security delivery . . . the actual delivery of key benefits . . . [and] the workings and effectiveness of each benefit . . .' Immediate changes it wants to make include extending the winter fuel allowance and to restore benefits to 16–17 year olds (SNP 2001a: 13). The proposals are hedged with caution using phrases like 'as resources become available', indicating that no rapid expansion of the Scottish social security budget (£9.2bn in 1998–9) is planned. It also appears that there is a hope that examination of the bureaucracy will release money to be spent directly on benefits.

What would happen to these benefits under independence would be a matter of acute concern to most Scots, especially pensioners. The SNP evidently intend that achieving independence should mean no disruption to benefit payments at all, a difficult but not impossible task. The infrastructure of benefit delivery (through local offices of the department for work and pensions, post offices, and so on) is already present. What would need to be added are financial systems to manage the inflow of revenue from taxation and the outflow of payments, which would be managed through a Scottish treasury, and a social security policy directorate.

Total UK spending on social security benefits in 1998–9 was £93.4bn. An additional £3.3bn was spent on administration,[19] 3.37 per cent of all social security spending. Applying this proportion to Scottish social security spending implies that £310m of the Scottish budget is administration costs.

The economies of scale effect can be seen by comparing these figures with Northern Ireland where administration of social security is devolved to the Secretary of State for Northern Ireland. There is little additional policy-making bureaucracy in Ulster as a policy aim is ensuring benefits parity with the rest of the UK. Nevertheless, the administrative costs of delivering social security spending to Northern Ireland's 0.8m people in 1998–9 was 4.3

per cent of a total £3.2bn social security budget.[20] In the Republic of Ireland, administration costs were 4.8 per cent of a budget of £5.3bn in 2000 delivered to 3.7m people (GoI 2001).[21] Applying these proportions to the Scottish budget implies that administrative costs would rise to £395m (4.3 per cent) or £440m (4.8 per cent), an increase of between £85m and £130m.

– The additional institutional cost –

Would the additional institutions that an independent Scotland would need exceed the £3.2bn cost to Scotland of these institutions in their present UK form? The major difficulty in answering that question is in knowing whether the SNP estimate of £1.7bn for defence costs is reasonable. If it is reasonable, that would represent a saving of about £260m on the present Scottish contribution to defence spending. But as yet, the SNP has not presented a detailed defence policy that would allow such an estimate to be made. An interim defence policy, where Scotland would make a payment to the rUK government for continued defence cover by the existing UK defence forces would imply that no saving would be made.

Nevertheless, even if it was possible to keep the Scottish defence budget within £1.7bn, this study has shown that there are other costs which would push the additional institutional cost above £3.2bn. These are the costs of borrowing, departments to manage economic policy, and a department to manage social security spending. These items look like costing somewhere between £400m and £500m. A diplomatic service would not necessarily cost more than is presently spent (although it would be a much smaller service than is presently provided), but meeting the SNP aspiration for an international aid budget would add another £280m.

This study has not been exhaustive in its analysis of all the extra institutions that would be required. Major items would be the establishment of Scottish Inland Revenue and Customs and Excise services. There are a myriad of small institutions such as the TV Licensing Authority. Collectively, they cost Scotland about £700m as now run on a UK basis. Establishing all these institutions on a Scottish basis would involve the loss of economies of scale. This might add between £50m and £150m to costs.

The additional costs which have been identified in this chapter and in other sections of this part of the book can now be added up. Figure 13.1 shows the low and high estimates of these costs in terms of what would have to be added and subtracted from Figure 10.1. The UK debt payment item derives from the additional proportion of UK debt (above that set out in Figure 10.1) that Scotland would assume at the date of independence, and follows the conclusion of Chapter 11. In line with that argument, the low estimate is a population-based share and the high estimate is a GDP-based share.

Figure 13.2. The costs (savings) of independence (£m).

Additional item	Low estimate	High estimate
EU payments	200	200
UK debt payment	80	230
Scottish borrowing	300	400
Treasury and National Statistics	15	30
Defence	(260)	0
Foreign Affairs	(15)	0
International Aid	0	280
Social Security	85	130
Other Institutions	50	150
TOTALS	**455**	**1420**

In round terms, it seems probable that independence could add between £0.5bn (0.7 per cent of GDP) and £1.5bn (2.1 per cent of GDP) to the expenditure side of the Scottish public sector balance sheet. These estimates are likely to come under heavy criticism as either ludicrous exaggerations (by supporters of independence) or woeful under-estimates (by opponents of independence). Political partisanship apart, there are a number of valid criticisms which can be made.

Some of the items – EU payments, UK debt payments – would depend on the outcome of negotiations which are hard to second-guess. Some of the items – Scottish borrowing – would depend on the state of the economy at the time. Some – defence, international aid, foreign affairs – would depend on political choices made by a Scottish government. Given the hazards of estimation, these figures are but one set of estimates amongst many others that could be made. Commonsense says, however, that when two defence systems are being created out of one, two social security systems out of one, and so on, costs must rise as, indeed, the cost of political representation rose with devolution.

Some general points should also be made. None of the potential costs of uncertainty discussed in Chapter 12 have been factored in. Neither can a start be made to estimating them until much more is known about the nature of independence that would be sought by the SNP. More needs to be known about the currency Scotland would have, how much integration with the UK single market would remain, and so on. If there was no knowledge about these matters, the costs of uncertainty would be high.

This part of the analysis also simply adds costs to one side of the balance sheet as though these costs would arrive in one lump. It would not be like that in reality. The costs would start to rise gradually, although most would probably be incurred by two years after the date of independence. It is also fair to note that independence would also create the opportunity to make changes which would affect the revenue side of the balance sheet. Scottish taxation revenues could not be assumed to remain static.

– A SCOTTISH OIL FUND –

The SNP have long proposed that a new institution should be created. They have suggested that a proportion of North Sea oil revenues, perhaps as much as 75 per cent should be put aside in a fund invested in international bonds and equities (SNP 2001b: 2). The SNP idea is modelled on a fund of this type which has been in existence in Norway since 1990. Based on the returns achieved by the Norwegian fund, and on certain assumptions about future oil price and production levels, the SNP contend that Scottish oil revenues could be worth about £4bn a year for the next 10 years. Investing 75 per cent of this revenue in a fund could generate an income 'worth more than £1bn per annum within 5 years'. Without re-investing the income in the fund, the annual income generated after 10 years 'could be worth as much as £5bn per year'.

Such a fund looks like a good idea. There is one in Scotland already. Shetland Islands Council, because of a special deal it got from the Government in the 1970s, is able to levy a royalty over every barrel of oil landed at the Sullom Voe oil terminal in Shetland. Until 2000, the royalty was about a third of a penny per barrel; since then, it has been reduced. But funds have been built up which totalled about £700m in 2001. The income from the funds goes to provide enhanced social services for the elderly and disabled, and has built a lot of sports facilities for all of Shetland's 23,000 people.[22] Apart from the Shetland and the Norwegian funds, the Canadian province of Alberta and the American state of Alaska also have such funds. Comparison of the two North American and the Norwegian funds enables some useful lessons to be learned.

– Alaska Permanent Fund –

Oil wealth first arrived in Alaska in 1969, when the state government (which collects revenues from mineral exploitation) earned $US900m from auctioning drilling licences. This money was soon spent, so in 1976, when oil and revenues began to flow it was decided to invest 25 per cent of the revenues in a permanent fund. There were three reasons: that when the oil revenues dried up, 'there would still be a major source of state revenues'; that 'the fund would remove a significant portion of the oil revenues from the legislative spending stream, thus reducing the opportunities for excessive spending by the legislature'; and that the fund would convert non-renewable oil wealth into 'a renewable source of wealth for future genera-tions of Alaskans' (APFC 2001a: 6–7).

Between 1976 and 2001, Alaska earned $55bn in oil revenues. Payments into the fund began in 1979 and in June 2001, the Fund's value stood at just over $US26bn (about £18.3bn) (APFC 2001b: 7). The fund is mainly invested in long-term low-risk investments. Income from the fund can be paid into the state government's general account for public spending, but in 25 years only $US300m has been spent this way. Just under half of the income is distributed as a straight annual dividend cheque to every eligible Alaskan. Since 1982, when the dividend was first paid, $US10.9bn has been paid out. In 2001, the individual dividend was $US1,850.28. The remaining 55 per cent of income has been ploughed back into the fund (APFC 2001a: 29–31).

Nearly all the fund's revenue comes from one very large oilfield, Prudhoe Bay, which passed peak production in 1988. That year, revenue from the fund exceeded the state's oil revenues for the first time, a position which is likely to become permanent after 2003. There is now concern that the fund should be protected, especially against inflation, to provide for the state's prosperity well into the future. A goal is that the fund should produce $US5bn a year income in 2026. The funds trustees have proposed that pay-outs should be limited to a maximum of 5 per cent of the fund's five-year average market value APFC 2001a: 44).

– Alberta Heritage Savings Trust Fund –

This was established in 1976, when oil revenues were high and the Canadian province's economy was booming, in order to provide a source of revenue when state oil and gas revenues started to fall. It appears that there were no fixed rules about how much should be placed in the fund and most major payments into it were made in 1976–7 by the end of which period it had $Can2.2bn of assets. By 1987, the fund reached a value of $Can12.7bn (about £6.7bn). Since then, the fund has not done so well. In March 2001, its value was $Can12.3bn (AHSTF 2001: 1).

All the income from the fund has gone into general spending by the provincial government. Some has been used for capital projects, such as building a children's hospital, some for research, such as work on renewable energy, and some for social purposes, such as dealing with drug abuse problems. The Alberta Government, which is obliged to balance its budget, now uses above-budget income from oil revenues to pay off the state's borrowings faster than they would otherwise be repaid.

In 1995, prompted by the static value of the fund, the Government re-thought its investment strategy. Hitherto, most of the fund appears to have been invested in bonds with the aim of producing high levels of income. The decline in long-term interest rates prompted a shift into equities with longer-term capital growth potential. The move in being done gradually and is expected to be completed by 2003 (AHSTF 2001: 6).

This shift into equities means that the investment income has become more volatile. In 2001, the Alberta Government received $Can706m revenue from the fund. This was sharply down from the previous year when $Can1,169m was received (AHSTF 2001: 3). In 2002, the Government proposed to hold a major public debate on the future of the fund once provincial debt has been eliminated. People will be asked whether they want the fund to be used for tax reductions or increased spending, investment in Alberta or just to be saved for the future.

– Norway's Government Petroleum Fund –

The Norwegian fund, again to provide for the future when oil revenues start to fade, was set up in 1990. The rules of the fund are that its income consists of the government's net cash flow from oil taxes, plus income from the sale of government shares in Statoil, plus the income from the funds investments. Its expenditure consists of transfers to the government budget needed if taxes from the non-oil mainland economy fall short of the public spending budget. No other spending is allowed and only the income earned in any one year can be spent. The capital cannot be touched (GoN 2002: 18). In effect, the fund operates simply as a budget balancing mechanism, creaming off any government tax surplus or making up any spending deficit.

The first payment into the fund did not occur until 1996 after Norway's non-oil budget moved into surplus in 1995. The non-oil budget remained in surplus until 2001 when it moved into a small deficit. A larger deficit is forecast for 2002. Oil revenues have gone into the fund every year since 1996 and were especially large in 2000 and 2001, years of high oil prices. By end 2001, the market value of the fund's investment was NOK613.7bn (about £47.6bn), of which NOK567.2bn was payments by the government into the fund (Norges Bank 2001: 7).

Until 1999, the returns achieved by the fund, which is invested outside Norway in a mixture of equities and bonds, were spectacular, averaging 9 per cent. Since then, interest rates have fallen, equity markets have weakened and the Norwegian krone has strengthened. In 2001, the fund's investments shrank in value by 2.5 per cent and the real annual average return 1998–2001 was only 3.6 per cent when measured in international currency.[23] Siphoning off the fund's income in order to bridge the government's non-oil budget deficit will also reduce its growth unless oil prices are particularly high.

Nonetheless, the fund is a valuable asset, worth about 43 per cent of Norway's GDP in 2001. The long-term goal is to deal with Norway's growing pension problem. The proportion of pensioners in the population is growing, and as pensions are paid out of current taxation, they will become a heavier burden. The government expects pension and disability payments to double as a percentage of GDP by 2030 and hopes the Petroleum Fund will help solve this problem (GoN 2002: 13). It is, in effect, Norway's pension fund. However, this nest-egg does cause some problems. The deficit-bridging oil money being pumped into the non-oil economy in 2002 will cause inflation. Monetary policy will have to be tightened either by raising interest rates or allowing the krone to rise in value which may squeeze traditional export industries. There is also public pressure to see some of the money spent now on hospitals and schools.[24]

– Oil fund prospects for Scotland –

Scotland's fiscal position is rather different from these three examples. Alaska's first US$900m receipt from the sale of drilling licences was eight times the state's routine spending, which was US$112m in 1969 (APFC 2001a: 1–2). By 1980, when annual oil revenues swelled to more than US$2bn, they had become 90 per cent of all the state's revenues and since then they have never dropped below 73 per cent of all revenues.[25] Although Alberta is a larger oil producer, oil revenues are not such a large proportion of the provincial government's income. From 1993–4 to 1999–2000, state oil revenues averaged Can$3.4bn a year, about 15 per cent of the state's total revenue. In 2000–1, revenues climbed to Can$10.6bn, or 41 per cent of all revenues. In 2002–3, oil revenues are expected to be 18 per cent of total revenue.[26] Norway's oil revenues also form a high proportion of state income. In 2000, they were 26 per cent of total revenues and in 2001, they were 34 per cent of all revenues (GoN 2001: 11).

On the 1990s record, oil revenues would be a much smaller proportion of the Scottish budget. From the data in Figures 10.1 and 10.2, oil revenues would have been 5.7 per cent of all Scottish revenues in 1998–9 down from a peak of 10.8 per cent of all revenues in 1996–7. There is therefore much less scope for periods of high oil revenues to produce the kind of surpluses that they have in Norway, Alaska and Alberta.

Scotland would also have to deal with its fiscal deficit before it could contemplate an oil fund. It took Norway six years after it first set up its fund to deal with its deficit before it could begin paying in to its fund. Norway's deficit, moreover, was of a lesser order (peaking at 2 per cent of GDP in 1991 (GoN 2001: 9)) than Scotland's deficit has been in recent years. If, as is implied by the SNP, a Scottish government simply began paying in 75 per cent of revenues, this would worsen a deficit which is already struggling to comply with the Maastricht criteria for EU and euro entry. That implies that creation of an oil fund would have to go hand-in-hand with a programme of tax increases and/or spending reductions which would be very difficult to achieve politically.

Although these practicalities make it very unlikely that there would be the revenue means to set up a Scottish oil fund, that does not make it a bad idea. On the contrary, there are several reasons why it is a good idea and should be held in reserve by a Scottish government, should there be periods when oil revenues unexpectedly rise.

First, it would forestall politicians from splurging unexpected oil bonuses, one of the reasons that Alaska created its fund. Second, it would prevent sudden dollops of oil money from causing distortions in the Scottish economy. Svein Gjedrem, Governor of Norway's Central Bank, has noted that oil price fluctuations cause Norway's terms of trade to vary widely. But much of the Petroleum Fund is invested in foreign equities and bonds. This means, he said, that 'changes in the oil price influence the size of the fund, but have little effect on the domestic use of petroleum revenues. The Petroleum Fund acts as a buffer against fluctuations in the oil price, which stabilises the krone exchange rate.'[27] Third, if such a Scottish fund were to be created with substantial sums, it could provide a dowry for future Scottish governments to use to deal with the same problem that Norway has – an ageing population which will make increasing demands on pension and disability payment budgets. And fourth, the existence of such a fund would improve Scotland's international credit ratings, cutting the interest it would have to pay on borrowings.

The experience of the Norwegian, Alaskan and Albertan funds and developments in equity markets since 1999 also shows that the SNP forecast that the capital invested in a Scottish fund could grow at 8 per cent a year is far too optimistic. Even with the careful management that the Norwegians demonstrated in out-performing various international bench–marks in the late 1990s, they could not avoid a shrinkage in the fund in 2001. Since the fund invested in equities in 1998, its annual average real return (after management costs) has been 3.6 per cent. The 2001 report stated: 'There are hardly grounds for expecting that the high return figures recorded in capital markets in the 1990s will be repeated in this decade' (Norges Bank 2001: 5).

– SCOTLAND'S ROOM FOR FISCAL MANOEUVRE –

There are several broad conclusions to be drawn from this analysis. The first is that even with gaining control of oil revenues, Scotland would have very little fiscal flexibility. The surpluses that Scotland would have enjoyed in the 1980s would have turned into deficits in the 1990s. If EU membership remains the goal for an independent Scotland, these deficits have, for the most part, been larger than the 3 per cent of GDP permitted under the Maastricht entry criteria.

The detailed work for this analysis stops in the fiscal year 1998–9. When the statistics are calculated for subsequent years, it appears likely that high oil prices would have reduced the deficit to below 3 per cent of GDP in 1999–2000, and that in 2000–1 there would be a small surplus, relapsing back into a small deficit again in 2001–2. The data for these three years is very likely to suggest that Scotland would have much more room for fiscal manoeuvre – more ability to raise and lower taxes and spending – than has been suggested here.

This, however, only serves to underline the point that an independent Scotland is very dependent on the erratic behaviour of oil prices throwing up a few years of high oil prices in order to gain a favourable wind for independence. It is a roll of the dice which few finance ministers in the modern world are prepared to rely on, even in jurisdictions where oil is a much more important part of the economy than in Scotland. For example, when presenting the 2002 budget for the Canadian province of Alberta, Patricia Nelson, the Finance Minister, said:

> Those who dare to guess the price of natural gas for the next three years, peg it anywhere from $2.65 a mcf to $4.60. Each 10 cent fluctuation means $163m more or less for the provincial coffers. Oil price forecasts range from a low of $18 a barrel to a high of $26.50. And for each dollar difference, we could gain or lose $108m. Mr Speaker, some would say 'just wait and see. Things will pick up'. We can't. We won't take that risk. We can't base a budget on this week's price of oil. And we will not put the future of essential programmes and services at risk while we sit with our fingers crossed, wishing and hoping that optimistic forecasts will come true. This year's budget is based on the price of gas remaining at about $3 and oil hovering around $20 a barrel.[28]

The finance minister of an independent Scotland would need to be equally cautious. Such a minister would also have to cope with the second conclusion of this study – the probability that independence would have pushed up the costs of delivering essentially the same public services that existed pre-independence. If this minister was lucky, and arrived in office to find that oil revenues were happily gurgling out of the North Sea, there would still be a difficult choice to make. Should this money be used for tax cuts or spending increases, when next year the flow might have dried up again? Or should it be tucked away for a future rainy day?

Economies do change. The Scottish economy may well change in the first decade of the twenty-first century to the point where the mainland non-oil public sector is in balance rather than showing a deficit. The UK national debt may reduce to a point where it would be no longer such an onerous burden nor such a contentious issue. These changes have happened, ironically enough, in Quebec since the 1995 referendum.

Since 1995, the Parti Québécois has taken to issuing glossy brochures. They are filled with economic statistics showing how real GDP per inhabitant is growing faster than in adjacent Ontario, charts showing how the provincial debt which was such an economic nightmare in 1995 had gone by 1999, and figures showing how more jobs have been created in Montreal than in Toronto (PQ 2000). Developments of a similar nature may well happen in Scotland. If they did, it would make the economics of independence much happier reading for Scottish nationalists.

There is still, however the problem of the third broad conclusion – the costs of uncertainty. The evidence presented in Chapter 12 showed that the two-week period right at the end of the 1995 Quebec sovereignty referendum caused considerable economic disruption. How much worse would that disruption be if it was spread over several months following a 'Yes' to independence vote in a referendum and then negotiations before a settlement became clear? How much extra economic growth would be needed to recover the ground lost to uncertainty? And how much less room would there be for the kind of fiscal manoeuvering needed to produce the stimulus required to produce that extra growth?

This analysis has not attempted to answer these questions. Rather, it has pointed to a solution aimed at minimising uncertainty and its problems. This fourth conclusion is, admittedly, not immediately appealing to a Nationalist. It is to point out that the root cause of uncertainty is change and that the problem of independence is that it promises, not just lots of change, but lots of unknown change. Therefore, to reduce uncertainty to a minimum, the possibility of change and the threat of unknown change has to be removed. It means saying that independence won't actually make any difference, not immediately at any rate.

This may seem a perverse conclusion for a section of a book which opened with the observation that independence would have little meaning if it were not to make a difference. But this is to confuse politics with economics. The economic evidence from a developed country such as Canada, where escape from oppression is not a motive for seeking independence, is that independence promises major changes to established and familiar economic structures. Those who are involved with that established economic structure recoil from that change and economic disruption is the result. But it is still possible to offer political change without economic change.

Three examples may illustrate the point. When the Labour Party, trading as New Labour, won the 1997 British general election, it did so promising that things could only get better and that there would be major constitutional reform. Alongside that promise was another – that a Labour Government would stick with the spending programme set out by the previous Conservative Government for at least two years. It promised political change, but little economic change, for a while anyway.

When the new Government held referendums in Scotland and Wales in devolution in 1997, it also promised major political change. But it also said that it would keep all the major economic levers of control – political change, but little economic change. This is also a trick which the SNP have used. In 1988, they re-defined independence to mean 'Independence in Europe'. It meant that independence did not mean some bleak isolation, but membership of the warming family of European nations. Or, as one party critic put it, 'an escape into a Utopia . . . where great changes could be achieved without much being changed' (Marr 1992: 191–3). In the context of this discussion about independence, this means offering political change without much economic difference. No difference to the UK internal market, no currency frontier, no different sets of regulations, no break with ties to the EU and its single market, and so on.

– Fiscal freedom –

This seems to be a route which the SNP started to test under John Swinney, elected as SNP leader in 2000. In a speech made shortly after becoming leader, he concentrated on one power which the Scottish Parliament lacked and which he believed lay at the heart of tackling Scotland's problems:

> I want the Scottish parliament to have full fiscal freedom – control over all of the revenues generated in Scotland and the ability to spend that money in Scotland. The power to take responsibility for our income and expenditure and pay Westminster for whatever remaining services we receive from the United Kingdom. I want that power urgently – to allow us to give our pensioners a decent income, to create a fair deal for disabled people, to create an economy that creates new jobs and new businesses, to enable us to properly invest in Scotland's ailing roads and rail links, to be at the forefront of investing in new developments in wind and wave power. As a Nationalist, I accept that fiscal autonomy is not independence. But I also accept it would be progress for Scotland (Swinney 2000).

This policy has not been much developed since then, save to suggest that any tax cuts under this regime would benefit business with the aim of stimulating economic growth. If this, despite Swinney's disavowal, is in practice a new definition of independence, it deals with a lot of the uncertainty problems. It would also generate much less additional cost. Rather interestingly, it has attracted interest from other parts of the political spectrum including parts which have been traditionally opposed to Nationalism. It corresponds to the Liberal Democrat's ideas for a federal Britain, being a form of fiscal federalism. It also corresponds to traditional Conservative notions of self-reliance. Some right-wing Conservatives acknowledge that their support for this idea looks odd:

> Of course, fiscal freedom has always presented a political paradox in that it takes Scotland far closer to independence than unionists have supported in the past. Bravely, supporters of the idea argue it is only by making a Scottish Parliament more responsible and more accountable for its financial commitments that the union will be preserved (Monteith 2001).

Examples of degrees of fiscal freedom can be found in many federal political systems around the world. In Europe, the freedom given to regional governments tends to be limited; in North America it is much greater (Hughes Hallett 2001). But where the concept as it has been voiced in Scotland goes beyond these examples is in severing the financial link between central and regional government. It raises the political question of what point would there be in continuing with the British state if one of its fundamental reasons for existing – to distribute public spending to all parts of the country to ensure equality of public services – has been taken away. Apart from that, and on the evidence presented in this book, fiscal freedom would disadvantage Scotland at times of low oil prices. At such periods, Scotland would have to resort to borrowing to maintain public spending, or cut spending.

A much more detailed blueprint is needed before a proper assessment can be made of the merits of fiscal freedom. Also needed is better information about taxation patterns in Scotland. All that exist at the time of writing are estimates rather than collected data. An assessment needs to be made about the ability of governments to use fiscal mechanisms to real economic effect. This would be to answer questions such as: how much do business taxes need to be cut in order to stimulate business growth and can such cuts be financed?

Scottish Nationalists quite rightly argue that the dynamic effects of independence need to be taken into the equation. Assessing whether independence would make an economic difference is not just a matter of totting up the current balance sheet. An assessment needs to be made of what changes can be made and what effect they would have on future balance sheets and the prosperity of individual citizens. This requires three things: a set of proposals, some solid economic data, and economic models in which the proposals can be tested. Unfortunately, none of these things exist to the required degree of sophistication. This study cannot go much beyond the point of saying that the available information suggests that the place from which an independent Scotland would start does not look to be a favourable one.

It also has exposed a fundamental economic problem which makes fiscal freedom look very difficult to implement. This is to do with borrowing and debt. The concept of fiscal freedom as expressed by Swinney must imply that the Scottish government would have the power to borrow. Maintaining tight control of borrowing is an essential tool of macro-economic management. If it goes out of control, it can cause inflation to rise, affecting interest rates. Since Scotland, on Swinney's definition, would not be independent, the UK would still be held responsible internationally for keeping control of borrowing. Scotland, on this analysis would be more liable to require unexpected levels of borrowing because it would be more reliant on volatile oil revenues than is the UK government. How could Scottish borrowing be kept under control so that it did not affect UK inflation and interest rate policy?

A related problem is to do with the national debt. The UK has good credit ratings because it has demonstrated its capacity for good economic management and it has close to 100 per cent control over the country's capacity to generate wealth and the income needed to repay the debt. But under the fiscal freedom proposal, the UK would lose control over about 10 per cent of its wealth-generating capacity. There is the additional problem of default risk. While the fiscal freedom agreement might provide for Scotland continuing to make a contribution to the UK Treasury for debt servicing costs, it is hard to envisage a mechanism that would prevent Scotland from defaulting on these payments. With the economic management problems noted above, the UK's credit rating would be down-graded, pushing up debt interest charges. This would be a burden that would fall on all UK taxpayers, not just Scottish ones.

This point highlights a fifth conclusion. This is that Scottish independence is something which affects all UK citizens, not just Scottish ones. Independence is sometimes imagined to be simply a matter of the Scots politely closing the door on the rest of the UK, leaving everyone else in peace except for the occasional noisy meeting on a football or rugby pitch.

In fact, this study has shown that there would be major consequences for all other UK citizens, most notably from the costs of uncertainty.

Ways of mitigating this effect have been suggested. But they lead to the sixth and final conclusion. This is that independence, if it is to be a realistic and practical proposal, cannot be a 'big bang' upheaval. Scottish Nationalists are often categorised into two types – fundamentalists and gradualists.[29] Fundamentalism can be typified as meaning a belief that independence, and consequent immediate change, can be achieved in one event by winning an election or a referendum. Gradualism, on the other hand, is taken to mean that achieving independence is a slow process. Devolution of UK power to a Scottish Parliament and then gaining more powers for that parliament is a gradualist approach.

This study, however, strongly argues that fundamentalist-style independence is probably unattainable in a modern, developed economy. This does not just derive from one set of circumstances; that, as the Scottish economy and the public sector balance sheet stand, there is not the room to make the major economic and fiscal changes that a Nationalist might want or believe are necessary. It derives from the evidence of Chapter 12 that event-style independence causes such economic disruption that it would set back the aim of achieving economic gain and improvement, possibly by many years. That has the further consequence of making it undesirable to those who would be expected to vote for it.

This, however, is not to conclude that independence is necessarily a bad thing in economic terms. Neither is it a conclusion that in order to achieve independence, Nationalists must forswear use of all the economic tools that independence would be expected to bring. It is a conclusion that both the definition of independence sought, and the means chosen to get it, require careful thought in order to avoid consequences that are economically and politically damaging. In this sense, there is only gradual independence.

– Conclusions –

- If an independent Scotland wished to be a member of the EU, it would have to accept the euro as its currency. Scotland's position as a country without its own currency is anomalous in EU entry terms, so some special terms of entry may have to be negotiated.
- Scotland's easiest solution to the currency issue would be if the UK is already a member of the euro at the time of independence. If it is not, Scotland's best course would be to remain with sterling and hope to enter the euro at the same time as sterling.

- Any other currency solution raises the level of economic risk and the cost to the Scottish economy of independence.
- Establishing the institutions required for a devolved government to become an independent government would be costly. Much of the cost of running such institutions is already budgeted for, but additional spending of between £0.5bn and £1.5bn would be incurred.
- The establishment of a Scottish oil fund into which excess oil revenues could be placed as an investment for the future is a good idea. However, it seems improbable that there would be any revenue in the early years of independence which could be placed in such a fund.
- The economic starting position for an independent Scotland does not look favourable. Unless independence coincided with a period of high oil prices, Scotland's public finances would be in deficit. Scottish public finances would be much more dependent on volatile oil prices than is the UK economy.
- In order to mitigate the costs of uncertainty and prevent these costs making independence unpalatable to the Scottish electorate, a Scottish government would have to be prepared to forego the prospect of making radical changes to the Scottish economy, at least in the short term.
- The concept of fiscal freedom is one way of moving to independence and reducing the costs of uncertainty. A substantial amount of work needs to be done elaborating this idea into a policy and overcoming major problems before it can be shown to be workable.
- Scottish independence would have an economic effect on all UK citizens. The implications of this need to be carefully assessed.
- Independence as a single country-changing event is probably unattainable in a modern developed economy. Independence is more likely to be attained as a gradual process.

– NOTES –

1. Information from Scottish Financial Enterprise.
2. Central Bank of Ireland (2001), 'Annual Report 2000', Dublin. (Note IR£ values expressed in GB£ values at average annual exchange rates.)
3. Norges Bank (2001), 'Annual Report and Accounts 2000', Oslo, p. 38. (Note: NOK values expressed in GB£ values at average annual exchange rates.)
4. HM Treasury (1999), 'Debt Management Report 1998–99', The Stationery Office.
5. Debt Management Office (2001), 'Annual Report and Accounts 2000–01', The Stationery Office, HC24.
6. Scottish Executive (2001), 'Annual Expenditure Report 2000–01 to 2002–03', Edinburgh: The Stationery Office.
7. Scottish Executive (2000), 'Government Expenditure and Revenues in Scotland 1998–99', pp. 20–1.
8. Scottish Parliament Official Report, 13 November, 2001, 'Finance Committee, Meeting 22', Cols 1508 and 1491.

9. Scottish Parliament Official Report, 7 March, 2000, 'Finance Committee, Meeting 7, Col. 444.
10. Note that all IR£ values cited in this publication have been converted to GB£ value at 2000 average exchange rate.
11. Information from Norwegian Embassy, London.
12. Office of National Statistics (2000), 'ONS Annual Report and Accounts 1999–2000', London: The Stationery Office.
13. Ibid. p. 22.
14. Visited 7 August 2001.
15. Foreign and Commonwealth Office (2000), 'Departmental Report: The Government's Expenditure Plans 2000–01 to 2001–02', London: The Stationery Office, Cm. 4609.
16. Information from Royal Danish Embassy, London.
17. United Nations, 1997, 'Agenda for Development', General Assembly Resolution A/RES/51/240, 20 June, 1997.
18. Department for International Development, 2000, 'Departmental Report, Government Expenditure Plans 2000–01 to 2001–02', The Stationery Office, London, Cm 4610.
19. HM Treasury (2001), 'Public Expenditure Statistical Analyses 2001–02', Tables 1.16 and 1.17, London: The Stationery Office, Cm. 5101.
20. Northern Ireland Office, (1998), 'Northern Ireland Expenditure Plans and Priorities 1999–2000 to 2001–02', London: The Stationery Office.
21. Government of Ireland (2001), 'Statistical Information on Social Welfare Services 2000', Pn. 10042, Dublin: Government Publications.
22. The Economist, 'Lonely but rich', 18 August 2000, p. 28.
23. Norges Bank press release, 6 March 2002, at http://www.norges–bank.no/pressemelding/en/2002.
24. Financial Times, 'Oil prices hold key to short-term economic outlook', 26 October 2001, p. 11.
25. Alaska Department of Revenue Tax Division (2001), 'Spring 2001 Revenue Sources Book', Appendix F. (Read at http://www.tax.state.ak.us/SourcesBook/2001fallsources/fall01index.htm)
26. Information collated from various Government of Alberta publications – Annual Reports, Budget announcements – available at: http://www.treas.gov.ab.ca/publications.
27. Gjedrem, S. (14 March 2002), 'Address to the Board of Directors of the National Insurance Fund', Oslo. (Read at http://www.norges–bank.no/english/speeches)
28. Nelson, P. L. (19 March 2002), 'Budget Speech', Edmonton, Alberta. (Read at http://www.treas.gov.ab.ca/publications/budget/budget2002/speech.html)
29. For a discussion in the recent political context, see Mitchell (1996).

Part Four: The Realities and the Limits of Independence

Jo Eric Murkens (Chapter 14) and
Michael Keating (Chapter 15)

Scotland and the Rest of the United Kingdom

– INTRODUCTION –

Scottish independence would herald a new era of rapprochement with rUK. Geographically, of course, Scotland and rUK would remain close neighbours; but emotionally too there will be ties – centuries of intermarriage, intermingling and immigration will see to that. Furthermore, assuming that Scotland and rUK are both members of the EU, there will be significant co-operation at that level with free movement of people, goods and capital guaranteed.

At the sub-government level, the level of private organisations, the ties are even closer. Almost 20 per cent of voluntary organisations (ranging from sporting bodies through Churches to Trades Unions and Charities) are organised on either an all island basis (ignoring the North–South split) or on all Archipelago basis (Whyte 1983: 300).

This chapter will examine the possibility of Scotland and rUK adopting Nordic-Council style arrangements which could grant additional rights and duties to their citizens.[1] The EU would have an important impact here because its non-discrimination provisions may mean that co-operation between Scotland and rUK is constrained by having to offer similar terms to nationals of all Member States; the United Kingdom has recently had to reduce some of its reciprocal arrangements with Ireland for this reason. Thus, whilst the two countries might wish to allow each other's nationals access to the highest posts in their respective civil service, they would not be able to under existing EU legislation, without offering similar opportunities to all EU nationals.

The other sections will try to illustrate how independence would make a difference to ordinary Scots and British people. Will people be free to live and work where they want? What will Scottish independence change in their lives? The focus will be on the provision of health care under the NHS, as well as the payment of social security and pensions after independence. Again, European Community legislation now provides the background to these discussions and both best-case and worst-case scenarios are analysed.

– CITIZENSHIP OPTIONS –

– Scotland's choices –

An independent Scotland could grant citizenship to all residents of its territory, including immigrants and people born in Scotland but resident elsewhere. It could also allow dual citizenship for those wishing to remain citizens of the United Kingdom. Alternatively, Scotland could treat all residents not born in Scotland, including the British, as aliens or non-Scottish. However, this would be greatly damaging to popular support for independence. A system of dual-nationality would be the most liberal model. The United Kingdom would then have to engage in corresponding action as it is the UK Government that determines British citizenship.[2] All British people resident in Scotland (but not born there) and all people born in Scotland who reside in rUK would then retain UK citizenship. Critics would then doubt the true extent of independence if all current British citizens retained a common citizenship.

The SNP's policy on citizenship is 'open and inclusive . . . The automatic right of citizenship will be open to all those living in Scotland, all those born in Scotland and all those with a parent born in Scotland. All others are free to apply'.[3] In many ways this is a progressive and liberal policy on citizenship. But is the scope really quite as wide as this statement suggests?

Would the SNP's policy include, for instance, legal immigrants (that is those with Indefinite Leave to Remain) who do not hold British citizenship? Would it extend to those on temporary visas or those without any legal status at all? Admittedly, those cases are relatively easy to deal with. But it gets more complicated. What about, for example, a naturalised British citizen who had been resident in Scotland for many years but who had moved to England a few years before independence? With most British citizens, it is easy to identify which part(s) of the United Kingdom they derive their citizenship from (place of birth, their parent's place of birth and so on) but registration and naturalisation of people is all done through one source in the UK (these days, the Home Office at Liverpool). Jeremy Jenkins, who is an independent researcher, gives an interesting example of those living overseas with Scottish grandparents. At the moment, they cannot get British citizenship, and unless they are Commonwealth citizens (which excludes US-Americans) they cannot even get an ancestry visa to work in the UK. Would Scotland offer them citizenship (as Ireland does)? If so, then they would be able to work in rUK or elsewhere in the EEA.

– rUK's choices –

The rUK could allow Scots to retain UK citizenship (and the concurrent right to move freely into rUK). The question is whether there would be any support for the suggestion that Scots can stay British whilst also being citizens of Scotland? Would they be given a two-year period, say, in which to choose? Conversely, if the majority of Scots had just voted for independence, would they want to retain British citizenship even if it was offered to them?

In the past, when British colonies became independent, the normal practice was that where a citizen of the UK and Colonies became a citizen of the newly independent nation, she lost UK/Colonies citizenship unless she retained links (birth, descent, residence and so on) to the UK or a place that remained a colony. The same principle applied would see someone losing British citizenship if she became a Scottish citizen upon independence unless she also had links to England, Wales or Northern Ireland. For example someone born in London but living in Edinburgh would become Scottish (unless she opted out) but would also retain British citizenship due to her birthplace.

However, there is no reason why the law could not provide for some additional facility to make a specific declaration of retention of British citizenship as well for those who did not stand to keep it automatically. Jeremy Jenkins takes the analogy further: someone born of entirely Scottish ancestry in Scotland would lose British citizenship upon becoming Scottish unless she made some sort of declaration to the UK Government asking to keep it (assuming this option was available).

Alternatively, rUK could renounce the loyalty of unionists in Scotland by cutting off their UK citizenship rights. A brief look at the Belfast (or Good Friday) Agreement of 10 April 1998 is helpful in this respect. Under Article 1(vi), The British and Irish Governments:

> recognise the birthright of all the people of Northern Ireland to identify themselves and be accepted as Irish or British, or both, as they may so choose, and accordingly confirm that their right to hold both British and Irish citizenship is accepted by both Governments and would not be affected by any future change in the status of Northern Ireland.

In other words, the two governments guarantee British citizenship in the event of Northern Ireland becoming part of the Republic. According to

Simon Partridge, who is a political analyst and writer on British–Irish relations, devolution and inter-ethnic conflict transformation, it would be highly anomalous if unionists in Ireland could remain British and those in Scotland could not. That said, any guarantee of British citizenship for unionists in either Scotland or Northern Ireland after secession from the UK could only ever be a political pledge that the UK Government could renege on at any time in the future if it chose to do so.[4] Moreover, it can be questioned whether the political conditions for common citizenship will prevail after Scottish independence. In the context of Quebec's secession, Robert Young points out that, 'the act of separation, by definition, would fracture any existing sense of common citizenship' (Young 1998: 85).

Citizenship is an area that was not settled during the Czech–Slovak negotiations in 1992. Each republic passed its own laws. The Czechs wanted an 'alien regime' whereby Slovaks in the Czech Republic would be treated as foreigners, and vice versa. The Slovaks, on the other hand, wanted a 'union regime' which would confer common citizenship on the citizens of both republics. The Czechs rejected this as well as proposal to introduce dual nationality.

The same point came up in the abortive attempt to split Quebec from Canada in 1995. The Parti Québécois introduced Bill 1 ('An Act respecting the Future of Quebec') shortly before the referendum. The Bill included a provision which stated that the Quebecois could retain their Canadian passports and citizenship if the province became independent. Most federalists staunchly refused to speculate about the consequences of Quebec's secession in the run-up to the referendum. But in 1998, the policy of the Reform Party, the official opposition in Canada's parliament which recently became the Canadian Reform Conservative Alliance, was that if a province chose to leave Canada, then 'the Canadian citizenship and Canadian passports of the people of that province choosing to leave Canada should be revoked'.[5]

There are two possibilities on either end of the spectrum as regards Scottish relations with rUK after independence. A 'maximalist' and a 'minimalist' view will illustrate the options, which leave ample room to slide up and down the scale between them.

– A maximalist view –

Scotland and rUK could develop intergovernmental bodies to pursue matters that remain of mutual interest post-independence. The governments might wish to meet before EU meetings to try to arrange a common position on upcoming issues (as Nordic Council members do) or co-operate on areas as diverse as running a joint heart–lung transport operation or civil service exchange (as the British and Irish Governments do). Scotland and rUK may also wish to co-operate in foreign affairs (including sharing embassies like the Czech and Slovaks) and defence. This co-operation might take place bilaterally or more broadly, and include the Irish Republic through the Council of the Isles. Given the range of interests that Scotland, Ireland and rUK will have in common, it is possible to foresee pressures for the Council of the Isles to act as the body at the centre of a confederal arrangement of the countries of the British Isles.

Citizenship is not central to the development of intergovernmental bodies. The Nordic countries do not have common citizenship, although they have reciprocal citizenship rights. Up until recently, their citizenship laws were framed in a similar way, although with effect from 1 July 2001 Sweden has allowed unrestricted dual citizenship, while the others only tolerate dual citizenship in very limited circumstances.

On the other hand, a maximalist view would clearly favour common citizenship. The relationship between Britain and Ireland since 1921 is instructive in this regard. The Ireland Act 1949 (of the UK Parliament), which recognised the Republic of Ireland, ended Irish dominion status and guaranteed citizens of the Republic those rights that they had hitherto enjoyed in the UK. It stated that the Irish Republic was not a foreign country. Moreover, although people born in the Irish Republic are not British citizens, they are not to be considered as 'aliens' either. Because of Great Britain's historic connections with Ireland and the Commonwealth, the definition of 'alien' did not apply to the Irish even when southern Ireland became an independent republic and left the Commonwealth in 1949. Henceforth, persons born in the Republic of Ireland ceased to be British subjects, although anyone who was a British subject prior to the British Nationality Act 1948 was allowed to retain their citizenship by giving written notice to the Secretary of State of his desire to do so.[6]

The relationship between the two countries today remains closer than with other EU Member States with, for example, a common travel area (for people and pets) which is generally not immigration controlled. Moreover, Irish citizens resident in the UK have full voting rights and can hold public office (for example become an MP) even without becoming British citizens. Ireland is also the only country outside the Commonwealth whose citizens can join the British armed forces.

But are the rights to vote and join the army reciprocal? Intriguingly, they are not. The National Parliament (Oireachtas) passed a law in 1983 permitting British citizens to vote in Irish elections but the Supreme Court struck it down as being unconstitutional. The sections of the Irish constitution dealing with voting referred only to the voting rights of 'citizens' in

Ireland, not residents or people. After the adoption by referendum of the Ninth Amendment to the Constitution , Article 16.1.2.ii now permits non-citizens to vote, 'as may be permitted by law' (see Gwynn Morgan 1990). This means that British citizens resident in the Republic of Ireland are entitled to vote in Dáil, European Parliament and local elections. But they cannot vote in presidential elections or constitutional referendums (there is no UK equivalent to these polls). Nor can they stand for the Dáil, unless they take out Irish citizenship, which is possible after five years residence in the Republic of Ireland. As for the Irish army, the right of UK citizens to be selected by general recruitment is subject to a residency requirement, which is met after six months. However, only Irish citizens can rise to officer level.

If the Scots follow the Irish example, many individuals and organisations may find it convenient to act as if independence had not occurred. Of course, they will not be able to ignore it completely, but the relationship between rUK and Scotland and its citizens could vary from extremely close – a truly special relationship – to that of just neighbours. Scottish independence would probably not lead to any great changes in the internal citizenship arrangements. Indeed, according to Simon Partridge, given the historical integration of Scotland within the British Empire (both in its home and overseas manifestations – it was an Anglo–Welsh–Scots project with a goodly Irish input), it is likely to have even less impact than Irish independence did.

– The minimalist view –

In the event of a complete breakdown of good neighbourly relations, or where the Scots themselves decide that their relations with rUK should resemble those of, say, Denmark rather than Ireland, what status will Scots have when they go to rUK to travel or work? In other words, what are the minimum rights and guarantees that Scots can rely on if Scotland and rUK fail to conclude bilateral agreements? Citizenship rights will then assume central stage in this worst case scenario.

Matters relating to citizenship range from the symbolic (community membership) to the practical (rights and benefits). Whilst it is still for the individual States to lay down their own citizenship rules, within the European Union rights and benefits are also granted on supranational level. As a practical matter, this section will examine whether Scots would have a right to live and work in rUK. It is assumed that an independent Scotland would apply to join the EU and be admitted as a new Member State.[7] European Community law gives nationals of the European Economic Area (EEA)[8] a right to live and work in the United Kingdom. This is called a right of residence which is granted if the EEA national:

- works in the United Kingdom; or
- does not work in the United Kingdom but has enough money to support herself throughout her stay without help from public funds (such as Income Support, Housing Benefit and Council Tax Benefit).[9]

So at a minimum, Scottish nationals (as EEA nationals) would have continued rights to live in rUK, accept offers of work, and work as an employee, in self-employment or in business. Moreover, they could set up a business, manage a company or set up a local branch of a company without needing a work permit.

Public sector restrictions

If Scottish independence means that citizens of Scotland and citizens of rUK have different nationalities and no common nationality, then this will impact on the ability of Scots to work for the UK Government. The Act of Settlement of 1700 provides, in section 3, that no person born out of the kingdoms of England, Scotland or Ireland or the dominions thereto belonging should be capable of enjoying any office or place of trust, either civil or military. This prohibition does not apply to Commonwealth citizens or citizens of the Irish Republic (section 52(6) and Schedule 5 of the British Nationality Act 1981) or to British protected persons employed in a civil capacity (section 1(1) of the Aliens' Employment Act 1955).

However, even if Scots enjoyed the same rights as the Irish that would no longer give Scots privileged access rights to the UK civil service. The European Communities (Employment in the Civil Service) Order 1991 amended the 1955 Act so as to allow nationals of Member States of the European Communities (and their spouses and certain children) to take up civil employment under the Crown. The exception is Article 39(4) TEC (ex Article 48(4) EC), which excludes from the freedom of movement of workers posts in the 'public service').

In 1996 the United Kingdom made an amendment to the Civil Service Management Code to restrict Commonwealth and Irish nationals from being employed in posts which were reserved for UK nationals.[10] This put Commonwealth citizens and Irish nationals in the same position as nationals of other Member States of the EEA as regards certain posts in the civil service, the Ministry of Defence, and the Foreign and Commonwealth Office which are reserved for UK nationals. However, as Jeremy Jenkins points out, the majority of Irish citizens living in the United Kingdom have lived there long enough to be eligible to apply for British citizenship by naturalisation if they wish.

The effect of the existing rules, therefore, is that after independence

Scottish nationals may be employed abroad in any civil post under the Crown (which includes the Diplomatic Service) if the Minister considers it appropriate. As regards civil employment under the Crown within rUK, Commonwealth Citizens, British protected persons and nationals of Member States of the EEA can be employed in posts other than reserved ones. Nationals of other countries may be employed in non-reserved posts only if a certificate is in force.

European Union citizenship

Citizenship rights today have to be discussed against the background of European developments which one day may overtake national citizenship rights. There are three possible models: nation-state based, EU based, or a mixed model combining elements of each within existing EU and Member State definitions and arrangements. The latter model is the favoured one in the EU. The Treaty on European Union signed in Maastricht in February 1992 established the status of citizenship of the Union in Articles 8–8e EC (now Articles 17–22 TEC). The opening provision, Article 17 TEC reads:

> Citizenship of the Union is hereby established. Every person holding the nationality of a Member State shall be a citizen of the Union. Citizenship of the Union shall complement and not replace national citizenship.

EU citizenship raises a number of questions that need to be addressed. Three areas that are fundamental to the debate might be categorised as (a) the hierarchy of norms, (b) the content of citizenship rights and (c) obligations and eligibility.

First, there is no consensus within the EU as to whether and how fundamental civil and political rights ought to be strengthened on EU level. What, for example, would be the relationship between the EU and the European Convention of Human Rights and Fundamental Freedoms?

Second, which obligations, if any, of EU citizens would need to be spelled out? Arguably, a modern definition of citizenship would have to include social rights. As a first step the European Social Charter could be integrated into the Treaty. But that would be a highly controversial move in light of the possible costs involved and the strong opposition by some Member States to new European competencies in this area.

The final point is about eligibility: who should have the right to EU citizenship? Obviously citizens of EU Member States would qualify. But should it mean that third country nationals who are resident in a Member State are excluded from the right to free movement of persons, not to mention the other rights of European citizens? What would be the relationship between EU citizenship, nationality, and the rights of other residents in the EU?

In sum, discussions of citizenship are currently taking place not on the level of the nation-state but on a European and even global level. The search is for alternatives to nationality. Do human rights, for instance, provide an adequate source of 'constitutional patriotism' which could act as the central element to define the right to citizenship? How desirable is 'global citizenship' or 'citizenship of the world' which, as Professor Jürgen Habermas (1992; 1996) claims, is the ultimate goal of the whole idea of Community membership?

So far citizenship has always referred to a state-like system of membership. The danger is that a supranational conception would lose its policy-making and people-binding potential. Furthermore, there is no sign that European governments will ever cede their citizenship laws. There is far too much diversity of approach at the moment (on issues like citizenship by birth, by descent beyond the first generation and dual citizenship) and the issues cut to the core of a nation's view of itself in the world.

_ WOULD SCOTS BE ABLE TO RECEIVE FREE TREATMENT _ ON THE NHS AFTER INDEPENDENCE?

This section will examine the rights of Scots to receive medical treatment in the manner they are accustomed to. A distinction must be made between primary and secondary medical care.

– Primary care –

Eligibility to receive medical primary care (that is basic medical treatment and non-hospital care)[11] is determined by whether a person is ordinarily resident in the United Kingdom and is not related to the person's nationality, or the payment of national insurance contributions or taxes. When overseas visitors (that is those not ordinarily resident in the UK) require emergency treatment a GP is required to provide immediately necessary medical treatment free of charge. In such a case no distinction is made on grounds of nationality or residence.[12] It should be noted that the obligation does not extend to the provision of non-emergency medical treatment.

GPs have a discretion whether to offer patients from EEA countries medical treatment on a free or private basis. To receive free treatment overseas patients need the approval of their insurer and should produce a E112 form. It is up to each EEA Member State to cover the costs of treatment provided to its insured nationals elsewhere in the EEA. The costs will be reimbursed between Member States by cash transfers at central government level.

In sum, if Scotland became independent, citizens and residents of Scotland would no longer automatically be able to access free healthcare (other than perhaps immediately necessary GP treatment) under English NHS law unless a reciprocal agreement were established between the two countries. Regulation (EEC) 1408/71 applies to all EU Member States, and co-ordinates social security and healthcare rights for people moving around the EU. Should Scotland decide to remain in the EU, rights to healthcare in England would arise under this Regulation. However, Scotland would have to reimburse England for care provided to those EEA nationals covered by the NHS in Scotland, and England would have to reimburse Scotland for healthcare provided in Scotland to those covered by the NHS in England.

– Secondary care –

As regards secondary care (hospital treatment), a NHS Patient's Guide[13] stipulates that under Regulations which first came into effect on 1 October 1982, visitors to the United Kingdom are liable to be charged for NHS hospital treatment. A visitor is defined as someone not ordinarily resident in the UK. According to Category 3fi, EEA nationals are exempt from charges for treatment the need for which arose during a visit.

The United Kingdom has reciprocal agreements with a number of countries.[14] Each agreement is negotiated between government officials. Currently, reciprocal agreements between the UK and non-EEA countries apply to Scotland. They would continue to apply to an independent Scotland – unless repudiated by Scotland (succession to international treaties is analysed elsewhere at pp. 159–65).

– SOCIAL SECURITY –

The United Kingdom is a unitary state in which central government substantially directs most government activity. However, the structure of services provided throughout the UK differs in certain respects. Social security law in Scotland is the same as for England and Wales. The administrative structure in Northern Ireland, however, is significantly different: personal social services are the responsibility of the Health Board (as they are in the Republic of Ireland), and the Northern Ireland Housing Executive manages public housing.

Scotland's social security system is currently integrated with the social programmes of the United Kingdom, financed through the state budget and regulated from London. Social security benefits are either contributory or non–contributory. Contributory benefits are funded from the National Insurance Fund which is a single fund for the United Kingdom. If Scotland was to move towards independence, there would have to be a financial adjustment of the Fund.

Child support, war pensions and the regulation of occupational and personal pensions provided by the private sector are also matters currently reserved to Westminster. If Scotland were to move towards independence it would need to consider suitable arrangements in respect of these matters in addition to social security benefits. After independence, Scotland would have to administer pensions, and social insurance cash benefits through itself. The reservation relating to social security in Schedule 5 of the Scotland Act excepts the subject matter of Part II of the Social Work (Scotland) Act 1968 which deals with some forms of social assistance. For that reason Scotland already has competence in relation to a range of social services.

As a practical matter, housing benefit and council tax benefits (unlike other social security benefits) are funded and administered by local authorities (which receive subsidy for those benefits from Westminster). That is, Scottish local authorities are currently administering housing benefit and council tax benefit although responsibility for policy-making and legislating does not rest with them.

As regards social security schemes for its citizens abroad an independent Scotland that acceded to the EU would need to apply Community law but, in addition, could enter into a reciprocal agreement with the rUK, which would itself need to take account of Community law.

– Community law –

Social security in the European context is governed by two Council Regulations (EEC) No. 1408/71, on the application of social security schemes to employed persons, to self-employed persons and to members of their families moving within the Community, and (EEC) No. 574/72, on the procedure for implementation of Regulation No. 1408/71.

The EC Regulations ensure that Scots would receive the same treatment in social security matters as nationals of those EEA States where they go to work. The regulations allow periods of social insurance in any of these countries to be combined so that a worker may qualify for a benefit or pension. Moreover, family members can receive the accrued benefits in any EEA country. The EC Regulations in general only cover workers and people getting social security benefits who are nationals of any EEA country, people with the status of stateless people or refugees living permanently in an EEA State, and the dependants and survivors of these people.

– Bilateral arrangements –

Generally the Agreements on Social Security are based on the principle of equal treatment between the nationals of the contracting party while residing in the territory of the other contracting party, as well as on the totalisation of the periods of insurance completed under the legislation of the contracting party to establish the right to entitlement for a benefit under the Social Security system of one or both countries. An independent Scotland would be free to legislate over and above the EC floor. Ireland, for instance, has bilateral Agreements with Austria and the United Kingdom who are also members of the EU. The bilateral agreements between Ireland and these countries continue to apply where:

1. The person is not covered by the personal scope of the EC Regulations, for example, non-nationals of the EEA (other than those who have the official status of refugee or stateless person who are residing permanently in the EEA or their survivors or dependants);
2. The provisions of the agreement provide greater assistance to a claimant than EC Social Security Regulations Nos 1408/71 and 574/72 and the right to use the bilateral agreement was acquired before the EC provisions applied to Ireland (1/4/73) or the other country. The EC provisions apply to the UK from 1/4/73 and to Austria from 1/1/94.[15]

– Relevance for Scotland –

Unravelling the social security system will raise many questions: What would happen to those people who reside in Scotland now but have spent most of their working lives in England? Or conversely, what would happen to the English person who worked in Scotland and then returned? Would special provision be needed in Community law to regulate those cases? This is not clear because, unlike other applicant states, Scotland does not have its own social security system now. The EC Regulations are co-ordinating measures that provide for exportability of benefits.

Another area of uncertainty is also the future liability of rUK. As people currently pay into UK pension funds, rUK may have a continued responsibility to pay social security and pensions after Scottish independence. Could the responsibility be divided? What scope is there for Scotland doing more for its pensioners?

– APPENDIX –

Existing British–Irish Co-operation.

	Rights of Irish Citizens in the UK	Rights of UK citizens in Ireland	Exceptions for Channel Islands and Isle of Man	European Union rules
TRAVEL visiting	there is a common travel area so people (and pets) may travel without a passport, although they may need to produce identification			free movement of persons (subject to certain restrictions and the holding of a EU Member State passport)
residence	no restrictions on residence between UK and Ireland, but UK nationals who were not born in the UK need to register with the authorities in Ireland		UK and Irish citizens have no right of residence in Channel Islands or the Isle of Man. Acquisition of residency can be a lengthy and expensive process. Channel Islanders and those from the Isle of Man are not restricted from residing in the UK or Ireland	EU nationals have right of residence in any Member State, subject to notification to authorities, and to restrictions imposed on public order grounds or for carriers of certain diseases. Non-workers (students retired etc.) may also have to demonstrate independent means
deportation	Irish Citizens may be deported from the UK, unless they were resident in the UK before 1973	British citizens (unless they were not born in Britain) may not be deported from Ireland		EU nationals may be deported from Member State back to their home on, for example, security grounds

	Rights of Irish Citizens in the UK	Rights of UK citizens in Ireland	Exceptions for Channel Islands and Isle of Man	European Union rules
VOTING	can vote or stand in any election	can vote or stand in European, and Local Elections, vote in parliamentary elections but not vote or stand in Presidential elections or referendums	Channel Islands and Isle of Man are not represented in the UK parliament	EU nationals can vote and stand in European and local (but not national) elections in any Member State

	Rights of Irish Citizens in the UK	Rights of UK citizens in Ireland	Exceptions for Channel Islands and Isle of Man	European Union rules
JOBS lawyers	Irish solicitors may practise in England and Wales but not Scotland	Scots lawyers (but not English and Welsh) must take Irish law test before practising	all jobs subject to stringent residence requirements. Non-residents may get temporary residence if skill shortage (e.g. surgeons)	EU nationals can look for work in any Member State although some public jobs may be reserved for nationals. Furthermore, although many qualifications (e.g. doctors, dentists) do transfer across Member States, others which require specific knowledge may not
civil servants	from June 1996 25% of UK civil service posts reserved for UK nationals (or for those foreign nationals who were already civil servants)	Irish civil service is open to all regardless of nationality		
army	Commonwealth and Irish (but not other EU) citizens may join the army at any rank	UK citizens may not join commissioned ranks		

	Rights of Irish Citizens in the UK	Rights of UK citizens in Ireland	Exceptions for Channel Islands and Isle of Man	European Union rules
SOCIAL RIGHTS	a bilateral agreement of 1971 allows for the transferability of social security benefits between the UK and Ireland. The 1971 rules are similar but not identical to the later EU regulations. Thus, for example, those (e.g. from Isle of Man) who rely on the 1971 agreement must work in Ireland for 6 weeks before being entitled to draw unemployment benefit whilst EU rules require only 1 week	the Isle of Man and Channel Islands are not covered by the EU rules and the Channel Islands are also not covered by the 1971 agreement	EU rules allow for the transferability of contributions across Member States (subject to innumerable conditions and exceptions)

Source: *The British–Irish Council: Nordic Lessons for the Council of the Isles*, The Constitution Unit, 1998, Appendix C.

– NOTES –

1. See The Constitution Unit *The Nordic Council: Lessons for the Council of the Isles* (London: The Constitution Unit, 1998).
2. We argued in Chapter 4 that rUK would be the continuing state, and that Scottish independence would not result in the creation of two new states but just the one. For the reasons given in that chapter it is now suggested that British citizenship would continue as well, and that a new Scottish citizenship would be created.
3. *Heart of the Manifesto*, 2001, p. 3.
4. This was the case with St Helena, whose citizenship situation is soon to be remedied by virtue of the British Overseas Territories Bill which is currently passing through the UK Parliament. The point to note is that the 'Saints' assumed citizenship had been given to them irrevocably, and have been demanding full British citizenship ever since the British Nationality Act 1981 restricted their rights.
5. Reform Party of Canada Blue Book, 1998, NATIONAL UNITY Section – Secession Contingency Plans.
6. Section 31(1) of the British Nationality Act 1981 affirmed this right.
7. This assumption is not made casually. For an extensive analysis of Scotland's membership in the EU see Chapters 6–8.
8. The EEA includes all EU Member States plus Iceland, Liechtenstein and Norway
9. This second restriction does not currently apply to Irish citizens, who are deemed to have Indefinite Leave to Remain (ILR) immediately, and to other EEA nationals once they have been working in the UK for 4 years, where again they are deemed to have ILR.
10. Civil Service Management Code, Section 1.1.7: http://www.cabinet–office.gov.uk/civilservice/managementcode/csmc.pdf. [visited 25 July 2001].
11. This includes general or family practitioners, professions ancillary to medicine (including dentistry, optics and pharmacy) and domiciliary health care (home nursing, occupational therapy).

12. *Overseas Visitors' Eligibility to Receive Free Primary Care*, NHS Executive, Series number: HSC 1999/018, February 1999, paragraphs 6–8.
13. *National Health Service Hospital Charges to Overseas Visitors – Patient's Guide*, NHS Executive, Department of Health, May 1999.
14. Anguilla, Australia, Barbados, British Virgin Islands, Channel Islands, Falkland Islands, Iceland, Isle of Man, Montserrat, Poland, Romania, St Helena, Sweden, Turks and Caicos Islands.
15. Department of Social, Community and Family Affairs, Dublin.

CHAPTER 15

Independence in an Interdependent World

– INDEPENDENCE IN THE MODERN WORLD –

The debate on the independence of small nations is predicated on the idea that independent statehood is a clear status carrying with it (a) a monopoly of legitimate authority within the territory and (b) a degree of real power and functional autonomy which otherwise would not be available. Yet, with the transformation of the state in recent decades, these features are increasingly in doubt and with this have come doubts about the meaning of independence itself. The idea that the state is the sole source of legitimate authority has always been questioned in some quarters. Small nations adjacent to large and powerful ones have rarely developed doctrines of absolute sovereignty, preferring to put their faith in traditions of shared and diffused authority and overarching orders (Puig 1998). Scotland is no exception and its traditions of limited sovereignty have in recent years been refurbished to cope with membership both of the United Kingdom and of the European Union (Keating 2001b). While there are those who portray the EU as nothing more than an association of sovereign states, the better arguments seem to lie with those who see it as a normative order in its own right, profoundly affecting the sovereignty of the states within it (MacCormick 1999). As for the functional power and autonomy of states, this has been steadily eroded from above by the complex of processes known as globalisation as well as by European integration; from below by decentralisation, devolution and challenges to its authority from stateless nations and other territorial movements; and laterally by the expansion of the market and of civil society. States, it is widely accepted, are not so much independent as interdependent.

Nationalist parties in stateless nations have been among the first to realise the limitations of traditional sovereignty doctrine and few of them now espouse statehood in the classical nineteenth century sense. Movements in

Catalonia, Scotland, Wales and the Basque Country (apart from the extreme nationalists) believe in European integration, while the Parti Québécois has produced successive formulas for achieving Quebec 'sovereignty' without cutting the main economic, social and even political ties to the rest of Canada (Keating 2001a). Public opinion in stateless nations has also shown itself very reluctant to make a hard and fast distinction between independence and advanced forms of devolution, while being much clearer on just what powers they would like to see exercised at which level (Keating 2001b). Indeed in the case of Quebec, some sovereigntists and federalists seem to share a remarkably similar vision of the future of Quebec, only differing on the way to get there, whether by leaving Canada and negotiating their way partly back in, or by staying in Canada and negotiating themselves partly out.

Yet, when all of this has been said, there is a difference between being an independent state and not being one. It is just that the difference was not was it was and, paradoxically, exercising the powers that come with independence may now require embracing a high degree of external dependence. We can probe this question by asking just what Scotland could do as an independent state within the European Union (since few are arguing for independence outwith the EU) and as a self-governing nation within the United Kingdom.

– THE INDEPENDENCE SCENARIO –

An independent Scotland would repatriate the functions presenting reserved to Westminster. These fall into three main categories: defence and foreign affairs; fiscal and monetary policy; and social security. Its ability to exercise these powers freely would be constrained by external influences from the global system, from Europe and from the proximity of England and Wales.

Scotland's options in defence and foreign affairs would be real but limited. Scotland, like other small European countries, would not be able to defend itself against external attack. SNP policy is for withdrawal from NATO although this was due to be considered by the party conference before the events of 11 September 2001 intervened. Outside NATO, its options would be to join a future European defence and security system, although this would in practice be linked to NATO, or to declare neutrality and free–ride on defence, secure in the knowledge that England, the United States and Europe would be unlikely to tolerate a hostile power occupying Scotland and posing a threat to themselves. Arguably, this is what the Republic of Ireland has done in recent decades. Scotland would be a minor player in world politics but could enhance its position by becoming a moral conscience, taking a role in peacekeeping, or setting an example in development aid as has been done at various times by Ireland, Canada and the Nordic countries, carving out a role for small but developed countries in areas in which the large powers cannot or will not take the lead. Otherwise, Scotland would need to work closely within a future European foreign and security policy (CFSP) in order to influence the big issues of world politics. Even this would be subject to limitations, since the CFSP is intergovernmental rather than supranational and there are recurrent indications that it may be guided by a 'directorate' of the large states with significant military forces, Germany, France and the United Kingdom. This would suggest that an independent Scotland could gain security within a European framework but that it would be unlikely to have much influence over policy direction.

Membership in other international organisations might also be mediated by Europe. This is most clearly true of the World Trade Organisation (WTO) in which the EU negotiates as a unit, and in global negotiations on the environment. In other bodies, like UNESCO, Scotland might be able to carve out a more distinctive position, in alliance with other small nations.

An independent Scotland would assume control over monetary and fiscal policy, a major change from the present position, but its scope for independent action would be constrained. I will not refer to the vexed question of whether Scotland presently benefits from fiscal transfers or makes a net contribution to the United Kingdom, since this would require a work of its own. I merely note that if an independent Scotland were to depend too heavily on oil revenues, this could be a destabilising factor, given the volatility of oil prices. It could also lead to imbalances in the domestic economy such as are found in Norway, where the service sector is seriously underdeveloped, to a degree that would be unacceptable to Scottish consumers. An independent Scotland seeking to attract mobile investment capital would be under heavy pressure to keep business taxation low, as in Ireland, which would imply higher levels of personal and sales taxation. Just how far it would be obliged to cut business taxes is, however, an open issue since high taxation small independent countries, like Denmark, do survive in world markets. More broadly, the risk is that dependence on the United Kingdom would be replaced by dependence on the international market, with Scotland unable to do anything that might frighten investors who, contrary to the tenets of neo-classical economics, do not always behave rationally. So ironically the demand for distinctive economic policies that drive much of the demand for independence could be frustrated by the very condition of independence. This is an issue that has arisen in Quebec, where some people are aware that the protective shield of the Canadian state allows the provincial government to do things that might be more difficult for an independent state. These include practices in economic policy which the NAFTA agreement bans for states but not for regions. Membership of the Canadian federation also protects Quebec farmers, notably its milk producers, from US competition, something that would be impossible where Quebec a full member of NAFTA. This effect is not so strong in Europe, where market competition rules apply to sub-state governments as well as states, but an independent Scotland would still be subject to more international scrutiny than at present.

An independent monetary policy for Scotland seems a non-starter since almost nobody is proposing that it have its own currency. If Scotland were to retain the British pound, as the Parti Québécois has proposed keeping the Canadian dollar, then it would be subject to the monetary policy of the Bank of England. Many people already criticise the Bank of England for ignoring economic conditions in Scotland (and the North of England) but after Scottish independence there would be no need to pay the Scots any attention.

It is almost certain, then, that an independent Scotland would adopt the euro. This would change, but not necessarily diminish, the pattern of interdependence. Scotland would be subject to monetary policies designed for the larger populations of Europe and could find that they did not meet its needs, as Ireland has discovered. If Scotland were to enter the euro while England and Wales remained outside, then it would be vulnerable to fluctuations in the pound since the rest of the old UK would be by far its largest trading partner. If England and Wales were also to adopt the Euro or at least enter the Exchange Rate Mechanism, this would be an element of stability. There would also be a higher possibility that European monetary policy would be tied more to the interests of the island of Britain (if still not always sensitive to the differences within it). Another implication of joining the Euro is that Scotland would be subject to the Stability Pact, which imposes strict limits on government deficits (not more than 3 per cent of GDP).

Apart from currency considerations, an independent Scotland would still face a high degree of economic interdependence with the rest of the UK. Scotland's trade with the rest of the UK is about one and a half times as great as that with the rest of the world. The experience of Ireland in the first fifty or sixty years of independence was of an even higher high degree of economic dependence on Great Britain. Canada, which relies on the United States for some eighty per cent of its trade, is highly vulnerable to changes in the US economy, one of the main effects being an accentuation of booms and slumps. Since it depends so highly on a rather open border with the USA, Canada has recently been under pressure to secure its external borders with the rest of the world, to keep out terrorists and illegal immigrants, especially since 11 September. An influential school of academics has argued that trade dependence also means that Canada and its provinces cannot allow their taxation to get out of line with that in the USA, which has serious implications for maintaining the Canadian welfare state (Courchene 2001). One of the principal arguments against the US–Canada Free Trade Agreement of 1988 (precursor of the North American Free Trade Agreement) was that economic dependence would produce political dependence. Against this it was argued that Canada is economically dependent on the United States in any case and that the FTA provided an overarching set of rules that would bind both parties and protect Canada from US unilateralism, an argument bearing some affinity to arguments made for the Union in Scotland in 1706–7. This type of bilateral interdependence may be attenuated in the case of Scotland, as it has been in Ireland, by membership of the European Union and a progressive diversification of its trade. Such a diversification is possible but it would be a long process and imply a rather drastic restructuring of the Scottish economy which would be unlikely to be painless.

Assuming control of the social security system would be a massive responsibility for Scotland but not a technical impossibility. It would have the disadvantage that liabilities for economic downturns and economic shocks within the UK would no longer be pooled, which could pose strains at times of economic slump. On the other hand, the opportunity could be taken to integrate social security more effectively with active labour market policy, on the lines of the Nordic countries, so reducing long term unemployment. This would imply a capacity to adapt rapidly to change that Scotland has not shown over recent decades, and a major commitment on the part of the social partners. Given this commitment, which Ireland has (at least to some degree) achieved, Scotland could join the ranks of small, activist democracies able to use their social integration to adapt quickly to change and maintain a degree of manoeuvre in an interdependent world (Katzenstein 1985). This would require a major change in relations among government, capital and labour which, in Scotland, have tended to follow the UK rather than the continental model.

– Scotland in Europe –

It is almost universally accepted that an independent Scotland should be a member of the European Union and other transnational organisations including the Council of Europe, adhering to the European Convention for the Protection of Human Rights, and the Organisation for Security and Co-operation in Europe. This, as most people also accept, entails considerable limits on Scottish sovereignty and independent action. Yet in an inter-dependent world the important question is less the capacity to act independently than the need to maximise the nation's capacity to govern itself, and to exercise influence within the new networks of power and decision-making. For a small country this may imply the need to accept massive amounts of transnational integration, positioning itself at the core of a united Europe. An attempt to establish a 'semi-detached' status within Europe on British or Danish lines could produce the worst of both worlds, a marginalisation of Scotland within European decision making circles, without a corresponding increase in autonomy. Denmark's position in relation to the single currency is instructive here. Unable to support a truly independent currency, Denmark has tied its krone to the euro, so accepting European monetary discipline without gaining a vote in the European Central Bank or a place on the committee of finance ministers when single currency issues are under discussion.

While, in the absence of the UK, Europe might provide the market access and mobility that Scotland needs, there is one important exception. Like Ireland, Scotland could not adhere to the Schengen regime on open borders, without closing its border with England unless England too adhered. England and Wales are unlikely to join Schengen in the medium to long term, and the erection of a hard border with passport controls between England and Scotland would be extremely difficult to sell to the public on either side. The prospect is therefore for a continuing free travel area with England and Wales and with Ireland, but the retention of border controls with the rest of Europe.

Independence in Europe involves swapping classic sovereignty for influence within a complex system of decision-making. The question here has always been whether Scotland can gain more influence as a small part of a larger member state of the EU, or as a small member state itself. Clearly, independence does make a difference in giving Scotland a seat in the Council of Ministers, guaranteed representation on the whole network of committees and no doubt a larger number of members of the European Parliament. There would also be the opportunity to press for different policies from those favoured by England and Wales and to forge coalitions with other like-minded nations. On the other hand, Scotland would probably find itself siding with England on many occasions, simply because of shared problems and conditions. The more tightly Europe integrates, the more attractive the option of separate Scottish membership becomes and, as suggested above, an independent Scotland would have an interest in yet further integration.

Enlargement of the Union to include the countries of central and eastern Europe along with Cyprus further reinforces the case for independence, since it would become difficult to explain why Slovenia should have a voice in the Council of Ministers and Scotland should not. Yet enlargement is to be accompanied by a reform of the structure of the Union, on lines that are only beginning to come clear. The Nice Treaty was designed to ensure that coalitions of small states could not easily outvote the large states in the Council of Ministers and there is persistent talk of a 'directorate' of large states, more likely informal than formal. Those who trust UK governments to represent Scottish interests will use this as an argument against independence; others will draw the opposite conclusion and it is unlikely that either will convince the other.

The argument would, however, change completely were a Europhobic Conservative Party to return to office in the United Kingdom, seeking to stop further European integration or even reverse it. Scots, it is true, have only been relatively less Eurosceptic than the English (Keating 2001b) but among the political leadership there is very little of the anti–Europeanism found in England. A sharp turn to Euroscepticism on the part of a British government could polarise the issue on national lines and force Scottish political, economic and social elites to choose between the UK and Europe. In that case, the arguments for independence would be strengthened. If a future British government were to propose withdrawal from the EU altogether, replacing it with a loose free trade area or, as favoured by some voices on the right, adhering to the North American (or Atlantic) Free Trade Area, this could clinch the argument.

– THE HOME RULE SCENARIO –

If independence in the modern world is not what it was, then there may be opportunities to build on the present settlement to enhance Scottish autonomy and influence without formally separating from the UK. This is the strategy that has been pursued for the last twenty years by the government of Catalonia under the leadership of the nationalist but not separatist *Convergència i Unió*. It is also the line taken by successive Liberal governments in Quebec from the 1960s onwards.

Contemporary developments, as I have argued elsewhere (Keating 2001c) permit an unpacking of sovereignty and its dispersal across multiple levels of authority and government. Statehood is no longer an absolute but a collection of symbols, competences and capacities for action that are continually changing and being renegotiated. In a confused way, this was understood before the rise of the modern state, by the framers of the Acts of Union, which provided for Scotland to retain some attributes of statehood while abolishing both its parliament and that of England in favour of a common monarchy and parliament. The Union has undergone periodic strains and demands for renegotiation to which the state has responded with greater (in the late 1990s) or lesser (between 1885 and 1922 and between 1979 and 1997) wisdom. With the fluidity of power and authority in the modern era and especially given the building of Europe, the need for adjustment is likely in the future to be more frequent. A definitive constitutional settlement, such as Canadian and Quebec governments have sought over the last thirty or more years, is unlikely ever to be possible. To manage this new politics of continual adjustment and change, certain elements are necessary.

The first is the recognition of Scotland as a self-determining nation within the Union. Curiously, successive British governments have recognised this and then tried to deny the consequences. In his White Paper on Scotland John Major declared that 'no nation can be kept in a union against its will', implying the right of self-determination, but then refused to accept the broad consensus on favour of home rule as a condition for remaining within the Union (Major 1992). Labour has been equally inconsistent, signing the Claim of Right asserting that the sovereignty rested with the Scottish people (Campaign for a Scottish Assembly 1988), but then insisting in its devolution legislation that the sovereignty of Westminster remained unabridged. Yet whatever the protestations of Westminster politicians and the wording of the Scotland Act, almost nobody in Scotland believes that the Parliament is a mere subordinate legislature, a creature of Westminster statute. Its claims to original authority are twofold: its basis in the referendum of 1997 as an act of self-determination; and the residual traditions of Scottish constitutional law and practice which never accorded untrammelled sovereignty to Westminster. Recognition of Scottish self-determination does not, however, mean Scottish independence. Like other rights, those of self-determination are limited by the rights of others, judgements about what is in the interest of the nation itself and practical considerations. It does, however, entail that Scotland should take charge of its own constitutional future and that the Scottish Parliament should be recognised as a partner of Westminster in the constitution. Changes in the constitutional settlement should therefore be negotiated and not imposed unilaterally. Holyrood could also be given an expanded constituent autonomy, with control over matters that affect only Scotland, like the number of members in the Scottish Parliament. This is a common feature in federations and devolved states, including Canada and, to a certain degree, Belgium and Spain.

Another element is that of symbolic recognition and here it must be said that Scotland has gained a lot more than other stateless nations such as Catalonia or Quebec. The name of the state (despite the infuriating tendency of foreigners and many English people to get it wrong) recognises the multinational nature of the polity, as do matters like flags and protocol. There may be some scope for further development here, especially if the monarchy is to be retained but what is missing is a constitutional practice to underlie this symbolic recognition of plurinationality.

Thirdly, there are specific powers that could be devolved to Scotland to enhance its self-governing capacity. Both Canada and Spain have seen a gradual devolution of competences to the sub-state level, both for reasons of functional efficiency and to satisfy the demands of the minority nations. These have allowed provinces and autonomous communities to shape their own welfare states within the broad lines of national policy. Occupational training has been devolved in most federal and regionalised states since the 1980s in response to recognition that it is best administered within regional labour markets and integrated with economic development promotion. This can be treated as a pragmatic question rather than a matter of doctrine. It is likely that the financial settlement will be revisited at some stage and Scotland allowed, or required, to assume greater responsibility for taxation. The interface between the social security system and devolved matters may create difficulties requiring and adjustment of functions, and there may be scope for more devolution in broadcasting. Other matters that could be revisited are the divisions within transport, with Scotland taking over regulation of airports and railways; consumer protection; and energy. It might also be possible to devolve responsibility for equal opportunities, with Scotland able to make firmer provision within the limitations of European law. The almost complete absence of a debate in Scotland on defence or foreign policy would seem to suggest that these are not areas where there is a strong demand to diverge from UK policy.

Even without changing the devolution legislation, Scotland could gain power by taking its own line on matters in which it now largely follows the English lead. It could decide to diverge from English policies in fields like higher education or transport, if the demand should arise. The main limitations on policy divergence in such matters is likely to be the limited policy making capacity within Scottish government, a problem that is endemic to small nations whether they are independent states or not.

Fourthly there is the external dimension, particularly the ability of a non-independent Scotland to project itself in Europe. There are two dimensions to this, action through the UK government, and autonomous action within Europe. The present arrangement for Scottish participation in the UK delegation at the Council of Ministers and in committees is regulated by concordat and, essentially, gives the last word to Whitehall. It is a rollover of the pre-devolution arrangements for the Scottish Office and designed for a situation in which both governments are in the hands of the same political party. In the event of divergence of party control in Edinburgh and London, the concordat system would be unlikely to survive but this does not mean the end of the union. It merely means that some other, more institutionalised, mechanism would have to be put in its place. Scotland's capacity to act alone in Europe is limited by its not being a state, but there is now a considerable network of regions and stateless nations across the EU, and a great deal of activity in the interstices of the state system. Some of the mechanisms for non-state influence, like the Committee of the Regions, have been a disappointment, but alliances of like-minded regions and nations have gained a certain protagonism. There is a huge array of regional associations and alliances, based on common economic interests, geographical proximity or shared political aspirations and Scotland has the potential to be involved in most of them. Gradually, the stronger European 'regions' are differentiating themselves from the rest with initiatives like the Regions with Legislative Power, or the Constitutional Regions, demanding recognition for their special needs. The White Paper on European Governance proposes partnerships with sub-state authorities on the design and implementation of European policies.

A distinction is often made when analysing the foreign activities of non-sovereign governments between paradiplomacy, which tends to be functionally driven and focused on low-key matters, and protodiplomacy, which is more politicised, seeks recognition from outside and may be preparing the way for secession. States have felt threatened by the latter, but have varied in their willingness to allow their constituent parts to play the game of paradiplomacy. In Belgium, the regions and language communities have complete external competence corresponding to their internal competences, allowing them wide leeway in European and foreign matters. Spain has been more reticent but the UK since devolution has been rather relaxed. It seems, perhaps surprisingly, that the Foreign Office has been particularly relaxed compared to domestic departments such as the Department of Trade and Industry, which are apprehensive about competing Scottish efforts in investment and trade promotion. Suggestions have been made recently in Catalonia that non-state governments which have exclusive responsibility for education and culture should be represented in some way in UNESCO. This would certainly include Scotland.

The Good Friday Agreement in Northern Ireland provides another outlet for Scotland as an independent actor, through the British–Irish Council (sometimes referred to as Council of the Isles). It is unlikely that the Council will make a big dent in the sovereignty claims and practice of the UK government, but it does provide an opportunity for the devolved governments to talk to themselves and the government of the Republic of Ireland. Were personal and policy networks to form around this, it could provide yet more chances for Scotland to forge alliances and enhance its governing capacity.

Finally, Scottish autonomy depends on the ability to mobilise social and economic forces around a development project that promises growth combined with social justice and environmental sustainability. This is not just a matter of acquiring formal governmental competences but of establishing a vision and generating consensus around it. Small countries can compensate for their lack of power and resources by their ability to sustain internal debate, their short lines of communication and the ease of adaptation to change. The debate on Scotland as a society and its place in Europe has been notable by its absence, compared with other stateless nations contemplating their future. It is as though the energies expended in achieving devolution had been exhausted, or else saved up for a forth-coming struggle over independence. Yet independent or not, Scotland still has to face the challenge of adaptation to a rapidly changing economic and social context in conditions that it will never itself control.

– A THIRD WAY? –

Small independent states and devolved nations and regions, despite their different constitutional status, share many of the same opportunities and constraints. There is an expanding literature building on this to explore the prospects of a third way between independence and decentralisation, much of it emanating from Quebec, where sovereigntists and federalists have argued themselves to a standstill (Gagnon and Tully 2001). Inspired by the literature on globalisation and territorialisation, Alain Gagnon has floated the idea of the 'regional state' a self-governing entity able to manage its own insertion into the global economy and other networks but not requiring full statehood in its traditional sense (Gagnon 2001). The term 'regional state' carries overtones that would be unacceptable in Scotland but the substance of the proposal is recognisable in other concepts such as 'stateless nation-building' (Keating 1997). It is also present in various forms in the political arena. The Good Friday Agreement on Northern Ireland suspends most of the rules of state sovereignty and unity, separates state from nation, recognisable multiple identities, and provides an open–ended process for resolving the problem of authority. Proposals from Catalan and Basque political movements go in the same direction.

Public opinion in Scotland, as in other stateless nations of Europe and in Quebec, shows an apparent ambivalence on the question of independence (Keating 2001b). On the on hand, there is a yearning for more recognition and something more than regional autonomy; on the other there is little desire to take on the burdens of full statehood. While some might see this as evidence of confusion in the minds of the citizenry, it is better understood as a rejection of the old categories of statehood and a search for new forms of autonomy. To this corresponds a sense of multiple identity, in which people can be Scottish, British and European at the same time, using these varied identities in their appropriate contexts. Tom Nairn has objected to the post-sovereignty scenario for Scotland on the grounds that nations have to go through a sovereignty phase first, and that there is no post-sovereign order yet in place to which Scotland could accede (Nairn 2000). It would indeed be an exaggeration to claim that a third way now exists for restructuring multinational states but there is an evolving political practice and set of ideas which at least tell us that the old stark choices between independence or not no longer exhaust the possibilities. The old sovereignty talk voiced both by British Eurosceptics and by many Scottish nationalists looks ever more out of touch with both historic practice and future realities.

Devolution has been described as a process rather than an event, and experience from elsewhere sustains this view. Scotland's Parliament and government may evolve as a way of allowing marginal adjustments to UK policy lines, as happened under the old Scottish Office but this is unlikely, especially since opinion polls show large majorities in favour of enhancing their powers. Instead the choice will be between independence and stronger home rule, following the third way traced by other stateless nations. There is, despite all the weakening of state sovereignty, a difference between these positions, but there is also an underlying similarity. Both require that Scotland equip itself not merely with a constitution, but also that it develop a societal project, bringing together questions of economic competitiveness, social cohesion and environmental sustainability, in the face of European and global forces. These are the vital conditions for autonomy in the modern world.

Chronology of Czechoslovakia

1918　11 November: Establishment of the Czechoslovak state at the end of World War I.

1938　September: Loss of Sudeten German territory of Czechoslovakia to Hitler's Germany under the Munich Agreement; Vienna Award gives Slovak territories to Hungary.

1939　Czech lands become a German protectorate; Slovakia becomes a separate State under German sponsorship for the duration of World War II (1939–45).

1944　Slovak national uprising.

1945　Czechoslovakia reunited; establishment of the Second Czechoslovak Republic (1945–8).

1948　25 February: Seizure of power establishes communist regime in Czechoslovakia.

1968　Prague Spring reform era, ended by the Soviet invasion; federation of the Czechoslovak Socialist Republic.

1989　November: Velvet Revolution against communist rule.

1990　19 April: Czechoslovakia officially renamed the Czech and Slovak Federative Republic.

　　　8–9 June: First fully free elections after communism.

1992　23 July: Klaus and Meciar conclude agreement for separation of state

　　　13 November: Law on the separation of the Federation passed; includes provisions for the division of federal property between the two constituent republics.

1993　1 January: Dissolution of Czechoslovakia into two states, Czech Republic and Slovakia.

Sources: Fawn, R. (2000); Leff, C. S. (1996).

Chronology of Quebec

1867   The British North America Act is adopted and the Canadian Constitution takes effect on 1 July. It is a pact between the two founding peoples – the English and the French – that sealed the sharing of powers within the new Canadian federation between a federal parliament and new provincial legislatures. French speakers would remain a minority in the federal parliament but would be a majority in Quebec's legislature.

1968   15 October: Sovereigntist forces in Quebec unite to form a new political party, the Parti Québécois (PQ), with René Lévesque, a prominent former minister in the Liberal government of Jean Lasage, as its leader.

1970   In the provincial election, the PQ elects its first members to the National Assembly.

1973   The PQ becomes the official opposition in the National Assembly.

1976   15 November: The PQ wins a majority of seats in the National Assembly and forms the new Government of Quebec with René Lévesque as premier.

1980   20 May: The PQ Government holds a referendum on Quebec sovereignty. 40.4 per cent voted Yes, 59.6 per cent voted No.

1981   The PQ is returned to power.

1982   The federal government patriates the Constitution from the UK Parliament and adds a new amending formula. Quebec opposes the patriation. It regards the forced patriation of the Constitution as a rupture of the 1867 pact between the two founding peoples.

1987   The Meech Lake Accord (named after the Prime Minister's holiday cottage on the shore of Meech Lake) is signed by the Prime Minister of Canada, Brian Mulroney, and the premiers of the ten provinces (including Quebec), which recognises Quebec as a 'distinct society'. The Accord sparks strong opposition, particularly in the English speaking provinces. Manitoba and Newfoundland go back on their signatures and the Accord results in failure.

1990 May: Lucien Bouchard, federal minister for the environment, and others resign from the Progressive Conservative Party in protest over the federal government's attempts to limit the scope of the distinct society clause in an eleventh hour attempt to save the Meech Lake Accord. They form the Bloc Québécois, the federal counterpart to the PQ.

1991 July: The provinces and the federal government reach a new constitutional agreement called the Charlottetown Accord (named after the capital city of Prince Edward Island where the Accord was signed).

1992 26 October: The Accord is rejected by 57 per cent of voters in Quebec (because it fell short of their demands) and 54 per cent elsewhere in Canada (because voters felt it gave too much away to Quebec).

1993 25 October: Quebecers elect a majority of sovereigntist MPs to the federal parliament. The Bloc Québécois (BQ) headed by Lucien Bouchard wins 54 seats – over 70 per cent of all those in Quebec. The BQ becomes the Official Opposition in the House of Commons

1994 September: The Parti Québécois, headed by Jacques Parizeau, wins a majority of seats in the National Assembly and forms the government. Its platform called for a referendum to be held on Quebec sovereignty during its term of office.

1995 30 October: The people of Quebec vote for a second time on sovereignty. The turnout is 93.52 per cent. The Yes side gets 49.4 per cent of the votes, the No side 50.6 per cent.

1996 September: The federal government refers three questions to the country's highest court, the Supreme Court. It asks, in essence, whether Quebec has the right to decide alone its sovereignty.

1998 20 August: The Supreme Court releases its Reference opinion.

2001 January: Quebec Premier Lucien Bouchard resigns and is replaced by Bernard Landry.

Source: 'Québec . . . on the road to nationhood', Bloc Québécois (1998); Gough (1999).

Chronology of Greenland

1953 Greenland becomes an integral part of Denmark through an amendment in the Constitution.
1973 Denmark joins the European Economic Community (EEC).
1979 1 May: Home Rule established in Greenland.
1983 With the introduction of home rule Greenland is offered the option of leaving the European Community (EC). On 23 February, 52 per cent of the Greenland electorate choose for their territory to leave the European Community. On particular reason is the desire to obtain political control over fishing in Greenland waters.
1985 1 February: Greenland withdraws from the EEC but remains affiliated to the Community through the OCT-arrangement (Overseas Countries and Territories), combined with a special fishing agreement running for 10 years (1985–95).

Source: *Greenland*, Royal Danish Ministry of Foreign Affairs.

Chronology of Ireland

1916 Decision of Irish Republican Brotherhood (IRB) for an insurrection against British rule in Ireland later known as the Easter Rising, Dublin; leaders are executed.

1917 Sinn Fein supports an independent republic.

1918 General Election in which Sinn Fein wins the majority of seats.

1919 Meeting of the first Dail Eireann. Eamon de Valera elected president of Ireland.

1919 War of Independence/Anglo–Irish War between 'republicans' and
–21   British forces.

1920 Government of Ireland Act passed by Westminster Parliament providing for two Home Rule parliaments in Belfast and Dublin.

1921 Anglo–Irish War ended by peace treaty. Articles of Agreement establish basis for an independent Irish Free State in southern 26 counties.

1922 Anglo–Irish Treaty approved; Irish Free State constitution passed, retaining allegiance to British Crown and membership of British Empire.

1922 Civil War between pro–treaty Irish Free State forces and anti-treaty
–3   'republicans'/Sinn Fein.

1925 Irish Free State government confirms the border between the states of Ireland to remain as laid down in the 1920 Act.

1937 New constitution, *Bunreacht nah Eireann*, approved by referendum.

1949 Republic of Ireland Act proclaims the southern state a republic while the British Government's Ireland Act gives the new constitutional guarantee to the Northern Ireland parliament that Irish unity would not occur without consent.

Source: Bew et al. (1989) and misc. sources

Bibliography

Abbreviations:
AHSTF – Alberta Heritage Savings Trust Fund
APFC – Alaska Permanent Fund Corporation
DTI – Department of Trade and Industry
GoI – Government of Ireland
GoN – Government of Norway
OECD – Organisation for Economic Co-operation and Development
PQ – Parti Québécois
SCDI – Scottish Council Development and Industry
SNP – Scottish National Party

APFC, (2001a), *Alaskan's Guide to the Permanent Fund – 25th Anniversary edition*, Juneau, Alaska. (Read at *http://www.apfc.org/library/2001guide.cfm*).
APFC, (2001b), *Annual Report 2001*, Juneau, Alaska. (Read at *http://www.apfc.org/library/anreport.cfm?s=5*).
AHSTF (2001), '2001 Annual Report', Edmonton, Alberta. (Read at *http://www.treas.gov.ab.ca/business/ahstf/publications.html*).
Anderson, M. (1996), *Frontiers: Territory and State Formation in the Modern World*, Cambridge: Polity Press.
Aust, A. (2000), *Modern Treaty Law and Practice*, Cambridge: Cambridge University Press.
Avery, G. and Cameron, F. (1998), *The Enlargement of the European Union*, Sheffield: Academic Press.
Bennett, Andrew P. W. (1998), *Political instability and poor economic performance in Quebec: Is there a correlation?* University of Edinburgh: Institute of Governance.
Bew, P., Hazelkorn, E. and Patterson, H. (1989), *The Dynamics of Irish Politics*, London: Lawrence & Wishart.
Blum, Y. Z. (1992), 'Russia Takes Over the Soviet Union's Seat at the United Nations', 3 *European Journal of International Law* 354.

Bogdanor, V. (1997), *The Monarchy and the Constitution*, Oxford: Clarendon Press.

Boothe, P. Johnstone, B. and Powys-Lybbe, K. (1991), 'Dismantling Confederation: The Divisive Question of the National Debt', in J. McCallum (ed.), *Closing the Books: Dividing Federal Assets and Debt if Canada breaks up*, Toronto: C. D. Howe Institute.

Bordo, M. and Jonung, L. (2000), *Lessons for EMU from the History of Monetary Unions*, London: Institute of Economic Affairs.

Bossuyt, M. J. (1987), *Guide to the 'Travaux Préparatoires' of the International Covenant on Civil and Political Rights*, Dordrecht: Martinus Nijhoff Publishers.

Brazier, R. (1999), 'Constitutional Reform and the Crown', in M. Sunkin and S. Payne (eds), *The Nature of the Crown: A Legal and Political Analysis*, Oxford: Oxford University Press.

Brownlie, I. (1995), *Principles of International Law* (4th ed.), Oxford: Clarendon Press.

Buchanan, A. (1998), 'Democracy and Secession', in M. Moore (ed.), *National Self–Determination and Secession*, Oxford: Oxford University Press.

Buckle, M. and Thompson, J. (1998), *The UK Financial System: Theory and Practice* (3rd ed.), Manchester: Manchester University Press.

Butler, D. and Ranney, A. (eds) (1978), *Referendums: A Comparative Study of Practice and Theory*, Washington DC: American Enterprise Institute for Public Policy Research.

Campaign for a Scottish Assembly (1988), 'A Claim of Right for Scotland', in Owen Dudley Edwards (ed.), *A Claim of Right for Scotland*, Edinburgh: Polygon.

Chalmers, M. and Walker, W. (2001), *Uncharted Waters: the UK, Nuclear Weapons and the Scottish Question*, East Linton: Tuckwell Press.

Clark, G. (1999), 'Scottish Devolution and the European Union', *Public Law*, 504.

Clinton, K. and Zelmer, M. (December 1997), *Constraints on the conduct of Canadian monetary policy in the 1990s: Dealing with uncertainty in financial markets*, Bank of Canada Research Paper.

Courchenc, T. (2001), *A State of Minds. Toward a Human Capital Future for Canadians*, Montreal: Institute for Research in Public Policy.

Cox, R. H. and Frankland E. G. (1995), 'The Federal State and the Breakup of Czechoslovakia: An Institutional Analysis', *Publius: The Journal of Federalism* 25:1.

Crawford, J. (1979), *The Creation of States in International Law*, Oxford: Clarendon Press.

Crawford, J. (1998), 'State Practice in International Law in Relation to Secession', *British Yearbook of International Law* 85.

Crawford, J. (2001), 'The Right of Self-Determination in International Law: Its Development and Future', in P. Alston (ed.), *People's Rights*, Oxford: Oxford University Press.

Davies, R. (1999), *Devolution: A Process Not An Event*, Cardiff: Institute of Welsh Affairs.

Dawson, M. (1999), 'Reflections on the Opinion of the Supreme Court of Canada in the Quebec Secession Reference', *National Journal of Constitutional Law*, November 1999.

De Grauwe, P. (1997), *The Economics of Monetary Integration* (3rd ed.), Oxford: Oxford University Press.

Denver, D., Mitchell, J., Pattie, C. and Bochel, H. (2000), *Scotland Decides: The Devolution Issue and the Scottish Referendum*, London: Frank Cass.

Denver, D., Pattie C., Bochel H. and Mitchell J. (1998), 'The Devolution Referendums in Scotland', *Representation*, Vol. 35, Number 4, 210.

Denza, E. (1998), *Diplomatic Law: Commentary on the Vienna Convention on Diplomatic Relations* (2nd ed.), Oxford: Oxford University Press.

DTI (2001), *Development of UK Oil and Gas Resources 2001* (The Brown Book), London: The Stationery Office.

Dupuis R. and McNeil K. (1995), *Volume 2: Domestic Dimensions*, Ottawa: Minister of Supply and Services.

Fawn, R. (2000), *The Czech Republic: a Nation of Velvet*, Amsterdam: Harwood Academic Publishers.

Fidrmuc J, and Horvath J. (1998), *Stability of Monetary Unions: Lessons from the break-up of Czechoslovakia*, University of Tilburg: Center for Economic Research.

Fitzpatrick, M. (2001), 'Calculating a Fiscally Autonomous Scotland', in Policy Institute, *Calling Scotland to Account*, Edinburgh.

Flanagan, T. (1996), 'Should a Supermajority be Required in a Referendum on Separation?', in Trent, J. E., Young, R. and Lachapelle, G. (eds), *Quebec–Canada: What is the Path Ahead?*, Ottawa: University of Ottawa Press.

Fortin, Pierre (2001), *Has Quebec's standard of living been catching up?* Université du Québec à Montréal: Mimeo.

Frowein, J. A. (1991), 'Germany United', *Zeitschrift für ausländisches öffentliches Recht und Völkerrecht*, 333.

Gagnon, Alain-G. (2001), 'Le Québec, une nation inscrite au sein d'une démocratie étriquée', in Jocelyn Mclure and Alain–G. Gagnon (eds), *Repères en mutation. Identité et citoyenneté dans le Québec contemporain*, Montreal: Québec-Amérique.

Gagnon, Alain-G. and J. Tully (eds) (2001), *Multinational Democracies*, Cambridge: Cambridge University Press.

Gay, O. (1999), 'Devolution and Concordats', Research Paper 99/84, House of Commons Library.

Gibson, H. (ed) (1997) *Caledonian Blue Book 1997, National Accounts for Scotland 1951–96*, Glasgow: Glasgow Caledonian University.

Glenny, M. (1993), *The Rebirth of History. Eastern Europe in the Age of Democracy* (2nd ed.) Harmondsworth: Penguin.

Gough, B. M. (1999), *Historical Dictionary of Canada*, London: Scarecrow Press.

GoI (2000), *Revised estimates for public services 2001*, Dublin: Government Publications, Pn. 9044.

GoI (2001), *Statistical Information on Social Welfare Services 2000*, Dublin: Government Publications, Pn. 10042.

GoN (2001), *Staatsbudsjettet [National Budget] 2002*, Oslo: Ministry of Finance (Read at *http://www.statsbudsjettet.dep.no/pdf/english.pdf*).

Grant, J. P. (ed.) (1976), *Independence and Devolution: the Legal Implications for Scotland*, Edinburgh: W. Green & Son.

Gwynn Morgan, D. (1990), *Constitutional Law of Ireland* (2nd ed.), Dublin: Round Hall Ltd.

Habermas, J. (1992), 'Citizenship and National Identity: Some Reflections of the Future of Europe', *Praxis International*, 12(1), 1.

Habermas, J. (1996), 'The European Nation State. Its Achievements and Its Limitations. On the Past and Future of Sovereignty and Citizenship', *Ratio Juris*, Vol. 9, No. 2, 128.

Happold, M. (2000), 'Independence: In or Out of Europe?', *International and Comparative Law Quarterly* Vol. 49, 15.

Harhoff, F. (1983), 'Greenland's Withdrawal from the EC', *Common Market Law Review*, 406.

Hawthorn, J. (1996), 'Some Thoughts on an Independent Scottish Defence Force', Occasional Paper No. 1, University of Glasgow: Scottish Centre for War Studies.

Hazell, R. (ed.)(1999), *Constitutional Futures: A History of the Next Ten Years*, Oxford: Oxford University Press.

Hazell, R. and O'Leary, B. (1998), 'A Rolling Programme of Devolution: Slippery Slope or Safeguard of the Union?', in R. Hazell (ed.), *Constitutional Futures: A History of the Next Ten Years*, Oxford: Oxford University Press.

Hendry and Wood (1987), *The Legal Status of Berlin*, Cambridge: Grotius.

Himsworth, C. M. G. and Munro C. R. (1999), *The Scotland Act 1998*, Edinburgh: W. Green/Sweet & Maxwell.

Hood, N. (1999), 'Scotland in the world', in J. Peat and S. Boyle (eds) (1999), *An Illustrated Guide to the Scottish Economy*, London: Duckworth.

Howse, R. and Malkin, A. (1997), 'Canadians Are a Sovereign People: How the Supreme Court Should Approach the Reference on Quebec Secession', 76 *Canadian Bar Review* 186.

Hughes Hallett, A. (2001), 'Fiscal autonomy and power sharing', in Policy Institute (2001) *Calling Scotland to account*, Edinburgh.

Innes, A. (1997), 'The Breakup of Czechoslovakia: The Impact of Party Development on the Separation of the State', *East European Politics and Societies*, Vol. 11, No. 3, 393.

Innes, A. (2001), *Czechoslovakia: The Short Goodbye*, New Haven: Yale University Press.

Jacqué, J.-P. (1991), 'German Unification and the EC', *European Journal of International Law* 11.

Jeffery, C. (2000), 'Sub-National Mobilisation and European Integration: Does it Make any Difference?', 38 *Journal of Common Market Studies* 1.

Johnson, C. (1996), *In with the euro, out with the pound*, London: Penguin.

Kamminga, M. T. (1996), 'State Succession in Respect of Human Rights Treaties', 7 *European Journal of International Law* 469.

Katzenstein, P. (1985), *Small States in World Markets. Industrial Policy in Europe*, Ithaca: Cornell University Press.

Keating, M. (2001a), *Nations against the State. The New Nationalism in Quebec, Catalonia and Scotland* (2nd ed.), Basingstoke: Palgrave. S'L- 320.5409. NAT

Keating, M. (2001b), *Plurinational Democracy. Stateless Nations in a Post-Sovereignty Era*, Oxford: Oxford University Press.

Keating, M. (2001c), 'Nations without States: The Accommodation of Nationalism in the New State Order', in M. Keating and J. McGarry (eds), *Minority Nationalism and the Changing International Order*, Oxford: Oxford University Press.

Kellas, J. G. (1998), *The Politics of Nationalism and Ethnicity* (2nd ed.), London: Macmillan Press.

Kemp, A. G. and Stephen, L. (1999), *Expenditures in and Revenues from the UKCS: Estimating the Hypothetical Scottish Shares 1970–2003*, North Sea Study Occasional Paper No. 70, Department of Economics, University of Aberdeen.

Klima, K. (1994),. *Constitutional Law of the Czech Republic*, Pilsen: University of West Bohemia.

Koskenniemi, M. (1994), 'National Self-Determination Today: Problems of Legal Theory and Practice', 43 *International and Comparative Law Quarterly* 241.

KPMG (8 February 2001), 'Corporate Tax Rates Continue to Tumble', Tax Press Release, KPMG. Available at: *http://www.kpmg/uk/press/detail.cfm?pr=846*.

Kuyper, P. J. (1994), 'The Community and State Succession in Respect of Treaties', in D. Curtin and T. Heukels, *Institutional Dynamics of European Integration. Essays in Honour of Henry G. Schermers Vol. 2*, Martinus Nijhoff Publishers.

Laidler, D. E. W. and Robson, W. B. P. (1991), *Two Nations, One Money? Canada's Monetary System following a Quebec Secession* (Canada Round Series No. 3), Toronto: C. D. Howe Institute.

Lane, R. (1991), "Scotland in Europe': An Independent Scotland in the European Conmmunity', in Finnie, W., Himsworth, C. M. G., and Walker, N. (eds), *Edinburgh Essays in Public Law*, Edinburgh: Edinburgh University Press. D346 EDI

Leddin, A. and Walsh, B. (1998), *The Macro-Economy of Ireland* (4th ed.), Dublin: Gill & Macmillan.

Leff, C. S. (1996), *The Czech and Slovak Republics: Nations Versus State*, Boulder: Westview Press.

Macartney, A. (1985), 'Autonomy in the British Isles', 54 *Nordisk Tidskrift for International Ret* 10.

MacCormick, N. (1999), *Questioning Sovereignty: Law, State and Nation in the European Commonwealth*, Oxford: Oxford University Press.

MacCormick, N. (2000), 'Is There A Constitutional Path to Scottish Independence?', 53 *Parliamentary Affairs* 721.

Major, J. (1992), 'Foreword by the Prime Minister' in Secretary of State for Scotland, *Scotland and the Union*, Edinburgh: HMSO.

Malanczuk, P. (1997), *Akehurst's Modern Introduction to International Law* (2nd ed.), London: Routledge.

Marr, A. (1992), *The Battle for Scotland'*, London: Penguin. 320.9411 MAR

Mason, K. (1983), 'Greenland – withdrawal from the EEC', 13 *Georgia Journal of International and Comparative Law* 865.

McCorquodale, R. (1995), 'Negotiating Sovereignty: The Practice of the United Kingdom in Regard to The Right of Self-Determination', *British Yearbook of International Law*, 283.

McCrone, G. (1999), 'Financing Scottish Government', in J. Peat and S. Boyle (1999) *An Illustrated Guide to the Scottish Economy*, London: Duckworth.

McRoberts, K. (1997), *Misconceiving Canada*, Oxford: Oxford University Press.

Midwinter, A. (1998), 'Government Expenditure and Revenue in Scotland: Accounting for the Fiscal Deficit in 1996–97', *Quarterly Economic Commentary*, Vol 24: 1, University of Strathclyde.

Mitchell, J. and Seyd, B. (1999), 'Fragmentation in the Party and Political Systems', in R. Hazell (ed.), *Constitutional Futures: A History of the Next Ten Years*, Oxford: Oxford University Press.

Mitchell, J. (1996), *Strategies for Self-Government*, Edinburgh: Polygon.

Mitchell, J. D. B. (1968), *Constitutional Law* (2nd ed.), Edinburgh: W. Green & Son.

Monahan, P. J. (2000), *Doing the Rules – An Assessment of the Federal Clarity Act in Light of the Quebec Secession Reference*, CD Howe Institute (Commentary 135).

Monteith, B. (2001) 'A different path to fiscal freedom', in Policy Institute (2001), *Calling Scotland to account*, Edinburgh

Moore, M. (1998) (ed.), *National Self-Determination and Secession*, Oxford: Oxford University Press.

Mullerson, R. (1993), 'The Continuity and Succession of States, by Reference to the Former USSR and Yugoslavia', 42 *International and Comparative Law Quarterly* 473.

Munro, C. (1994), 'The Union of 1707 and the British Constitution', in *Scotland and the Union, Hume Papers on Public Policy: Vol. 2 No. 2*, Edinburgh: Edinburgh University Press.

Nairn, T. (2000), *After Britain: New Labour and the Return of Scotland*, London: Granta Books.

Nash, M. L. (1996), 'The Greenland Option', 146 *New Law Journal* 1019.

Norges Bank (2001), *The Government Petroleum Fund Annual Report 2001*, Oslo (Read at *http://www.norges–bank.no/english/petroleum_fund/reports/2001/index.html*)

O'Connell, D. P. (1967), *State Succession in Municipal Law and International Law*, Vol. 1, Cambridge: Cambridge University Press.

O'Connell, D. P. (1979), 'Reflections on the State Succession Convention', *Zeitschrift für ausländisches öffentliches Recht und Völkerrecht* 725.

Oeter, S. (1991), 'German Unification and State Succession', *Zeitschrift für ausländisches öffentliches Recht und Völkerrecht* 349.

OECD (December 2000), 'Economic Outlook', Paris.

Parti Québécois (2000), *Le Québec, un nouveau pays pour un nouveau siècle.*

Peat, J. and Boyle, S. (eds) (1999), *An Illustrated Guide to the Scottish Economy'*, London: Duckworth.

Pitchford, R. and Cox A. (eds) (1997), *EMU Explained: Markets and Monetary Union*, London: Kogan Page.

Policy Institute (2001), *Calling Scotland to Account*, Edinburgh.

Poole, G. B. and Westerterp, D. (1996), *Financial Markets and Instability: Market Response to the Quebec Referendum*, Department of Economics, University of Western Ontario: Mimeo.

Puig i Scotoni, P. (1998), *Pensar els camins a la sobirania*, Barcelona: Mediterrània.

Quane, H. (1998), 'The United Nations and the Evolving Right to Self–Determination', 47 *International and Comparative Law Quarterly* 537.

Rowlands, D. (1997), 'International Aspects of the Division of Debt under Secession', *Canadian Public Policy – Analyse de Politiques*, Vol. 23, No. 1, 45.

Rowlands, D. (2001), 'Negotiating Debt under Secession: The Case of Quebec and Canada', in D. Carment, J. F. Stack, F. Harvey (eds), *The International Politics of Quebec Secession: State Making and State Breaking in North America*, Westport, Connecticut: Praeger.

Russell, M. and Hazell, R. (2000), 'Devolution and Westminster: Tentative Steps Towards a More Federal Parliament', in R. Hazell (ed.), *The State and the Nations: First Year of Devolution in the United Kingdom*, London: Imprint Academic.

Schachter, O. (1993), 'State Succession: The Once and Future Law', 33 *Virginia Journal of International Law* 253.

Scottish Centre for Economic and Social Research (1996), *Scotland's Government – the transition to Independence*, Peterhead: SCESR.

Scottish Constitutional Convention (1995), *Scotland's Parliament. Scotland's Right*, Edinburgh: Scottish Constitutional Convention.

SCDI (December 1999), *Survey of Scottish Primary Sector Exports 1998/99*, Edinburgh.

SCDI (April 2001), *Survey of Scottish sales and exports in 1999/2000*, Edinburgh.

Scottish Executive (1999), *Government Expenditure and Revenues in Scotland, 1997–98'*, Edinburgh: Scottish Executive.

Scottish Executive (2000), *Government Expenditure and Revenues in Scotland, 1998–99*, Edinburgh: Scottish Executive.

Scottish Executive (2001), *Input–Output Tables and Multipliers for Scotland 1998*, Edinburgh: Scottish Executive.

SNP (May 1995), *Scottish Budget Balance relative to the UK, 1995–96* (Press Release), Edinburgh: SNP Publications.

SNP (December 2000), *Scotland's 21st Century Opportunity, Government Expenditure and Revenues in Scotland 2000–2002*, Edinburgh: SNP Publications.

SNP (2001a), *Manifesto/01*, Edinburgh: SNP Publications.

SNP (2001b), *The Scottish Fund for Future Generations*, Edinburgh: SNP Publications.

Scottish Office (1992), *Government Expenditure and Revenues in Scotland*, London: HMSO.

Scottish Office (1997), *Government Expenditure and Revenues in Scotland 1995–96*, Edinburgh: HMSO.

Scottish Office (1998), *Government Expenditure and Revenues in Scotland 1996–97*, Edinburgh: HMSO.

Seymour, M. (2000), 'The anti-democratic drift of the federal government: A brief concerning Bill C–20', http://pages.infinit.net/mseymour/a–frame/a__pol-doc.html [visited 23 February 2001].

Shaw, M. (1994), 'State Succession Revisited', *Finnish Yearbook of International Law* 34.

Shaw, M. N. (1997), *International Law* (4th ed.), Cambridge: Cambridge University Press.

Shepherd, R. H. E. (2000), *Czechoslovakia: the Velvet Revolution and Beyond*, Basingstoke: Macmillan.

Shihata, I. F. I. (1999), 'Matters of State Succession in the World Bank's Practice', in Mojmir Mrak (ed.), *Succession of States*, The Hague: Martinus Nijhoff.

Simpson, D., Main, B., Peacock, A. and Zuleeg, F. (1999), *Report on the Economic Aspects of Political Independence*, Edinburgh: The David Hume Institute.

Sloat, A. (2000), 'Scotland and Europe: Links Between Edinburgh, London and Brussels', 31 *Scottish Affairs* 92.

Smith, T. B. (1957), 'The Union of 1707 as Fundamental Law', *Public Law* 99.

Spence, D. (1991), 'Enlargement Without Accession: The EC's Response to German Reunification', *RIIA Discussion Papers No. 36*, London: The Royal Institute of International Affairs.

Stanic, A. (2001), 'Financial Aspects of State Succession: The Case of Yugoslavia', 12 *European Journal of International Law* 751.

Streinz, R. (1983), 'Succession of States in Assets and Liabilities – a New Régime? The 1983 Vienna Convention on Succession of States in respect of State Property, Archives and Debts', 26 *German Yearbook of International Law* 198.

Sullivan, L. M. (2000), 'International Law and the Break-Up of the United Kingdom: Towards a Democratic Theory of Secession', Ph.D. Thesis, Sidney Sussex College, Cambridge.

Sweeney, P. (1998), *The Celtic Tiger*, Dublin: Oak Tree Press.

Swinney, J. (2000), *St Andrew's Day speech*, Edinburgh: SNP Press Office.

Thatcher, M. (1993), *The Downing Street Years*, London: HarperCollins.

Thomas, H. (1991), 'Perestroika in the Western Wing – Nationalism and National Rights within the European Community', in W. Twining (ed.) *Issues of Self-Determination*, Aberdeen: Aberdeen University Press.

Timmermans, C. W. A (1990), 'German Reunification and EC Law', *Common Market Law Review* 438.

Tomuschat, C. (1990), 'A United Germany Within The European Community', *Common Market Law Review* 415.

Toope, S. J. (1999), 'Case note on the Reference re Secession of Quebec', 93 *The American Journal of International Law* 519.

United Nations (1974), 'Report of the International Law Commission to the General Assembly', A/9610/Rev. 1, in *Yearbook of the International Law Commission* 1974 Vol. II, Part One.

Wallace, W. (1997), 'Rescue or Retreat? The Nation State in Western Europe, 1945–93', in P. Gowan and P. Anderson (eds), *The Question of Europe*, London: Verso.

Walters, M. D. (1999), 'Nationalism and the Pathology of Legal Systems: Considering the Quebec Secession reference and its Lessons for the United Kingdom', 62 *Modern Law Review* 371.

Watts, R. L. (1998), 'Examples of Partnership', in R. Gibbins and G. Laforest, *Beyond the Impasse: Toward Reconciliation*, Montreal: Institute for Research on Public Policy.

Weiss, F. (1985), 'Greenland's Withdrawal from the European Communities', 10 *European Law Review* 173.

Whyte, J. (1983), 'The Permeability of the United Kingdom–Irish Border: A Preliminary Reconnaissance', *Administration*, Vol. 31, No. 3, 300.

Wicks, E. (2001), 'A New Constitution for a New State? The 1707 Union of England and Scotland', 117 *The Law Quarterly Review* 109.

Williams, P. (1994), 'The Treaty Obligations of the Successor States of the Former Soviet Union, Yugoslavia and Czechoslovakia: Do They Continue in Force?', *Denver Journal of International Law & Policy*, Vol. 23, 1.

Williams, P. R. (1994), 'State Succession and the International Financial Institutions: Political Criteria v. Protection of Outstanding Financial Obligations', 43 *International and Comparative Law Quarterly* 776.

Williamson, E. D. and Osborn, J. E. (1993), 'A U.S. Perspective on Treaty Succession and Related Issues in the Wake of the Breakup of the USSR and Yugoslavia', 33 *Virginia Journal of International Law* 261.

Woodliffe, J. (1992), *The Peacetime Use of Foreign Military Installations under Modern International Law*, Kluwer Academic Publishers.

Young, R. (1994), *The Breakup of Czechoslovakia, Research Paper No. 32*, Kingston, Ontario: Institute of Intergovernmental Relations, Queen's University.

Young, R. (1997), 'How Do Peaceful Secessions Happen?', in D. Carment, and P. James (eds.), *Wars in the Midst of Peace: The International Politics of Ethnic Conflict*, Pittsburgh: University of Pittsburgh Press.

Young, R. A. (1998), *The Secession of Quebec and the Future of Canada*, McGill–Queen's University Press.

Zahraa, M. (2001), 'Prospective Anglo–Scottish Maritime Boundary Revisited', 12 *European Journal of International Law* 77).

Index